JOURNAL FOR THE STUDY OF THE OLD TESTAMENT
SUPPLEMENT SERIES

48

JSOT Press
Sheffield

Professor Frank Charles Fensham

TEXT and CONTEXT

Old Testament and Semitic Studies for F.C. Fensham

edited by

W. Claassen

Journal for the Study of the Old Testament
Supplement Series 48

Published by JSOT Press
JSOT Press is an imprint of
Sheffield Academic Press Ltd
The University of Sheffield
343 Fulwood Road
Sheffield S10 3BP
England

Typeset by Sheffield Academic Press
and
printed in Great Britain
by Billing & Sons Ltd
Worcester

British Library Cataloguing in Publication Data

Text and context : Old Testament and Semitic
studies for F.C. Fensham.— (Journal for
the study of the Old Testament. Supplement
series, ISSN 0309-0787; 48).
1. Bible. O.T.—Criticism, interpretation,
etc.
I. Fensham, F. Charles II. Claassen, W.
III. Series
221.6 BS1171.2

ISBN 1-85075-040-8

CONTENTS

A TRIBUTE TO FRANK CHARLES FENSHAM

Text and Context was conceived, solicited and prepared as an expression of sincere gratitude to our teacher and colleague Frank Charles Fensham, on the occasion of his sixtieth birthday, October 13, 1985. Judged by his own standards of modesty and gentleness, he himself would never have thought of being honoured by a Festschrift. The mere fact that his friends and colleagues from different continents, as well as his students, have reacted with such promptness and alacrity in contributing to this Festschrift, only underscores their esteem, appreciation and unreserved loyalty and affection towards Charles Fensham. To us, who know him so well, he is indeed the epitome of kindness and scholarly competence.

The title of this Festschrift reflects in some way or other Fensham's comprehensive approach to and understanding of the Old Testament in its World. He has mastered a variety of topics with such resilience, skill and resourcefulness that he truly merits the qualification as an all-rounder—hard to find in these days of intensive specialization. Fensham is one of the few South African scholars who have gained scholarly acceptance and acknowledgment on an international level. He has been invited to lecture at several international congresses and at universities in Rome, Uppsala, Bern, Tel-Aviv, Jerusalem, Leiden, Utrecht, Groningen, Amsterdam, Oxford, Cambridge, Zürich, Basel, Tübingen, Munich and Berlin, apart from those in South Africa. Owing to a major operation he had to cancel an invitation to act as guest professor at Cambridge in 1969. Having been awarded both the prestigious Fulbright and the Smith-Mundt scholarships in 1958, he completed a second doctorate at Johns Hopkins University (Baltimore) under the famous W.F. Albright who ardently wished to retain Fensham on his staff. This very tempting offer he declined, as was later also the case when he was offered a chair in Old Testament Theology by his alma mater (University of Pretoria).

Fensham saw his task as being in South Africa and especially at the University of Stellenbosch. Here he has attracted students from all over the country. His success in engendering the students' interest in his subject and in stimulating them to do research is quite remarkable. Presently, a substantial number of his students, who hold master's and doctor's degrees (26 and 17 respectively) fill important positions at universities all over South Africa (Stellenbosch, Western Cape, Port Elizabeth, Fort Hare, Orange Free State, University of South Africa, The University of the North etc.). They form a formidable 'school' that exerts a dominating influence in the fields of Old Testament Theology and Semitics in South Africa.

The wide variety of doctoral subjects and the diversity of treatment, i.e. Hebrew Philology, Ugaritic Mythology, Wisdom Ethos, Old Babylonian Economy, Israelite History, Literary Analyses, Archaeology, etc., reflect Fensham's interests in the texts, literature, languages, cultures, histories, religions and theologies of the Bible world, forming a kaleidoscope of Old Testament and Semitic studies. He has also introduced his students to international scholarship. In fact, the majority of his doctoral students have submitted their dissertations to be examined by internationally renowned scholars.

Throughout his career Fensham has also remained a trustworthy friend and sympathetic confidant of many a minister in the Dutch Reformed Church. Although he has served this Church in many official ways, his indirect service to and quiet influence on many of her leaders is perhaps far greater than can ever be accounted for. He displays a balanced view of Scripture, and teaches his students to work respectfully but scientifically with the text, to be critical, to ask historical questions and to ignore irrelevant scholastic and systematic issues. In a certain sense Fensham's coming to Stellenbosch in 1951 marked the beginning of a new direction in biblical research, the subsequent fruits of which can clearly be observed in the Church today. He also served as pastor of the local Rhenish congregation for many years. Perhaps this accounts for his most influential article: 'Widow, Orphan and the Poor...'.

The work and life of Charles Fensham can never be described without referring to his invaluable service to and enhancement of the Afrikaans culture. He played a leading role in the tricentennial festivities commemorating the founding of Stellenbosch. His Bos-orchestra (he himself plays the concertina) did and still does much to enrich folk music. He wrote a vast number of popular articles dealing with the cultural heritage of the Afrikaner. As chairman of the Stellenbosse Heemkring he has contributed immensely to the conservation of important documents and folklore, and to the restoration of buildings and *objets d'art*. His role as the national chairman of the Afrikaanse Skrywerskring is also praiseworthy as well as his enthusiastic encouragement of authors, both young and old, to publish their works. He was also co-editor of the first major general encyclopedia (10 volumes) in Afrikaans. Presently he is the chairman of a committee which organizes the festivities to commemorate the coming of the French Huguenots to South Africa in 1688.

Fensham's quality of leadership as well as his esteem as an academic were observed at a very early stage of his career. He took a leading role in student activities and on student councils at the Pretoria University during the late forties when the political situation of the post-war era was very tense. At Stellenbosch he soon became an influential member of the Faculty of Humanities and later was elected dean. He subsequently has been appointed in many committees, including the Executive Committee. His service was regarded as of such value and excellence that he became a member of the Council of the University of Stellenbosch. He also served as a member of the Councils of the Universities of the Western Cape and of Port Elizabeth.

Fensham's stature as an academic was duly acknowledged when he was elected as the national chairman of the South African Academy of Science and Arts ('Die Suid-Afrikaanse Akademie vir Wetenskap en Kuns'). Again, his remarkable qualities of leadership, good humour and scholarly approach to matters of national interest have won him considerable success and recognition. Despite such demanding circumstances and time-consuming obligations Fensham wrote commentaries (on Exodus [POT series], Ezra-Nehemiah [NICOT series]. Hebrews [Afrikaans series]), monographs (on Israelite History, Archaeology, the Dead Sea Scrolls, etc. in Afrikaans) and articles (see bibliography), and rendered most valuable service to the New Afrikaans Bible Translation project. He was, as a consequence, awarded the prestigious Totius prize by the South African Academy in 1984, for his decisive role in fostering Biblical studies, languages and history.

Charles Fensham is married to Yvonne Theron. They have three children and two grandchildren. One is always impressed by the love, understanding and kind generosity that mark their family and household. Of course, students like to visit the Fenshams, not only to borrow a rare book from his private library in which he has invested a whole fortune, but simply to talk and to listen to this so rare an example of a true master and teacher.

Thus, *Text and Context* is dedicated to F. Charles Fensham, in respectful tribute to a fellow-student, teacher, colleague, collaborator, critic, mentor and close friend.

The editors
15th June 1985

ABBREVIATIONS

AB	Anchor Bible
AfO	*Archiv für Orientforschung*
AHw	*Akkadisches Handwörterbuch*
AOAT	Alter Orient und Altes Testament
ATANT	Abhandlungen zur Theologie des Alten und Neuen Testaments
ATD	Altes Testament Deutsch
AS	*Anatolian Studies*
BA	*Biblical Archaeologist*
BAR	*Biblical Archaeology Review*
BASOR	*Bulletin of the American Schools of Oriental Research*
BDB	Brown, Driver & Briggs, *A Hebrew and English Lexicon of the Old Testament*
BH	*Biblia Hebraica*
BHS	*Biblia Hebraica Stuttgartensia*
Bib	*Biblica*
BibOr	*Bibliotheca orientalis*
BTB	*Biblical Theology Bulletin*
BWANT	Beiträge zur Wissenschaft vom Alten und Neuen Testament
BZ	*Biblische Zeitschrift*
BZAW	Beihefte zur Zeitschrift für die alttestamentliche Wissenschaft
CAD	*The Assyrian Dictionary*
CBQ	*Catholic Biblical Quarterly*
CRAIBL	Comptes rendus de l'Académie des inscriptions et belles-lettres
CSEL	Corpus scriptorum ecclesiasticorum latinorum
DBS	*Dictionnaire de la Bible Supplément*
ETR	*Etudes théologiques et religieuses*
FRLANT	Forschungen zur Religion und Literatur des Alten und Neuen Testaments
GK	Gesenius–Kautzsch, *Hebräische Grammatik*
GKC	Gesenius–Kautzsch, *Hebrew Grammar*, ed. Cowley
HAT	Handbuch zum Alten Testament
HKAT	Handkommentar zum Alten Testament
HUCA	*Hebrew Union College Annual*
ICC	International Critical Commentary
IDB	*Interpreter's Dictionary of the Bible*

IEJ	*Israel Exploration Journal*
JANES	*Journal of the Ancient Near Eastern Society*
JAOS	*Journal of the American Oriental Society*
JBL	*Journal of Biblical Literature*
JCS	*Journal of Cuneiform Studies*
JJS	*Journal of Jewish Studies*
JNES	*Journal of Near Eastern Studies*
JNWSL	*Journal of Northwest Semitic Languages*
JSOT	*Journal for the Study of the Old Testament*
JSS	*Journal of Semitic Studies*
JTS	*Journal of Theological Studies*
KAI	*Kanaanäische und Aramäische Inschriften* (Donner & Röllig)
KAT	Kommentar zum Alten Testament
KHCAT	Kurzer Handcommentar Altes Testament
MDOG	*Mitteilungen der Deutschen Orient-Gesellschaft*
NICOT	New International Commentary on the Old Testament
OLZ	*Orientalische Literaturzeitung*
OTL	Old Testament Library
OTS	*Oudtestamentische Studiën*
PEQ	*Palestine Exploration Quarterly*
RA	*Revue d'assyriologie et d'archéologie orientale*
RB	*Revue Biblique*
RiBib	*Rivista Biblica*
SBM	Stuttgarter biblische Monographien
SVT	Supplements to Vetus Testamentum
TD	*Theology Digest*
THAT	*Theologisches Handwörterbuch zum Alten Testament*
ThLZ	*Theologische Literaturzeitung*
ThV	*Theologia Viatorum*
TrThZ	*Trierer theologische Zeitschrift*
TWAT	*Theologisches Wörterbuch zum Alten Testament*
TZ	*Theologische Zeitschrift*
UF	*Ugarit-Forschungen*
UT	*Ugaritic Textbook* (Gordon)
VT	*Vetus Testamentum*
VuF	*Verkündigung und Forschung*
WdO	*Welt des Orients*
WMANT	Wissenschaftliche Monographien zum Alten und Neuen Testament
ZA	*Zeitschrift für Assyriologie*
ZAW	*Zeitschrift für die alttestamentliche Wissenschaft*
ZDPV	*Zeitschrift des Deutschen Palästina-Vereins*
ZThK	*Zeitschrift für Theologie und Kirche*

CONTRIBUTORS

1. Frank Andersen is Professor of Studies in Religion, University of Queensland, St Lucia, Queensland, Australia.

   David Noel Freedman is Arthur F. Thurnau Professor of Biblical Studies, University of Michigan, USA.

2. Johann Cook is Senior Lecturer, Department of Semitic Languages, University of Stellenbosch, South Africa.

3. Ferdinand E. Deist is Professor of Old Testament and Head of the Department of Old Testament, University of South Africa, Pretoria, South Africa.

4. Herbert Donner is Professor for Old Testament Study, Theologische Fakultät der Christian-Albrechts-Universität, Kiel, West Germany.

5. J.A. Emerton is Regius Professor of Hebrew, St John's College, Cambridge.

6. Paul A. Kruger is Senior Lecturer, Department of Semitic Languages, University of Stellenbosch, South Africa.

7. A. Malamat is Professor of Biblical and Ancient Jewish History, Hebrew University of Jerusalem, Israel.

8. William McKane is Professor of Hebrew and Oriental Languages, St Mary's College, University of St Andrews, Fife, Scotland.

9. Patrick D. Miller, Jr, is Professor of Old Testament Theology, Princeton Theological Seminary, Princeton, New Jersey, USA.

10. L.M. Muntingh is Senior Lecturer, Department of Biblical Studies, University of Stellenbosch, South Africa.

11. M.J. Mulder is Professor for Old Testament Exegesis, Faculty of Theology, Rijksuniversiteit, Leiden, Netherlands.

12. Philip Nel is Professor of Semitic Languages, University of the Orange Free State, Bloemfontein, South Africa.

13. Antoon Schoors is Professor in the Departement Oriëntalistiek, Katholieke Universiteit, Leuven, Belgium.

14. J.A. Soggin is Professor for Hebrew Language and Literature, University of Rome (La Sapienza); honorary Professor, Waldensian Theological Seminary, Rome; and visiting Professor, Pontifical Biblical Institute, Rome, Italy.

15. J.B. van Zijl is Professor of Semitic Languages, University of Port Elizabeth, South Africa.

16. Moshe Weinfeld is Professor of Biblical and Ancient Near Eastern Studies, Hebrew University of Jerusalem, Israel.

17. Hannes Olivier is Professor of Old Testament, Faculty of Theology, University of Stellenbosch, South Africa.

18. Adam S. van der Woude is Professor of Old Testament, University of Groningen, Netherlands.

19. Walter Gross is Ordinarius for Old Testament Exegesis, Katholisch-Theologische Fakultät, Eberhard-Karls-Universität, Tübingen, West Germany.

20. P.A. Verhoef is Emeritus Professor of Old Testament, University of Stellenbosch, South Africa.

21. Siegfried Mittmann is Professor of Biblical Archaeology, Evangelisch-Theologische Fakultät, Eberhard-Karls-Universität, Tübingen, West Germany.

22. Walter T. Claassen is Professor of Semitic Languages, University of Stellenbosch, South Africa.

1

THE ORTHOGRAPHY OF THE ARAMAIC PORTION OF THE TELL FEKHERYE BILINGUAL

Francis I. Andersen and David Noel Freedman

The purpose of this paper is to describe the orthography of the Aramaic section of the recently published bilingual inscription from Tell Fekherye (Abou-Assaf 1981, 1982). On the whole, it is our judgment that the orthography is consistent with the general principles and procedures derived from the study of Northwest Semitic inscriptions, but at the same time there are numerous unusual and novel features which warrant special attention.

In the following study of the text we shall examine all the words in which vowel letters (that is, consonant signs used to represent vowel sounds) or potential vowel letters occur, as well as those in which vowel letters might or should have been used and were not. On the basis of the information we shall then tabulate the results, and summarize the findings in the form of inductive rules or guidelines. In making the selection and in examining the material, the following are our presuppositions, which in turn are confirmed by the data:

(1) In the inscription, all final vowels are marked by the appropriate vowel letters, of which there are three: *he*, *waw*, *yod*. *Alef* is not a vowel letter in this inscription, either in the final or in any medial position. It is either a true consonant (a root phoneme) in medial or in final position; or, in some instances, a marker of the emphatic state in final position, and presumably also consonantal (or at least not demonstrably only a vowel letter), since the purely phonetic spelling of word-terminal long /a/ is regularly *he*. To judge from later Aramaic texts written in syllabic cuneiform, the use of the 'A (glottal) sign at the end of emphatic nouns

The Aramaic portion of the Tell Fekherye bilingual (Abou-Assaf, Bordreuil and Millard)

1 *dmwt’ | zy | hdys‘y : zy : šm : qdm : hddskn*

2 *gwgl : šmyn : w’rq : mhnḥt : ‘sr : wntn : r‘y*

3 *wmšqy : lmt : kln : wntn : šlh : w’dqwr*

4 *l’lhyn : klm : ’ḥwh : gwgl : nhr : klm : m‘dn*

5 *mt : kln : ’lh : rḥmn : zy : tṣlwth : ṭbh : ysb*

6 *skn : mr’ : rb : mr’ hdys‘y : mlk : gwzn : br*

7 *ssnwry: mlk : gwzn : lḥyy : nbšh : wlm’rk : ywmwh*

8 *wlkbr : šnwh : wlšlm : byth : wlšlm : zr‘h : wlšlm*

9 *’nšwh : wlmld : mrq : mnh : wlmšm‘ : tṣlwth : wl*

10 *mlqḥ : ’mrt : pmh : knn : wyhb : lh : wmn : ’ḥr : kn*

11 *ybl : lknnh : ḥds : wšmym : lšm : bh : wzy : yld : šmy : mnh*

12 *wyšym : šmh : hdd : gbr : lhwy : qblh : ṣlm : hdys‘y*

13 *mlk : gwzn : wzy : skn : wzy : ’zrn : l’rm ẇrdt : krs’h*

14 *wlm’rk : ḥywh : wlm‘n : ’mrt : pmh : ’l : ’lhn : w’l ’nšn*

15 *tyṭb : dmwt’ : z’t : ‘bd : ’l : zy : qdm : hwtr : qdm hdd*

16 *ysb : skn : mr’ : ḥbwr : ṣlmh : šm : mn : yld : šmy : mn : m’ny’*

17 *zy : bt : hdd : mr’y : mr’y : hdd : lḥmh : wmwh : ’l : ylqḥ : mn*

18 *ydh : swl : mr’ty : lḥmh : wmwh : ’l : tlqḥ : mn : ydh : wl*

19 *zr‘ : w’l : yḥṣd : w’lp : š‘ryn : lzr‘ wprys : l’ḥz : mnh*

20 *wm’h : s’wn : lhynqn : ’mr : w’l : yrwy : wm’h : swr : lhynqn*

21 *‘gl : w’l : yrwy : wm’h : nšwn : lhynqn : ‘lym : w’l : yrwy*

22 *wm’h : nšwn : l’pn : btnwr : lḥm : w’l : yml’nh : wmn : qlqlt’ : llqṭw : ’nšwh : š‘rn : l’klw*

23 *wmwtn : šbṭ : zy : nyrgl : ’l : ygtzr mn : mth*

The Aramaic portion of the Tell Fekherye bilingual, vocalized

1 *damûta' zî Hadysis'î zî śam qudm Hadad Sikan*

2 *gugal šamayn wa'arq (ḍ) mahanḥat 'usr wanātin ri'î*

3 *wamašqî lamāt kullan wanātin šilâ wa'adaqur*

4 *la'ilāhîn kullam 'aḥwih gugal nahar kullam ma'addin*

5 *māt kullan 'ilāh raḥmān zî taṣlûtuh ṭābâ yāsib*

6 *Sikan māri' rab māri' Hadyis'î malk Guzan bir*

7 *Sasnûrî malk Guzan laḥayyay nabšah walama'rak yawmwih*

8 *walakabbar šanawih walašallam baytah walašallam zar'ah walašallam*

9 *'anāšwih walamallad mariq minnih walamašma' taṣlûtah wala-*

10 *malqaḥ 'imrat pumih kānin wayahab lih waman 'aḥir kan*

11 *yabil lukāninah ḥadas wašumîm luśam bih wazî yal(l)id šumî minnih*

12 *wayaśîm šumah Hadad gabbār luhawî qābiluh ṣalm Hadyis'î*

13 *malk Guzan wazî Sikan wazî 'Azaran l'rm wrdt karsi'ih*

14 *walama'rak ḥayyawih walama'n 'imrat pumih 'il 'ilāhīn wa'il 'anāšîn*

15 *tayṭab damûta' za't 'abad 'l zî qudm hawtir qudm Hadad*

16 *yāsib Sikan māri' Ḥabûr ṣalmah śam man yalid šumî min ma'nayya'*

17 *zî bēt(!) Hadad mār'î mār'î Hadad laḥmah wamawih 'al yilqaḥ min*

18 *yadih Sala mār'atî laḥmah wamawih 'al tilqaḥ min yadih walu-*

19 *zara' wa'al yaḥṣud wa'alp śi'ārîn luzara' waparîs lu'aḥaz minnah*

20 *wami'â si'wān luhayniqān 'immir wa'al yirway wami'â sawr luhayniqān*

21 *'igl wa'al yirway wami'â nišwān lahayniqān 'alîm wa'al yirway*

22 *wami'â nišwān lu'apān batannûr laḥm wa'al yamalli'ānih wamin qalqalāta' lulaqaṭû 'anāšwih śi'ārīn lu'akalû*

23 *wamawtām šibṭ zî Nirgal 'al yigtizar min mātih*

suggest that a distinctive pronunciation was being recorded, although the same device served also to mark some word-terminal long vowels as such.

(2) Both *waw* and *yod* are used as medial vowel letters (but not *he*). *Waw* is used for primal /u/ (long or short [?]) and also for the diphthong /aw/. *Yod* is used for primal /i/ (whether long or short [?]) and for the diphthong /ay/.

These premises do not exclude other possibilities, but represent the point of departure for the study. Whether *waw* and *yod* were always used for all such vowels remains to be determined.

Since the objective is to establish the governing principles of the spelling in the inscription, we shall avoid areas of controversy concerning readings and interpretations, since it is essential to base the findings on clear cases and consensus readings as much as possible. Fortunately the text is mostly in excellent shape, and the presence of an equally readable Assyrian text makes most of the readings and interpretations secure.

We may now proceed to a word-by-word analysis of the text in terms of its orthography. In order to establish orthographic practice and rules, it is necessary to try to vocalize the text; and while this is all too often a fruitless and thankless job, it has to be attempted. It should be pointed out, however, that we are not concerned about the actual quality of many of the vowels, in particular those short unstressed vowels that are not and would not be represented in the orthography. Thus whether the vowel connecting prepositions to the following words is *a* or *i* or some indistinct sound does not matter in this inquiry. So we have chosen somewhat arbitrarily and trust that our reconstruction of such vowels will not be misunderstood. We make no claim to secret wisdom here, and would be happy to be corrected. In some cases where we think there is a reason for the selection of one vowel over another (the possible survival of old case-endings is a frequent instance), we shall offer explanations of our choices. In matters affecting orthography we shall take up that task in earnest.

The inventory of words, with comments on spelling

1. *dmwt'* (line 1), *damûta'*, 'the image'. The form seems quite regular, f. s. emphatic of *damût* (Heb. *dĕmût*).

The older the inscription is, the less confident we can be that a word such as this one already had the vocalization which we only know from much later attestation. Arguments from comparative-historical grammar can lead to more than one possibility and their contending claims cannot be settled. It is only at a later period that the suffix *-ût* is generally productive for abstract nouns. This one is concrete. The ending probably arose in the first place from the etymological /w/ in third-weak roots, as with this word, spreading to nouns with strong roots by analogy. Hence the possibility exists that in early times, and perhaps still surviving in the early first millennium BC, a word like this one was pronounced **dimwut-*, or the like. **Damawt-* is less likely, because that diphthong would either hold up or yield /o/. But theoretically the possibility that the *w* in *dmwt'* represents a diphthong cannot be entirely ruled out.

Converging evidence can be brought for this possibility. (i) The survival of words with primal consonant /w/ in such a position. (ii) The prominence in Aramaic of a consonant /w/ either in this position (*ḥaywān*, 'animals') or as an extension of a strong root (*malkĕwān*, 'kingdoms'). (iii) The early preference for *plene* spellings of Hebrew infinitives construct of third-*yod*/*waw* verbs in /-*ôt*/ suggests derivation from *damawatu*, or the like. (iv) Some strange spellings in the Hebrew Bible point to the possible existence of a consonantal *waw* in the third root position of some derivatives of weak roots. The ***ketib*** *qṣwwtw* (Exod. 37.8; 39.4) points to a variant plural *qiṣwōt-*. The word 'testimonies' (*'ēdōt*) is sometimes pointed with *shewa* to yield *'ēdwōt-* (1 Kgs 2.3; 2 Kgs 17.15; 23.3; Jer. 44.23; Ps. 119.14, 31, 36, 99, 111, 129, 144, 157; Neh. 9.34; 1 Chron. 29.19; 2 Chron. 34.31).

The existence of an analogous *w* in other words in this inscription (see below II A) requires that this possibility be taken into account. See also the discussion of No. 33. Even so, the probability is that the word was pronounced approximately as we have vocalized it. The reconstruction of the first stem vowel is admittedly conjectural.

The final *alef* is a consonant, marking the emphatic state. How it was pronounced at that time cannot be determined solely from the inscription (i.e. it may have quiesced in the final position). Such an *alef* can be considered to be a vowel letter only when it has no history as a consonant. There are no such cases in this inscription. In fact there are only two other cases of the emphatic in the whole inscription, *m'ny'* (line 16) and *qlqlt'* (line 22). The medial *waw*, however, is almost certainly a vowel letter, representing long /u/, which was evidently considered by the scribe to be the dominant or significant vowel in the word. It may be noted that only two vowel letters were in use in the middle of words (*he* is never so used) and so the choice is limited. With a possible exception noted below (No.

141), *a*-type vowels are never indicated medially, so we would expect to find only *u*- and *i*-types represented in the orthography.

Whether any vowels, considered phonetically, had been deflected to /o/ or /e/ at this stage is not germane. Nor can we prejudge the extent to which primal diphthongs /aw/ and /ay/ might have monophthongized in this dialect at this stage. If a vowel is known to be primally long, all the indications are that it would be stable, particularly in Aramaic. But the phonology of a previously unattested dialect should not be assumed hastily to be just like the rest of Aramaic. In particular there are two features of the present inscription that dictate caution. First, the letters used for writing certain consonants point to an early, if not archaic stage—typologically speaking. Second, the possible influence of Assyrian has to be kept in mind.

2. *zy* (1), *zî*, 'of'. This is the well-known particle used in various ways in Northwest Semitic inscriptions. The vocalization is certain and reflects the use of *y* as a final vowel letter for *-î*.

3. *hdys'y* (1), *hadyis'î*, 'Had-yis'i'. This is the name of the king who erected the statue memoralized in the inscription. Neither the vocalization nor the meaning proposed is certain, but both are plausible. In any case there seems to be little question about the final vowel sound, *î*, represented by the vowel letter *yod*. Naturally the initial *he* is a consonant, and so is the medial *yod*. The name, as most suggest, probably means 'Hadd (= Hadad) is my salvation', or the like. The etymology makes it virtually impossible to vocalize the medial *yod* as a vowel letter for *î*. The second part of the name cannot be a verb, for the *h* of the *hap'el* would be evident.

The other vowels in the name are short and require no comment.

4. *zy* (1), *zî* cf. No. 2. Here the particle is the relative pronoun meaning 'who'.

5. *śm* (1), *śam*, 'he set'. As expected, the short medial vowel receives no orthographic representation.

6. *qdm* (1), *qudm*, 'before'. All Northwest Semitic languages do not follow the same patterns with segholates. Eblaite complicates the picture even more. The vowel or vowels are short, however, and have no significance for this study.

7. *hdd skn* (1), *hadad sikan*, 'Hadad of Sikan'. On the basis of other instances of personal or place names in the inscription we might have expected, or at least not have been surprised, to see a medial *yod* in the name *skn*, since we find vowel letters in names of persons and places to facilitate identification and pronunciation. It does not seem to matter particularly whether the vowel was originally long or not: it is the quality that counts, and in general only /u/ and /i/ vowels are represented, and then, as this word shows, on a selective basis.

To judge from the rest of the inscription, it is more likely that a vowel written by means of a consonant was long, or at least stressed, rather than short. But that does not mean that all long (or stressed) vowels were so written; nor does it mean that every vowel so written must have been long. While rules are to be expected, and are certainly found, an element of convention operates in all writing systems, some variations are acceptable, and mistakes occur. Insofar as conventions, variants, and mistakes cause a text to fall short of absolute consistency, it is not valid to point to such marginal usage as evidence that there were no rules at all!

In the present text there is no word in which an expected terminal long vowel is not represented by a vowel letter, and there is no word in which such a vowel letter can reasonably be interpreted as a representation of a terminal short vowel. In view of remarks already made, we do not wish to state too dogmatically that this dialect had reached the stage, common throughout Northwest Semitic at this time, when all primal short terminal vowels had been lost, or else lengthened. But all the indications are that this was the state of affairs. To assert to the contrary that short terminal vowels were still pronounced, but never written, is to state something which is not only impossible to prove but which flies in the face of both historical-comparative grammar and the orthographic evidence. We are speaking about Aramaic, of course. How far a similar process had gone in Assyrian at this time is another question. But even if this loanword was *Sikanu* in Assyrian at this time, the odds are that it would be pronounced in an Aramaic text as Aramaic. The spelling of the word here supports this observation. Cf. Nos. 33, 63.

There is no reason to suppose that the place-name was pronounced *Sikanu*. As already remarked, loanwords would conform to Aramaic word patterns. Even if it could be proved that the Assyrians were saying *Sikanu*, it would not follow that Arameans did the same. The Assyrian spelling (*si-ka-ni* in line 20) proves nothing, since the final sign could equally represent vowelless terminal *-n*.

8. *gwgl* (2), *gugal*, 'water-master'. This is a loanword from Akkadian, so we are not surprised to find it equipped with a medial vowel letter. Again the selection is limited to vowels that can properly be represented by *waw* or *yod*, and we have noted that the scribe limits himself to not more than one vowel letter in the middle of a word. In this case the vowel seems to be short, but it may be under the accent. In any case we suggest that the vowel letter was intended to mark quality (and perhaps stress) rather than quantity.

9. *šmyn* (2), *šamayn*, 'heavens'. The *yod* here represents the diphthong /ay/. It is important evidence to support the view that the diphthongs /aw/ and /ay/ were preserved in this branch of Aramaic as was true of most of the Aramaic dialects. So far as we are aware, there is only one exception in this inscription to the practice of representing the diphthong by its consonantal element, and that is *bt* in line 17 (see below [No. 130] for discussion).

10. *w'rq* (2), *wa'arq*, 'and earth'. No comment is needed, except to note that representation of primal /ḍ/ by means of *q*.

11. *mhnḥt* (2), *mahanḥat*, 'the provider'. This form is analyzed as a *hap'el* participle of the root *nḥt*. The vocalization is not certain, but the vowels are all short, and we would not expect any orthographic representation of any of them.

12. *'sr* (2), *'usr*, 'riches'. The vocalization is based on later Aramaic *'utrā'*, but all that matters is that there are no vowels requiring or implying orthographic representation. Syriac *'awtrā'* is secondary. Note that in this dialect primal /ṯ/ is written *s* (cf. Nos. 3, 159).

13. *wntn* (2), *wanātin*, 'and the giver'. Here we seem to have the *pe'al* participle, m. s. The only point to be made is that long /ā̱/ here and elsewhere in the inscription is not represented in the orthography in the medial position.

14. *r'y* (2), *ri'î*, 'food, provender'. The vocalization is based on the Akkadian cognate, but biblical *rĕ'î* is also germane. For our purposes the important orthographic element is the representation of final *î* by *yod*. Theoretically the final syllable could be a diphthong; but this is most unlikely, and in any case it would not introduce any departure from standard practice.

15. *wmšqy* (3), *wamašqî*, 'and drink'. Here again the orthographically interesting information concerns the final *yod* which represents *î*.

16. *lmt* (3), *lamāt*, 'to the countries'. While the form of the noun is apparently singular, it serves as a collective with the following *kullan* ('all of them'). The word is found in Aḥiqar. It is not certain whether *mt* in other Old Aramaic inscriptions (where it often means 'man') might sometimes mean 'land(s)'. Whether a loan from Akkadian or not, the stem vowel was probably long, but is not represented in the orthography.

17. *kln* (3), *kullan*, 'all of them'. Here we have the particle *kl* plus the 3rd f. pl. pronominal suffix. Both vowels were probably short.

18. *wntn* (3), *wanātin* (cf. No. 13).

19. *šlh* (3). The form and meaning of this word are obscure. Whether connected with Sefire *šlw* (Sf III 5) or derived from one or other of the roots *šly* (Kaufman, p. 164), the terminal *he* is hard to explain. If a loan from Akkadian, *sil'u*, 'libation' (*AHw*, p. 1044), is the best candidate. It seems likely that the final *he* is a vowel letter, presumably for *-â*, but possibly for another vowel. In view of the availability of *waw* and *yod*, it can hardly be /u/ or /i/, and there is little ground for belief that either /o/ or /e/ yet existed in this dialect. The word was doubtless construed as feminine singular.

20. *w'dqwr* (3), *wa'adaqur*, '?'. This is another loanword from Akkadian, and therefore we are not surprised at the use of *waw* to indicate the significant medial vowel (the only one eligible for representation in this system). The *waw* represents an original short /u/, but whether it was under accent and possibly lengthened in its Aramaic guise cannot be determined.

21. *l'lhyn* (4), *la'ilāhîn*, 'for the gods'. There are two points of orthographic interest: (a) the long *î* in the final syllable is represented by *yod*; note that this example establishes the use of *yod* as a vowel in the medial position for *î*; the same word, apparently, is spelled without the medial *yod* in line 14 (*'lhn*). Cf. No. 105. (b) The medial long /a/ (third syllable) is not indicated in the orthography.

22. *klm* (4), *kullam*, 'all of them'. Particle with the 3rd m. pl. suffix. Cf. No. 17.

23. *'ḥwh* (4), *'aḥwih*, 'his brothers'. This is a difficult form, and our proposal is admittedly a stab in the dark. The important things to note are as follows. It is the consistent practice in this inscription to include a *waw* before the 3rd m. s. pronominal suffix when it is attached to masculine plural nouns. It also seems clear that this *waw* does not represent a vowel but has consonantal force, or reflects the consonantal element in a diphthong. We therefore regard the *waw* as a part of the plural form of nouns used with pronominal suffixes, in particular with m. pl. nouns with 3rd m. s. suffixes. To interpret this *waw* otherwise, to read it as /u/, for instance, creates problems. How could such a form develop? A consonant in the third root position of a word such as *'ḥ(w)*, 'brother', is understandable. Misdivision takes the syllable *-wi-* as the plural morpheme, extending it by paradigmatic analogy to strong roots. The result is standard in this inscription and in Sefire (convenient inventory in Fitzmyer 149). Fitzmyer vocalizes *'aḥawh*, etc. (p. 31), assuming a secondary suffix after the analogy of biblical Aramaic *-ôhî*. But the loss of the final vowel from a form with that history is a serious obstacle, in our opinion, to say nothing about the consonant cluster /wh/. In any case, whether *'aḥwih* or *'aḥawh* (or even *'aḥawih*), the *waw* is consonantal.

24. *gwgl* (4), *gugal*. Cf. No. 8.

25. *nhr* (4), *nahar*, 'rivers'. Another collective, since it is followed by *kullam*.

26. *klm* (4), *kullam*. Cf. No. 22.

27. *m'dn* (4), *ma'addin*, '?'. We take this to be a *pa'el* participle m. s. All the vowels are short, and none is represented in the orthography.

28. *mt* (5), *māt*. Cf. No. 16.

29. *kln* (5), *kullan*. Cf. No. 17.

30. *'lh* (5), *'ilāh*, 'god'. The final *he* here is a consonant; hence the preceding long /a/ vowel is not represented by a vowel letter. Cf. *'lhyn* (4) / *'lhn* (14).

31. *rḥmn* (5), *raḥmān*, 'the compassionate'. If the second vowel was

actually long /a/, then we have another example of a long medial /a/ not represented in the orthography.

32. *zy* (5), *zî*. Cf. No. 2.

33. *tṣlwth* (5), *taṣlûtuh*, 'his prayer'. Apparently a loan word from Akkadian, but adapted to Aramaic usage. The noun is feminine singular with a 3rd m. s. pronominal suffix. Since the noun is in the nominative case, we have supplied the nominative case ending as the connecting vowel between noun and suffix, but this is only a guess. There is a medial vowel letter, *waw*, which represents a long /u/, in the key syllable of the word.

34. *ṭbh* (5), *ṭābâ*, 'good'. The word is a predicate adjective f. s. abs., modifying the preceding noun *tṣlwth*. The final vowel, long /a/, is represented by *he*. The medial long /a/ is not represented.

35. *ysb* (5), *yāsib*, 'the dweller', or in this case perhaps 'the resident monarch'. We take this form as the *pe'al* participle m. s., and note the medial long /a/, unrepresented in the orthography.

36. *skn* (6), *sikan*. Cf. No. 7.

37. *mr'* (6), *māri'*, 'lord'. To judge from the vocalization eventually attested, this title is probably an original participle. The final *alef* is a root consonant. The long /a/ in the first syllable is not represented in the orthography.

38. *rb* (6), *rab*, 'great'.

39. *mr'* (6), *māri'*. Cf. No. 37.

40. *hdys'y* (6), *hadyis'î*. Cf. No. 3.

41. *mlk* (6), *malk*, 'king'. We take the word in its monosyllabic root form, although there are other possibilities, such as **malik* (which seems to be the Eblaite reading). Cf. No. 6.

42. *gwzn* (6), *guzan*, 'Guzan'. Since a foreign place-name is involved, the spelling is enhanced by the use of a vowel letter. The *waw*

represents an original short /u/ vowel, but whether it has been modified or lengthened under accent (if it is stressed) cannot be determined. The later pronunciation *Gozan*, as attested in Hebrew, does not settle the pronunciation here. All that can be said is that a medial vowel letter is used to represent a vowel which was originally short /u/. Cf. the discussion of *gwgl* (No. 8).

43. *br* (6), *bir* (later *bar*), 'son'.

44. *ssnwry* (7), *sasnûrî*, 'Sas-nuri'. The name seems clear enough, but the vocalization may be partially uncertain. For orthographic purposes, we are concerned with the latter part of the name only:

(a) The final vowel *î* of the 1st c. s. suffix is represented by *yod*.

(b) The medial vowel *û* is represented by *waw*.

The name as a whole is doubtless *sas* (for *sams*='sun')—*nûrî*='The sun (god) is my light' (lit. 'fire'). Both the suffix and the medial vowel are long.

45. *mlk* (7), *malk*. Cf. No. 41.

46. *gwzn* (7), *guzan*. Cf. No. 42.

47. *lḥyy* (7), *laḥayyay* or *laḥayyî*, 'to give life, to make live'. We take the form to be *pa'el* infinitive. The first *yod* is consonantal and part of the root. The form is archaic, since the standard form would be *laḥayyayâ*. Here the reading may be *ḥayyay*, but *ḥayyî* is not ruled out. In either case, the diphthong or vowel reflects a root consonant, so we have an example of historical or etymological spelling.

48. *nbšh* (7), *nabšah*, 'his soul/person'. We read this as the noun plus the 3rd m. s. suffix. Since the noun is in the objective case, we supply the accusative vowel *-a* as the connection between noun and pronominal suffix.

49. *wlm'rk* (7), *walama'rak*, 'and for extension'. We take this as a *pe'al* infinitive of the root *'rk*. The *alef* is etymological.

50. *ywmwh* (7), *yawmwih*, 'his days'. The meaning is certain, but the form is difficult. We interpret the form as a m. pl. noun with the 3rd

m. s. pronominal suffix. The form of the noun, with medial *waw*, may be unusual, but it is known in Aramaic from Panammu through Elephantine to Qumran. The first *waw* therefore represents the diphthong /aw/. The second *waw* is normal in this inscription for pl. nouns with 3rd m.s. suffixes. We consider it consonantal and vocalize accordingly. Cf. No. 23.

51. *wlkbr* (8), *walakabbar*, 'and to multiply'. We take this as a *pa'el* infinitive of the root *kbr*. No vowels are eligible for consonantal spelling. Short /i/ also is possible, but inconsequential.

52. *šnwh* (8), *šanawih*, 'his years'. We have here another example of the m. pl. noun with a 3rd m. s. pronoun suffix connected by a *waw* which marks the stem. We consider the *waw* a consonant and part of the morphology of plural nouns in this dialect. Cf. Nos. 23 and 50.

53. *wlšlm* (8), *walašallam*, 'and to give success to'. We take the form to be the *pa'el* infinitive of the root *šlm*. Cf. No. 51.

54. *byth* (8), *baytah*, 'his house'. Since the word is in the objective case, we have supplied the accusative case ending to connect it with the pronoun suffix. The spelling with the medial *yod* shows that the diphthong /ay/ of the original word is still represented. The variant spelling of this word in line 17 (*bt*) poses a problem. See No. 130.

55. *wlšlm* (8), *walašallam*. Cf. No. 53.

56. *zr'h* (8), *zar'ah*, 'his seed'. We take the form to be the noun with the 3rd m. s. suffix; the final *he* is a consonant, which is true of all 3rd m. s. suffix forms. The connecting vowel we have supplied is the accusative form. Cf. No. 54.

57. *wlšlm* (8), *walašallam*. Cf. No. 53.

58. *'nšwh* (9), *'anāšwih*, 'his men'. Another case of a m. pl. noun with a 3rd m. s. pronoun suffix. We take the *waw* to be a consonant and part of the plural form. Cf. Nos. 23, 50, 52.

59. *wlmld* (9), *walamallad*, 'and to efface'. We take the form as a *pa'el* infinitive. See also Nos. 80, 175.

60. *mrq* (9), *mariq*, 'plague(?)'. This word occurs in Sefire I A 29, and seems to be identical with later Aramaic *mĕra'*, cognate with Akkadian *marṣu*, Arabic *maraḍ*, 'illness'. In any case the stem vowels are almost certainly short, so the spelling contains nothing unexpected.

61. *mnh* (9), *minnih*, 'from him'. We interpret this form as the preposition *min* plus the 3rd m. s. pronoun suffix. The terminal *he* is consonantal (or historical spelling and hence of no special orthographic significance).

62. *wlmšm'* (9), *walamašma'*, 'and for listening or being heard'. We take this form to be the *pe'al* infinitive of *šm'*. Cf. No. 49.

63. *tṣlwth* (9), *taṣlûtah*, 'his prayer'. Except for the hypothetical connecting vowel, the form is the same as No. 33. See comments there.

64. *wlmlqḥ* (9-10), *walamalqaḥ*, 'and for receiving or accepting'. We take the form as the *pe'al* infinitive of *lqḥ*.

65. *'mrt* (10), *'imrat*, 'the utterance of'. This is the f. s. construct form before the absolute noun *pmh*.

66. *pmh* (10), *pumih*, 'his mouth'. We take this form to be the m. s. noun plus the 3rd m. s. suffix. We have supplied the genitive case connecting vowel. The final *he* is consonantal.

67. *knn* (10), *kannan*, or *kānin*, 'he built or constructed'. We take this to be a *pa'el* or else a *palil* form, perfect 3rd m. s., like Hebrew *kônēn*. See the discussion under No. 74. The medial long /a/ is not represented in the orthography.

68. *wyhb* (10), *wayahab*, 'and he gave'. This form seems to be a *pe'al* perfect 3rd m. s. from the root *yhb*.

69. *lh* (10), *lih*, 'to him'. This form is the preposition *l* with the 3rd m. s. pronoun suffix; the final *he* is consonantal.

70. *wmn* (10), *waman*, 'and if(?)'. The form is uncertain, and so is the

meaning; but in any case it has no particular orthographic importance.

71. *'ḥr* (10), *'aḥir*, 'another'. Conceivably it could be read as *'aḥar*, 'after(wards)'. Assyrian parallels favour this alternative. In either case there is nothing to be gained orthographically from the form except that it is consistent with the principles and practices so far observed or deduced.

72. *kn* (10), *kan(?)*, 'if or when'. The form and meaning are not clear, but the word is not important orthographically.

73. *ybl* (11), *yabil*, 'it wears out(?)'. It is hard to say just what this form is. The root *bly* (*blh* in Hebrew, *bl'* in Aramaic) means 'wear out', usually of clothes, but in an Elephantine text it refers to a boat in disrepair. If this root were involved, we would expect the third consonant to be represented. An apocopated form is not out of the question, but would be inconsistent with the morphophonemics of the rest of the inscription. See however No. 178. Derivation of *ybl* from the root *nbl*, 'decay' in Hebrew, commonly used of foliage; or *npl*, 'destroy' in Assyrian, is equally problematic, since /n/ does not assimilate in Aramaic. Bordreuil and Millard (Abou-Assaf 1982: 32) prefer the root *ybl*, 'remove', extending its meaning to 'deterioration'. Even then one would expect the first syllable to retain a diphthong. The existence of by-forms *bl* and *bll*, or at least some measure of semantic overlap between these roots, requires us to treat the form with caution. The grammatical objection that the subject ('image') is feminine suggests rather that the implied subject is 'my name', since it is the removal of the name on the statue—a vital detail—that is later enjoined. The Assyrian parallel uses the noun *anḫūtu*, 'dilapidation'. Other usage suggests that a general formula, used specifically of temples, is being applied to an object not so liable to natural wear and tear but vulnerable, nevertheless, to damage, often deliberate.

74. *lknnh* (11), *lukanninah*, perhaps *lukāninah*, 'let him build it'. We take this form as combination of the precative particle *lu* and the 3rd m. s. *palil* perfect of the verb *kn* (cf. No. 67), plus the 3rd f. s. suffix. We have supplied connecting vowels in keeping with the syntax. It is possible that the *lu-* form had developed into a kind of pseudo-preformative verb at this stage. But we think that a perfect is not

entirely ruled out. The use of the precative particle with preformative verbs in Akkadian does not necessarily prove the contrary, for they are preterit. Even so, in view of the cultural mix exhibited by this inscription, influence of Assyrian on this Aramaic dialect is very likely. Nor does the association of this kind of jussive later on in the text with a negated imperfect prove that it is derived from an imperfect, for part of the contrast lies in the difference in aspect between an act performed and one that does not happen. Precative *lu* is not the only candidate for ancestor of preformative *l*-. The history of this particle in Semitic is not well understood. Almost any vowel, short or long, is found with it (Huffmon 78-81; Dion 166-70). From the present inscription we can infer at least that the connecting vowel was short, especially if it was *lu*-. This is not likely if it came from *luyakannin*, or the like. But to say more than that would be mere speculation in the present state of knowledge. So far as the present investigation is concerned, we are indifferent to the correct identification of the stem of such verbs, whether preformative or afformative; for in each case the stem vowels are short, even if often indeterminate as to quality, and so are not eligible for consideration as potential occasions for the use of vowel letters.

So far as the present word is concerned, the twin consonants of such a root are manifest chiefly in *pa'el*, and later pronunciation consistently (but not quite universally) shows the doubling of the middle radical. So this form is probably *lukanninah*. The final *he* is a consonant and all the vowels are short.

75. *ḥds* (11), *ḥadas*, 'new'. The syntax is problematical. The matching form in the Assyrian versions is a verb. If this word is an adjective, it cannot refer to the statue. Perhaps it is an adverb—'anew'. In any case there is no reason to suspect that it contains long vowels, so the orthography is normal.

76. *wšmym* (11), *wašumî-m*, 'and my name'. This form consists of the conjunction plus the name *šum* with the 1st s. pronoun suffix *-î* and an enclitic *mem*, which makes the suffix a medial vowel. However, in this inscription some vowels of this kind are represented and here there would be an added reason to do so. Without the enclitic *mem* the word would certainly have been written with the *yod* representing the final vowel, so here it is retained, even though it is no longer final. In the relationship between No. 76 and No. 81 (*šmy*) we can see the

mechanism by which the early use of vowel letters for final vowels spread to the interior of words, first to the writing of a vowel which sometimes *is* terminal, then to long medial vowels which are never terminal.

We have adopted the normal Aramaic word for 'name', but there is no indication in the spelling as to how the stem was pronounced.

77. *lśm* (11), *luśam*, 'let him set'. We take this to be the same sort of form as No. 74 with precative *lu-* followed by the *pe'al* form of the perfect 3rd m. s. Kaufman (p. 150), however, supposes that *l-* is a preformative, as in later Aramaic, and therefore that the stem is *śim*. Compared with *yśym* (No. 83) he then infers from the difference in spelling that the supposed /i/ in No. 77 was reduced, and so not spelled with a vowel letter. Since we have not found any certainly short medial /i/ spelled with a vowel letter, the point remains somewhat moot. But in our opinion, the occurrence of the normal *yśym* in the same inscription makes it unlikely that *lśm* is a variant preformative. A diphthong is out of the question.

78. *bh* (11), *bih*, 'on it' or 'in it'. This form is the preposition *b* plus the 3rd m. s. suffix. We have supplied a vowel, but we are not prepared to argue for it. In any case the final *he* is a consonant.

79. *wzy* (11), *wazî*. Cf. No. 2.

80. *yld* (11), *yal(l)id*, 'he effaces'. The meaning is certain, since cognate verbs are used in the Sefire inscriptions. There, however, both *pe'al* and *hap'el* are attested (Fitzmyer 76). Here all forms (Nos. 59, 80, 175) are *pe'al*. The argument as to whether the root is *ldd* or *lwd* is inconclusive. The problem is similar to the one presented by *ybl* (No. 73), and the simplest resolution is to recognize a simple biconsonantal, rather than a 'hollow' root. 'He will die' is spelled *ymwt* at Sefire, and that *waw* must be a vowel letter (the attempt of Degen [p. 28] to explain it as a *Gleitlaut* is unconvincing). The fact that *yld* is not spelled similarly here does not necessarily mean that the orthography is inconsistent, as the root may be different. At Sefire both infinitive and imperative are spelled simply *ld*. In any event the vowels are short and the orthography is appropriate.

81. *šmy* (11), *šumî*, 'my name'. Here we have the noun plus the 1st s.

pronoun suffix. The final long /i/ is represented by *yod* in the orthography.

82. *mnh* (11), *minnih*, 'from it'. This appears to be the preposition *min* plus the 3rd m. s. pronoun suffix. The final *he* is a consonant. Cf. No. 61.

83. *wyśym* (12), *wayaśîm*, 'and he sets'. We take the form to be a *pe'al* imperfect 3rd m. s. from the hollow root *śym*. The first *yod* is a consonant, of course; but the second one is an internal vowel letter for long /i/. This is a parade example of the use of the vowel letter for an internal vowel. We cannot be absolutely certain that the vowel was long at this time, but the spelling strongly suggests that it was, and, by the same token the non-use of a vowel letter in *yld* (No. 80) suggest that its vowel was not long.

84. *šmh* (12), *šumah*, 'his name'. The form consists of the noun plus 3rd m. s. pronoun suffix. The final *he* is consonantal. We have supplied the connecting vowel *-a-*, an accusative case ending for the noun.

85. *hdd* (12), *hadad*. Cf. No. 7.

86. *gbr* (12), *gabbār*, 'hero, warrior'. The form is no doubt the D-stem for 'warrior', with long /a/ in the second syllable without orthographic representation.

87. *lhwy* (12), *luhawî*, 'let him become'. The form combines the precative particle with the *pe'al* perfect 3rd m. s. of the root *hwy*. Cf. No. 77, and the discussion there. The final *yod* stands as a vowel letter for long /i/, but it also constitutes the third consonant of the root, thus providing an example of the transition from historical to phonetic spelling. Cf. No. 47.

88. *qblh* (12), *qābiluh*, 'his enemy'. The form combines the m. s. noun or participle with the 3rd m. s. pronoun suffix. The final *he* is consonantal. We have supplied a connecting vowel reflecting the presumed nominative case of the noun.

89. *ṣlm* (12), *ṣalm*, 'the image of'. We assume that the word is the same as Hebrew *ṣelem*, hence originally monosyllabic. It is the m. s. construct form, and the stem vowel would be short.

90. *hdys'y* (12), *hadyis'î*. Cf. No. 3.

91. *mlk* (13), *malk*. Cf. No. 41.

92. *gwzn* (13), *guzan*. Cf. No. 42.

93. *wzy* (13), *wazî*. Cf. No. 2.

94. *skn* (13), *sikan*. Cf. No. 7.

95. *wzy* (13), *wazî*. Cf. No. 2.

96. *'zrn* (13), *'azaran*, 'Azaran'. The vocalization of the place-name comes from the Akkadian. Since there are only /a/ vowels in the word, no vowel letters are expected and none are used.

97. *l'rm wrdt* (13). The reading here is questionable, and while some sense can be made of the phrase in connection with the uncontested following word *krs'h*, 'his throne', we prefer to pass over these terms. It is not likely that the *alef* or the *waw* are candidates for vowel letters.

98. *krs'h* (13), *karsi'ih*, 'his throne'. This spelling with *reš* is somewhat surprising, but the form is well-attested in Aramaic for the word 'throne'. It has the 3rd m. s. suffix. The final *he* is consonantal. There are no vowel letters, and no long vowels.

99. *wlm'rk* (14), *walama'rak*. Cf. No. 49.

100. *ḥywh* (14), *ḥayyawih*, 'his life'. Again we have an example of a m. pl. noun with a 3rd m. s. pronoun suffix. We note the presence of medial *waw*, which we interpret as a consonant representing the plural form of the noun. We have supplied connecting vowels. The final *he* is consonantal. Cf. Nos. 23, 50, 52, 58.

101. *wlm'n* (14), *walama'n*, 'and so that'. Cf. Hebrew *lĕma'an*.

102. *'mrt* (14), *'imrat*. Cf. No. 65.

103. *pmh* (14), *pumih*. Cf. No. 66.

104. *'l* (14), *'il*, 'to' or 'for'.

105. *'lhn* (14), *'ilāhîn*, 'gods'. Here we have a m. pl. form in the absolute state, but without a vowel letter for the internal long /i/. The form is to be compared with *'lhyn* (No. 21 = *'ilāhîn*). It is a little surprising to find the same word spelled in two different ways in a short inscription, and it may reflect the fact that medial vowel letters were a relatively recent innovation and that older spellings persisted even after the more modern system had been introduced. The defective four-letter form would naturally be the older original spelling, whereas the five-letter form would be more up-to-date. It is also conceivable that the scribe, having written the word in the fuller, more correct form in its first occurrence, would not feel obliged to give the full spelling the second time (Andersen 1970). We have another example of this phenomenon in the varying spellings of the word *ś'ryn* (line 19) and *ś'rn* (22), both being the plural form of the word 'barley'; and the defective form follows the full spelling. Another possibility is that *'lhn* here is part of an old traditional expression (cf. Judg. 9.9, 13), and perhaps the phrase was simply copied from an older example or was written out in the older style in which it had originated. Note the two spellings of 'earth' in Jer. 10.11, one archaic (as in our inscription)—it sounds credal—one current. The parallel term *'nšn* (*'anāšīn*, 'men') also is written defectively. It will be noted that the long /a/ in *'lhn* is not represented in the orthography.

106. *w'l* (14), *wa'il*, 'and to' or 'for'. Cf. No. 104.

107. *'nšn* (14), *'anāšīn*, 'men'. Here we have another m. pl. noun corresponding to *'lhn* (*'ilāhīn*, 'gods') in the same line, and, like the earlier word, written defectively, that is, without a vowel letter for the long /i/ in the last syllable of the word. The same reasoning applies here as was proposed in No. 105. It may be observed that in the five examples of m. pl. nouns in the absolute state, two are written out fully or *plene* while three are not. Of all the graphic procedures examined in this inscription the treatment of the m. pl. ending (*-īn* or *-în*) is the least consistent.

108. *tyṭb* (15), *tayṭab*, 'may be good'. This word is a 3rd f. s. imperfect form of the *pe'al* stem of the root *yṭb*, a byform of the primal root *ṭb*.

The *yod* apparently represents the diphthong /ay/, if we assume that the verb followed the *yaqtal* pattern. Alternatively we could vocalize *tîṭab*, assuming a *yiqtal* formation. Cf. biblical Aramaic *yêṭab*, apparently derived from *yayṭab* in contrast with Hebrew *yîṭab* (*qal*). We would expect the *yod* to be written in either case, since it is one of the root consonants. The form, however, is new for Old Aramaic. The *hap'el* is well attested, consistently *hyṭb* in Old Aramaic, *hwṭb* at Elephantine. Ezra 7.18 attests the *qal*. The byform *yṭb* is generally used for derived stems and tenses, so the medial *yod* in the present form is historical spelling in that sense, whether representing the diphthong or long vowel.

109. *dmwt'* (15), *damûta'*. Cf. No. 1.

110. *z't* (15), *za't*, 'this'. It is the f. demonstrative adjective modifying the preceding noun *damûta'*. In this form the *alef* is a consonant and the /a/ vowel is short. Even if the *alef* had quiesced at this early period—there is no evidence for this—the preserved *alef* still could not be regarded as a vowel letter for the (probably) lengthened /a/, but only as an example of historical spelling. Such an *alef* cannot be regarded as a true or pure vowel letter until it is used in a word where it had no etymological or historical rootage.

111. *'bd* (15), *'abad*, 'he made'. This is a *pe'al* perfect 3rd m. s. verb.

112. *'l* (15), *'il*, '?'. This is some sort of particle in an idiomatic expression based on an Akkadian cliché, although it does not correspond exactly to the Assyrian parallel here. It was probably accommodated to Aramaic *'l*. Cf. Nos. 104, 106.

113. *zy* (15), *zî*. Cf. No. 2.

114. *qdm* (15), *qudm*. Cf. No. 6.

115. *hwtr* (15), *hawtir*, 'he has exceeded, i.e. done more'. This form is the *hap'el* perfect 3rd m. s. of the root *ytr* (primal *wtr*). It is noteworthy that the diphthong /aw/ has been preserved and is represented by its consonantal constituent *waw*.

116. *qdm* (15), *qudm*. Cf. No. 6.

117. *hdd* (15), *hadad*. Cf. No. 7.

118. *ysb* (16), *yāsib*. Cf. No. 35.

119. *skn* (16), *sikan*. Cf. No. 7.

120. *mr'* (16), *māri'*. Cf. No. 37.

121. *ḥbwr* (16), *ḥabûr*, 'Habur'. This is the name of the well-known river of Syria // Mesopotamia. Note the use of the vowel letter *waw* for the distinctive /u/ sound in the name. For similar practice in foreign names, cf. *gwzn* (Nos. 42, 46), and in words of foreign origin, cf. *gwgl* (Nos. 8, 24), *'dqwr* (No. 20) and *tṣlwth* (Nos. 33, 63). We believe that the *waw* is used to identify the quality of the vowel rather than its length or even its position under stress, although neither possibility is ruled out in adaptation to Aramaic word patterns. In time, if not immediately, the effect of the use of a vowel letter might have been to lengthen and accentuate the vowel so represented.

122. *ṣlmh* (16), *ṣalmah*, 'his image'. The form is the m. s. noun with the 3rd m. s. pronoun suffix. Since it is the direct object we have supplied an accusative connecting vowel /a/. The final *he* is consonantal. Cf. No. 89.

123. *śm* (16), *śam*. Cf. No. 5.

124. *mn* (16), *man*, 'whoever'. We suggest that this pronominal particle serves as the subject of the following verb. The vowel is short.

125. *yld* (16), *yal(l)id*, 'effaces'. Cf. No. 80.

126. *šmy* (16), *šumî*, 'my name'. Cf. Nos. 76, 81.

127. *mn* (16), *min*, 'from'. Cf. Nos. 61, 82.

128. *m'ny'* (16), *ma'nayya'*, 'the vessels'. Here we have a m. pl. noun in the emphatic state. We take the *alef* at the end of the word to be consonantal just as the medial *alef* is (as part of the root). Cf. No. 1

for discussion of the emphatic state in the inscription and No. 110 for discussion of possible quiescence of *alef* in different positions. There are apparently no long vowels in this word, and, as we expect, no vowel letters.

129. *zy* (17), *zî*. Cf. No. 2.

130. *bt* (17), *bēt*, 'house'. Here we have the only probable case of diphthong contraction in the whole inscription. The contraction is standard in Phoenician and other Canaanite dialects, including North Israelite and apparently Moabite; but it is not the rule in Aramaic inscriptions where the word is regularly spelled *byt*, showing preservation of the diphthong. Thus in this inscription we have the form *byth* (*baytah*, No. 54), which we would regard as normal for Aramaic of all periods. Elsewhere the diphthongs seem to have been preserved, since they are represented in the spelling. We might try to explain the phenomenon by saying that the diphthongs had contracted, but the consonantal elements *w* and *y* were kept through historical spelling. Then the form here, *bt*, could be explained as an instance of phonetic spelling against the prevailing conservatism of the orthographic system. The main objection to this explanation is that the practice of this dialect would run counter to our whole experience with classical Aramaic, and it is difficult to establish such a revolutionary idea on the basis of one reading, which itself is negated by at least the following examples of diphthongal preservation: *šmyn* (No. 9), *byth* (No. 54), *ywmwh* (No. 50), *tyṭb* (No. 108, probably), *hwtr* (No. 115), *wmwh* (Nos. 136, 144, plausibly), *swr* (No. 166), *lhynqn* (Nos. 160, 166, 172), *yrwy* (Nos. 163, 169, 175, probably), to say nothing about the universal spelling *byt* in Old Aramaic inscriptions, which makes this unique exception all the more remarkable. It is better to seek another explanation. Since at least one other inscription shares the problem of two different spellings of the same word (in the Mesha Inscription—*bt* [lines 23, 27, 30, 30; some in place names, but always with a word-divider], normal for Moabite; but *wbbth* [line 7] versus *bbyth* [line 25], the exception being the other way around from the Tell Fekherye inscription), we may reasonably suppose that two forms of spelling, if not two different pronunciations, of this word were current, rather than supposing that this word was somehow vulnerable to incorrect spelling. The normal Aramaic pronunciation would be *bayt*, alone

and in its various combinations. No theory about variations due to differences in stress, or in the construct state, however true for masoretic Hebrew, has held up with respect to the inscriptional evidence. The efforts of Bange along these lines were not successful. But it is possible that a reference to the temple of Hadad might ultimately derive from Canaanite sources, where Hadad played a central role. Thus 'the house of Baal/Hadad' in the Canaanite epics would inevitably be spelled *bt b'l/hdd* and perhaps that spelling in that combination became a fixed tradition, *bt* serving as a kind of logogram, a hangover of Phoenician spelling. In the Mesha Inscription something similar happened at second remove. Just as the Aramaeans received their writing system from the Phoenicians, with only a trace of Phoenician spelling showing up, as with *bt*, so the South-Canaanite dialects used a writing system already adapted by the Aramaeans, rather than one which they developed along similar lines (but independently) by direct borrowing from the Phoenicians. Aramaean cultural influence is evident in the palaeography, and the one occurrence of the spelling *byt* in the Mesha Inscription could represent a lone intrusion of Aramaic usage.

Beyond such speculation about all we can say is that this is the single exception to diphthongal representation in the inscription, so far as we are aware. Apart from this, the only other deviation from the standard Aramaic spelling of the word 'house' (*byt*, corresponding to Southern Judahite, familiar from standard biblical Hebrew) in the entire Aramaic corpus known to us is in a (very late) Hatra text (KAI 249, line 4).

It should be emphasized that the normal spelling of the same word *is* represented in this inscription, so that any explanation of one spelling must take into account the other, at the same time and in the same place, and carved by the same stone-carver from a cartoon made by the same scribe.

Yet this very circumstance draws attention to the fact that the present inscription consists of two distinct portions which cover much of the same ground. The four words which present archaic (Phoenician) spellings (*'lhn*, *'nšn*, *bt*, *ś'rn*) all occur in the second part and two of them (*'lhyn*, *byth*) occur with normal spelling in the first part. The second part contains formulaic material of a kind known from other Northwest Semitic inscriptions, such as Sefire. That is, these expressions were not original to the author of the present inscription, and even their spelling reflects derivation from older practice. Andersen (1966) pointed out a similar distribution of contrasting usage in the syntax of the Mesha Inscription.

131. *hdd* (17), *hadad*. Cf. No. 7.

132. *mr'y* (17), *mār'î*, 'my lord'. Here we have the m. s. noun and the 1st s. pronoun suffix. The final *î* is represented in the orthography by *yod*. Cf. No. 37 for *mr'*.

133. *mr'y* (17), *mār'î*. Cf. No. 132.

134. *hdd* (17), *hadad*. Cf. No. 7.

135. *lḥmh* (17), *laḥmah*, 'his bread'. The form consists of the m. s. noun plus the 3rd m. s. suffix. The final *he* is consonantal.

136. *wmwh* (17), *wamaw(i)h*, 'and his water'. Here we have a m. pl. (or dual) noun plus the 3rd m. s. suffix. The *waw* represents the plural or dual form and may preserve the diphthong of the dual ending as the *yod* does in Hebrew. We have suggested an appropriate vocalization, although it is also possible that the diphthong has been resolved. The final *he* is consonantal. Cf. Nos. 23, 50, 52, 58, 100 for this construction.

137. *'l* (17), *'al*, negative particle, 'let not'.

138. *ylqḥ* (17), *yilqaḥ*, 'let him [not] receive or take'. We read this as a *pe'al* imperfect 3rd m. s. verb.

139. *mn* (17), *min*. Cf. No. 127.

140. *ydh* (18), *yadih*, 'his hand'. Singular noun with 3rd m. s. pronoun suffix. The final *he* is a consonant. We have supplied the connecting vowel reflecting the genitive case of the noun.

141. *swl* (18), *sawl*, 'Sala(!)'. Admittedly this is a very difficult form, but we shall attempt an explanation. From the Assyrian version we know that this is a personal name and that it designates the goddess Shala, the consort of Hadad. Apparently it was felt that the key vowel, in fact the only vowel (we do not think that there would be a

final vowel in the Aramaized form), should be represented in the spelling of the names, especially exotic names, in the Aramaic version. Since the vowel was *a* (perhaps long *a*), there was no vowel letter available to represent it in a medial position. They might have tried a *he* in the middle of the word, but that would have violated their rules, since it certainly would have been considered a consonant or pronounced as such.

The only available signs were *waw* and *yod*. *Yod* could represent *î* or the diphthong *ay*. It would have been possible to write the name *syl* and pronounce it either *sîl* or *sayl*; the latter would have been vaguely similar to *sāl*, but obviously it was rejected. The alternative was not much more promising: use *waw* suggesting *û* or *aw*. The pronunciation *sûl* would not have met the need, but *sawl* would have been closer to the actual pronunciation; and so the spelling *swl* was adopted. The system did not permit a closer approximation, but the scribe clearly was determined to set the pronunciation, and the readers of the inscription were going to be helped, whether they needed it or wanted it or not.

142. *mr'ty* (18), *mār'atî*, 'my lady'. A f. s. noun with the 1st s. pronoun suffix. The final vowel *î* is represented by *yod*. The medial *alef* is consonantal and there are no other long vowels or vowel letters.

143. *lḥmh* (18), *laḥmah*. Cf. No. 135.

144. *wmwh* (18), *wamaw(i)h*. Cf. No. 136.

145. *'l* (18), *'al*, 'not'. Cf. No. 137.

146. *tlqḥ* (18), *tilqaḥ*, 'let her [not] receive or take'. 3rd f. s. *pe'al* imperfect of root *lqḥ*. Cf. No. 138.

147. *mn* (18), *min*. Cf. No. 127.

148. *ydh* (18), *yadih*. Cf. No. 140.

149. *wlzr'* (18-19), *waluzara'*, 'and let him sow'. The form is a combination of the precative particle *lu* plus the *pe'al* perfect 3rd m. s. of the root *zr'*; or possibly a pseudo-preformative jussive *luzra'* or *lizra'*.

150. *w'l* (19), *wa'al*. Cf. No. 137.

151. *yḥṣd* (19), *yaḥṣud*, 'let him [not] reap' or 'harvest'. The vocalization may be uncertain, but, so far as we can see, in this *pe'al* imperfect 3rd m. s. form of the root *ḥṣd* there are no long vowels.

152. *w'lp* (19), *wa'alp*, 'and a thousand (measures)'. The noun is probably monosyllabic; there are no vowels which might be represented by vowel letters.

153. *ś'ryn* (19), *śi'ārîn*, 'barley'. Here we have a m. pl. noun in the absolute state. The final syllable contains the long /i/ vowel marking the plural ending, and this is indicated by a *yod*. Cf. *'lhyn*, No. 21. Curiously enough, as in the case of *'lhyn* (No. 21), for which a variant spelling occurs in line 14 (*'lhn*, No. 105), without the vowel letter, the same is true of this word; the form without the vowel letter occurs in line 22 (*ś'rn*, No. 187). It is difficult to account for variant spellings of the same word in the same inscription, but these are not the only examples. For previous discussion, see Nos. 21, 105.

154. *lzr'* (19), *luzara'* or *luzra'*. Cf. No. 149.

155. *wprys* (19), *waparîs*, 'and a *parîs* (measure)'. This is apparently a loanword domesticated in Aramaic. In accordance with the established practice of this inscription or scribal school, the distinctive internal vowel (*î*) is marked by the appropriate vowel letter (*yod*).

156. *l'ḥz* (19), *lu'aḥaz*, 'let him grasp' or 'collect' or 'gather in'. We have a combination of precative particle (*lu*) plus the *pe'al* perfect 3rd m. s. from the root *'ḥz*; or else a pseudo-preformative jussive. There are no vowels needing attention.

157. *mnh* (19), *minnah* or *minnih*, 'from it (him)'. The antecedent or referent is not entirely clear. The person under the curse is described as going to collect from all his plantings some paltry yield. But the final 'from it' should refer to his previous efforts or to the person from whom he will gain his reward. In case the suffix is a 3rd f. s., then we would read *minnah*, but if it is 3rd m. s., as are all the others, then we would read *minnih*. In either event the final *he* is a consonant. Cf. Nos. 61, 82.

158. *wm'h* (20), *wami'â*, 'and a hundred'. This is the numeral, a feminine noun in the absolute state. The *he* is a vowel letter representing final long /a/.

159. *s'wn* (20), *si'wān*, 'sheep' (pl.). Here we have a feminine pl. noun in the absolute state. The vocalization is uncertain, being complicated by the presence of the *waw* which marks the plural form. Since, however, the fem. pl. in all Aramaic has the form *-ān*, there is no reason to think that the *waw* here is a vowel letter for a supposed *-ôn*. It should be regarded as a consonant, in conformity with its use with m. pl. nouns having suffixes. Cf. the comparable f. pl. noun *nšwn* (Nos. 171, 177).

160. *lhynqn* (20), *luhayniqān*, 'let them give suck'. Here we have the precative particle (*lu*) along with the *hap'el* perfect 3rd f. pl. of the root *ynq*; or a pseudo-preformative jussive. Two points should be noted: (a) the preservation of the diphthong /ay/ in the derived conjugation which is represented by the appropriate consonantal element *yod*; (b) the vowel in the last syllable is doubtless long /a/, but unrepresented in the orthography. This indicates strongly that the preceding word, *s'wn*, should not be vocalized as *si'ôn*, but rather as *si'wān*, or the like. Cf. No. 166.

161. *'mr* (20), *'immir*, 'lamb'. There are no long vowels and no vowel letters, as expected.

162. *w'l* (20), *wa'al*, 'and not'. Cf. No. 137.

163. *yrwy* (*20*), *yirway*, 'let it [not] be satiated'. We read this *pe'al* imperfect 3rd m. s. form of the root *rwy* as a *yiqtal* form with the resulting diphthong /ay/ at the end, preserved in the spelling with the consonantal element *yod*. It could also be read as a *yaqtil* form, *yarwî*. In the later case the final *yod* would be a vowel letter for long /i/. It would also in all likelihood have been preserved as a specimen of historical spelling, since the third root consonant was a *yod*.

164. *wm'h* (20), *wami'â*. Cf. No. 158.

165. *swr* (20), *sawr*, 'cattle'. Although the noun is normally masculine singular, here it is treated as f. collective and the subject of the verb

lhynqn which follows. From the orthographic viewpoint, the important feature of this word is the presence of medial *waw*, which represents the consonantal element in the diphthong /aw/, itself part of the primal form of this word. This spelling indicates that the diphthong has been preserved in this dialect. The formulaic nature of the language is evident. Similar expressions are used in Sefire—[*šb*ʿ] *šwrh yhynqn ʿgl w'l yśbʿ* (Sf I A 23). The close similarity to line 20 of our inscription highlights the anomaly of *swr* where Sefire has *šwrh*. There are several possible explanations: (a) The two words are the same, but Tell Fekherye (for once!) has not marked the final *-â*. This is hard to believe in view of the consistent spelling of 'hundred' in the context. (b) Similar to (a), it is a scribal error, and we should restore the missing *he*. This is always a possibility, and one mistake would not be unusual in a text of this size. (c) The term is generic, collective, as often in the Hebrew Bible, where it includes females (Lev. 22.28; Num. 18.17); necessarily so when the verb attributes giving birth (as in the Hebrew text) or giving suck (as here) to them.

166. *lhynqn* (20), *luhayniqān*, 'let them give suck'. Cf. No. 160.

167. *ʿgl* (21), *ʿigl*, 'calf'. There are no long vowels and no vowel letters.

168. *w'l* (21), *wa'al*, 'and not'. Cf. Nos. 137, 162.

169. *yrwy* (21), *yirway*, 'let it [not] be satiated'. Cf. No. 163.

170. *wm'h* (21), *wami'â*. Cf. Nos. 158, 164.

171. *nšwn* (21), *niswān*, 'women'. This is a f. pl. noun in the absolute state. We have vocalized the form in accordance with the standard rules for Old Aramaic and therefore treat the intervening *waw* as a consonant marking the plural form. Cf. No. 159 *s'wn* for a further discussion of this feature. On affinities of this morphology with Arabic, see Bordreuil and Millard (pp. 35f.) and Kaufman (p. 169).

172. *lhynqn* (21), *luhayniqān*, 'let them give suck'. Cf. Nos. 160, 166.

173. *ʿlym* (21), *ʿalîm*, 'a child'. This is a m. s. noun. Of orthographic

interest is the use of a vowel letter *yod* to represent medial long /i/ in the second syllable. The word is attested with the same spelling in Old Aramaic (Sf I A 22) and the vocalization is confirmed by Syriac. (The vocalization *'ulaym* [Cross and Freedman, p. 28], based on Bauer and Leander, should be abandoned.)

174. *w'l* (21), *wa'al*, 'and not'. Cf. Nos. 137, 162, 168.

175. *yrwy* (21), *yirway*, 'let it [not] be satiated'. Cf. Nos. 163, 169.

176. *wm'h* (22), *wami'â*. Cf. Nos. 158, 164, 170.

177. *nšwn* (22), *nišwān*, 'women'. Cf. No. 171.

178. *l'pn* (22), *lu'apān*, 'let them bake'. To judge from other similar forms in this inscription, this would be a combination of precative *lu* with the *pe'al* perfect 3rd f. pl.; or a pseudo-preformative jussive. The listing of such forms as apocopated imperfects or jussives (Bordreuil and Millard 49f.) is not compelling. A precative perfect is at least a possibility. The expected root here is *'py*, 'bake'. The absence of a third root consonant requires explanation, whether the form is preformative or afformative. Some other verb forms in this inscription present similar problems (cf. No. 73), but generally III-*y*/*w* roots retain the consonant, as such, or as long vowel reflex still evident in historical spelling. Cf. Nos. 15, 47, 87, 163, 169, 175. A biconsonantal byform cannot be entirely ruled out, so it may be better to recognize phonological changes within that family. The Sefire inscriptions, which represent the texts nearest to this one in content and style, present exactly the same mixture, with the expected *y* alongside a terminal *he* which seems to represent, not just the contraction of the diphthong (not represented in the spelling), but possibly a more radical change to long /a/. See Fitzmyer's vigorous statement (42). What this amounts to, then, is the development of a biconsonantal byform for some items in the paradigm, as in standard Aramaic (*'ăpô*) and Hebrew (*'āpû*). Whatever the root, the last syllable contains long /a/ which is not represented in the orthography.

179. *btnwr* (22), *batannûr*, 'in an oven'. We have here a prepositional phrase containing the familiar Northwest Semitic word for 'oven'. We note the use of the medial vowel letter *waw* to represent the long

/u/ of the second syllable. Several other common nouns in the inscription share this feature. Cf. Nos. 1, 8, 20, 33 and duplicates Nos. 24, 63, 109.

180. *lḥm* (22), *laḥm*, 'bread'. There are no long vowels and no vowel letters.

181. *w'l* (20), *wa'al*, 'and not'. Cf. Nos. 137, 162, 168, 174.

182. *yml'nh* (22), *yamalli'ānih*, 'let them [not] fill it up'. We take the form to be a *pa'el* imperfect 3rd f. pl. with a 3rd m. s. suffix. As a connecting vowel we have supplied the old jussive ending of the verbal form *-i*, but any vowel will do. The final *he* is consonantal.

183. *wmn* (22), *wamin*, 'and from'. Cf. No. 127.

184. *qlqlt'* (22), *qalqalāta'*, 'the baskets'. We analyse the form as a feminine plural noun in the emphatic state (cf. Nos. 1, 109, 128 for other examples). The final *alef* is a consonant. Note also the long /a/ vowel in the penultimate syllable, without representation in the orthography.

185. *llqṭw* (22), *lulaqaṭû*, 'let them gather'. We interpret the form as a combination of the precative particle *lu* plus the *pe'al* perfect 3rd m. pl. of the root *lqṭ*; or a pseudo-preformative jussive. The final vowel *-û* of the 3rd pl. is represented by *waw*. There are no other long vowels or vowel letters.

186. *'nšwh* (22), *'anāšwih*, 'his men'. Cf. No. 58.

187. *ś'rn* (22), *śi'ārīn*, 'barley'. This noun is the f. pl. absolute, written defectively, that is, without a vowel letter (*yod*) for the long /i/ in the plural ending. It is to be compared with the full spelling of the same word *ś'ryn* (No. 153). For further discussion see the pair *'lhyn* (No. 21) and *'lhn* (No. 105). Apparently the use of the medial *yod* in such circumstances was optional. Perhaps the most extraordinary feature of this pair of spellings is that the norm, to judge from actual specimens, is the *defective* spelling. It is the only spelling met at Elephantine, where the word occurs many times. In fact No. 153 represents the only known instance of the *plene* spelling of the plural

absolute of this word in the entire Aramaic corpus. Were it not for that fact, one would be tempted to interpret *ś'rn* as a regular feminine plural (the singular form is feminine). Still it may be further observed that the confusion over the gender and morphology of this word in Northwest Semitic is illustrated by the fact that in Ugaritic the singular is masculine, perhaps also in Hadad (line 5—it is clearly feminine in Bir-rakib lines 6, 9).

The total picture for the spelling of this word suggests another principle, commonly met in the history of spelling. The competition between historical and phonetic spelling goes on all the time. All that matters is that the word be identified unambiguously and that the reader be given as much help as needed. This help is clearly needed in the case of exotic words, less needed in the case of familiar words, for which conventional spellings, not necessarily completely phonetic (not using all the possible vowel letters), serve quite adequately as virtual logograms. The extraordinary tenacity of the archaic spelling of 'barley'—for centuries—illustrates the point, with the paradox that the only known case of what would usually be considered a 'modern' spelling occurs in one of the oldest known Aramaic inscriptions.

188. *l'klw* (22), *lu'akalû*, 'let them eat'. We interpret the form as a combination of the precative particle *lu* plus the *pe'al* perfect 3rd m. pl. of the root *'kl*. The final long *-û* vowel is represented by *waw* in the orthography (cf. for the other example No. 185). There are no other long vowels or vowel letters.

189. *wmwtn* (23), *wamawtān*, 'and *mawtān*'. Apparently this is a proper noun, but it seems to be derived from the root *mwt*, 'death', and is attested in the literature. We note the use of *waw* to represent the diphthong /aw/, or if the correct vocalization of the word is *mûtān*, it could stand for the vowel *û*. We are not sure of the final syllable but it seems to be the classic *-ān* nominal ending (which becomes *-ōn* in other dialects).

190. *šbṭ* (23), *šibṭ*, 'Demon'. This (proper) noun is apparently monosyllabic. There are no long vowels or vowel letters.

191. *zy* (23), *zî*. Cf. No. 2.

192. *nyrgl* (23), *nîrgal*, 'Nergal'. Here we have the name of the well-

known Assyrian deity. The medial vowel letter *yod* is supplied to represent the characteristic vowel *i* in the name. The other vowel is *a* and would not be represented in the orthography.

193. *'l* (23), *'al*. Cf. No. 137.

194. *ygtzr* (23), *yigtizar*, 'let him [not] be cut off'. Here we have an infixed *pe'al* imperfect 3rd m. s. of the root *gzr*. There are no long vowels or vowel letters.

195. *mn* (23), *min*. Cf. No. 127.

196. *mth* (23), *mātih*, 'his country'. This is the noun f. s., plus the 3rd m. s. suffix. The final *he* is a consonant. We have supplied the connecting vowel, in this instance an *i*, for the genitive case of the noun.

Summary

I. *Final Letters*

A. Consonants

1. *Alef* (') Emphatic state of nouns
   a. *dmwt'* (*damûta'*) : Nos. 1, 109.
   b. *m'ny'* (*ma'nayya'*) : No. 128.
   c. *qlqlt'* (*qalqalāta'*) : No. 184.

2. *He* (*h*) as 3rd m. s. pronoun suffix
   a. *'ḥwh* (*'aḥwih*) : No. 23.
   b. *tṣlwth* (*taṣlûtuh*) : No. 33.
   c. *nbšh* (*nabšah*) : No. 48.
   d. *ywmwh* (*yawmwih*) : No. 50.
   e. *šnwh* (*šanwih*) : No. 52.
   f. *byth* (*baytah*) : No. 54.
   g. *zr'h* (*zar'ah*) : No. 56.
   h. *'nšwh* (*'anāšwih*) : Nos. 58, 186.
   i. *mnh* (*minnih*) : Nos. 61, 82, 157.
   j. *tṣlwth* (*taṣlûtah*) : No. 63.
   k. *pmh* (*pumih*) : Nos. 66, 103.
   l. *lh* (*lih*) : No. 69.
   m. *lknnh* (*lukanninah*) : No. 74.
   n. *bh* (*bih*) : No. 78.

o. *šmh* (*šumah*) : No. 84.
p. *qblh* (*qābiluh*) : No. 88.
q. *krs'h* (*karsi'ih*) : No. 98.
r. *ḥywh* (*ḥayyawih*) : No. 100.
s. *ṣlmh* (*ṣalmah*) : No. 122.
t. *lḥmh* (*laḥmah*) : Nos. 135, 143.
u. *wmwh* (*wamaw*[*i*]*h*) : Nos. 136, 144.
v. *ydh* (*yadih*) : Nos. 140, 148.
w. *yml'nh* (*yamalli'ānah*) : No. 182.
x. *mth* (*mātih*) : No. 196.

B. Vowels

1. *He* (*h*) for *-â*.
a. *šlh* (*?*) : No. 19.
b. *ṭbh* (*tābâ*) : No. 34.
c. *wm'h* (*wami'â*) : Nos. 158, 164, 170, 176.

2. *Waw* (*w*) for *-û*.
a. *llqṭw* (*lulaqaṭû*) : No. 185.
b. *l'klw* (*lu'akalû*) : No. 188.

3. *Yod* (*y*) for *-î* (or *ay*).
a. *zy* (*zî*) : Nos. 2, 4, 32, 79, 93, 95, 113, 129, 191.
b. *hdys'y* (*hadyis'î*) : Nos. 3, 40, 90.
c. *r'y* (*ri'î*) : No. 14.
d. *wmšqy* (*wamašqî*) : No. 15.
e. *ssnwry* (*sasnûrî*) : No. 44.
f. *lḥyy* (*laḥayyî* or *laḥayyay*) : No. 47.
g. *šmy* (*šumî*) : Nos. 81, 126.
h. *lhwy* (*luhawî*) : No. 87.
i. *mr'y* (*mār'î*) : Nos. 132, 133.
j. *mr'ty* (*mār'atî*)—No. 142.
k. *yrwy* (*yirway* or *yarwî*)—Nos. 163, 169, 175.

II. *Medial Letters* (waw *and* yod).

A. Consonants

1. *Waw*
a. *'ḥwh* (*'aḥwih*) : No. 23.
b. *ywmwh* (*yawmwih*) : No. 50.
c. *šnwh* (*šanwih*) : No. 52.
d. *'nšwh* (*'anāšwih*) : Nos. 58, 186.
e. *lhwy* (*luhawî*) : No. 87.
f. *ḥywh* (*ḥayyawih*) : No. 100.
g. *wmwh* (*wamaw*[*i*]*h*) : Nos. 136, 144.

h. *s'wn* (*si'wān*) : No. 159.
i. *yrwy* (*yirway* or *yarwî*) : Nos. 163, 169, 175.
j. *nšwn* (*nišwān*) : Nos. 171, 177.

2. *Yod*
a. *hdys'y* (*hadyis'î*) : Nos. 3, 40, 90.
b. *lḥyy* (*laḥayyî*) : No. 47.
c. *wyhb* (*wayahab*) : No. 68.
d. *wyśym* (*wayaśîm*) : No. 83.
e. *ḥywh* (*ḥayyawih*) : No. 100.
f. *m'ny'* (*ma'nayya'*) : No. 128.

B. Diphthongs

1. *Waw* for *aw*
a. *ywmwh* (*yawmwih*) : No. 50.
b. *hwtr* (*hawtir*) : No. 115.
c. *swl* (*sawl* or *sûl* or *sôl*) : No. 141.
d. *swr* (*sawr*) : No. 165.
e. *wmwtn* (*wamawtān* or *wamûtān*) : No. 189.

2. *Yod* for *-ay*
a. *šmyn* (*šamayn*) : No. 9.
b. *byth* (*baytah*) : No. 54. See also *bt=bēt*—No. 130.
c. *tyṭb* (*tayṭab* or *tîṭab*) : No. 108.
d. *lhynqn* (*luhayniqān*) : Nos. 160, 166, 172.

C. Vowels

1. *Waw* for *û*
a. *dmwt'* (*damûta'*) : Nos. 1, 109.
b. *gwgl* (*gûgal*) : Nos. 8, 24.
c. *w'dqwr* (*wa'adaqûr*) : No. 20.
d. *tṣlwth* (*taṣlûtuh*) : No. 33.
e. *gwzn* (*gûzan* or *gawzan*) : Nos. 42, 46, 92.
f. *tṣlwth* (*taṣlûtah*) : No. 63.
g. *ḥbwr* (*ḥabûr*) : No. 121.
h. *btnwr* (*batannûr*) : No. 179.
i. *wmwtn* (*wamûtān* or *wamawtān*)—No. 189.

2. *Yod* for *î*
a. *l'lhyn* (*la'ilāhîn*) : No. 21; but see No. 105 *l'lhn*.
b. *wšmym* (*wašumî-m*)—No. 76; cf. Nos. 81, 126.
c. *wyśym* (*wayaśîm*) : No. 83.
d. *tyṭb* (*tîṭab* or *tayṭab*) : No. 108.
e. *ś'ryn* (*śi'ārîn*) : No. 153; but see No. 187 *ś'rn*.
f. *wprys* (*waparîs*) : No. 155.
g. *'lym* (*'alîm*) : No. 173.
h. *nyrgl* (*nîrgal*) : No. 192.

Conclusions

The importance and value of the new inscription for orthographic study can hardly be exaggerated. We have here an early text (not later than the ninth century BC and possibly earlier), well preserved with clearly written signs, and a parallel rendering in readable Akkadian to help with the difficulties of analysis and interpretation. It is written in a language close enough to standard Aramaic and other Northwest Semitic dialects to allow generally for positive analysis and interpretation. And there is considerable information from which spelling practices and underlying principles can be determined.

We can offer the following by way of summary and evaluation. The orthography of the Aramaic inscription is fairly regular and it is consistent generally with the practices and principles of neighbouring states using the Phoenician alphabet and similar Northwest Semitic languages. There are exceptional if not idiosyncratic features, but these for the most part have been incorporated into the system, which may be described as follows:

I. *Final vowels*

Final vowels are regularly represented in the orthography. The system is the same as employed all over the area, except in Phoenicia (or Canaan) proper, where vowel letters were avoided. The system is essentially the same as that used in Moab, Ammon, Israel and Judah.

Final vowels are represented in the following ways:

A. *He* (*h*) represents long *â* and possibly other vowels such as *ē* and *ō*; but we have no certain examples of the last two.
B. *Waw* (*w*) represents long *-û*.
C. *Yod* (*y*) represents long *-î*.

There are several examples of *he* for *-â*, only two of *waw* for *-û*, and many of *yod* for *-î*. There are no known exceptions, that is, every likely word-terminal vowel is so represented. We cannot prove that short final vowels were dropped, but if they were pronounced they were not considered important enough to record. We hold to the position that if final vowels were preserved in the spoken language they would have been indicated in the orthography, and failure to indicate them would mean that they were no longer preserved, or that they were in the process of being lost.

II. *Medial vowels*

Only two vowel letters were used medially, *waw* and *yod*. As with final vowels, they represent *û* and *î* respectively. There are enough examples to show that there was an effort to indicate the quality of those vowels which occasionally can be shown to be long and/or under stress, but not always. The usage is clearly not consistent or regular, although it is not merely sporadic. Short vowels are generally not indicated in any way, although there may be, originally, exceptions in the case of foreign and unusual words, especially names. In general the vowel *a* is not indicated at all when medial, whether short or long, stressed or unstressed. There are any number of examples of this non-representation for vowels known to be long. The reason is that no letter of the alphabet had been assigned to this function. *He* could have been tried; after all it was in use for word-terminal long *-â*. But apparently using it as a medial vowel letter would have been too confusing, since it is used so often as a true consonant. But, whatever the reason, it was not so used. And it would be centuries before *alef* was used as a vowel letter for any vowel in Semitic.

The explanation of the use of three letters for word-terminal vowels but only two for word-medial vowels is probably to be found in the fact that /w/ and /y/ were semi-vowels, and the corresponding consonant letters represented both the diphthongal offglide and the homorganic long vowel. But etymological /h/ preserved its consonantal pronunciation in post-vocalic positions, including the ends of words. Morphological factors were at work as well. Many verbs which end with a long vowel can receive an additional suffix, which then moves that vowel to the interior of the word. So the same vowel can be terminal or medial. Once the custom is established of spelling such a word in a particular way, whether suffixed or not, the principle of using a vowel letter for a medial vowel has taken root. This is illustrated in the present inscription by comparing *šmy* (Nos. 81, 126) with *šmym* (No. 76). Furthermore, this circumstance goes a long way to explain the fact that a long vowel which is always word-medial, such as the long /i/ of the m. pl. ending of nouns, can be spelled either way. Insofar as the identity of the word is sufficiently established by the consonantal spelling, its pronunciation is not likely to be in doubt. But purely consonantal spelling of verbs would not distinguish plural from singular.

In our inscription the only instances of word-terminal *-â*, always spelled with *he*, are f. s. nouns. This vowel does not survive suffixation, so that it becomes word-medial; the stem ending becomes *-at-*, so there is no need or use for any vowel letter. This conventional use of *he* for word-terminal long /a/ but not for word-medial long /a/ remained fixed in Northwest Semitic orthography. When, very much later, word-medial long /a/ was represented by a consonant letter, the one chosen was *alef*, particularly in Aramaic.

A certain selectivity is to be noted in the use of these internal vowel letters. For the most part they are used in loanwords, foreign or foreign-sounding names, and certain other terms, where identification of the vowel might be important. Since in certain cases at least the vowel is originally short (as in *gugal* and *'adaqur*) we emphasize the use of these vowel letters to mark quality in preference to quantity. The same will be true of stress since in some cases the vowel indicated by the vowel letter will not be in the normally stressed syllable. But by and large the vowel letters are used for long vowels in stressed syllables, at least if we follow the generally accepted rules governing long vowels and stressed syllables for Aramaic and Northwest Semitic in general.

A. *waw* (*w*) for *û*.

B. *yod* (*y*) for *î*.

A notable exception

We know of five cases of the absolute m. pl. noun, the final syllable of which is vocalized *-în*. In two cases the medial vowel letter *yod* has been used (full spelling). In three cases the *yod* has been omitted (defective spelling). Clearly the scribes felt that they had a choice, and it is not clear why they chose one way on one occasion and the other way on another, especially in cases where the same words are involved. Thus the word for 'gods' is spelled with the *yod* once and without it once: *'lhyn* // *'lhn*. There is no detectable difference in grammatical form or force. The same is true of *ś'ryn* // *ś'rn*. We do not observe the same situation with *waw* for *û*. In all the words in which medial *waw* is used as a vowel letter, the same word is always spelled the same way: *dmwt'* (Nos. 1, 109), *tṣlwth* (Nos. 33, 63), *gwgl* (Nos. 8, 24); *gwzn* (Nos. 42, 45, 92). The medial *waw* seems to be used more consisently than medial *yod*, but some instances where the former might have been used but was not may have escaped our notice. Our impression is that all vowels we can identify as long /u/ and/or short /u/ under stress have been marked by *waw*. The exceptions in the case of *yod* have been noted.

It is interesting in this connection to note a historical difference between the use of *waw* and *yod* as vowel letters. The use of *yod* to spell long /i/ has a basis in derivation, but the use of *waw* to spell long /u/ seems to have developed by analogy with the use of *yod* on purely phonetic grounds. Does this mean that *waw* for *û*, being only phonetic, was used more freely, whereas *yod* for *î* was still constrained by considerations of historical spelling, just as *alef* was for much longer?

III. *Diphthongs*

In general original and etymological diphthongs are preserved in the writing. That would be as true for diphthongs which are ultimately retained in known languages as for those which are ultimately contracted. Without being able to decide between actual and historical spelling we can say that the spelling is more like other Aramaic and Judahite inscriptions in which the diphthongs are preserved in the spelling, than it is like Phoenician and Israelite inscriptions, in which the diphthongs have been contracted and there is no trace of them in the spelling. There are enough examples of both kinds to show that the scribes were consciously representing them in the spelling of the words. The only significant exception to the use of *waw* and *yod* to represent diphthongs is the word *bt*, 'house' (No. 130). The fuller spelling of the same word, representing the diphthong, is *byth* (No. 54). It is difficult to account for the conflicting spellings in the same inscription, and we are inclined to regard the contracted spelling as exceptional and perhaps due to special circumstances which we cannot now reconstruct.

It might seem possible to turn the argument around and say that the spelling *bt* shows that the diphthong had been contracted and that the survival of the *yod* in the other cases such as *byth* is an instance of historical spelling. The same would be true of *waw*. We would then have to recognize that *yod* represents not *ay* but *ê* in such cases, and that *waw* represents not *aw* but *ô* when it marks an internal diphthong. We can consider here the opposite problem of *bt*, which has no consonantal marker (*yod*) where we would expect one. In the word *swl* (No. 144) we have such a marker (*waw*) whether for a vowel or diphthong, when we do not expect one. On the basis of the parallel Akkadian we know that the word is the name of the goddess *šala*, and that the vowel in the Aramaic form should be *a*. According to the system used in our text, this vowel is not marked in medial positions, but we have a marker in this word. The *waw* should represent either *û* or *aw* according to our thesis, but it is suggested that if *waw* represents the contracted diphthong *ô* < *aw*, it can represent *ô* here in this name. It is difficult to imagine the shift from *ā* to *ô* in Aramaic of this or any other period; but anything is possible.

Such a hypothesis opens the way for reconsideration of certain remaining problems in the text: e.g., the use of *waw* regularly in all m. pl. nouns which have the 3rd m. s. pronoun suffix. We have interpreted the *waw* as consonantal, but it might be a vowel letter for *ô*, followed by the 3rd m. s. suffix *h*, which would be pronounced *hī*, thus giving us a standard form of the suffix attached to plural nouns of later (biblical) Aramaic. This observation would also establish that at least some final vowels are not indicated orthographically.

It would also be possible to explain the f. pl. nouns which are written with internal *waw*: *s'wn* and *nšwn*. We have taken the *waw* as consonantal, but these forms could be read as follows: *si'ôn* (or *sa'ôn*) and *našôn* with a shift from the original long *ā*. But the assumption that *w* writes *ô* in such words is not only gratuitous; it cuts across all we know about historical Aramaic phonology. Further it is contradicted within this inscription, where other words containing primal long /a/, notably *pe'al* active participles, show no sign that this vowel had shifted to *ô*.

Perhaps it is impossible to decide such issues on the basis of available evidence. We believe that our analysis and conclusions are consistent with the data from this inscription and the whole corpus of related ones, and with our knowledge of the history of the languages of other Northwest Semitic dialects. Problems remain regardless of the hypothesis, and these may be resolved only with further research and more evidence.

[Completed July, 1983]

BIBLIOGRAPHY

Abou-Assaf, A.

1981 'Die Statue des HDYS^{c}Y, König von Guzana', *MDOG* 113, pp. 3-22.
with Bordreuil, P. and Millard, A.R.

1982 *La Statue de Tell Fekherye et son inscription bilingue assyro-araméenne*, Paris: Editions Recherche sur les civilisations.

Andersen, F.I.

1966 'Moabite Syntax', *Orientalia* 35, pp. 81-120.

1970a 'Orthography in Repetitive Parallelism', *JBL* 89, pp. 343-44.

1970b 'Biconsonantal Byforms in Biblical Hebrew', *ZAW* 82, pp. 270-74.

Bange, L.A.
1971 *A Study in the Use of Vowel-Letters in Alphabetic Consonantal Writing*, Munich: UNI-DRUCK.

Cross, F.M., and Freedman, D.N.
1952 *Early Hebrew Orthography: A Study of the Epigraphic Evidence* (AOS 36); New Haven: American Oriental Society.

Degen, R.
1969 *Altaramäische Grammatik* (Abhand. für die Kunde des Morgenlandes, 38/3) Wiesbaden: Steiner.

Dion, P. E.
1974 *La langue de Ya'udi. Description et classement de l'ancien parler de Zencirli dans le cadre des langues sémitiques du nord-ouest*, Waterloo, Ontario: Corporation for the Publication of Academic Studies in Religion in Canada.

Donner, H., with Röllig, W.
1962-64 *Kanaanäische und aramäische Inschriften; mit einem Beitrag von O. Rössler*, Wiesbaden: Harrassowitz.

Fitzmyer, J.A.
1967 *The Aramaic Inscriptions of Sefire* (Biblica et Orientalia, 19), Rome: Pontifical Biblical Institute Press.

Huffmon, H.B.
1965 *Amorite Personal Names in the Mari Texts: A Structural and Lexical Study*, Baltimore: Johns Hopkins Press.

Kaufman, S.A.
1982 'Reflections on the Assyrian-Aramaic Bilingual from Tell Fakhariyeh', *Maarav* 3/2, pp. 137-75.

2

NEW HORIZONS IN TEXTUAL CRITICISM

Johann Cook

The Textual Criticism of the Old Testament is experiencing a period of progress after it tended to stagnate in the first half of the twentieth century.[1] A major stimulating factor in this process has been the discovery of the Dead Sea Scrolls.[2] The main areas in which progress has been shown are in respect of the development of exegetical tools, which are based upon sound methodological grounds, the publication of Hebrew manuscripts and text witnesses, and reflection upon textual theories, which are fundamental to correct text-critical method. It is an honour to dedicate this article to Professor Fensham, who introduced the author to the exciting field of the ancient translations.

The Development of Exegetical Tools

The development which will have the greatest influence upon Textual Criticism—this holds true for Biblical Studies in general—is the development of tools for tenable analyses. In this respect the use of the computer for exegetical and concordantial purposes is a decisive development. Currently various computer-assisted projects are being directed in the scholarly world, concerned with the Hebrew text and the ancient versions. The most comprehensive project is probably the *Computer Assisted Tools for Septuagint Studies* (*CATSS*)[3] project which is being co-directed by R.A. Kraft and E. Tov from Philadelphia and Jerusalem respectively. The main purpose of this project is to create a flexible multi-purpose data-base containing the main types of data needed for the study of the LXX and its relation to the Masoretic Text and to other sources and literatures.[4] The progress in respect of this project has been significant over the last couple of years. The first visible fruits of this ambitious project were delivered at the last congress of *IOSCS* held at Salamanca (27-28 August 1983): E. Tov delivered a paper in which he made use of computerized data.[5] At the *European Science Foundation* (*ESF*) congress which took place in Jerusalem (10-13 September 1984), he once again delivered a paper based on similar data obtained from the computer,[6] this time concerning the study of the translation technique of the Septuagint.

The usefulness and versatility of the computer is demonstrated by its wide range of applications. Lexica and concordances, much-needed in various fields of biblical studies, are now being developed in various centres. The data-base devised in the *CATSS* project can ultimately be used for the development of concordances.

The author of this article is at present engaged in the development of a data-base/concordance of the Peshiṭta text of the Old Testament. Up to the middle of the twentieth century the biggest single problem confronting the researcher on the Peshiṭta was the lack of an authoritative text. This problem has now effectively been removed, as, according to M.J. Mulder, director of the Peshiṭta Institute, the publication of the Old Testament will be completed within five years.

The next task to be taken on is the construction of a concordance. Scholars[7] have previously realized that existing lexica have serious shortcomings. At the recent congress of *IOSOT/IOSCS* a decision was taken to attend to this problem. Professor McKane, of St Andrews, Scotland, called upon members to participate in this respect. The author of this article visited Leiden (among other places) after the congress and held formal discussions with Mulder at the Peshiṭta Institute concerning co-operation in respect of the production of a Syriac concordance. In co-operation with McKane it was decided that the computer will be used for the processing of data. A redaction committee was formed under the chairmanship of McKane, the chairman of the Peshiṭta project, one member of the Peshiṭta Institute, Mulder and the author of this article. It was also decided that a pilot study of the first six chapters of Genesis would be undertaken by this author. This study was performed in the department of Semitic Languages at the University of Stellenbosch, of which Professor F.C. Fensham is the head. The results of the study were subsequently discussed with the other members of the redaction committee in Jerusalem at the *ESF* congress. The results[8] satisfied the members of this committee[9] and consequently the project is being continued.[10]

In the research area *tools* there has thus been a dramatic change in the situation. These developments will give rise to the possibility of tenable and representative analyses in the near future. However, in order to execute such analyses a sound textual theory is required.

The Question of Sound Textual Theory

The Dead Sea Scrolls also played an important role[11] in respect of this issue. Some of the oldest available data (Hebrew texts and translations) have been discovered at Qumran. These data brought new insights into the complicated textual histories of the various texts and more specifically in respect of the nature of the relation between the diverse textual witnesses of the Old Testament. Existing and outdated theories came under scrutiny and new theories were formulated, whilst various pleas[12] were correctly delivered on behalf of the refinement of terminology used by scholars in connection with Textual Criticism.

Before the discovery of the Dead Sea Scrolls there seemed to be a consensus amongst scholars that the MT, LXX and Sam. Pent, as far as the Pentateuch is concerned, represented the three main streams of textual traditions available and that the MT and LXX represented the primary textual traditions regarding the other books of the Old Testament. Even after 1947 scholars tended to hold on to this tripartite scheme with the consequence that all available textual data are fitted into this system. The well-known *local text theory*,[13] developed by F.M. Cross, is based upon this dogmatic system. P.E. Kahle indeed succeeded in partly freeing himself from this tripartition. He was one of the first scholars to take the *diversity* of textual data seriously,[14] albeit with incorrect presuppositions.

Recently, a new proposal has been formulated for the rejection of this tripartite scheme as a theoretical possibility. The textual variety[15] which confronts the researcher has finally demonstrated the shortcomings of this division. It is not possible to fit all variant readings found in the Hebrew texts and translations into this system. A textual theory of a *multitude of texts* opens the possibility for the methodologically correct interpretation of variants and deviating textual readings in comparison with their *Vorlagen*.

The Publication of Texts

Concerning the publication of texts, there are two problem areas which need the urgent attention of biblical scholars. These problems are directly related to the theoretical premises on which the respective textual critics base their research. These premises, again, are determined by factors such as the textual theory applied by textualists and the interpretation of the text history of the various Hebrew texts and versions.

The first problem area is concerned with the theoretical premises upon which text editions rest. As is well known, two basic premises are used in the publication of existing text-publications, a *diplomatic text-concept*,[16] and a *critical text-concept*.[17]

Of the *diplomatic text-concept* there are many examples; as a matter of fact most of the existing text editions are based upon this model. In this case an existing manuscript is used as the basic text for collating other relevant manuscripts. As far as existing *Hebrew text editions* are concerned, the two main editions, the *Biblia Hebraica Stuttgartensia* (*BHS*), as well as the *Hebrew University Bible Project* (*HUPB*), are based upon such a principle.[18] For *BHS* Codex Leningradensis has been used as basic text, whereas for *HUBP* Codex Aleppo is used. The same premise was applied in the *Cambridge Septuagint Project*, where Codex Vaticanus served as a diplomatic text, in those passages where it was available.[19]

Of the *critical text-concept* there are two important examples, the *Göttingen Septuagint Project* and the *United Bible Societies Greek New Testament*, edited by K. Aland. In these instances no single manuscript was used as basic text. In the case of the LXX, an/the original text[20] is reconstructed on the basis of *all* existing manuscripts, versions and patristic citations.[21] In order to do this successfully, interrelationships between extant materials are determined. On account of rigid analyses textual families are determined which are of great importance for determining the history of a text, which again is decisive for the final evaluation of a variant reading.

From this it is clear that the text-critical apparatus has a determinative role to play as far as text editions are concerned. Consequently, the question which of these two basic premises should be preferred (or should they perhaps be combined?) will be attended to after the second problem area, the role of text-critical apparatuses, has been discussed.

This problem area may be described in terms of the formula *too little—too much*. There are text editions which have too little *useful* data combined in their text-critical apparatuses. A representative example is the *Biblia Hebraica* (*BH*) project. The various *BH* editions have been subjected to criticism[22] in the past. The most recent edition, *BHS*, is an improvement on the previous editions in some respects. This is true as far as the manuscript which is used as diplomatic text,[23] as well as the apparatus criticus, is concerned. The bipartition which was used in the *BH* editions has been done away with. All textual data have been incorporated into one critical apparatus. The usefulness of this edition is evident. It is the only complete edition of the Hebrew text of the Old Testament which can be used for research purposes.[24] However, it is also subject to conspicuous weaknesses.[25]

In the book of Genesis various examples of inconsistent, incorrect, unclear and incomplete utilization of textual data occur (needless to say it also contains many cogent proposals). O. Eissfeldt proposed various changes to the MT of Genesis 1, of which very few are sufficiently founded. On the strength of the Septuagint the phrase *wyhy-kn* is transposed to the end of v. 6 and added to v. 20. In like manner the phrase *wyr' 'lhym ky-ṭwb* is added to v. 7, inter alia, on account of the fact that the equivalent of this phrase occurs in the LXX in verse 8. In addition, the extensive plus found in v. 9 in the LXX is only mentioned in the text-critical apparatus of *BHS*, without any definite proposal. The same is true of the addition of *kai pantōn tōn ktenōn kai pasēs tēs gēs*, which occurs in the LXX in v. 28.

A contextual analysis of the whole of Genesis in the Septuagint disclosed the following approach[26] of the translator to his Hebrew *Vorlage*: the harmonization of conspicuous discrepancies, which includes the harmonization of parallel verses, the explication of ambiguous Hebrew phrases and an affinity for variation.

Genesis 1 in the Septuagint contains a harmonizing pattern which corresponds to the rest of the book. A problem concerning the structure of this chapter in MT is the discrepancy between the *six days* upon which the creation took place, and the *eight works* which were completed during these days. This, inter alia, contributed to the various discrepancies identified in the MT. In the LXX these discrepancies are cleared on the basis of internal and/or external considerations. The additions which are found in the Septuagint, and which have been discussed above, should be attributed to this harmonizing approach and not to a Hebrew *Vorlage(n)*. It is therefore incorrect to add these phrases to the MT.

Eissfeldt did not observe this typical translational approach of the LXX translator. This is also clear from his treatment of other passages. Verses 11 and 12 are harmonized internally in the LXX in Genesis 1; however, Eissfeldt mentioned only the *waw* preceding *'ṣ* in v. 11. He was probably misled by the fact that more than one textual witness had this addition. His interpretation of *lmynw* in v. 11 is unacceptable on similar grounds.

Another problem identified in the text-critical apparatus of *BHS* is the incomplete quotation of data. In Genesis 2 various examples occur. The equivalent of the inverted readings *šmym w'rṣ* occurs in the LXX, Sam. P., Pesh. and in some of the Targumim. Eissfeldt, however, only mentioned Sam. P. and the Pesh. The adverb *eti*, which occurs in Gen. 2.9 and 19 in the LXX, has no equivalent in MT. Yet in the text-critical apparatus of *BHS* only the addition in v. 19 is mentioned. Once again the text critic was misled by the fact that more than one version have the addition in v. 19 (Sam. P. has it added too). However, in Sam. P. the equivalent of this adverb is not added to v. 9. The reason for the additions in the LXX was clearly not understood. It was used in order to relate items which were said to be created from the earth in Genesis 2 and ultimately to Genesis 1, where the first account of the creation is found. This is once again in line with the harmonizational approach mentioned above.

Similar examples can be multiplied. In Gen. 8.19 an extensive addition occurs in the LXX which should also be ascribed to the harmonizational pattern above, yet in *BHS* it is proposed that its Hebrew equivalent should be added to MT.

It is hard to determine on what methodological grounds additions, etc., in the LXX are only quoted in the text-critical apparatus, or indeed proposed as additions etc. A contextual analysis of the various versions would have led to the avoidance of such incorrect interpretations.

The *HUBP* is an example of the *too much* approach. There are significant differences in approach between the *HUBP* and the *BHS*. The difference in diplomatic texts which are used in each case has been mentioned already. A major difference is concerned with the text-critical apparatus compiled in both editions. In the *HUBP*, contrary to *BHS*, an extensive apparatus criticus is used, in which as wide a variety of textual data as possible is utilized.

In the introduction[27] to the sample edition of Isaiah and in an article introducing[28] this new edition, the editor, M.H. Goshen-Gottstein, outlined the theoretical premises[29] upon which this project rests. The critical apparatus consists of four different apparatuses. The first contains data from the ancient versions. In the second are combined data from the Dead Sea Scrolls and quotations from rabbinic literature. The third apparatus contains medieval Hebrew biblical manuscript data, whereas in the fourth Masoretic details are dealt with.

The apparatus criticus of the *HUBP* is comprehensive and it reflects the encompassing intention of its directors. From a methodological point of view hardly any criticism[30] can be brought against this project. However, the comprehensiveness of this project seems to be its largest single drawback. After two decades of solid research limited results have been delivered. The second publication (Isaiah 22–44) in this series recently[31] appeared, while the final volume of the book of Isaiah[32] and the book of Jeremiah will be published in the near future.

To sum up this part of the discussion: The *BHS* edition is a vast improvement on former *BH* editions. Its greatest advantage is its usefulness. It is a handy tool for the biblical student. However, it does have one major disadvantage, the inconsistency[33] of its text-critical apparatus. The *HUBP*, on the other hand, is methodologically a sound undertaking. However, the fact that only a limited number of Old Testament books are available is a serious handicap.

It remains to offer a possible solution to the problems outlined above. As far as the first problem area is concerned, the *critical text-concept* as followed by the *Septuaginta Unternehmen* represents an ideal to pursue. It would not be possible to transplant the *Göttingen concept*[34] onto a critical edition of a Hebrew edition. In the first place the Hebrew text of the Old Testament has a different tradition history from that of the Septuagint. Second, there are many practical problems to be bridged. All existing Hebrew and manuscripts of the versions are not available[35] for general use. Much more textual data will have to be reworked, which will again have an influence upon the extent of the critical apparatus used.

Thus, much theoretical reflection will have to go into the development of such an edition. Nevertheless, the solution to these problems is found somewhere between the two Hebrew text projects discussed above. This can be done by limiting the amount of data included in the text-critical apparatus. For exegetical purposes medieval details are of secondary[36] importance. The ancient versions, the Dead Sea Scrolls data and all Hebrew manuscript data (excluding medieval manuscripts) should suffice for such a critical apparatus. On account of predetermined theoretical premises the editor of a given book may then execute contextual analyses of all data, before expressing relevant proposals in the apparatus criticus. This is evidently a comprehensive suggestion. However, as stated at the outset, current developments in the area of exegetical tools will make the realization of this proposition much more of a practical possibility.

Conclusion

I have endeavoured to demonstrate that much work still[37] needs to be done as far as the Textual Criticism of the Old Testament is concerned. This applies to an important aspect not treated here, the question of grammatical analysis, which includes the issue of translation technique. This field of study is closely related to the text-critical issue.

The Qumran data[38] are yielding remarkable results, opening new theoretical possibilities in respect of textual theory and textual history. These insights will ultimately have an impact upon the publication of texts.

NOTES

1. For a historical outline of the factors which led to this situation, cf. M.H. Goshen-Gottstein, 'The Textual Criticism of the Old Testament: Rise, Decline, Rebirth', *JBL* 102/3 (1983), pp. 365-99. Cf. also E. Tov, 'A Modern Outlook Based on the Qumran Scrolls', *HUCA* 53 (1982), pp. 11-17.

2. Goshen-Gottstein (*op. cit.*, p. 387) speaks of a 'post-Qumran discoveries' period. Cf. also E. Tov, 'A Modern Outlook. . . ' and *idem* (ed.), *The Hebrew and Greek Texts of Samuel*, Jerusalem: Academon, 1980. Unfortunately the publication of the Qumran data has not lived up to scholarly expectations (cf. D.N. Freedman, 'The Dead Sea Scrolls—Retrospective', *BA* 40 (1977), pp. 94-97 and G. Vermes, *The Dead Sea Scrolls; Qumran in Perspective* [Ohio, 1977], p. 24).

3. This project is the result of long-term planning and persistent research. The process was initiated in 1968 when the *International*

Organization for Septuagint and Cognate Studies (IOSCS) was established (cf. R.A. Kraft and E. Tov, 'Computer Assisted Tools for the Septuagint', *BIOSCS* 14 [1981], p. 22).

4. R.A. Kraft and E. Tov, *op. cit.*, pp. 1f. The author of this article is engaged in a joint project of the Dept of Bible of the Hebrew University and the Dept of Semitic Languages of the University of Stellenbosch, concerning the grammatical and text-critical analysis of the LXX.

5. 'Computer Assisted Alignment of the Greek-Hebrew Equivalents of the Masoretic Text and the Septuagint'.

6. 'Computer Assisted Analysis of the Translation Technique of the LXX'.

7. M.H. Goshen-Gottstein, 'Prolegomena to a Critical Edition of the Peshitta', *Text and Language in Bible and Qumran* (Jerusalem, 1960), pp. 163-204. Cf. also his 'The Textual Criticism of the Old Testament: Rise, Decline, Rebirth', *JBL* 102/3 (1983), p. 391.

8. Various assistants in the Dept of Semitic Languages worked on this project. B.A. Nieuwoudt should especially be mentioned.

9. Further developments which followed the *ESF* congress mentioned above, hold in store that the University of Bar-Ilan will probably also be involved in this joint project.

10. The author has received a grant from the *Human Sciences Research Council* of South Africa to carry on with this project.

11. Cf. the collection of F.M. Cross and S. Talmon (eds.), *Qumran and the History of the Biblical Text* (Cambridge and London, 1975). The *IOSCS* held a symposium on the implications of the Qumran data. Some of the papers read at this congress have been published in: E. Tov (ed.), *The Hebrew and Greek Texts of Samuel* (Jerusalem, 1980).

12. Cf. D.W. Gooding, 'An Appeal for Stricter Terminology in the Textual Criticism of the Old Testament', *JSS* 21 (1976), pp. 15-20 and E. Tov, 'A Modern Outlook . . . ', pp. 13ff.

13. His views are found in 'The Dead Sea Scrolls', *The Interpreter's Bible* (Nashville, 1957), XII, pp. 645-67; *The Ancient Library of Qumran* (London, 1968); 'The History of the Biblical Text in the Light of Discoveries in the Judean Desert', *Qumran and the History of the Biblical Text*, pp. 177-95; 'The Contribution of the Qumran Discoveries to the Study of the Biblical Text', *op. cit.*, pp. 278-92; 'The Evolution of a Theory of Local Texts', *op. cit.*, pp. 306-20; 'Problems of Method in the Textual Criticism of the Hebrew Bible', *The Critical Study of Sacred Texts*, W.D. O'Flaherty (ed.) (Berkeley, 1979), pp. 31-54.

14. 'Untersuchungen zur Geschichte des Pentateuchtextes', *TSR* 88 (1915), pp. 399-439. It was republished in Kahle's *Opera Minora* (Leiden, 1956), pp. 5-37.

15. E. Tov, *op. cit.*, p. 13.

16. The term *eclectic* should be abandoned in respect of text publications;

it should rather be used to describe the text character of manuscripts (cf. J.W. Wevers, 'Die Methode', *Das Göttinger Septuaginta-Unternehmen* [Göttingen, 1977], p. 12).

17. Not all scholars share the definition of a critical edition followed here. Goshen-Gottstein ('The HUBP Edition, An Introduction to Some Problems of Editing the Bible', *Fourth World Congress of Jewish Studies*, 1968, p. 165), is of the opinion that such an edition should contain a diplomatic text with 'critical apparati'.

18. In fact most existing text editions are based upon this premise.

19. In Gen. 1.1-46.8; 2 Sam. 2.5-7; 10.13; Codex Alexandrinus has been used.

20. I am leaving out of discussion what is meant by this and whether it is actually possible to reach this text.

21. Cf. the introduction of the book of Genesis in the Göttingen series which was edited by J.W. Wevers.

22. Cf. H.M. Orlinsky, 'The Textual Criticism of the Old Testament', in S. Jellicoe (ed.), *Studies in the Septuagint: Origins, Recensions, and Interpretations* (New York, 1974), pp. 240ff.; and F.E. Deist, *Towards the Text of the Old Testament* (Pretoria, 1978), p. 88.

23. Since the third edition of *BH* Codex Leningradensis has been utilized.

24. This edition is, for instance, used in the *CATSS* project, of which E. Tov, co-worker to the *HUBP*, is the co-editor.

25. At the *IOSCS* congress which took place in Salamanca in 1983, one afternoon session was put aside for a symposium with the title *The Use of the Versions in the Text Criticism.* Prof. J.W. Wevers from Toronto acted as chairman of this meeting. During the discussion this issue was attended to.

26. Cf. my paper which was delivered at Salamanca: 'The Translator of the Greek Genesis'. It will be published in the Proceedings of the Congress under the editorship of Natalio Fernandez Marcos.

27. *The Hebrew University Bible—The Book of Isaiah, sample edition with introduction*, vol. I; ed. M.H. Goshen-Gottstein (Jerusalem, 1965).

28. 'The HUBP Edition, An introduction to Some Probems of Editing the Bible', *Fourth World Congress of Jewish Studies* (1968), pp. 166f.

29. The authority with which he writes is evident from his nuanced discussion.

30. It is unclear why the Judean scrolls data and rabbinical quotations should be combined in one apparatus.

31. Cf. M.H. Goshen-Gottstein, 'The Textual Criticism of the Old Testament: Rise, Decline, Rebirth', *JBL* 102/3 (1983), p. 365.

32. *Ibid.*

33. It is of course true that the specialist who wants to work with the primary sources could analyze these separately in addition to the opinions

found in these apparati.

34. I do not share Diebner's criticism of the Göttingen endeavour: 'Wozu betreiben wir im akademischen Unterricht Textkritik?', *Dielheimer Blätter zum Alten Testament* 16 (1982), pp. 55f. It is interesting to note that his proposal to reconstruct a 'christliche Bibel' (p. 61) (he clearly overestimated the Christian influence upon the Septuagint) is in accordance with what Wevers formulated as an ultimate, realizable goal: 'Es sollte Einverständnis darüber herrschen, welchen Anspruch der hier vorgelegte Text erhebt. Die Hss, Übersetzungen und patristischen Zeugnisse, die uns zur Verfügung stehen, führen uns, abgesehen von seltenen und geringfügigen Ausnahmen, nicht weiter zurück als bis ins zweite christliche Jahrhundert!' (*Septuaginta Vetus Testamentum Graecum Auctoritate Academiae Scientiarum Gottingensis Editum*, vol. I, *Genesis* [Göttingen, 1974], p. 63).

35. Paul Kahle attempted, in connection with the third edition of *BH*, to obtain Codex Aleppo, but without success (cf. the third edition of *Biblia Hebraica*, edited by R. Kittel in 1937, p. xxix).

36. The specialist could examine these data in the original sources.

37. Within the limited scope of this article it was not possible to attend to all important textcritical research which is currently being done. A very important group to be mentioned, is the Hebrew Old Testament Text Project, in which scholars such as Barthèlemy, Rüger and J.A. Sanders participate. Cf. also the excellent article by E. Ulrich, 'Horizons of Old Testament Textual Research at the Thirtieth Anniversary of Qumrân Cave 4', *CBQ* 46 (1984), pp. 613-36.

38. The present author is developing a computerized database in co-operation with the Ancient Biblical Manuscript Center (Claremont, California). An article on this project will appear in *Textua*.

3

PARALLELS AND REINTERPRETATION IN THE BOOK OF JOEL: A THEOLOGY OF THE YOM YAHWEH?

Ferdinand E. Deist

The book of Joel abounds in parallel lexical items, constructions, expressions and ideas (cf. Bourke 1959: 5-31, 191-212). It is the primary goal of this contribution to investigate some of these parallel portions of the text in order to determine their function within the book (cf. Ellul 1979: 426-37) and only secondarily to provide a few suggestions as regards the possible origin of the book. In both respects I can offer little more than what Ackroyd (1979) has called 'rearranging my uncertainties'. But I hope to show that the book was not intended to 'refer' to any concrete event in history, but was rather compiled to serve as a 'literary theology' of the concept 'The Day of the Lord'.

1. *The parallelism 1.2-20 and 2.18-27*

2.18-27's repetition of lexemes, expressions, etc. from 1.2-20 seems to imply that Yahweh's intervention on behalf of his people (2.18)[1] leads to the liquidation of the lack created by the unprecedented calamity pronounced in 1.2-3. Consider the table overleaf.

The only lack described in ch. 1 that is not addressed in 2.18-27 is that of offerings in the temple—but see 4 below. The lack described in ch. 1 and liquidated in 2.18-27 seems at first glance to be of a very concrete nature, a concreteness tempting one to view ch. 1 as a description of a real locust plague (see, for such an interpretation, e.g. Kutsch 1962; Rinaldi 1968; Allen 1976, *ad loc.*). There are, however,

Areas affected during the creation of the lack (ch. 1)		Areas affected by the liquidation of the lack (ch. 2)	
Verse		*Verse*	
4:	[grasshoppers devour everything]	25:	[Yahweh restores everything that the grasshoppers have devoured (cf. v. 20)]
6, 10:	land, corn, wine oil	18:	land corn, wine, oil
10:	soil (ארמה)	21:	soil (ארמה)
12:	vineyard, fig-trees, trees	22:	trees, fig-trees, vineyards
16:	joy and gladness (שמחה וגיל)	23:	gladness and joy (גילי ושמחי)
16/17:	parched soil, dry dykes, withered corn, granaries deserted	23:	the rain does not fail: grain, wine, or oil will produce
19/20:	the open pastures (נאות מדבר)	22:	the open pastures (נאות מדבר)
20:	animals of the field (בהמות שדה)	22:	animals of the field (בהמות שדי)

obstacles in the way of such an interpretation. For instance, 1.12, 16-17,[2] 19-20 and 2.21-23 create the impression that a drought was also involved in the creation of the existing lack. But droughts and locust swarms do not occur simultaneously. Locust plagues normally only follow after good rains that break a period of drought (Møller-Christensen & Jørgensen [1960?]: 121), while the text treats these two calamities as simultaneous occurrences. Furthermore, it is strange that people living in a country where locust plagues occurred at regular intervals should be called upon to take note of this particular plague and, especially, to retell this to all generations to come. One could perhaps argue that this particular plague—if such were indeed intended here—was particularly severe. But even then it remains strange why *this* should be remembered forever.

The literal interpretation of Joel's locusts might be valid if such problems as the above-mentioned could be solved satisfactorily and should therefore not necessarily be ruled out completely. There is, however, another possible interpretation, namely, that the prophet did not speak about a literal plague and drought at all, but was merely creating a *literary* world of calamities[3] to serve as metaphors describing the character of the Day of the Lord. The 'genre' of the text thus *is* description, but then not of a 'real' phenomenon, but of a theological conception. That the intention of the text goes beyond the mere historical situation is clear from the 'conclusion' after the proclamation of Yahweh's intervention (2.26-27), a conclusion that sounds very much like Deutero-Isaiah's proofs of the incompatibility of Yahweh (cf. Isa. 41.17; 45.17-25). The impression of imagined reality is strengthened by a second set of parallels.

2. *2.1-17 and 1.1-15*

Consider the following table (from the perspective of 2.1-17):

	Chapter 2		*Chapter 1*
Verse		*Verse*	
2:	A big and mighty nation (עם)	6:	A mighty and innumerable nation (גוי)
2:	[A nation] whose like has never been known nor ever shall be in ages to come (דור ודור)	2–3:	[A thing] the like of which has never happened; pass it on to generations to come (לדור אחר)
3 a-b:	In front of them a fire devours (אכל) and a flame behind them	4:	The locusts devour (אכל) everything (cf. v. 19: a fire devours the pastures and a flame trees)
3c:	The land becomes a wilderness (שממה)	7:	God's vineyard becomes a wilderness (שמה)
4-10:	Description of the devastator and its devastation	4:	Description of the devastator and its devastation
11:	The day of the Lord is terrible and unbearable	15:	The day of the Lord is near: a day of devastation
12-14:	The offerings (מנחה ונסך) may be restored	8–13:	The calamities lead to a lack of offerings (מנחה ונסך) in the temple
15-17:	A great fast must be proclaimed and everybody should take part	5, 8, 13, 14:	Everybody should be pleading with God, a plea culminating in a day of fasting

Without this parallelism the connection between the two chapters would be obscure, since the only overt suggestion that the prophet may still be referring to the locusts of ch. 1 here, is that seven-fold כ in 2.4-7, which may indicate that the innumerable nation of 2.2 should perhaps not be taken literally. Since the real subject described in ch. 2 is never mentioned explicitly, the parallelism with ch. 1 and its locusts suggests that they remain the subject—although this 'link' may still prove to be only superficial, if not intentionally misleading (cf. note 7).

Parallelism is no mere repetition. A parallel text often provides oblique commentary on its 'antecedent', thereby deepening or even changing the meaning of its paradigm text (see Miscall 1978). That the approaching locusts of ch. 1 are pictured in military terms in ch. 2 is rather striking in the light of the—albeit much older—well-known locust similes in the Ugaritic texts of *Keret* and *Anat*. Compare the following table:

Joel 2.2-9, 16 (NEB)	*Ugaritic texts*
A mighty, countless host appears their like has never been known . . .	Your army, a great host: three hundred myriads, troops without number, soldiers uncountable (Krt 88-91)
On they come, like squadrons of horse like war-horses they charge . . . like a countless host in battle array	Like locusts they occupy the field, like grasshoppers the corners of the desert (Krt 103-105)
Like warriors they charge they mount the walls like men at arms each marching in line no confusion in the ranks	Arrayed in twos, look! in threes all of them (Krt 94-95)
They plunge through streams they burst into the city leap on to the wall climb into the houses entering like thieves through the windows	. . . and occupy the towns take over the cities. . . (Krt 110)
Gather the children, yes, babes at the breast; bid the bridegroom leave his chamber and the bride her bower.	The solitary man closes his home, the widow locks herself in, the sick man carries his bed, the blind man gropes his way. Even the new-wed groom goes forth, he drives to another his wife, to a stranger his well-beloved. (Ginsberg's translation in *ANET*, Krt 93-103)

Although the imagery of the Ugaritic texts was also known and employed in Israel (cf. Judg. 6.5; 7.2; Jer. 46.23; 51.27; Nah. 3.16-17), Joel used the imagery in exactly the opposite manner: soldiers are not likened to locusts, but locusts to soldiers. In doing so, he succeeded in bringing a new dimension to the description of the Day of the Lord, namely a military dimension (cf. Kutsch 1962: 82): it is not only a day of natural catastrophes, but *also* of military threats (cf. Wolff 1969: 55f.; Everson 1974: 331-37; Hoffmann 1981: 43-47). The listener/reader can easily be misled; nowhere in ch. 2 are the locusts explicitly mentioned. Given the 'normal' use of locust imagery for military enterprises and the absence of real locusts in the environment of the reader, the 'normal' interpretation of ch. 1 would be to understand it in military terms.[4] At the same time, however, the locusts of ch. 1 are still so fresh in the mind of the reader that he, because of the parallelism between the two chapters, still reads ch. 2 as referring to locusts. In this manner both interpretations, i.e. locust plague *and* military threat, 'hover' above the text, although ch. 2 focuses the attention on the military sphere: even the summons to the day of fasting reminds one of military conscription (cf. the summoning of the bridegroom in 2.16, and compare the Ugaritic parallel cited above).[5] The author succeeds in veiling the 'real' meaning of his text by letting the reader doubt the actuality of the locusts in ch. 1 as well as the actuality of the invading army (by the 'comparative' use of military imagery),[6] thereby suggesting that he is operating with imagery and not referring to the external world. The locust and drought imagery of ch. 1 enriches the military imagery of ch. 2 and vice versa. It is thus striking that the Day of the Lord is only briefly mentioned in ch. 1, but treated more extensively in ch. 2. That the scene described is changed from the countryside (ch. 1) to the city (ch. 2) shows that 2.18-27 is the focus of attention in 1.2–2.27.

3. *Preliminary conclusion*

a. Joel 1.2-20 and 2.18-27 stand parallel and reveal a functional relationship of lack (1.2-20) and liquidation of lack (2.18-27). Since 2.1-17 is not directly 'reflected' in 2.18-27 and the semantic relationship between 1.2-20 and 2.18-27 is of a primary nature, while the relationship between 2.2-20 and 2.1-17 is of a 'secondary' (that is re-interpretative) nature, we will have to look at 1.2-20 and 2.18-27 separately first. The relationship between the imagery of this portion of the text and a text like Hosea 2 is conspicuous. Consider the following examples:

	Joel 1–2 (NEB)		*Hosea 2* (NEB)
Verse (MT)		*Verse* (MT)	
9f.:	Mourn, you priests, . . . the fields are ruined, the parched earth mourns; the corn is ruined, the new wine is desperate, the oil has failed	10f.:	For she does not know that it is I who gave her corn, new wine, and oil . . . Therefore I will take back my corn at the harvest and my new wine at the vintage . . .
12:	The vintage is desperate, and the fig-tree has failed; . . . and none make merry over harvest	12f.:	I will ravage the vines and the fig-trees . . . and turn them into a jungle . . . I will put a stop to her merrymaking
		15:	I will punish her for the holy days when she burnt sacrifices to the Baalim . . .
	Joel 2		*Hosea 2*
Verse			
18-20:	Then the Lord's love burned with zeal for his land, and he was moved with compassion for his people . . . and said: I will send you corn, and new wine, and oil . . . I will expose you no longer to the reproach of other nations. I will remove the northern peril far away from you and banish them into a land far and waste . . .	16-19:	But now listen, I will woo her . . . there I will restore her vineyards, turning the Vale of Trouble into the Gate of Hope . . . and I will wipe from her lips the very names of the Baalim; never again shall their names be heard . . .
22-27:	Be not afraid, you cattle in the field; . . . the trees shall bear fruit, the fig and the vine yield their harvest. O people of Zion, rejoice and	20-25:	Then I will make a covenant . . . with the wild beasts . . . so that all living creatures may lie down without fear. I will betroth you

be glad in the Lord your God, who gives you good food in due measure and sends down rain as of old. The threshing-floors shall be heaped with grain, the vats shall overflow with new wine and oil . . . and you shall eat . . . and praise the name of the LORD your God . . . and you shall know that I am present in Israel, that I and no other am the Lord your God . . .

to myself for ever . . . and you shall know the LORD. At that time I will give answer . . . I will answer for the heavens and they will answer the earth, and the earth will answer for the corn, the new wine and the oil, and they will answer for Jezreel . . . And I will . . . say to Lo-ammi: 'You are my people', and he will say: 'Thou art my God'.

The close agreement between these two texts suggests that there may be a common tradition behind them, that they stem from the same kind of theological background, and that the idea expressed by some, namely that the Day of the Lord also had its roots in the polemic against the Baal cult, may be right (cf. Ellul 1979: 428, 431, 433; Cathcart 1978: 48-59; Hoffmann 1981: 44f.). One may term the theological conception behind the Day of the Lord in Joel 1.2-20 and 2.18-27 'anti-Canaanite theology'. Whether this theology of the Day of the Lord should be located in Ephraimite tradition is, however, an open question, since the same theological frame of mind can also be detected in Isaiah 24, the opening chapter to the problematic 'Isaiah Apocalypse'. It is not the purpose of this investigation to go into this question. What seems certain is that the theological reference system that lies behind Hosea 2 has very much in common with Joel 1 and 2.18-27.

b. The parallelism between 1.2-20 and 2.1-17 reveals a functional relationship of reinterpretation/redescription (as seen from the perspective of 2.1-17). The Day of the Lord is here described in imagery drawn from the theology of theophany (cf. Weiss 1966: 29-60) which, via the idea of the Divine Warrior (and the idea of the Holy War), was clothed in military imagery (cf. Everson 1974: 335-36; Kutsch 1962: 89-92). Even the cosmic perspective attached to the theology of the Yom Yahweh in 2.6, 10 is common to this theological tradition (cf. Kutsch 1962: 83, 86-88). It is thus quite obvious that the theological framework of 2.1-17 differs substantially from that of 1.2-20 and 2.18-27.

However, through the literary parallelism between 1.2-20 and 2.1-17 the anti-Canaanite and theophanic theologies are intertwined: The more 'earth-bound' perspective of the first theology is built into a more cosmic one, that which was on an 'agricultural-rural' level is reinterpreted in city terms, and perhaps that which was Ephraimite is 'Jerusalemized'. The fact that 2.1-27 'splits up' 1.2-20 and 2.18-27 makes it imperative to view the whole in terms of this central portion, since the whole is now structured according to the 'pivot point' pattern (cf. Watson 1976). What precedes and what follows this pivot point should be read in terms of that point, so that the whole, as it stands now, should be interpreted in military terms as well. It is perhaps at this 'stage' that a comparison with Isaiah 24 becomes more fruitful, since in that chapter we encounter both the elements occurring in Joel 1 and 2: agricultural *and* military disaster.[7]

4. *Joel 1–2 and 3*

Although ch. 3 does not show the same amount of parallelism with the preceding and subsequent texts of the book as we have encountered up to now (and which we will also find in connection with ch. 4), there are, nevertheless, some points in this chapter that link it with what precedes it, albeit more covert and on a theological level (cf. Ellul 1979: 435-36). The והיה אחרי כן of 3.1 seems to interpret the sequence of *waw*-consecutives in 2.18 (see note 1) as referring to *future* salvation, since it is clearly intended to link up *logically* and chronologically with 2.18: after the material blessings (2.18-27) spiritual blessings will follow (3.1-5). The order in which the recipients of the blessings are mentioned reminds us of the order in which the people were summoned to the national day of fasting:

2.16	*3.1*
The whole congregation	All flesh
The children and sucklings	The elders
The elders	Your sons and daughters
The bridegroom and bride	The soldiers
(in the sense of military conscription?)	

while the addition of slaves in 3.1 does not really constitute a 'plus' in the sense of more people, but only in the sense that it functions as an additional social category of people. Similarly, the mention of the sun and the moon in 3.4 recalls their mention in 2.10, while the Day of the Lord in 3.4 reminds us of 1.15 and 2.11 and Zion (3.5) recalls the Zion of 2.1. That which we have to assume in 2.18-27, namely that only those who call on Yahweh will be saved, is made explicit in 3.5. But what is more important is that 3.1-15 supplies a necessary complement to 2.18-27.

The order of the calamities in ch. 1 is natural–spiritual (if one takes the frequent mentioning of the shortage of offerings in the temple to indicate a spiritual need as does Ellul [1979: 428]). 2.18-27 does not, however, 'take care' of the spiritual needs of the people. These are only addressed in 3.1-5. But then the liquidation of the spiritual lack goes far beyond what was implied in ch. 1 and in that sense 3.1-5 constitutes a major 'plus' to 1–2. On the one hand 3.1-5 creates the impression of a (later) eschatological addition to 1–2, as was frequently observed in the past. (The idea of material blessings followed by spiritual blessings is often found in Deutero-Isaiah [cf. Isa. 55]). On the other hand this 'Deutero-Isaianic eschatological outlook' of 3.1-5 is precisely that which links 3.1-5 to 2.17-28, since 2.27 already shows much affinity with the Deutero-Isaianic 'proof of Yahweh's uniqueness' (cf. 41.17; 45.17-25). But then 3.1-5 also goes beyond Deutero-Isaiah in that its imagery concerning the changes that will occur in the sun and the moon suggests something of an 'apocalyptic' nature (3.4—cf. 2.10; 4.15 as well as the language of theophany in 3.3; cf. 2.2). These descriptions of the future actions of Yahweh seem to exceed the Deutero-Isaianic eschatological expectations, which are more accurately reflected in 2.18-27. Nevertheless, one can term the theological framework within which the Day of the Lord is interpreted in 3.1-5 'eschatological'.

5. *2.10-11 and 4.14-17*

Consider the table overleaf. The re-occurrence of key concepts of 2.10-11, (17) in 4.14-17 is conspicuous, as is the chiastic rearrangement of the structure in which the parallel elements occur. Ellul (1979: 433) spots another interesting chiastic pattern created by this parallelism: the agricultural catastrophe reflected in 1.1-14 is expressed in military terms (see note 4) while the destruction of the nations by an army is depicted in agricultural imagery (4.10).

Apart from the parallels in vocabulary, it is interesting to note the parallel between the summons to the national day of humiliation in

2.10-11			4.14-17
לפניו רגזה ארץ רעשו שמים	(1)	(4)	כי קרוב יום יהוה בעמק החרוץ
שמש וירח קדרו וככבים אספו נגהם	(2)	(2)	שמש וירח קדרו וככבים אספו נגהם
ויהוה נתן קולו לפני חילו	(3)	(3)	ויהוה מציון ישאג ומירושלם יתן קולו
כי רב מאד מחנהו כי עצום עשה דברו כי גדול יום יהוה ונורא מאד מי יכילנו	(4)	(1)	ורעשו שמים וארץ ויהוה מחסה לעמו ומעוז לבני ישראל
2.17 : וידעתם כי בקרב ישראל אני ואני יהוה אלהיכם ואין עוד ולא יבשו עמי לעולם	(5)	(5)	וידעתם כי אנכי יהוה אלהיכם שכן בציון הר קדשי וזרים לא יעברו בה עוד

ch. 2 and the summoning of the nations to the Valley of Decision in ch. 4. In ch. 2 the inclusion of the bridegroom and the bride in the list of summoned people creates—within the military framework of 2.1-17—the impression of total war. This impression is not, however, allowed to develop into a literal 'meaning' of that phrase in ch. 2, since the narrower context is that of the cult. Chapter 4 now 'picks up' that possibility and overtly uses the imagery of total war (cf. van Selms 1979/80). It is, furthermore, interesting to note that 4.9-18 responds to the calamities described in chs. 1–2 in reverse order and interprets the mysterious 'power from the north' as actual foreign nations. In chs. 1–2 the need of the people is described in the order agricultural–military. In ch. 4 these two lacks are liquidated in the order military salvation–agricultural abundance (4.9-14, 18).

Despite these parallels—in which the process of reinterpretation is already clear—the extensions of and additions to the elements common to 2.10-11 and 4.14-17 (as underlined above) are also conspicuous. The additions and alterations show a clear affinity with the Zion ideology (cf. the additions/alterations in the elements (3—3) and (4—1) above). This has often been noted in the past. The main difference between the two passages is reflected in the elements (3—3): whereas Yahweh was the commander of the foreign power directed *against* Jerusalem in 2.1-17, he is in (4) roaring *from* Jerusalem-Zion. Whereas the Day of the Lord was understood as an event directed *against* Israel-Judah in ch. 2, it is here interpreted as a day of (final) salvation *for* Judah. Chapter 4 takes up the military imagery of ch. 2 and interprets it as military actions performed in favour of Israel on the Yom Yahweh. This shift in meaning is even clearer when one compares the two chapters on a broader scale. Consider the following examples:

Joel 1–2	*Joel 4*
The city is (as yet?) intact (2.15-17; cf. 1.2; 2.1) and its inhabitants (still?) in it (1.2; 1.13f.; 2.16).	The city is destroyed (4.15, 17b) and its inhabitants dispersed (4.2-3, 6).
Yahweh is acting against his people (2.11) and is the leader of the attacking foreign power.	Yahweh is acting for his people (4.1, 16f., 21) and initiates a war against the foreign nations.
The congregation should be sanctified to pray and fast (2.16) in order to prevent a (military) defeat.	A war should be sanctified against the nations (4.9).
Yahweh is spoken to in the second person or referred to in the third person (נחלתיך; ארצו; עמו—2.17-8; cf., however, 2.1).	Yahweh speaks in the first person throughout (cf. however 4.16; cf. נחלתי; ארצי; עמי).
Yahweh spares his land and his people (2.18).	Yahweh changes the plight of his people.
The ensuing 'peace' is of a concrete and historical (i.e. 'this-sided') nature (2.18-20, 21-27).	The ensuing peace is of an eschatological nature, although seemingly still within history (4.15-21).

The resemblance between 4.15-21 and Zech. 14.8-12 is very strong. This hints in the direction of understanding the theological framework of Joel 4 as standing in close connection with apocalyptic, or perhaps proto-apocalyptic thought.

As was the case with ch. 1, ch. 4 (especially 4.3-6) creates the impression that real extra-textual events are being referred to. The difficulties experienced in 'locating' and dating these events and the contradictory nature of scholarly opinion on this matter[8] may show that these 'references' should not be taken as references at all and that one does right in following Hanson's opinion (1979: 318) that the author simply employed a series of stereotyped apocalyptic phrases. The chapter simply moulds the imagery of ch. 2, which shows definitive signs of the Divine Warrior Hymn (cf. Hanson 1979: 123-26), into a more apocalyptic style. It seems as if 4.1, like 3.1, does not take 2.18 to refer to a concrete historical event of salvation. For if it does, it will lead to a contradiction: in 2.18 Yahweh will already have changed the plight of his people, and if he now, as 4.1 says, (again) changes the plight of his people, this second change will not be for the good of his people. Chapter 4 clearly takes chs. 1–2/3(?) as referring to the future, reinterprets the theology of the Day of the Lord contained in the first half of the book and frames it in apocalyptic thought. In doing so the author almost reverses the meaning of chs. 1–2.

As suggested earlier, it may be saying too much to call Joel 4 apocalyptic (in the strict sense of the word) (cf. Meyers 1962: 192). The resemblance between this chapter and texts like Trito-Zechariah and Ezekiel is common knowledge and the theological framework of this chapter would therefore suit Hanson's category of proto-apocalypticism.

6. *Conclusion*

The book of Joel consists of at least three parallel passages: 1.2-20 // 2.18-27; 1.2-20 // 2.1-17; 2.10-11 // 4.14-17. In the first case the parallel passage liquidates the lack described in the paradigm text. In the second instance, the parallel passage reinterprets the paradigm text's description of natural disasters in military and theophanic imagery and narrows down the scope to the city of Jerusalem, while it simultaneously provides a cosmic perspective to the whole. In the last case the parallel passage, situated in a textual environment that almost contradicts that of the paradigm text, completely reinterprets the military imagery of the paradigm text in proto-apocalyptic terms. At the same time it stands in the functional relationship of the final liquidation of the lacks described in chs. 1–2.

The odd section in the parallel structuring of the book seems to be 3.1-5, although it fits neatly into the whole and provides an extensive spiritual reinterpretation of 2.18-27 in an eschatological fashion.

All four chapters evade historical interpretation in the sense of linking them with concrete historical events, and therefore it seems that we cannot date them. But they are linked together by a common theme, namely the Day of the Lord. The different theological environments in which the Day of the Lord is mentioned in these chapters seem to suggest that the book consists of at least three, if not four, interpretations of that concept. Whether these theological perspectives should be viewed as of different historical and/or geographical origins cannot be answered in this study and it may be worthwhile investigating such possibilities. However, this study does suggest that the book of Joel is better understood if it is not read 'referentially' in terms of locusts, droughts, military threats and battles, but as a compilation—albeit artistically composed—of different theologies of the Yom Yahweh arranged in such a manner that they may be read as reinterpretations of each other. Given ch. 4 as the outer circle of this process of reinterpretation, the book as a whole can, in its final form, only be understood 'apocalyptically'. Without ch. 4 the book would still make good sense, but it would then have to be read 'eschatologically'. With chs. 3 and 4 isolated from 1-2, the latter section will still make sense, but will then have to be interpreted in terms of theophany and judgment. Should one remove 2.1-17, the remainder would still form a meaning unit, but it would then have to be read in terms of anti-Canaanite theology.

The book of Joel, therefore, can be understood as a theology of the Yom Yahweh or as theologies of the Yom Yahweh, depending upon the portion of text under investigation. Perhaps this approach to the book may also explain why, in such a brief booklet, the term Yom Yahweh occurs no less than four of the sixteen times it occurs in the whole corpus of prophetical writings.

NOTES

1. 2.18 is widely acknowledged as an *Umbruch* in the book of Joel, but very little attention has been paid to the problems attached to the interpretation of this verse within the context of the book. If one takes the locust plague and drought of ch. 1 and/or the military threat of 2.1-17 literally, 2.18 presupposes a literal day of humiliation, since the oracle of salvation in 2.18-27 can only follow on such a day. Yet there is no evidence in the book that such a day was indeed kept. There are various calls to such a day, but no indication of them being met. (Cf. the various ways in which scholars approached or evaded this problem, e.g. Budde 1919; Wolff 1969: 6; Rimbach 1981: 308; Ellul 1979: 430, 435. Kutsch [1962: 93] merely assumes that such a day was kept: 'In einer grossen Bussfeier ergeht—ähnlich wie in 2 Chron. 20,4-19—an das versammelte Volk wohl durch den Propheten ein

Heilsorakel'.) There are a number of (poorer and better) solutions to this problem: one may argue that the personal lament of 1.19-20 provides the necessary ground for accepting 2.18 as referring to a concrete oracle of salvation addressed to the congregation as Amos's intervention on behalf of his people (Amos 7.1-3) prevented a similar disaster. But then Amos could still intervene, since in his case we have to do with a vision and not with a real plague that has already started, as is the case in Joel. One could also argue that 2.12-14 provides an indication of such a day. But not only does a further call to a fast follow on that text, 2.12-14 also forms such an integral part of 2.1-17 and is phrased in such eloquent and traditional (Deuteronomistic) phraseology (cf. Wolff 1969: 57) that one would really have to use a very sharp literary-critical knife to reconstruct a reference to such a day from 2.12-24. One may also follow the solution presented by Ogden (1982; 1983), namely to accept the book as a collection of oracles of salvation. In that case there is no need for a day of humiliation within the text, since we have only to do with oracles. This solution may help us forward, but then we have already conceded that the book itself no longer refers to historical circumstances. One may also follow another course. The consecutive imperfect forms of 2.18 create the impression of historical narration (cf. GKC §111a) and are—interpreted thus—the source of the problem. One may, however, also understand them as expressing *logical*, rather than chronological, sequence (cf. GKC §111 i-l). Then the chronological problem falls away. Or, which is perhaps even better, one may follow Theodotion by reading these forms not as consecutives but as copulatives—a reading seemingly presupposed by 3:1 and 4:1 (see paragraphs 4 and 5 of the text). Then it is impossible to read the text as 'referring' to external events, since the logic of the text is simply that ch. 1 and 2.1-17 are continued here: *if* a day of lament were kept, the consequences would be as described in 2.18-27.

2. Wolff (1969: 40) accepts these verses as referring to a real drought and thereby he presupposes the simultaneous occurrence of locusts and drought. But Jepsen has sensed the problem involved in such a view and has tried to divide Joel 1 into a 'locust' layer and a 'drought' layer (Jepsen 1938).

3. The idea that the book of Joel is more than 'normal' prophecy or even that the book should be viewed more from a literary perspective has been proposed more than once in the past. Wolff (1969: 15f.) speaks of the book as 'learned' prophecy; Müller (1965/66) views 1.2-4, 2.18 and chs. 3–4 as literary reworkings of an earlier oral Joel; Rinaldi (1968) even speaks about the book as a possible midrash on Ps. 65 and Ogden (1963) views at least ch. 4 as an oracle of salvation that presupposes other literature, thereby departing from the view that the book can be read 'historically'. Many scholars have also pointed to the fact that the book—like the prayer in Jonah 2—creates the impression of a compilation of prophetical utterances, since it so often 'quotes' from other prophetical books (see Meyer 1962: 193 and the

literature cited by him).

4. It is indeed possible to interpret many an image of Joel 1 as 'results' of a military siege. In those days it was standard procedure to destroy the vegetation of a besieged city in order to force the inhabitants to surrender. To get an idea why invaders were likened to grasshoppers in those days, one has only to think of Shalmaneser's boastful reports about his campaigns against foreign kings and the humanitarian laws of Deut. 20.19-20 and of the shortage of food in Jerusalem during the Babylonian siege of that city (Jer. 37.2; 38.9; cf. 2 Kgs 6.24-29). Shalmaneser said (in Wiseman's translation): 'I smote 14,000 of their men with weapons, falling on them like Adad pouring down a hailstorm' (Kurkh Stele ii); and 'I cut down his plantations (and then) marched as far as the mountains of Hauran. I destroyed, tore down, and burnt with fire numberless villages. . . ' (Black Obelisk). And Deuteronomy ruled: 'When you are at war, and lay siege to a city for a long time in order to take it, do not destroy its trees by taking the axe to them, for they provide you with food; you shall not cut them down. . .' (NEB). See also note 7 below.

5. In this regard compare Herrmann (1958: 220): 'Zweifellos . . . fördern die beiden hier einander gegenübergestellten Texte [i.e. 1 Krt II: 96-103 and Deut. 20.5-7] gegenseitig die Erklärung, und es wird deutlich, dass der ugaritische Text an markanten Beispielen sagen will: soweit es möglich ist, sollen alle Kräfte für den Kriegszug des Königs Keret aufgeboten werden'.

6. Ellul is right in asserting, 'Si elle est au v. 11 clairement l'armée de Yhwh, on ne sait pas aux v. 2b-9 s'il s'agit des armées célestes ou de l'armée des insectes' (1979: 429), while Meyers (1962: 191) might just have walked right into the 'trap' set by the author by interpreting his army all too literally.

7. If the assumption that Joel 1 presents us with an anti-Canaanite version of the theology of the Yom Yahweh holds true, an interesting question may arise. Seeing that locusts nowhere play a role in that 'theology' one may well ask whether the locust imagery of Joel 1 is 'original' in Joel 1 or whether it was inserted into ch. 1 to link this chapter to the second, since the locust imagery is only encountered explicitly in 1.4 and its parallel in 2.25 (and perhaps in 1.6?). The rest of the chapter can easily be understood as a description of the consequences of a severe and prolonged drought only. There is thus a possibility that the locust theme was introduced into ch. 1 to provide a link with ch. 2 and that these 'locusts'—because of the well-known suggestive power of this image—had to 'signal' *military threat* right from the outset. This would also make the 'enemy from the north' in 2.20 more comprehensible (cf. Childs 1959), while the mention of this 'enemy'—given its links with the chaos tradition—would supplement the polemics against Canaanite tradition in ch. 1 in a very meaningful manner. But at this stage this can be no more than a guess.

BIBLIOGRAPHY

Ackroyd, P.R.
1979 'Faith and its Reformulation in the Post-exilic Period', *TD* 27, pp. 323-46.

Allen, L.C.
1976 *The Books of Joel, Obadiah, Jonah and Micah*. Grand Rapids: Eerdmans.

Bourke, J.
1959 'Le jour de Yahvé dans Joël', *RB* 66, 5-31, pp. 191-212.

Brodie, L.
1978 'Creative Writing: Missing Link in Biblical Research', *BTB* 8, pp. 34-39.

Budde, K.
1919 'Der Umschwung in Joel 2', *OLZ* 22, pp. 104-10.

Cathcart, K.J.
1978 'Kingship and "Day of YHWH" in Isaiah 2.6-22', *Hermathena* 125, pp. 48-59.

Childs, B.S.
1959 'The Enemy from the North and the Chaos Tradition', *JBL* 78, pp. 187-98.

Dorn, L.
1978 'Chronological Sequence in Two Hebrew Narratives', *Bible Translator* 29, pp. 316-22.

Ellul, D.
1978 'Introduction au livre de Joel', *ETR* 54, pp. 426-37.

Everson, A.J.
1974 'The Days of Yahweh', *JBL* 93, pp. 329-37.

Hanson, P.D.
1979 *The Dawn of Apocalyptic* (rev. edn), Philadelphia: Fortress.

Herrmann, W.
1958 'Das Aufgebot aller Kräfte. Zur Interpretation von 1 K II 96-103=IV 184-191 und Dtn 20 5-7', *ZAW* 70, pp. 215-20.

Hoffmann, Y.
1981 'The Day of the Lord as a Concept and a Term in the Prophetic Literature', *ZAW* 93, pp. 37-50.

Jepsen, A.
1938 'Kleine Beiträge zum Zwölfprophetenbuch', *ZAW* 56, pp. 85-96.

Kutsch, E.
1962 'Heuschreckenplage und Tag Jahwes in Joel 1 und 2', *ThZ* 18, pp. 81-94.

Martin, W.J.
1969 '"Dischronologized" Narrative in the Old Testament', *SVT* 17, pp. 179-86.

Meyers, J.M.
1962 'Some Considerations Bearing on the Date of Joel', *ZAW* 74, pp. 177-95.

Miscall, P.D.
1978 'The Jacob and Joseph Stories as Analogies', *JSOT* 6, pp. 28-40.

Møller-Christensen, V. & K.E. Jordt Jørgensen
[1960?] *Dierenleven in de Bijbel* (transl. J.M. Vreudenhil), Baarn: Bosch & Keuning.

Müller, H.P.
1965/6 'Prophetie und Apokalyptik bei Joel', *ThV* 10, 231-52.

Ogden, C.S.
1982 'Prophetic Oracles against Foreign Nations and Psalms of Communal Lament: The Relationship of Psalm 137 to Jeremiah 49.7-22 and Obadiah', *JSOT* 24, pp. 89-97.
1983 'Joel 4 and Prophetic Response to National Laments', *JSOT* 26, pp. 97-106.

Reicke, B.
1970 'Joel und seine Zeit', *ATANT* 59, pp. 133-41.

Rimbach, J.A.
1981 'Those Lively Prophets—Joel ben Pethuel', *CMT* 8, pp. 302-304.

Rinaldi, G.
1968 'Gioele e il Salmo 65', *BibO* 10, pp. 113-22.

Rudolph, W.
1967 'Wann wirkte Joel?', in *Das ferne und nahe Wort* (Festschrift für L. Rost), Berlin: Töpelmann, pp. 193-98.

4

PSALM 122

Herbert Donner

Psalm 122 is a pilgrim song.[1] As far as that is concerned, nearly all scholars agree.[2] No agreement, however, can be stated as to the explanation and translation of three key-verses which are important for the interpretation of the Psalm as a whole: vv. 2, 3, and 5. In v. 2 the tense of the participle phrase *'ōmᵉdôt hāyû raglēnû* is controversial: is it present tense ('our feet are standing')[3] or past tense ('our feet were standing')[4] or even future tense ('our feet will be standing')?[5] In v. 3 the difficult clause *kᵉ'îr šeḥubbᵉrâ-llāh yaḥdāw* is debated: does it refer to Jerusalem as a place of pilgrimage ('like a city where people come together in unity')[6] or to Jerusalem's strong and compact walls ('like a city that is closely compacted together')?[7] In v. 5 tense is again in doubt: *did* the 'thrones for judgment' stand in Jerusalem,[8] or *do* they actually stand there?[9] And which sort of thrones are the 'thrones for judgment, the thrones of the house of David?' Interpreters are well advised to consider these problems mainly from the grammatical and stylistic points of view—as Charles F. Fensham did in most of his articles and books, teaching his pupils and colleagues not to go too far in historical or theological presuppositions and assumptions. The following short reflections are cordially and warmly dedicated to him on the occasion of his sixtieth birthday.

I

The reason why the tense of the phrase *'ōmᵉdôt hāyû raglênû* is regarded as unclear can hardly be comprehended, especially since the ancient versions rendered it correctly, using the past tense.[10] Interpreters' different views seem to be caused by preconceived opinions on the character and situation of the pilgrim song. The syntactical structure of the phrase in question is quite clear: it is a *nominal* clause with inverted word order (complement of the predicate-subject) having a perfect form of the root *hyh* as so-called *copula*. In the whole OT there is only one exact parallel: 1 Sam. 17.34, *rō'ē hāyâ 'abd^ekā*—'a shepherd was your servant'. But it is, of course, grammatically correct to refer to similar clauses in as much as they show a participle connected with a perfect form of *hyh*. The following types are attested:

1. participle as complement + perfect of *hyh* (grammatical subject missing): e.g. Deut. 9.7, *mamrîm h^eyîtem 'im YHWH*—'you have been rebellious against the Lord'. The instances: Exod. 39.9; Deut. 9.22, 24; 31.27; 1 Sam. 25.7; Ezek. 16.22; 36.13; Ps. 69.9; Lam. 4.8; Neh. 13.26; 2 Chron. 26.10.
2. perfect of *hyh* + participle as subject: e.g. Gen. 40.13, *hāyîtā mašqēhû*—'when you were his cupbearer'. The instances: 2 Sam. 3.17; 5.2; 1 Kgs 12.6; 2 Kgs 17.33; Isa. 10.14; Pss. 30.8; 126.3; Dan. 8.7; Neh. 5.18; 6.14, 19.
3. perfect of *hyh* + participle as complement: e.g. 1 Kgs 10.3, *lō'-hāyâ dābār ne'lām min-hammelek*—'nothing was hid from the king'. The instances: 2 Sam. 10.5; 1 Kgs 11.4; 2 Kgs 18.4.
4. subject + perfect of *hyh* + participle as complement: e.g. 1 Kgs 5.1, *ûš^elōmōh hāyâ mōšēl*—'and Solomon was ruler'. The instances: Gen. 37.2; 39.22; Exod. 3.1; Judg. 1.7; 1 Sam. 2.11; 2 Sam. 3.6; 1 Kgs 18.3; 22.35; 2 Kgs 3.4; 4.1; 6.8; 7.3; 9.14; Jer. 26.18; 26.20; 32.2; Ezek. 27.7f.; 43.6; Zech. 3.3; Job 1.14; Dan. 8.5; 10.2, 9; Neh. 3.26; 2 Chron. 15.17; 22.4.
5. complement + perfect of *hyh* + participle as subject: Lam. 4.19, *qallîm hāyû rōd^epēnû*—'our pursuers were swift'. (This is the only instance.)

In all these 57 cases the perfect of *hyh* is the indicator of past tense.[11] This principle does not seem to hold true in the following items:

1. Gen. 42.11, *lō'-hāyû ^abādêkā m^eragg^elîm*—'your servants are no spies' and 42.31, *lō' hāyînû m^eragg^elîm*—'we are no spies'. Both verses belong to Joseph's questioning of his

brothers: he charges them with espionage, but they plead not guilty, claiming to have come only to buy food. The perfect forms *hāyû/hāyînû* clearly reply to Joseph's allegation that they have entered Egypt 'to see where the land is unprotected',[12] i.e. that the brothers had been spies from their arrival in Egypt until this moment. That is untrue; the brothers were no spies, therefore they are no spies. The forms *hāyû/hāyînû* are forms of static-resultative perfect.

2. Another example of a similar kind can be found in Isa. 59.1-2a: 'behold, the arm of the Lord is not too short to save, nor his ear too heavy to hear, but your iniquities separate between you and your God' (*kî 'im-ʿᵃwōnōtêkem hāyû mabdîlîm bēnēkem lᵉbên *ᵉlōhêkem*). The suggestion that Yahweh might be unable to help is contrasted with the statement that people's sins caused the non-appearance of Yahweh's help. The iniquities have already done so, and therefore we have to translate: 'but your iniquities have separated between you and your God' (correctly so in RSV and NIV). This interpretation is clearly supported by the following perfect forms: *histîrû* (v. 2b), *nᵉgōᵃlû, dibbᵉrû* (v. 3).

3. The 'shepherds of Israel' in Ezek. 34.1 are charged with false conduct. The description of what they did is given to show what they are like. Therefore, however, the attributive clause *ᵃšer hāyû rōʿîm 'ōtām*, 'who fed themselves' (34.2), seems to be doubtful.[13] Probably one should prefer the Septuagint version: μὴ βόσκουσιν οἱ ποιμένες ἑαυτούς = *hᵃyirʿû rōʿîm 'ōtām*—'shall shepherds feed themselves?'[14] But if this is not so, we have to translate the phrase in the past tense, as some of the ancient versions did.[15] This would be in harmony with vv. 4-6: a retrospective glance at the behaviour of the shepherds in the past. Verse 10 reads as follows: *wᵉlō'-yirʿû ʿôd hārōʿîm 'ōtām* 'and the shepherds shall no longer feed themselves', i.e. after Yahweh's judgment. Things are, consequently, similar to Gen. 42.11, 31 and Isa. 59.2a.

4. Ps. 10.14, *yātôm 'attā hāyîtā ʿōzēr*—'you have been the helper of the orphan'—presents no difficulty. Within the passage vv. 12-15 we read in v. 14 a retrospect on the individual fate of the worshipper, obviously in the past tense:

'You, O God, have seen trouble and grief, you considered to take (it) in your hand. The helpless committed himself unto you; the orphan, you have been a helper for him'.[16]

5. Lam. 1.11, *r^e'ēh* YHWH *w^ehabbîṭā kî hāyîtî zōlēlā*—'look, O Lord, and consider that I was despised' is the final verse of the passage 1.7-11 in which Jerusalem remembers the bygone catastrophe. All verbal forms of this passage are to be translated in the past tense.[17]
6. Lam. 1.16 describes the poet's reaction to the catastrophe: 'This is why I weep, and my eyes overflow with tears, for a comforter that should restore my spirit is far from me. My children are desolate, because the enemy has prevailed' (*hāyû bānay šōmēmîm kī gābar 'ōyēb*). This is indeed the only exception to the rule: here the connection of a participle with the perfect of *hyh* means the present tense. Or does the poet intend to say that his children were desolate when they saw the power of the enemy at that time, at the time of Jerusalem's destruction?

Apart from Lam. 1.16 which is not clear, the following rule can be well established: the perfect of *hyh* used in connection with a participle is an indication of the past tense. We have to translate Ps. 122.2: 'Our feet were standing in your gates, O Jerusalem'. This is a backward glance at the great moment of the pilgrim's arrival in the holy city. Naturally, the pilgrim's feet did not stand in all of Jerusalem's gates at the same time, but in one of them only. The plural is an indicator of liturgical style, quite similar to the Anacreonticon No. 20, 1a of the Patriarch Sophronius of Jerusalem:

Ἅγιον πόλισμα θεῖον	Holy city of God,
Ἱερουσαλήμ, τ' ἐς νῦν	Jerusalem, how I long to stand
ἐθέλων πύλας παρεῖναι	now at your gates
ἵν' ἀγαλλιῶν εἰσέλθω	and go in, rejoicing![18]

II

What is the meaning of *y^erûšālayim habb^enûyā k^e'îr šeḥubb^erā-llāh yaḥdāw* (v. 3)? Grammatical considerations are not very helpful in solving this problem, for the structure of the phrase is both clear and unclear, so to speak. It is obviously a nominal clause, the subject of which is Jerusalem.[19] The complement of the predicate is either (a) the comparative phrase *kᵉʿîr šeḥubbᵉrā-llāh yaḥdāw*, translated: 'the rebuilt Jerusalem is like a city . . .',[20] or (b) the passive participle *habbᵉnūyā*, translated: 'Jerusalem is rebuilt (lit.: is the rebuilt one) as a city . . .'[21]

In both cases the root *bnh* is used in the sense of 'to rebuild'; for the fact that a city has been built is self-evident and need not be said. The Psalm speaks of the post-exilic Jerusalem. But this is only true on condition that the root *ḥbr* is not used in an architectonic sense. If that were the case, we should indeed translate: 'Jerusalem is built as a city that is compacted together'. We would have to suppose a solemn procession of the pilgrims around the city walls, as attested in Ps. 48.13f., and the verse would describe the pilgrim's admiration for the well-built city with its strong walls and solid towers.[22] The meaning and use, however, of the root *ḥbr* does not support this quite familiar interpretation: neither in biblical Hebrew nor in post-biblical Hebrew texts, nor in other Semitic languages, is *ḥbr* used as an architectonic term, as far as I can see.[23] Moreover, the ancient versions did not understand it in such a way. Septuagint: Ἰερουσαλὴμ οἰκοδομουμένη ὡς πόλις ἧς ἡ μετοχὴ (A οἱ μέτοχοι) αὐτῆς ἐπὶ τὸ αὐτό—'Jerusalem, built like a city, the communion (or convention, assembly) of which is ἐπὶ τὸ αὐτό—whatever ἐπὶ τὸ αὐτό may mean. Jerome translated: *iuxta* LXX: *Hierusalem quae aedificatur ut civitas cuius participatio eius in id ipsum*; and *iuxta Hebr.*: *Hierusalem quae aedificaris ut civitas cuius participatio eius simul*. The assumption of a nominal form like *šeḥebrāh* or *šeḥebrā-llāh*, presupposed by the Septuagint, is highly improbable, for the nouns *ḥeber* 'company, band' (Hos. 6.9; Prov. 21.9; 25.24) and *ḥebrā* 'company' (*hapax* in Job 34.8) are rendered differently by the Septuagint, whereas the *puʿal* of *ḥbr* is translated μέτοχοι at least in Hos. 4.17. In other words, the ancient versions made a paraphrase of the same text we have in MT. They considered, however, the root *ḥbr* as relating not to the city but to the people who are 'connected, united' there, i.e. who came together in Jerusalem. This interpretation is preferable, particularly because v. 4 explicitly speaks of the Israelite tribes wandering to Jerusalem. Among modern scholars it was advocated by B. Duhm only:

> Gewöhnlich übersetzt man: die du neugebaut bist, so recht wie eine Stadt, die allzumal in sich zusammengefügt ist. Was soll das aber heissen? Sollte der Verf. für nötig gehalten haben, zu versichern, dass Jerusalem nicht aus einer Zahl unzusammen-

> hängender Ortschaften besteht, dass es eine Stadt, nicht ein Land ist? Wem musste oder wollte er das auseinandersetzen? Oder will der Verf. sagen, dass Jerusalem wieder eine Mauer bekommen hat, die es vor dem Auseinanderfallen schützt? Thut eine Mauer das? Und wenn ja, warum erwähnt der Verf. das und noch dazu in so künstlicher Weise, dass nur ein Exeget das herauskonstruieren kann? Hat *ḥubbᵉrā* Jerusalem zum Subjekt, so wäre der natürliche Sinn doch wohl der, dass die Bürgerschaft einmütig verbunden ist, aber man begreift wieder nicht, warum das erwähnt würde. Mir scheint, Subjekt ist 'es', nämlich alles, was Jude heisst, was zu den Stämmen Jahwes gehört. In Jerusalem fühlen sich alle Juden, mögen sie geboren sein, wo sie wollen, als Genossen, als Blutsverwandte vgl. Ps. 87.[24]

This is indeed much more probable than the architectonic interpretation and confirms supplementarily Luther's ingenious translation: 'Jerusalem ist gebaut, daß es eine Stadt sei, da man zusammenkommen soll'.

III

The meaning of v. 5 is not easily intelligible. B. Duhm[25] already was astonished at the striking nationalistic motivation: people come together in Jerusalem because Jerusalem was formerly the capital of the Davidic empire and will be so again in Messianic times. But we need not understand *kî* as a causal particle; it is rather affirmative. What sort of thrones, however, are the 'thrones for judgment, the thrones of the house of David'? Obviously thrones on which judges are accustomed to sit, or thrones on which kings sit who are judges as well.[26] F. Baethgen[27] assumed that civil cases were adjudicated on the occasion of a pilgrimage; the court of superior authority, seemingly, was seated in Jerusalem, and the judges were members of the Davidic family. But this is nothing but a mere assumption, inferred from Ps. 122.5. Those interpreters who favour a pre-exilic date for the Psalm usually argue in a similar way: Jerusalem is said to have been the central sanctuary of the Israelite amphictyony in monarchic times, the Davidic king was chief justice, and amphictyonic law and jurisdiction was administered to the Israelite tribes on the occasion of a pilgrimage.[28] This theory, however, is more than doubtful. The hypothesis of an Israelite amphictyony can no longer be upheld.[29] As to Israelite jurisdiction being a matter of the city council, the role of the king was rather scanty.[30] The root *špṭ* in connection with the king usually does not mean 'to judge' but 'to rule'.[31] Finally, the question remains unanswered why there should have been several Davidic thrones or even thrones for judgment. The Davidic kings in Jerusalem had one throne only,[32] and if the chair on which they sat for judgment was a piece of furniture distinct from the throne, it was just one piece, not more than one.[33]

Furthermore, let us look at the perfect *yāšᵉbû*, which can be interpreted as present or past tense. In cases of doubt usage is decisive. From an examination of the connection of *šāmmā* or *šām* with perfect forms in the OT we get the following results:

(a) *šāmmā* + perfect as past tense is attested 5 times: Gen. 25.10; 49.31; Ezek. 23.3; Ps. 76.4; Cant. 8.4.

(b) *šām* + perfect as past tense is attested 34 times: Gen. 11.9; 21.31; 35.7; Exod. 15.25; Josh. 19.13; Num. 9.17; 11.34; 13.33; 21.12f.; Deut. 10.6f.; 1 Sam. 7.17; 2 Sam. 1.21; 20.1; 2 Kgs 2.25; Isa. 57.7; Ezek. 23.3; Hos. 6.7, 10; 9.15; 10.9; Pss. 14.5; 53.6; 66.6; 133.3; 137.1, 3; Neh. 13.5; 2 Chron. 1.3; 20.26; 28.9; 32.21.

There are three real or possible exceptions. Ps. 36.13, *šām nāpᵉlû pōᶜᵃlê 'āwen*—'there the evildoers fall (or: will fall?)'—does not fit in with its preceding context. Maybe it is an addition, and if so, we cannot say anything about the tense. Job 39.29, *miššām ḥāpar 'ōkel*—'from there he (sc. the eagle) seeks out the food' is obviously present-durative, consequently a real exception from the rule. Isa. 34.15, *šāmmā qinnᵉnā qippōz wattᵉmallēṭ*—'the arrow-snake will nest there and lay (eggs?)', and 34.14, *'ak-šām hirgīʿā lîlît*—'Lilith only will repose there' and *'ak-šām niqbᵉṣū dayyōt*—'vultures only will gather there', all these instances belong to an announcement of Yahweh's coming judgment; they are future tense. These few exceptions, however, cannot contend with the mass of examples which produce evidence for the following rule: the connection of the local adverb *šām/šāmmā* with perfect forms has to be interpreted in the sense of past tense.

In consequence, we have to translate Ps. 122.5: 'Yea, there stood[34] thrones for judgment, the thrones of the house of David'. But why *did* they stand there in the past, if there were real legal proceedings in Jerusalem, whether in pre-exilic or in post-exilic times? There is no point in that. It would, however, be quite intelligible on the premise that it was a matter of some kind of 'historical' reminiscence: later pilgrims were told that thrones for judgment had been placed there in former times. In fact, the wording *šāmmā yāšᵉbū* is reminiscent of the style of Latin Christian documents on pilgrimage.[35] The pilgrims wrote down what they saw and what they were told at the holy places; they liked to introduce biblical reminiscences with formulas like *ubi fuit, ibi erat* etc. Here are some selected examples:

> *Itinerarium Burdigalense* 13 (CSEL 19.21; Do. 52): *ibi sedit Achab rex et Helias prophetauit*, 'there sat king Ahab and Elijah prophesied'; 13f. (CSEL 20.4f.; Do. 53): *ibi positum est monumentum, ubi positus est Ioseph*, 'there is the tomb where Joseph was buried'; 14 (CSEL 20.16; Do. 53): *ibi fuit rex Hieroboam*, 'there was king Jeroboam'; 15 (CSEL 21.19–22.1; Do. 55f.): *et in aede ipsa, ubi templum fuit, quem Salomon aedificauit*, 'and in the building itself, where the temple was which Solomon had built'; 16 (CSEL 22.14; Do. 57): *ubi fuit domus Caifae*, 'where the house of Caiaphas stood'; 20 (CSEL 25.11f.; Do. 63): *ubi Abraham habitauit et puteum fodit*, 'where Abraham lived and sank a well'; *Etheria* 4.2 (CSEL 41.13f.; Do. 88): *nam hic est locus Choreb, ubi fuit sanctus Helias propheta*, 'for this is the place Horeb where St Elijah the prophet was'; *Theodosius* 1 (CSEL 137.7f.; Do. 199): *ibi erat domus Raab publicanae, quae excepit exploratores*, 'the house was there which belonged to Rahab the prostitute, who received the spies'; *Antoninus Placentinus* 20 (CSEL 205.11f.; Do. 281): *et ibi sunt septem cathedrae marmoreae seniorum*, 'there are also seven marble seats for the elders'.

It does not require much conceptual power to imagine similar circumstances on the sacred area of the post-exilic temple. Pilgrims came from everywhere, and local guides showed them all objects of interest in Jerusalem and, of course, near the temple itself. 'There stood thrones for judgment, the thrones of the house of David', they said; and that is, so to speak, the prototype of a 'biblical' reminiscence.[36] The astonishing plural can be well explained by this assumption. Still at present there is a plurality of 'Davidic' memorials on the *Ḥaram aš-Šarīf*: *maḥkamat an-nabī Dā'ūd*, 'the seat for judgment of the prophet David', in the *Qubbat as-Silsila* east of the Dome of the Rock, and *kursī* (or *taḥt*) *Sulēmān*, 'Solomon's throne', in the eastern enclosure. Other places of this kind in the sacred area: *miḥrāb Dā'ūd* (and *Sulēmān*), 'the prayer-place of David (and Solomon)', in the cave beneath the sacred rock (*aṣ-ṣaḫra*); *rummān an-nabī Dā'ūd maṣnū' biyadihi*, 'the pomegranate of the prophet David made by his own hand'; *qabr Sulēmān*, 'Solomon's tomb', in the Dome of the Rock itself; *miḥrāb Sulēmān*, 'Solomon's prayer-place', in the *al-Aqṣā*-Mosque; *qubbat Sulēmān*, 'the dome of Solomon', near the northwest corner of the sacred area; and *miḥrāb Dā'ūd*, 'David's prayer-place', in the southern wall of the so-called Solomon's stables.[37] These places, of course, are not kept holy because of their assumed 'Davidic' origin, but because they are reminiscent of great prophets, venerated in Islam. Nevertheless, the 'owners' are the first two members of the 'house of David'. Why should not the development of such memorial places in the temple area have begun in Persian times? Naturally, it is highly improbable that the 'thrones of the house of David' (Ps. 122.5) were identical with one or several of the Islamic places mentioned above, particularly because some of them are situated on spots that were outside the sacred area in pre-Islamic times.[38] The religious-phenomenological pattern, however, seems to be the same both here and there.

Ps. 122 is a pilgrim song in more than one respect. It is a retrospective glance at the pilgrimage to Jerusalem, composed in liturgical style and ready for use by pilgrims of different times and origins. In addition, it is an early example of the religious mentality of pilgrims at holy places. Finally, it is the oldest text we know of which shows the veneration of quasi-historical holy places, an early predecessor of later Jewish, Christian, and Islamic documents on pilgrimage.

NOTES

1. See H. Gunkel and J. Begrich, *Einleitung in die Psalmen* (2nd edn, 1966), pp. 309-11.

2. See the comprehensive book of K. Seybold, *Die Wallfahrtspsalmen. Studien zur Entstehungsgeschichte von Psalm 129–134* (Biblisch-Theologische Studien, 3), 1978. A critical position is held by H. Seidel, *Auf den Spuren der Beter. Einführung in die Psalmen* (1980), pp. 41f.: Pss. 120–134 are 'Verkündigungsgedichte' or 'Kurzandachten' with the elements thesis, meditation, and benediction or intercession.

3. So, for example, the Zurich Bible, the Revised Luther Bible, the Einheitsübersetzung (1980), RSV, NIV, and among the interpreters: M.L. de Wette (1836), E. Reuss (1893), Fr. Baethgen (1904), C.A. and E.G. Briggs (1907), E. Kautzsch (1910), W. Staerk (1911), R. Kittel (1922), H. Herkenne (1936), F. Nötscher (1947), D. Michel (1960), E.J. Kissane (1964), C.C. Keet (1969), K. Seybold (1978). No claim is made for the completeness of this list.

4. E.g. The Interpreter's Bible, and F. Delitzsch (1874), H. Hupfeld (1888), B. Duhm (1899), H. Schmidt (1934), M. Dahood (1970), H.-J. Kraus (1978), A. Weiser (1979).

5. So, as far as I know, only the Luther Bible, e.g. in the last original edition of 1545.

6. The Luther Bible, and B. Duhm (1899), H. Herkenne (1936), E.J. Kissane (1964), Rogerson–McKay (1977), A. Weiser (1979).

7. The Zurich Bible, the Einheitsübersetzung, RSV, NIV, the Interpreter's Bible, and F. Delitzsch (1874), H. Hupfeld (1888), F. Baethgen (1904), C.A. and E.G. Briggs (1907), E. Kautzsch (1910), W. Staerk (1911), R. Kittel (1922), H. Schmidt (1934), F. Nötscher (1947), D. Michel (1960), C.C. Keet (1969), H.-J. Kraus (1978).

8. The Zurich Bible, and F. Delitzsch (1874), H. Hupfeld (1888), B. Duhm (1899), E. Kautzsch (1910), W. Staerk (1911), R. Kittel (1922), E.J. Kissane (1964), C.C. Keet (1969), K. Seybold (1978).

9. The Luther Bible, and Einheitsübersetzung, RSV, NIV, the Interpreter's Bible, M.L. de Wette (1836), E. Reuss (1893), F. Baethgen (1904), H. Schmidt (1934), F. Nötscher (1947), D. Michel (1960), H.-J. Kraus (1978), A. Weiser (1979).

10. Septuagint: ἑστῶτες ἦσαν οἱ πόδες ἡμῶν; Vulgate: *stantes erant pedes nostri*.

11. See Gesenius–Kautzsch, *Hebr. Grammatik* [GK] §116r; G. Bergsträsser, *Hebr. Grammatik* II §13i; R. Meyer, *Hebr. Grammatik* §104.2g (for the Middle Hebrew §101.7b). Correspondingly, the imperfect of *hyh* is an indicator for the present and future tenses, consecutive imperfect for the narrative past tense.

12. Verses 8, 12; lit.: 'to see the nakedness of the land'.

13. W. Zimmerli translated on p. 825 of his commentary (BK XIII/11 [1963]), 'die sich selber weiden', on p. 827, however, 'die sich selber weideten'.

14. Cornill, Bertholet *et al.*; rejected by Zimmerli, *op. cit.*, p. 827.

15. Vulgate: *qui pascebant semet ipsos*; see also Peshitta and Targumim.

16. Correctly Kittel, Baethgen, Duhm, Weiser *et al.*; wrongly, H.-J. Kraus.

17. Against the interpreters! But compare Septuagint: ὅτι ἐγενήθην ἠτιμωμένη; less distinctly, Vulgate: *quoniam facta sum vilis*.

18. See H. Donner, *Die anakreontischen Gedichte Nr. 19 and 20 des Patriarchen Sophronius von Jerusalem* (Sitzungsberichte d. Heidelberger Akad. d. Wiss., phil.-hist. Kl. Nr. 10; 1981), pp. 12, 23, 35. The English translation follows J. Wilkinson, *Jerusalem Pilgrims Before the Crusades* (1977), p. 91.

19. The Septuagint and, corresponding with it, both versions of the Psalter by Jerome, do not consider v. 3 a complete phrase but an exclamation—a less probable interpretation which does not affect our exegesis.

20. The so-called *kaph veritatis* of the old grammarians; see GK §118v. Strictly speaking, this *kaph* is not a particle introducing the predicate but a particle of emphatic comparison.

21. See GK §116o/q. Examples: Gen. 2.11; 45.12; Isa. 14.27; 66.9; Ezek. 20.29; Zech. 7.6.

22. Among the ancient versions Peshitta thought of it: *šwr'*, 'the wall', for *yaḥdāw*.

23. With the exception of the derivatives: Heb. *maḥbᵉrōt*, 'joists' (2 Chron. 34.11) and 'cramps of iron' (1 Chron. 22.3), Arab. *ḫābūr* 'hob, pin, wedge'. These words, however, do not refer to walls of stones or bricks.

24. B. Duhm, *Die Psalmen* (KHC XIV; 1899), pp. 270f.

25. *Op. cit.*, p. 271.

26. See Yahweh's throne in Ps. 9.5.

27. *Psalmen* (HKAT II/2; 1904), p. 377.

28. See, e.g., H.-J. Kraus, *Psalmen* (BK XV/11; 1960), pp. 840f.

29. See H. Donner, *Geschichte des Volkes Israel und seiner Nachbarn in Grundzügen* (EATD 4/1; 1984), pp. 62-70.

30. See C. Macholz, 'Die Stellung des Königs in der israelitischen Gerichtsverfassung', *ZAW* 84 (1972), pp. 157-82; 'Zur Geschichte der Justizorganisation in Juda', *ibid.*, pp. 314-40.

31. See W. Richter, 'Zu den "Richtern Israels"', *ZAW* 77 (1965), pp. 40-74, esp. 58-70.

32. See 1 Kgs 7.7.

33. K. Seybold, *op. cit.*, p. 24, regards v. 5b as an addition, eliminating the 'house of David' from the original verse. But are the arguments really sufficient for elimination?

34. Lit.: 'sat'; the root *yšb* is used metonymically (transmitted from the judges to the thrones).

35. The Latin documents on pilgrimage are published by P. Geyer, *Itinera Hierosolymitana* (CSEL 39; 1898) [referred to in the text as CSEL]. Translation into German and commentary: H. Donner, *Pilgerfahrt ins Heilige Land. Die ältesten Berichte christlicher Palästinapilger* (*4-7. Jahrhundert*) (1979) [referred to in the text as Do.].

36. R. Kittel, *Die Psalmen* (KAT XIII; 1922), p. 392, gave a very similar interpretation.

37. See the antiquated but still very useful article by C. Sandreczki, 'Die Namen der Plätze, Strassen, Gassen usw. des jetzigen Jerusalem', *ZDPV* 6 (1883), pp. 43-77, esp. 72-76.

38. That is true, for example, in regard to 'Solomon's throne' (*kursī Sulēmān*).

5

A CONSIDERATION OF TWO RECENT THEORIES ABOUT BETHSO IN JOSEPHUS'S DESCRIPTION OF JERUSALEM AND A PASSAGE IN THE TEMPLE SCROLL

J.A. Emerton

Josephus refers in the *Jewish War* 5.4.2 (§145) to the wall of Jerusalem in the first century AD as it ran from the tower called Hippicus (in the west) southwards and then towards the east. It 'extended through the place called Bethso to the Gate of the Essenes, and then turned southwards above the spring of Siloam...' The purpose of the present article is to consider two recent attempts to identify the location of Bethso and to relate it to a passage in the Temple Scroll. It is a pleasure to dedicate it to my friend Professor F.C. Fensham.

I

In an article published in Hebrew in 1972,[1] and in English translation in 1976, the late Yigael Yadin suggested that the statement of Josephus about Bethso should be combined with information that he gives us about the Essenes, and also with a passage in the Temple Scroll. He developed the theory in his first (Hebrew) edition of the Temple Scroll in 1977, and again in the revised (English) edition of 1983 (and the latter is cited here), in ch. V.II.7 (pp. 294-304). Like the majority of scholars, Yadin identifies the Qumran sect with the Essenes. Although the identification is more problematical than is sometimes recognized, I shall not discuss the question further in this article but shall treat the theory as if it were proved—and, in any case, the evidence from Qumran certainly has much in common with what Philo and Josephus tell us about the Essenes. Yadin accepts the theory of E. Robinson, J. Schwartz and others about the meaning of Bethso. The first element of the word, which appears in Greek as *bēthsō*, appears to be the common Hebrew and Aramaic *bêt*, 'house' or 'place', in the construct state. It is suggested that the second element is *ṣô'â*, 'excrement', and that the whole phrase denotes a latrine. Yadin notes that both *hṣw'h* and *btym*, the plural of *byt*, are found in close proximity in the Temple Scroll, col. XLVI, lines 13-16:

> And you shall make[2] them a place for a 'hand' (*mqwm yd*), outside the city, to which they shall go / out, to the northwest of the city—roofed houses [*btym mqwrym*] with pits within them, / into which the excrement [*hṣw'h*] will descend, [so that] it will [not] be visible at any distance (*rḥwq*) / from the city, three thousand cubits (Yadin's translation; 1983, p. 294).

The phrase 'a place for a hand' recalls Deut. 23.13-15, which commands that, when the Israelites go out to war, they shall have a place (*yād*) outside the camp where they shall empty their bowels and cover their excrement (*ṣē'â*). Thus, God will not see (*yir'eh*) *'erwat dābār*. Following Deuteronomy's injunction, the War Scroll 7.6-7 lays down that there shall be a space (*rwḥ*) between all the camps and the 'place of the hand' (*lmqwm hyd*) of about 2000 cubits, so that no *'rwt dbr* may be seen (*yr'h*). Yadin suggests (1962, pp. 73-74; 1983, pp. 298-301) that the distance of 2000 cubits was derived from Josh. 3.4, where it is the distance between the ark and the people of Israel, and he notes rabbinic evidence for relating the sabbath limit of 2000 cubits to that verse. Why, then, does the Temple Scroll speak of 3000 cubits, in contrast to 2000 in the War Scroll? The answer probably lies, partly at least, in the point made by Yadin: 'it is the Temple city, and not just any city' (1983, p. 299). Deuteronomy, the War Scroll and the Temple Scroll all stress that the aim of the law is that the use of the latrines should not be seen (and the verb *r'h* is used in all three passages). Yadin suggests that more than purely topographical considerations may be involved. He notes that there are references to both 1000 and 2000 cubits in the description of the pastoral limits of Levitical cities in Num. 35.4-5, that they were understood in different ways by different rabbis, and that some of them added the two figures together to get 3000 cubits.

Yadin's explanation of the significance of the 3000 cubits in the Temple Scroll, and of its probable origin, is convincing.

Yadin also reminds us (1976, p. 91) of the description by Josephus, *Jewish War* 2.8.9 (§§147-49) of the way in which the Essenes emptied their bowels: they dug a hole and afterwards covered it over again (cf. Deuteronomy). On the sabbath, however, they refrained from emptying their bowels, presumably because digging a hole was work and was therefore forbidden.

How is this related to the topography of Jerusalem? Contrary to the view of, for example, M. Avi-Yonah, Yadin argues that the Gate of the Essenes was not at the south-east corner of the city, but faced south-west—and that theory certainly seems to fit what Josephus says about its location. Yadin is cautious about the precise position of the gate, but thinks it may be the gate discovered by H. Maudsley in the south-western part of the city. Other scholars had previously favoured such an identification (e.g. Bliss and Simons). Yadin suggests that the Essenes went out through the gate in this part of Jerusalem to walk to the latrines 3000 cubits away to the north-west of the city. He favours a site somewhere to the north-west of the tower known as Hippicus (not far from the present Jaffa Gate). He also comments that it 'is quite possible that the strange phenomenon of the Essenes using this small gate relatively near the "hand" to go outside the wall to relieve themselves prompted the people of Jerusalem to call it "the Gate of the Essenes"' (1983, p. 303). It is also possible, he thinks, 'that the Essenes living in Jerusalem preferred to dwell in the vicinity of the gate leading to the latrines, and that in course of time this gate was named after the residents of the small quarter they created there' (p. 304).

II

Bargil Pixner, whose article on the subject was published in 1976, knew of Yadin's article of 1972 and developed the theory in his own way (though Yadin, 1983, p. 303, 'cannot accept some of his more detailed conclusions'). He agrees with Yadin that Bethso was the place where the Essenes' latrines were to be found, and that the second element in the name is *ṣw'h*. His principal disagreement with Yadin concerns the location of Bethso. It seems to him unlikely that the latrines were 3000 cubits (1.5 km.) from the city. 'If we consider', he says, 'that such visits to the Bethsô had to be made summer and winter, day and night, by men and women, not to speak of the old and the sick, I believe that not even the great insistence on the holiness of the "City of the Sanctuary" would have made the Essenes submit to the physical ordeal connected with such a walk' (p. 256). He therefore suggests that 'the area *within* which the latrines had to be placed' was 3000 cubits from the city, not that they had to be at a distance of 3000 cubits away from the city. Similarly, he thinks that 1QM 7.7 means that 'A large space should be left between their camps *for* (instead of '*to*') the place of the hand of about 2,000 cubits', and that the 'basic idea of the prescription was that in the area around the camp all human refuse had to be concealed' (p. 257).

Accepting the identification of the Gate of the Essenes with the gate excavated by Maudsley, Pixner believes that Bethso must be near it, and claims to find help for the identification of the site in the Copper Scroll from Qumran (3Q15). Col. 8.10, 14 refers to *hšw'* or *hśw'*, which J.T. Milik (1962, p. 274) earlier identified with Bethso. Pixner prefers the reading *hśw'*, with a *sin* not a *shin*, and seeks to account for the difference between *św'* and *ṣw'h* in a way that will be considered below in section III. On this view, it lies north-west of the Gate of the Essenes, and Pixner thinks that the words 'to the north-west' (*lṣpwn hm'rb*) in the Temple Scroll refer to the direction taken by someone leaving the Gate of the Essenes and making for the latrines, not to the position of Bethso in relation to the city. He agrees with Allegro (pp. 155-56) that the probable site is 'in the vicinity of Birket es-Sultan, which is just below Bishop Gobat School' (p. 259). Further, he notes that the Copper Scroll speaks of *bšlp šl hśw'* and *bryn*[3] *šl hśw'*, which he supposes to mean 'in the unploughed land of the So' and 'in the irrigated land of the So', respectively. He believes that the descriptions of the two parts of the So' fit the topography of the area near the former Bishop Gobat School. Further, the Copper Scroll also uses the word *bṣywt* (if that is the correct reading; Milik reads *bṣwyh*) in close proximity to the second occurrence of *hśw'*, and Pixner suggests that it is the preposition *b* with a plural of *ṣw'h*. Other sites described in this part of the Copper Scroll are also identified by Pixner with places in the same area, and he believes that there was an Essene quarter (Hebrew *maḥ*^{a}*neh*, 'camp') in this part of Jerusalem. Two other pieces of evidence are regarded by him as relevant to the theory that there was an Essene quarter in this part of Jerusalem. One is the presence in the area of ritual baths resembling what is found at Qumran (pp. 269-74), including one with a ridge down the middle of the steps. The other is the poetic text known as the Apostrophe to Zion (11QPs[a] 22.1-18).[4] It shows the Essene devotion to Jerusalem, but perhaps Pixner implies more than that. It is possible that he thinks that it testifies to the love of the Essenes for the part of the city where he supposes the Essene quarter to have been. He maintains on p. 245 that, in the Roman period, Mount Zion was identified with the western hill, as it was for many centuries later, although modern scholars recognize that it was originally the name of the eastern hill south of the temple. It is thus possible that Pixner thinks that the fact that 11QPs[a] 22.1-18 mentions Zion is evidence for an Essene connexion with the western hill. It is unnecessary to consider here Pixner's speculative theories about the early church in this region (see the appendix at the end of this article).

III

In an attempt to evaluate the two theories, we shall begin with that of Pixner.

First, the presence of ritual baths in the region believed by Pixner to have been the Essene quarter is inconclusive. The Essenes did, indeed, regard ceremonial purity as important, but so did other observant Jews, who also had ritual baths, and there is nothing about the baths in the relevant part of Jerusalem to indicate that they were Essene. Similar ritual baths have been discovered elsewhere, and it is unlikely that they were all made by Essenes.[5]

Second, if Pixner's reference to the Apostrophe to Zion is intended only as evidence for Essene devotion to Jerusalem, its relevance cannot be denied. If, however, he intends it to support the location of the supposed Essene quarter on the western hill, the argument is open to question. While the *Jewish War* 5.4.1 (§137) suggests that Josephus mistakenly identified Mount Zion with the western hill, it does not follow that the author of the Qumran text took the same view. It is possible, for example, that he used the word as a virtual synonym of Jerusalem, as it often is in the Old Testament. Further, Pixner recognizes (p. 245) that as late as 1 Macc. 4.37; 5.54; 7.33 the name Zion was associated with the temple mount, not the western hill. 1 Maccabees is to be dated near the end of the second century BC or in the early decades of the first. Sanders (1967, p. 11) dates 11QPs[a] to the first half of the first century AD on palaeographical grounds but thinks that the Apostrophe to Zion 'may date from the fourth or third century B.C.'; and Vermes (p. 58) dates even the manuscript to the second century BC. It would be unwise to assume that the author cannot have held the earlier view.

Third, the identification of the gate discovered by Maudsley with the Gate of the Essenes fits what Josephus says, but it is still uncertain and Yadin is right to be cautious. We cannot be sure that Josephus gives us a complete list of gates, and it is possible that there was another gate that would also fit his description. The uncertainty does not, however, seriously affect Pixner's argument. If the Gate of the Essenes were further east, it would still be compatible with his location of Bethso. The identification of the Gate of the Essenes with Maudsley's gate is, indeed, the most plausible part of Pixner's theory.

Fourth, Pixner's treatment of the element *so* is open to objection. The suggestion of Yadin and his predecessors that the second element of Bethso is to be explained as *ṣô'â* is attractive, though the absence of the feminine ending is a problem, especially since the Temple Scroll has the full form *ṣw'h* in line 15. On the other hand, the identification of *ṣw'h* with *hśw'* or *hšw'* is more difficult. In addition to the absence of the feminine ending *-h* in the latter word, the two words begin with different sibilants. Pixner offers two explanations (p. 260). The first is that, if the writer came from the north,[6] he 'did not distinguish well between the pronunciation of' *ṣ* and *ś*. Pixner offers no evidence for this theory that someone from the north would have been likely to confuse the two sibilants, and without such evidence the theory is implausible. The second explanation, which Pixner appears to prefer, is that a 'change in pronunciation occured [sic] in the Jerusalem area itself... by the second half of the first century A.D., simply by losing its guttural sound'. Once again, no evidence is offered. Nor is it clear what understanding of the nature of emphatic consonants underlies the strange reference to 'its guttural sound'. Such flimsy arguments are weakened further by Pixner's suggestion that *bṣywt* (with *ṣ*) in the Copper Scroll is a form of the same word. If the *ṣ* had changed to *ś*, how did the writer come to use the former consonant here so soon after failing to use it in *hśw*? The obvious way of understanding *ṣw'h*, on the one hand, and *św'* or *šw'*, on the other, is that they are different words. The latter word is probably to be identified with *šw'* in the Genesis Apocryphon 12.14, where *'mq hšw'* is identified with *'mq* *mlk' bq't byt krm'*. The word is probably *šāwē'*, 'plain', not *śô'*, and it is not clear to me how Milik, who recognizes the Copper Scroll to have the same word as the Genesis Apocryphon, can identify it with the second element of Bethso. Where is *byt krm'* to be located? Fitzmyer (pp. 173-74) thinks it may be Beth-haccherem, the modern Ramat Raḥel, though Milik (1962, p. 274) favours an area immediately to the south-west of Jerusalem (cf. Allegro, pp. 90-92), and *hšw'* or *hśw'* in 3Q15 8.10, 14 appears to be different from *byt hkrm* in 10.5. It is thus possible that *hšw'* is in the region favoured by Pixner, but most unlikely that it is to be identified with *ṣw'h*. It may be added that the identification of sites mentioned in the Copper Scroll is difficult (as, indeed, is the problem of the nature of the whole scroll). Incidentally, both the reading *bryn* and its interpretation are problematical, as Pixner recognizes, and the view that it means 'on the irrigated land' is not a secure foundation for an identification of the site.

Fifth, Pixner's theory that 3000 cubits in the Temple Scroll and 2000 cubits in the War Scroll refer to areas within which excrement must be covered, rather than to the distances that the latrines must be from the camp or city, is improbable. If it were true, it would imply that outside those areas excrement could be left uncovered. That, however, would contradict the command in Deut. 23.13-15 and what Josephus says about Essene practice in the *Jewish War* 1.8.9 (§147). Yadin's interpretation of the evidence is much more probable: the War Scroll wishes to keep such pollution 2000 cubits from the camp, and the Temple Scroll prescribes that it shall be 3000 cubits from the holy city. We may grant that the distance would make the convenience highly inconvenient in the middle of a winter's night for an aged and ailing Essene (and even for a young and healthy one), but it is doubtful whether such rigorists as the Essenes would have been deterred by such considerations where the putting into practice of the biblical law was concerned. A sect capable of forbidding the emptying of the bowels on the sabbath is unlikely to have let humanitarian considerations stand in the way of keeping the camp and, *a fortiori*, the sacred city free from pollution.

Pixner's theory is thus to be rejected. The Gate of the Essenes may well have been where he locates it, though we cannot be certain, and there may well have been Essenes living near it, though Josephus does not tell us how the gate got its name. It may be doubted, however, whether that justifies us in postulating an Essene quarter—

at least, if we are to think of anything comparable to the present Muslim, Christian, Armenian and Jewish Quarters of the Old City of Jerusalem. It is possible that Bethso was where Pixner thinks it was, but much of the reasoning connected with the identification is unconvincing. His attempt to link *ṣw'h* with *hśw'* (or *hšw'*) has failed, and so has his interpretation of 3000 cubits in the Temple Scroll and 2000 cubits in the War Scroll.

IV

Yadin's theory can be dealt with more briefly. As I have maintained above, his interpretation of 2000 cubits in the War Scroll and 3000 cubits in the Temple Scroll is convincing. They indicate the distance that the latrines must be placed from the camp and the city, respectively, not the area within which excrement must be covered. He is also right in refusing to identify *ṣw'h* with *hšw'* or *hśw'*, and the second word is probably to be read as *hšw'* and identified with *šw'* in the Genesis Apocryphon. He is right yet again to be cautious about identifying the gate excavated by Maudsley with the Gate of the Essenes, while regarding the identification as not unlikely. On the other hand, his location of Bethso is improbable. Although his interpretation of the relevant passage in the Temple Scroll is probably correct, his attempt to correlate it with what Josephus says about Bethso is difficult. The difficulty lies in Josephus's words about the relation of the wall to Bethso. He says that the wall ran *dia* (followed by the genitive) 'the place called Bethso'. The preposition often means 'through', 'across', or the like, and I translated it 'through' at the beginning of this article. If that is the meaning, then Yadin's interpretation is impossible. He, however, quotes (1983, p. 302) Thackeray's translation 'past the place called Bethso'. M. Avi-Yonah (*Israel Exploration Journal* 18 [1968], p. 121) appeals to Herodotus (4.39) in support of the possibility of this meaning and argues that it is found, not only in the passage now being discussed, but also shortly afterwards in the *Jewish War* 5 §147, where he maintains that the Third Wall is said to run 'past' the royal caverns. Even if, however, the Second Wall is said in §145 to descend 'past the place called Bethso', the statement is scarcely to be reconciled with Yadin's theory. To say that the wall descended 'past' Bethso suggests that the two were in close proximity, and it may be doubted whether the statement would fit the latrines mentioned in the Temple Scroll, which were to be 1.5 kilometres from the city. With the help of K.H. Rengstorf (ed.), *A Complete Concordance to Flavius Josephus*, vol. I (Leiden, 1973), pp. 440-42, I have worked through Josephus's uses of *dia*, and I can find no examples of this preposition with the sense that would be required by Yadin's interpretation. When Josephus wrote of Bethso, he is most unlikely to have been referring to the area suggested by Yadin.

V

What conclusions may be drawn from the above discussion, which has found difficulties in the theories of both Yadin and Pixner? First, Yadin's interpretation of the Temple Scroll 46.13-16 is correct, but his attempt to correlate it with what Josephus says about Bethso is unconvincing. Second, Pixner's attempt to correlate the information given in the Temple Scroll with that of the Copper Scroll and with the topography of the south-west corner of Jerusalem, and to base on it a theory of an Essene quarter of the city, must be rejected. On the other hand, it is quite likely that the identification of the Gate of the Essenes with the gate discovered by Maudsley is correct, and some Essenes may have lived near it. What are we to think of Bethso? Pixner may be correct in following those who locate it near the site of the former Bishop Gobat School to the west of Maudsley's gate, but his theory that it should be related to the Temple Scroll's command to make a place for 'hand' must be judged mistaken. We still do not know for certain the meaning of the second element in Bethso, but it does not seem to have anything to do with the latrines mentioned in the Temple Scroll, which were probably intended to be—whether or not the intention was ever realized in practice—1.5 kilometres outside the city (much to the discomfort of the sectarians on chilly nights). If the word 'Bethso' denotes 'latrine', the reference may be to lavatories used by inhabitants of Jerusalem other than the Essenes. In any case, the meaning of what Josephus says about Bethso must be treated as a different problem from that of the Temple Scroll's location of latrines outside Jerusalem. The attempts to link the two problems have proved failures.

Appendix: Pixner's discussion of the primitive church

It is beyond the scope of the present article to discuss in detail Pixner's speculative attempt (pp. 245-46, 276-93) to link the setting of the primitive church in Jerusalem with the 'Essene quarter' that he postulates. A brief reference to its weaknesses is, however, appropriate, lest it be thought that it offers confirmation of the rest of his theory. He cites no Christian evidence that is certainly earlier than the fourth century AD for the location in the first century of the church on the western hill. Moreover, even if there was Essene influence on the early church (e.g. in the sharing of possessions—which Pixner himself differentiates on p. 281 from the practice of the Essenes), it does not necessarily imply that Christians and Essenes lived in the same part of the city. Further, some of the evidence is too flimsy to be taken seriously. Why, for example, should it be supposed that the 'pious men' living in Jerusalem of Acts 2.5 or the 'great multitude of priests' of Acts 6.7 were Essenes? It is true that the priests are unlikely to have been Sadducees (though conversion to Christianity may have completely changed their outlook), but Josephus, *Ant*. 20.8.8 (§§179-81) refers to the distinction, indeed antagonism, between the high priests (who were presumably Sadducees) and ordinary priests. Pixner also cites uncertain variant readings in Acts 2.1 and 21.22 in support of his theory. In any case, his understanding of the former verse (if the plural reading 'days' is accepted) to refer to the different days on which Pentecost was celebrated according to different calendars (including that of the Essenes) is apparently based on the view that the verb used here means 'had come to an end' (p. 279), whereas it probably means simply 'had come'—see W. Bauer, W.F. Arndt, and F.W. Gingrich, *A Greek-English Lexicon of the New Testament and Other Early Christian Literature* (Cambridge and Chicago, 1957), p. 787—and there is insufficient evidence to associate the 'multitude' of the latter verse (and other verses in Acts) with the *rabbîm* of the Qumran texts. In Acts 15.16-18, James (of whose position in the church we know too little to enable us to identify it with that of the sectarian *m^{e}baqqēr*) quotes Amos 9.11-12, and Amos 9.11 is cited in CD 7.16 and 4QFlor 1.12, but the point of James's quotation is the mention of the Gentiles in Amos 9.12, whereas the point of the other references is the mention of David in Amos 9.11; Acts gives no hint that James' Davidic ancestry, as distinct from his relationship to Jesus, was a subject of any significance for the early church.

Postscript

I am indebted to Mr M.N.A. Bockmuehl, of Wolfson College, Cambridge, for drawing my attention to an article by R. Riesner, 'Essener und Urkirche in Jerusalem', *Bibel und Kirche* 40 (1985), pp. 64-76, which appeared some months after the present article had been submitted to the editors of this volume. In general, Riesner follows Pixner and differs from him only in details. Riesner is aware of the discovery of a number of ritual baths since the publication of Pixner's article, and he recognizes that ceremonial washing was important for all pious Jews in the New Testament period, and that the presence of ritual baths is not in itself a strong argument in favour of an Essene quarter (p. 73). He appears to suppose, however, that the number found in the relevant part of Jerusalem still supports the hypothesis of an Essene origin in this case. But if all pious Jews needed ritual baths, then the presence of such baths, even the presence of several such baths, has no value as evidence unless there are other reasons to postulate the presence of Essenes. Riesner believes that there is such evidence but—apart from the existence of the Essene Gate—it depends on the correlation of the statement of Josephus about Bethso with what the Temple Scroll says about the place for a 'hand'. He rightly sees that Yadin's theory places Bethso too far from the city wall to fit Josephus's words (p. 72), but he fails to recognize the superiority of Yadin's interpretation of the distances mentioned in the Temple Scroll to that of Pixner. If, as the present article has argued, the attempt to correlate the statements in Josephus and the Temple Scroll fails, then Riesner's argument in support of Pixner loses its force.

NOTES

1. A list of the principal works cited will be found at the end of the article.

2. *w'śyth* is plainly second person masculine singular, and it is surprising that Pixner translates it 'And they shall make . . . ' (p. 255).

3. Milik (1962, p. 292) reads *brwy* but indicates that the reading of the last two letters is uncertain, and allows (p. 292) that *bryw* and *bryn* are also possible. The interpretation is also uncertain.

4. Pixner, pp. 267-68. The text is published by Sanders (1965, pp. 43, 85-89; and 1967, pp. 76-77).

5. For ritual baths at Masada, see Y. Yadin, *Masada: Herod's Fortress and the Zealots' Last Stand* (London, 1966), pp. 164-67; at Jericho: E. Netzer, *BASOR* 228 (1977), pp. 2-4, 6, and his article 'Ancient Ritual Baths (*Miqvaot*) in Jericho', in L.I. Levine (ed.), *The Jerusalem Cathedra*, II (Jerusalem and Detroit, 1982), pp. 106-19, and p. 106 mentions ritual baths at Gezer and the Herodion; in the Jewish quarter of the Old City of Jerusalem: N. Avigad, *Discovering Jerusalem* (Nashville, 1983; ET of a work published in Hebrew in Jerusalem, 1980), pp. 139-43. Not all the baths excavated have a ridge running down steps, but Avigad, p. 142, mentions such a ridge, and it is clearly visible on the photograph on p. 143. Miss J.M. Hadley, to whom I am indebted for two of the above references, informs me that a ritual bath with such a ridge has also been discovered at Ramat Raḥel.

6. Pixner refers on p. 260 to Milik, 1959, p. 329.

PRINCIPAL WORKS CITED

Allegro, J.M., *The Treasure of the Copper Scroll* (London, 1960).

Bliss, F.J., 'Third Report on the Excavations at Jerusalem', *Palestine Exploration Fund Quarterly Statement* for 1885, pp. 9-25.

Fitzmyer, J.A., *The Genesis Apocryphon of Qumran Cave I* (2nd edn; Rome, 1971).

Milik, J.T., 'Le rouleau de cuivre de Qumrân (3Q 15). Traduction et commentaire topographique', *Revue Biblique* 66 (1959), pp. 321-57.

—in M. Baillet, J.T. Milik, and R. de Vaux, *Les 'Petites Grottes' de Qumrân* (Discoveries in the Judaean Desert of Jordan, III; Oxford, 1962).

Pixner, B., 'An Essene Quarter on Mount Zion?', *Studia Hierosolymitana in onore del P. Bellarmino Bagatti*, 1. *Studi Archeologia=Studium Biblicum Franciscanum*, Collectio Maior, 22 (Jerusalem, 1976), pp. 245-85.

Sanders, J.A., *The Psalms Scroll of Qumrân Cave 11* (DJDJ, IV; Oxford, 1965).

—*The Dead Sea Psalms Scroll* (Ithaca, 1967).

Simons, J., *Jerusalem in the Old Testament* (Leiden, 1952).

Thackeray, H. St J., *Josephus, III, The Jewish War, Books IV-VII* (The Loeb Classical Library; London and New York, 1928).

Vermes, G., *The Dead Sea Scrolls: Qumran in Perspective* (London, 1977).

Yadin, Y., *The Scroll of the War of the Sons of Light Against the Sons of Darkness* (Oxford, 1962; ET of a work published in Hebrew in Jerusalem, 1955).

—'The Gate of the Essenes and the Temple Scroll' [Hebrew], *Qadmoniot* 5 (1972), pp. 129-30=ET *Jerusalem Revealed: Archaeology in the Holy City 1968–1974* (New Haven, Conn., London, and Jerusalem, 1976), pp. 90-91.

—*The Temple Scroll* [Hebrew] (Jerusalem, 1977; 2nd edn and ET Jerusalem, 1983).

6

THE SYMBOLIC SIGNIFICANCE OF THE HEM (*KĀNĀF*) IN 1 SAMUEL 15.27

Paul A. Kruger

Symbolic language or gestures are much resorted to by the peoples of the ancient Near East in the communication of their thoughts, feelings, in legal matters and everyday activities. Symbolic actions are, for instance, attested in the following fields of life: in sale contracts,[1] acts of disinheritance,[2] servitude and manumission,[3] in treaties,[4] and in oath-taking'.[5]

Over and above the significance of the symbolic gesture in legal formulae, it was also of vital importance in worship, supplication, and other emotional circumstances as expressed by movements of the body. In this regard several significant studies have been published concerning gestures in these spheres of life, of which the best may be the exhaustive treatment of M.I. Gruber, *Aspects of Nonverbal Communication in the Ancient Near East* (Columbia University, 1977). The great advantage of his study is the fact that he also took into account semantic parallels from the Akkadian and Ugaritic cultures, something H. Vorwahl in his 'Die Gebärdensprache im Alten Testament' (Diss. Berlin, 1932) failed to do. It must, however, be noted that the symbolic gestures collected by Gruber shed light only on the gesture in one sphere of life, namely the emotional-expressive side. These gestures form part of a much larger family of such ways of expression in the ancient Near East. A comprehensive investigation of all the symbolic acts of the peoples of this region such as that of C. Sittl, *Die Gebärden der Griechen und Römer* (Leipzig, 1890), where gestures in art were also incorporated, has not yet been undertaken. It would also be of great use to consult the symbolic language of the Egyptians, since they participated in a certain sense in the same universality of ancient Near Eastern symbolism in literature and art.[6] This was convincingly proved by Keel[7] in his iconographic approach to the conceptual and the symbolic world of the peoples of the ancient Near East.

The purpose of this article is to inquire only into the symbolic significance of the hem of the cloak (*kānāf*) in 1 Sam. 15.27. It is a privilege and a pleasure to dedicate this study to a great scholar and teacher whose contributions were and still are a stimulus to many students.

The Symbolic Value of the Garment

Before we proceed to study the meaning of the symbolic act in this Old Testament passage, it is important to make a few notes on the symbolic significance of the garment in the ancient Near East in general, and of the hem of the garment in particular, as a background against which the significance of the hem in 1 Sam. 15.27 can be better understood.

The judgment of the peoples of the ancient Near East on clothing differs radically from that of our Western conception of it. For them clothing is an extension of a person's personality. The removal of clothes is considered as much more serious than a mere physical matter. This is proved by a number of texts. The stripping or removing of the garment could mean (a) that someone has been lowered in status,[8] or (b) it could proclaim the dissolution of an existing alliance or relationship,[9] or (c) it could serve as legal evidence in the conclusion of contracts.[10]

The Symbolism of the Hem in the Ancient Near East

A piece of clothing that is of particular symbolic importance in a variety of life spheres is the skirt or the fringe of the garment. It is associated with magic spells, procedures for divorce, vassal treaties, legal formulae and religious language.

Evidence of its symbolic meaning is attested in the whole of the ancient Near East. It appears in Akkadian and West-Semitic (Aramaic, Hebrew and Ugaritic) literature. The most relevant terminology in this connection is:

(a) (1) In Akkadian various words are used to denote the hem: *sikku*,[11] *sissiktu*,[12] *garnu/gannu*.[13]

(2) In West Semitic the tip of the garment is generally rendered by *knf*: 1 Sam. 15.27; 24.6; Ruth 3.9; Ezek. 16.8; Zech. 8.23; *The Words of Ahikar* (Aramaic), line 171;[14] and the *Panammuwa Inscription* from Samual, line 11.[15] The comparative Ugaritic word is *sin* (CTA 6 [1 AB] 2.10).

(b) The most important symbolic acts connected with the hem are as follows:

(1) The 'seizing of grasping of the hem' (in Akkadian the words *ṣabātu*[16] and *kullu*[17] are used).

(2) For the same symbolic acts in West-Semitic: *ḥzq* or *'ḥz* in its different interdialectal variants:

Hebrew: *ḥzq* (Hi) *(bknf)*, 1 Sam. 15.27; Zech. 8.23;

Aramaic: *'hz (bknf)*, Panammuwa II.11; *'ḥd (bknfy)*, Ahikar 171;

Ugaritic: *'ḫd (bsin)*, CTA 6 (1 AB) 2.9-10.

(c) The negative counterpart of the 'seizure of the hem' (*sissiktu ṣabātu*) is the 'cutting of the hem' (*sissiktu batāqu*). To indicate the same symbolic act in Hebrew the word *krt* is employed (*krt 't knf*, 1 Sam. 24.6).

(d) The 'cutting of the hem' in Akkadian can be compared with another symbolic act associated with the hem in the Old Testament, viz. the 'spreading of the hem over someone' (*prś knf*, Ruth 3.9 and Ezek. 16.8).

In the following section some examples of the symbolic gestures referring to the hem, and to the different categories in which they appear, are offered.

The Hem as Personal Surety Sign

The hem was regarded as an extension of the owner's personality and authority.[18] Through lack of a personal seal when concluding a contract or other agreement, an impress of the hem on a clay tablet would suffice as a personal 'signature'.[19]

The Mari correspondence provides evidence of a similar practice in the prophetic communications to the king. Clear indication of this unusual custom is found in seven Mari letters[20] where the sending of a lock of hair and a piece of the fringe of the garment of the person are proof of the owner's identity.

The Hem in Treaty Relationships

Regarding the fact that the hem of the robe was so closely associated with the identity of the wearer, it is understandable why this piece of drapery also figures so prominently in treaty agreements. Apparently symbolic acts relating to the hem were performed by the contracting parties on the occasion of the treaty ceremony. These are: 'to bind the *sissiktam*' (*sissiktam rakāšu*), 'to hold the *sissiktam*' (*sissiktam kâllu*), and 'to seize the hem of the garment of X' (*qaran ṣubat X ṣabātu*).[21] These gestures are attested in agreements between superior and inferior parties and in parity relationships. 'The seizure of the hem of the garment' refers to the symbolic gesture of submission by the vassal to his Great King, whilst 'the abandoning of the hem' is an act of defection.[22] This practice is attested in treaty documents from the second millennium down to Neo-Babylonian times.[23]

The Hem in the Religious Sphere

In Mesopotamia, when a pious worshipper is making a petition to his god, it is often said that 'he seizes the border (*sissiktum*) of the cloak of his god'. We may picture the suppliant before his god (the statue), placing his hand upon or possibly grasping some part of the garment with which the image may have been clothed.[24] The 'grasping of the hem of the god' by the petitioner indicated one of the stations of the worshipper's religious service to his god. The different activities proceed according to a fixed chronological order: the worshipper is 'seeking' the face of his god, he 'appears' in front of the god, 'prostrates' himself at his feet, and 'grasps the hem of his cloak'.[25]

Evidence of a similar gesture is also encountered in the prayers of the Assyrian and Babylonian kings.[26]

Seizing the Hem as a Gesture of Supplication in an Ugaritic Text

The Ugaritic literature contains one example of the 'grasping of the hem' (CTA 6 [1 AB], 2.9-10). The dramatic actors in this case are the god Mot and the goddess Anat. The circumstances which lead to the performance of the gesture are as follows: Mot has temporarily slain Baal. Baal's sister, Anat, after a period of mourning, seeks out Mot in the hope of reviving her brother (CTA 6 [1 AB] 2.4-8). Then, suddenly, she encounters the culprit and in a desperate attempt to persuade him to restore Baal she performs the following symbolic act:

tiḫd. m (*t*) (10) *bsin. lpš.*	She seizes Mo(tu) by the hem of (his) garment,

tšṣq[nh] (11) *bqṣ.all.*	she presses (him) by the edge of (his) robe (CTA 6 [1 AB], 2.9-11).[27]

This gesture by Anat can best be understood as a symbolic act denoting the earnestness of her supplication.[28] Such an interpretation is confirmed by her entreaty of the god accompanying this symbolic act (line 12): *'at.mt.tn.'aḥy,*[29] 'Will you, Mot, surrender my brother?'

The Hem of the Cloak in Marriage

The hem was also of symbolic significance in divorce procedures in the ancient Near East. In a number of texts recording divorce procedures, the hem of the wife's garment was 'cut' (*batāqu*) to effectuate the dissolution of the marriage alliance. By cutting the hem, the husband symbolically 'cuts' the bond of marriage.[30]

The Import of the Hem in 1 Samuel 15.27

In the preceding section an attempt was made to set the scene against which the symbolic significance of the hem in 1 Sam. 15.27 can be viewed. The next step is to examine this passage in its context.

The account in this chapter illustrates the survival of the ancient symbolic gesture of the seizing of the hem.[31] It contains the dramatic scene of Saul's failure to impose the ban (*ḥrm*, v. 3), as commanded by Yahweh, on everything captured during his campaign against the Amalekites. When Saul encounters Samuel on his return from Carmel, he does not seem to realize the gravity of his fault and he tries to pass over the matter by insisting that it was the army who spared the animals (v. 21). Then follows Samuel's classic rebuke of Saul's conduct, reminding him that Yahweh requires diligent obedience rather than observance of outward cultic ceremonies:

> Does Yahweh take pleasure in burnt-offerings and sacrifices as in obedience to the voice of Yahweh? Obedience is better than sacrifice, to listen (is better) than the fat of rams (v. 22).

Saul, apparently realizing that he has violated Yahweh's instruction, then confesses his sin (v. 25). He thereupon implores Samuel to come back with him so that he can worship (*ḥwh*) Yahweh (v. 25). Samuel refuses to listen to Saul's request (v. 27a). At that moment when 'Samuel turned to leave, *he seized the hem of his garment*' (*ḥzq bknf m'ylw*, v. 27b).

The text, as it stands, is ambiguous regarding the initiator of this symbolic act. The RSV and NEB understand it to be Saul; according to the AV, Samuel seized Saul's hem. Grammatically and stylistically speaking either Samuel or Saul could be the subject of the act in view of the fact that Hebrew prose does not always clearly specify the new subject in the case of a rapid change of subject.[32] In an attempt to resolve the unclarity in the MT, the LXX and Peshitta inserted 'Saul': 'And Samuel turned his face to depart, and *Saul* caught hold of the skirt of his garment'. That this is the only plausible interpretation[33] of the text in order to understand the real significance of the gesture, will become evident from the discussion below.

On the significance of this gesture, different opinions have been offered:

1. It was a mere accident, 'ein zufälliges Geschehen', as Stoebe[34] puts it, with no symbolic significance.
2. Several scholars assume that the act has a magical significance.[35] According to this theory the seizing of the border of Samuel's garment by Saul signifies that he gained symbolic power or domination over Samuel. This is in accord with the custom in the ancient Near East by which the disposal of someone's hem implies in actual fact to have command over the person himself. A similar line of reasoning is also implicit in Conrad's explanation of the act.[36] He collects several Mari 'prophetic' texts to prove his hypothesis that Saul, as was the case in Mari where the possession of the hem and the hairlock of the prophetic communicator was guarantee enough to keep him under state control, performs this gesture to dishonour Samuel and to deprive him of his power.[37] But the reaction of Samuel to Saul's symbolic act can in no way be interpreted so as to support Conrad's notion.[38] From the passage it is very clear that Samuel was not humiliated but in full control of the situation.[39]
3. Some explain the gesture in terms of its political significance in the ancient Near East, where it denotes the submission of a vassal before his overlord, as was the case in the treaties.[40]
4. Recently it was suggested by Brauner[41] that the gesture referred to an act of 'supplication, importuning and submission'. While this seems to be the most plausible

> explanation of the act put forward so far, it is not without its own difficulties. In support of his thesis, Brauner adduces a random selection of several references to the 'seizure of the hem' from different spheres of life in the ancient Near East, and applies these different notions to the one symbolic act in the Samuel passage. However, over and above the fact that he fails to distinguish sharply between the changing symbolic import of the symbolic act in the different fields of life, his viewpoint that the symbolic act in 1 Samuel 15 refers, at the same time, to *three* different significations, is also questionable.

In order to grasp the symbolic meaning of the act, it is important to take note of what happened after the performance of the gesture. Samuel immediately turned the act symbolically against Saul as an indication that Yahweh would tear his kingdom away from him (v. 28). Saul, apparently still on the ground with the rent hem in his hand (to take hold of the hem of Samuel's garment,[42] Saul must have bowed down very low—most likely he was on his knees), then repeated his request of v. 25 (v. 30). Against all expectations Samuel hearkened to his petition and listened to his plea (v. 31). It is important to note that Saul repeated his request twice in exactly the same manner, once before and once after the symbolic act. The fact that Saul's request was granted the second time after the performance of the symbolic act clearly indicates that the symbolic act could not have been accidental. The sudden change in Samuel's attitude can only be accounted for by assuming that he took to heart the significance of Saul's gesture as one of supplication, and that this act on Saul's part persuaded Samuel of the earnestness of the king's request. Such an interpretation is also consistent with the concept of this act in religious texts from Mesopotamia and in the Ugaritic document referred to above.

A comparable custom in post-biblical Judaism is provided by the Babylonian Talmud *Ta'an*. 23b. In this passage the *ṣîṣit* (the tassel on the flowing ends [*knfy*]) of a person's robe was seized on making an earnest appeal. The text records a certain Ḥānān who was so well-known for his piety that the Rabbis were accustomed to sending schoolchildren to him. They seized him by the borders (*špyly*) of his mantle and implored him to ask God for rain.[43]

Conclusion

In the preceding discussion an attempt has been made to interpret the obscure symbolic act of the 'grasping of the hem' in 1 Sam. 15.27 on the strength of comparative evidence from the neighbouring cultures. It has been found that the act of the 'seizure of the hem' elsewhere in the ancient Near East can contribute greatly to a clearer understanding of the symbolic significance of a similar gesture in 1 Sam. 15.27. With regard to the passage it has been established that the 'grasping of the hem' there can best be explained as an act of supplication. This is in accord with the notion which this particular symbolic gesture also evinces in comparative religious material from Mesopotamia and Ugarit.

NOTES

1. This included actions such as raising the seller's foot from the property sold, and placing the buyer's foot in its place (E.M. Cassin, 'Symboles de cession immobilière dans l'ancien droit mésopotamien', *Année Sociologique*, 1954, pp. 120ff.); the transfer of a shoe as a symbol of an owner's right (D.A. Leggett, *The Levirate and Goel Institutions in the Old Testament* [Cherry Hill, 1974], pp. 249ff.), and the 'passing on of the pestle', *bukāna(m) šūtuqu* (D.O. Edzard, 'Die *bukānum*-Formel der altbabylonischen Kaufverträge und ihre sumerische Entsprechung', *ZA* 60 [1970], pp. 8ff.).

2. In this connection the removal of the garment played an important role (A. Draffkorn-Kilmer, 'Symbolic Gestures in Akkadian Contracts from Alalakh and Ugarit', *JAOS 94* [1974], p. 181).

3. *CAD* Z 29, lines 9-11, and E. Kutsch, *Salbung als Rechtsakt im Alten Testament und im Alten Orient* (BZAW 87, 1963).

4. Kilmer ('Symbolic Gestures', p. 183 n. 24) collected some of these acts. Cf. also the paper delivered by J.C. Greenfield to the 1967 *RAI* ('The Symbolic Act in Ancient Near Eastern Treaties'); M. Weinfeld, 'The Covenant of Grant in the Old Testament and in the Ancient Near East', *JAOS* 90 (1970), pp. 198ff.; J. Munn-Rankin, 'Diplomacy in Western Asia in the Early Second Millennium BC', *Iraq* 18 (1956), pp. 91f. For the act of handshaking, cf. Z. Falk, 'Gestures Expressing Affirmation', *JSS* 4 (1959), pp. 268f.; for the same symbolic act in the iconography, cf. O. Keel, *Die Welt der altorientalischen Bildsymbolik und das Alte Testament* (3rd edn, Neukirchen-Vluyn, 1980), figures 122, 123.

5. Weinfeld, 'The Covenant of Grant', pp. 198f. For a detailed study on the oath in the history of religion, cf. 'Eid', in *TRE* 9 (eds. G. Krause and G. Müller; Berlin, 1976–), pp. 373ff. In the Old Testament two gestures in

connection with oath-taking are recorded, viz. 'the lifting of the hand' (*nś' yd*, Exod. 6.8; Num. 14.30; Deut. 32.40; and often), and 'the placing of the hand under someone's thigh', only attested in the patriarchal narratives (Gen. 24.2, 9; 47.29). For an attempt to explain the symbolic significance of the last act, cf. R.D. Freedman, 'Put Your Hand Under My Thigh', *BAR* (1976), pp. 3ff.

6. For a general approach on certain symbolic gestures in the Egyptian literature, cf. E. Brunner-Traut, 'Gesten', *LdÄ*, II (eds. W. Helck and W. Westendorf; Wiesbaden, 1975–), pp. 573ff., and H. Müller, 'Darstellungen von Gebärden auf Denkmälern des Alten Ägypten', *MDAIK* 7 (1937), pp. 57ff.

7. The first edition of his pioneer work (1972), referred to in note 4, marks a turning point in Old Testament Psalm exegesis. For a list of his other publications, where the same principles are applied, cf. the third edition of the same work (1980), p. 348.

8. Cf. the Old Babylonian text BRM IV.52 (Ḫana). For the text and translation, cf. C. Kuhl, 'Neue Dokumente zum Verständnis von Hos. 2.4-15', *ZAW* 52 (1934), pp. 102ff. For different opinions expressed on the symbolic meaning of the gesture in the text, cf. *CAD* E 320 b, and S. Greengus, 'A Textbook Case of Adultery in Ancient Mesopotamia', *HUCA* 40 (1969), p. 41 (n. 21).

9. In the Hittite Laws (par. 171) the removal of the son's robe by his mother denotes the severing of family ties. For a translation, cf. R. Haase, *Die keilschriftliche Rechtssammlungen in deutscher Übersetzung* (Wiesbaden, 1963), p. 89. Cf. also the symbolic act attested in *RS* 17.159 (S. Rummel, 'Clothes Maketh the Man—an Insight from Ancient Ugarit', *BAR* 2/2 [1976] p. 7), and in Ezek. 26.16.

10. Cf. the various references brought together by H. Petschow, 'Gewand(saum) im Recht', *RLA*, III (eds. E. Weidner and W. von Soden; Berlin, 1971), pp. 318f., and Y. Muffs, *Studies in the Aramaic Legal Papyri from Elephantine* (Leiden, 1969), p. 102.

11. W. von Soden, *Akkadisches Handwörterbuch* (*AHw*), II (Wiesbaden, 1972), p. 1042a.

12. Von Soden, *ibid*., p. 1050.

13. Von Soden, *ibid*., p. 904, §8.

14. For the text and translation, cf. A.P. Cowley, *The Aramaic Papyri of the Fifth Century B.C.* (Oxford, 1923), pp. 218, 225.

15. H. Donner and W. Röllig, *Kanaanäische und aramäische Inschriften* (Wiesbaden, 1962-64), no. 215.

16. Von Soden, *AHw* III (1981), p. 1067, §3b.

17. Von Soden, *AHw* I (1965), p. 502, §1a.

18. R.A. Veenker, 'Hem', in *IDB Suppl.* (ed. K. Crim; Nashville, 1976), p. 401.

19. H. Kühne, *Das Rollsiegel in Syrien* (Tübingen, 1980), p. 24; F.J.

Stephens, 'The Ancient Significance of *ṣiṣith'*, *JBL* 50 (1931), pp. 59ff.; Petschow, 'Gewand(saum)', pp. 320f. For a fragment of such a clay tablet on which the hem is impressed, cf. fig. H 11, in *IDB Suppl.*, p. 402. This custom was carried down from Old Babylonian to Hellenistic times (M. San Nicolo, *Beiträge zur Rechtsgeschichte im Bereiche der keilschriftlichen Rechtsquellen* [Oslo, 1931], p. 140, and K. Oberhuber, *Die Kultur des Alten Orients* [Frankfurt a.M., 1972], pp. 226f.).

20. *ARM* (*T*) VI 45; *ARM* X 7; X 8; X 50; X 81; *ARMT* XIII 112, and *ARM HC A* 455. For a discussion and translation of the relevant parts, cf. F. Ellermeier, *Prophetie in Mari und Israel* (Herzberg, 1968), pp. 102ff. Scholars do not concur on the significance of the gesture. For M. Noth ('Remarks on the Sixth Volume of Mari Texts', *JSS* 1 [1956], p. 328) it has a magical rather than a legal meaning. Cf. also the viewpoints of J.F. Craghan, 'The *ARM X* 'Prophetic' Texts: Their Media, Style and Structure', *JANES* 6 (1974), pp. 39ff.; A. Malamat, 'Prophetic Revelations in New Documents from Mari and the Bible', *VTS* 15 (1966), pp. 207ff.; and more recently E. Noort (*Untersuchungen zum Gottesbescheid in Mari* [AOAT 202; 1977], p. 85) who is apparently in favour of a magical explanation (cf. his term 'Kontrollzwecken').

21. Munn-Rankin, 'Diplomacy in Western Asia', p. 91.

22. In the Mari letters the expressions are: *qaran ṣubât X ṣabâtum* ('to seize the corner of the garment of X') and *qaran ṣubât X wuššurum* ('to let go the fringe of the garment of X'). Cf. G. Dossin, 'Une mention de Hattuša dans une lettre de Mari', *RHA* 5, fasc. 35 (1939), p. 72.

23. For references, consult Munn-Runkin, 'Diplomacy in Western Asia', pp. 91f.; Dossin, 'Une mention de Hattuša', p. 72; and D.J. McCarthy, *Treaty and Covenant* (Rome, 1978), p. 89.

24. Stephens, 'The Ancient Significance', p. 61.

25. W. Mayer, *Untersuchungen zur Formensprache der babylonischen 'Gebetsbeschwörungen'* (Rome, 1976), pp. 122f. According to him 'the grasping of the hem' is a 'Geste des Hilfesuchens' (p. 128). The action is interpreted in like manner by von Soden (*AHw*, II, p. 1051, §7): 'Bittgestus'. Note also the suggestion of Stephens, 'The Ancient Significance', p. 67: 'a symbol of the earnestness of the worshipper's petition'.

26. For references, cf. M.-J. Seux, *Épithètes royales akkadiennes et sumériennes* (Paris, 1967), p. 327 (n. 320); *CAD* Ṣ (*ṣabātu* 3g2b); *AHw*, II, p. 897b (*qannu* lc), and p. 1051a (*sissiktu* 7b). For the Neo-Babylonian kings, cf. S. Langdon, *Die neubabylonischen Königsinschriften* (*VAB* IV, 1912), pp. 110f., 142f., and 262f.

27. For the text and translation, cf. E.L. Greenstein, '"To grasp the Hem" in Ugaritic Literature', *VT* 32 (1982), p. 217.

28. As an act of supplication it was already recognized by T.H. Gaster in 1950 (*Thespis: Ritual, Myth and Drama in the Ancient Near East* [New York] p. 200).

29. For the transliteration of this part, cf. J.C.L. Gibson, *Canaanite Myths and Legends* (Edinburgh, 1978), p. 76.

30. K.R. Veenhof, 'The Dissolution of an Old Babylonian Marriage according to *CT* 45, 86', *RA* 70 (1976), p. 159. Cf. also document no. 900 from the Newell Babylonian Collection at Yale, which was published by the late J.J. Finkelstein, 'Cutting the *sissiktu* in Divorce Procedures', *WdO* 8/2 (1976), pp. 236ff., and Greengus, 'The Old Babylonian Marriage Contract', *JAOS* 89 (1969), p. 515 (n. 44).

31. The question whether vv. 27-31 were part of the original narrative unit 15.1-35, or whether they were a later interpolation (H.P. Smith, *The Book of Samuel* [ICC; Edinburgh, 1899], p. 139, and A. Weiser, *Glaube und Geschichte im Alten Testament* [Göttingen, 1961], p. 204), is not discussed here. For a survey of the different opinions, cf. H.J. Stoebe, *Das Erste Buch Samuelis* (KAT VIII/1; Gütersloh, 1973), pp. 278ff.

32. D. Conrad, 'Samuel und die Mari-'Propheten'. Bemerkungen zu I Sam. 15.27', *ZDMG Suppl.* I (1969), p. 275.

33. Most scholars agree on the point that it was Saul who tore Samuel's hem (Stoebe, *KAT* VIII/1, p. 291; P.K. McCarter, *I Samuel* [AB 8; Garden City, N.Y., 1980], p. 268; C.J. Goslinga, *Het Eerste Boek Samuël* [COT; Kampen, 1968], p. 305; Conrad, 'Samuel und the Mari-"Propheten"', p. 275, and H. Seebass, '1 Sam. 15 als Schlüssel für das Verständnis der sogenannten königsfreundlichen Reihe 1 Sam. 9.1–10.16, 11.1-5 und 13.2–14.52', *ZAW* 78 [1966], p. 151).

34. *KAT* VIII/1, p. 291. He is, however, not clear as to what he regards as 'ein zufälliges Geschehen'—the *act* performed by Saul, or *the tearing away* of the hem? Note also the assumption of Goslinga, *Het Eerste Boek Samuël*, p. 305: 'Saul heeft ongewild een symbolische handeling verricht'.

35. Cf. for instance, Stephens, 'The Ancient Significance', p. 69, and A. Jirku, 'Zur magischen Bedeutung der Kleider in Israel', *ZAW* 37 (1917-18), p. 117.

36. Cf. his study in note 32 above.

37. Conrad, *op. cit.*, pp. 278, 280.

38. R.A. Brauner, '"To Grasp the Hem" and 1 Sam. 15.27', *JANES* 6 (1974), p. 37. Cf. also the scepticism of Stoebe (*KAT* VIII/1, p. 291), and Mayer (*Formensprache*, p. 149 n. 35) concerning Conrad's suggestion.

39. Conrad's view can further be doubted because it is based on a very small collection of texts from only *one* field of life ('prophetic' texts), while other examples of this widely attested gesture are not considered at all.

40. For example, Veenker, 'Hem', p. 402. It is very unlikely that the prophet as the representative of Yahweh would have submitted himself to the authority of the king in such a radical manner, expecially in this critical stage in the Israelite monarchy. Cf. also Conrad, 'Samuel und die Mari-"Propheten"', p. 275.

41. Cf. his study quoted in note 38. This suggestion is accepted by

McCarter in his recently published commentary on Samuel (p. 266). Cf. note 33 above.

42. The Hebrew word used here to denote the garment is *m'yl*. It was an outer garment worn by men of rank (Jonathan: 1 Sam. 18.4; David: 1 Chron. 15.27; the princes: Ezek. 26.16; Job: Job 1.20; 24.14; the friends of Job: Job 2.12; and Samuel: in the passage under discussion and in 1 Sam. 28.14. Cf. H.W. Hönig, *Die Bekleidung des Hebräers* [Zürich, 1957], pp. 60ff.). Seemingly the garment extended to the feet (LXX ad Exod. 28.4, 31) with a skirt (*kānāf*) at the lower end. For suggestions as to what the *m'yl* may have looked like, cf. E. Haulotte, *Symbolique du vêtement selon la Bible* (Paris, 1966), figures 20-22; G. Dalman, *Arbeit und Sitte in Palästina*, V (Hildesheim, 1964), pp. 228ff., and H. Weippert, *BRL* (ed. K. Galling; 2nd edn; Tübingen, 1977), p. 187.

43. The passage was quoted from the Talmud by the Strack–Billerbeck commentary ([München, 1954-56], I, p. 520) on Mt. 9.20. Cf. also Veenker, 'Hem', p. 402, and Stephens, 'The Ancient Significance', p. 69. Another OT passage which may be consulted with regard to a similar symbolic gesture is Zech. 8.20-23. For the NT passage (Mt. 9.20), cf. further H. van der Loos, *The Miracles of Jesus* (Leiden, 1965), pp. 317ff.

7

THE KINGDOM OF JUDAH BETWEEN EGYPT AND BABYLON: A SMALL STATE WITHIN A GREAT POWER CONFRONTATION*

A. Malamat

The present essay is based on several of my studies on the final years of the Kingdom of Judah, though now from a specific geopolitical or geostrategic point of view. Attention to this particular facet, which finds expression in the 'power game' of the day, can sharpen our observation, especially since we may resort here to Political Science and International Relations. Admittedly, we must be wary of the pitfalls in submitting to anachronistic concepts. To mention but one example, the concept of a 'State' of Judah is an obvious anachronism, yet one certainly would not forego this terminology. Nevertheless, our distinct awareness of anachronistic perceptions is bound to curb the methodological difficulty in using categories of modern disciplines. Indeed, such contemporary categories prove efficient analytical tools when applied to ancient phenomena as well.

A word on the source material is in order, considering its ramifications on the historical method to be applied to this period. A wide range of sources for this tense period provides a particularly detailed insight into much of the political situation and development in Judah; besides the relevant biblical books the contemporaneous epigraphical material in Hebrew is plentiful and varied, more so than in any earlier period. One need only refer to the Lachish and now the Arad ostraca, the over fifty inscribed bullae, just prior to Nebuchadnezzar's conquest, from a Jerusalem archive published only recently, and the further hoard of two hundred bullae from this period, now by Professor Avigad, the most thrilling being 'Berachyahu ben Neriyah ha-sofer', the scribe of Jeremiah mentioned in the Bible. The effects of the political-military events have revealed utter destruction in the archaeological excavations throughout Judah, from Tell Batash (Timnah) in the west to Ein Gedi in the east, from Jerusalem in the north to Lachish in the south.

Yet a proper perspective for evaluating the historical factors underlying the final fate of Judah—factors which determined the policies of its rulers—is to be obtained *only* from sources beyond Palestine, primarily the Neo-Babylonian Chronicles and, to a lesser degree, Egyptian documentation. The combination of biblical data with external sources—especially the detailed framework of dates they contain—enables a sort of micro-analytic study of this period. Thus when we can trace the historical process in time units much more minute than is generally feasible for the Israelite period—in terms of a specific year, month or even day—we gain the fascinating immediacy that is microhistory. Here, as well as in the likewise fascinating macrohistorical analysis, new issues can sometimes be detected and raised by the astute historian from sources long considered over-exploited. The originality of the historian often lies in his ability to make these sources talk and reveal new insights.

Finally, a note on chronology. The chronological method applied here has more than once influenced our reconstruction of the chain of events. Though there is an almost general consensus that the post-dating system, involving accession years, was employed in Judah at this time, another point is still particularly controversial—the month of the Judean regnal new year. Our reckoning is based on an autumnal calendar beginning on 1 Tishri, and not on the spring calendar accepted by a majority of scholars and which was in general use in Babylonia. On previous occasions I have sought to demonstrate the preference of this Tishri reckoning in Judah, and its propensity for reconciling the majority of the variegated data, at least for our period. So I shall not enter here on a discussion of that matter. Rather, it is international politics and grand strategy, involving the various actors, with which we are here concerned.

With the decline of the mighty empire of Assyria, toward the end of the seventh century BC and the striking victories of the young Nebuchadnezzar in the summer of 605 BC, a most reluctant Judah was swept into the ensuing confrontation that erupted between the Neo-Babylonian empire and Egypt. These two powers were a keen and novel political phenomenon in the Near East. North of Judah, the up-and-coming Neo-Babylonian, or rather Chaldean, empire, had become a decisive military and political factor in Mesopotamia, while to the south, the Pharaohs of the twenty-sixth dynasty in Egypt (Psammetich I, Necho II, Psammetich II, Hophra) were now renewing intervention in Asia, as the occasion arose, whereas previously Egypt had long abandoned its *Ostpolitik*. The struggle between the two powers alternated from open military conflict to 'cold war'. The small state of Judah, located at the particularly sensitive crossroads linking Asia and Africa, was influenced more than ever before by the international power system, now that the kingdom's actual existence was at stake.

In Political Science terms, Judah was now poignantly caught up in a bi-polar system, meaning that the exclusive control of international politics was concentrated in two powers, solely responsible for preserving peace or making war. Though the ancients clearly lacked such a modern concept as bi-polarity, they were nevertheless empirically aware of this power system category; thus, for example, Thucydides' approach to the struggle between the two centres—Athens and Sparta. Similarly, the prophet Jeremiah expresses the idea metaphorically: 'And now what do you gain by going to Egypt, to drink the waters of the Nile? Or what do you gain by going to Assyria to drink the waters of the Euphrates?' (Jer. 2.18); and later in the same chapter: 'How lightly you gad about, changing your way! You shall be put to shame by Egypt as you were put to shame by Assyria' (Jer. 2.36). (The political circumstances reflected in these passages are occasionally dated to the years 623–617 BC, a time when both Assyria and Egypt could have been considered potential allies of Judah.) Hence, bi-polarization of power had entered biblical consciousness.

Apparently, a multi-polar system accommodates small or secondary states, insofar as it is more capable of maintaining the fragile balance of power, thus deterring violation of the states within the region. However, the bi-polar system, whose stability as such is still debated by political scientists, also entails tranquility for secondary states, granting that the big states adopt policies of peaceful coexistence. Once the equilibrium is disturbed or upset by one of the partners seeking hegemony, the secondary power, lacking sufficient economic and military potential, turns to inexpensive diplomatic means to alleviate its plight.

Such was the fate of Judah. In the last two decades of its existence, the rapid pace of the international scene demanded of the Judean rulers exceedingly skilful manoeuvring in order to cope with kaleidoscopic situations. A series of no less than six critical turning points in Judah's foreign policy can be discerned, marking drastic shifts in loyalty from one major camp to the other—all within these twenty years. In other words, the political orientation of Judah alternated radically at an average frequency of every three years. In reacting to external temptations, the little kingdom eventually succumbed not only to international intrigues, but to her own risky policies as well. What were these six crucial stages, alternating between loyalty and rebellion?

1. The chain of events in Judah's fate began with the Battle of Megiddo in the summer of 609 BC, though this incident occurred several years prior to Judah's direct involvement in the Egyptian-Babylonian conflict. Possibly, the budding bi-polar system already influenced Josiah's decision to halt Pharaoh Necho, who was rushing northward in support of his previous rivals, the Assyrians, in their deteriorating struggle against the newly rising Babylonians. It is difficult to ascertain, but possibly Judah was somehow acting in concert with Babylonia to hinder this Egyptian aid.

There were several factors in Judah's favour: the newly enthroned Pharaoh Necho II was as yet inexperienced; the Egyptian army was far from its base when the Judeans chose to launch their surprise attack near Megiddo; above all, only half a year before the Egyptians had sustained a setback in the Euphrates region by the up-and-coming Babylonians—a fact generally overlooked. At any rate, this is a rare example of bold military initiative taken by a relatively small state, Judah, against the army of the biggest power of the day, Egypt of the twenty-sixth dynasty.

At this point, I shall take the opportunity of drawing attention to a possible additional source for the Battle of Megiddo, namely a fragmentary ostracon from Arad. The 'curious case of ostracon' no. 88 whose left half is missing, has received two different interpretations and restorations, one by the late Professor Aharoni and the other by the late Professor Yadin, the only attempts as far as I am aware, and both are, in my opinion, rather dubious. The Hebrew text reads:

I have come to reign in all . . .	אני.מלכתי.בכ
Take strength and . . .	אמץ.זרע.ו
King of Egypt to . . .	מלך.מצרים.ל

Aharoni (in his book on the Arad inscriptions, 1975) assumed that it refers to the enthronement of Jehoahaz, as successor of Josiah, while Yadin (*IEJ*, 1976) suggested it was a declaration of Asshur-uballit, the last king of Assyria. Since neither version seems acceptable, I risk an alternative proposal and restore:

> אני מלכתי בכ[ל הגויים] (בכ[ל הרי יהודה])
> I reign over all the nations (or: all the mountains of Judah)
> אמץ זרוע ו[צא לקראת] (ו[התחזק נגד])
> Take strength and go up against (or: muster your forces against)
> מלך מצרים ל[הלחם בו] (ל[בקעת מגידו])
> The King of Egypt to make war against him (or: to the Valley of Megiddo)

This daring military initiative at Megiddo was rooted in military ideology, as it finds expression in the book of Deuteronomy, Josiah's guiding light. Furthermore, we can confidently conjecture that this initiative received the support and encouragement of the prophetic circles. To judge primarily by the style of the inscription, I submit we have here a prophetic-political text, where God speaks through his prophets, apparently encouraging Josiah to go to war against Egypt. This is no king of flesh and blood, as both Aharoni and Yadin had assumed—but God speaking: אני מלכתי. The very style of the wording implies this: the verb מלכתי is inscribed in the past tense, but understood here in the present, as is frequently found with Biblical tenses (Blake, *A Resurvey of Hebrew Tenses*, Rome, 1951). Our restoration is supported by such verses as Ps. 47.9: 'God *reigns* over the nations; God *sits* on his holy throne'—מָלַךְ אלהים על גוים אלהים יָשַׁב על כסא קדשו , or 1 Chron. 16.31: 'Let the heavens be glad, and let the earth rejoice, and let them say among the nations, The Lord *reigns!'*—ישמחו השמים ותגל הארץ ויאמרו בגוים ה׳ מָלָךְ .

In the second line, note the word זרוע, 'arm'. This type of exhortation is repeated time and again especially in the political prophecy of Ezek. 30.22-26:

> Therefore thus says the Lord God: Behold, I am against Pharaoh king of Egypt, and will break his arms, both the strong arm and the one that is broken; and I will make the sword fall from his hand. I will scatter the Egyptians among the nations, and disperse them throughout the lands. And I will strengthen the arms of the king of Babylon, and put my sword in his hand; but I will break the arms of Pharaoh, and he will groan before him like a man mortally wounded. I will strengthen the arms of the king of Babylon, but the arms of Pharaoh shall fall; and they shall know that I am the Lord....

The completion in lines 2 and 3 is based on what we know of the Battle of Megiddo from 2 Chronicles 36. If this restoration, as well as the dating of the ostracon (on this point, I agree with Yadin), are in fact correct, then it seems that this is a prophetic proclamation in the name of the Lord, dispatched to the cities of Judah for the purpose of recruiting military aid in the campaign against Egypt. Finally, reinforcing my belief that this may be the true reconstruction is the harmonious spacing and outline of the Hebrew letters, obviously written by a mature, professional scribe and characteristic of a public decree; none of the numerous other ostraca found at Arad can compare with this one in elegance and beauty of script.

We return now to the first of our six stages. Despite the failure at Megiddo, this should not, *a priori*, be considered a suicidal undertaking, as is so often done, but rather a carefully calculated political move within the international power game, as I have pointed out elsewhere. However, the chance death of Josiah in the Plain of Megiddo put an effective end to the renewed prosperity of the Judean kingdom.

Judah's territory was once again 'cut down to size', reduced to its minimal dimensions. Egypt now controlled the entire region west of the Euphrates, or, in biblical phraseology, 'from the Brook of Egypt unto the river Euphrates, all that pertained to the king of Egypt' (2 Kgs 24.7). But its hegemony was short-lived.

2. The second fateful turning point occurred four years later, in the summer of 605 BC when Egypt was utterly defeated by King Nebuchadnezzar, the rising star of Babylon, in the Battle of Carchemish on the Euphrates, on the present Turkish-Syrian border. This renowned battle was a superb demonstration of sheer Babylonian military superiority, and in fact, by determining the power set-up in the Near East for years to come, sealed the fate of Syria and Palestine.

Nonetheless, the Judean leadership failed to grasp the shift in balance of power, and continued to cling to the dubious image of a strong Egypt which would rush to the aid of its allies in time of need. That other states in Palestine sought Egyptian aid against Babylonia is recorded in an Aramaic letter from Saqqara (Memphis in Egypt). In this letter, a ruler, most likely from Ekron in Philistia, approaches Pharaoh for urgent military assistance against the impending Babylonian onslaught, reminding his suzerain of his treaty obligation.

This document possibly concerns one of the Babylonian expeditions against Philistia either in the summer of 603 or the winter of 601/600 BC. Further proof may be found in the new excavations of Tel-Miqneh-Ekron, where a total destruction level was discovered from the end of the sixth century BC. Thus, in antiquity, probably more so than in modern times, a small state had difficulty in correctly assessing early warning signals of a shift in the 'global' power structure. According to the common assumption in International Relations, small states conduct prudent relations in foreign affairs. Judah's behaviour during this period contradicts this model and demonstrates that small states may in their ineptness, coupled with the inherent lack of a developed intelligence system, adopt high-risk policies, often with fatal consequences.

In this light, we can appreciate all the more the deep foresight and realistic historical perspective of the prophetic circles in Judah, who had a genuine understanding of the international scene at that time. The great prophets of the day, Jeremiah and Ezekiel (or Uriah, the son of Shemaiah from Kiriath-jearim, who prophesied 'in words like those of Jeremiah', Jer. 26.20) were entirely free of the 'establishment' line of thought, unlike the false prophets, and were thus able to grasp the situation in more realistic terms. Therefore, theirs was a sober and unbiased appreciation of the situation, for the long-range benefit of the nation, as opposed to the immediate, feasible interests so typical of the establishment and its supporters, the false prophets, such as Hananiah. In Ezekiel's words Egypt resembled 'a staff of reed to the house of Israel... when they leaned upon you, you broke' (Ezek. 29.6-7), and in her threats against Babylonia, but a 'paper tiger': 'Pharaoh with his mighty army and great company' will be of no avail in battle (Ezek. 17.17). Ezekiel was distressed by Egypt's enticement of Judah, likening Egypt to a harlot, who could only tempt but could not sustain (Ezek. 16.26; 23.21, 27). International relations in prophetic imagery, especially that of Ezekiel, are likened to prostitution. On the other hand, Jeremiah, who regarded Nebuchadnezzar as 'God's chosen rod' (of chastisement) realized that the opportune moment had passed: now only voluntary submission to the Babylonians could save Judah; it was the choice between 'the way of life and the way of death' (Jer. 21.8-9). We reject the widely accepted assumption that the prophets' outspoken stands were merely the machinations of later redactors, to make them conform with the outcome of events. On the contrary, we believe their orientation, as expressed in the biblical sources, reflects the reality of their views.

In modern terms, these prophets served—*with due recognition of their far more profound motives*—as analysts and commentators, quite independent of official policy and general consensus. In doing so, they played an active role in the acute issue of foreign political orientation, which had gradually intensified the polarity between the pro-Egyptian and pro-Babylonian factions. This polarity crossed lines—from the royal court onward, through state officials and priestly circles down to the masses. Likewise, political orientation and ideology proved the main bone of contention between the true and false prophets. Indeed, small states in general are more preoccupied with external than domestic affairs, a phenomenon known as *das Primat der Aussenpolitik*.

The Babylonian subjugation of Judah was not long in coming, although its exact date is still disputed. Judah seems to have held out for another two years after the Battle of Carchemish, surrendering only in the winter of 603 BC even though Nebuchadnezzar had already reached as far as Ashkelon and utterly destroyed it a year earlier. (Of this destruction, we now have archaeological proof from the first seasons of excavations at the site.) In view of this Babylonian threat, Egypt earnestly sought to bring Judah back into its fold, which introduces us to the third turning point, again entailing direct military confrontation between Egypt and Babylonia.

3. Some two and a half years after submitting to Babylonia, King Jehoiakim found an opportune moment to throw off its yoke. In the winter of 601/600 the Babylonian king waged his most ambitious campaign—an attack on Egypt proper, a major historical event revealed only relatively recently through publication of the Babylonian Chronicle from the time of Nebuchadnezzar (known as the Wiseman Chronicle). This official historical record conceals neither the Babylonian shortcomings during this campaign, which led to heavy losses on both sides, nor the subsequent, empty-handed Babylonian retreat. It was this Babylonian failure which, presumably exploited by Egyptian propaganda, encouraged the Judean leadership to rebel and defect to the Egyptian camp. For the next two years the Babylonians were unable to retaliate against Judah, and they concentrated on recouping their strength, and above all re-equipping the chariot force.

4. Only in the winter of 598/597 BC did Nebuchadnezzar strike at Judah, in a show of strength which, no doubt, served as a warning to Egypt and her other allies. The first Babylonian siege of Jerusalem, well documented in the Bible, was the fourth turning point. The biblical account is now fully borne out by the Babylonian Chronicle, which even specifies the precise day of the city's surrender by Jehoiachin (the son of Jehoiakim who died under obscure circumstances)—on 2 Adar or March 16, 597 BC.

This precise date now enables us to reappraise the actual course of the siege and the ensuing exile from Judah. Jerusalem had apparently been under siege for several weeks prior to the arrival of Nebuchadnezzar and his choice troops, an event which broke the spirit of the defenders, who were already demoralized by the lack of any sign of Egyptian aid forthcoming. Though the Judean king's surrender saved Jerusalem from physical destruction, and Judah from the status of a conquered country within the Babylonian empire, its human resources were seriously depleted—ten thousand of its inhabitants having been exiled to Babylonia, including the elite of the nation, the 'good figs' in Jeremiah's prophecy (ch. 24), and the higher military echelons.

Nebuchadnezzar's policy of deportation and 'heavy tribute' ultimately proved shortsighted. The very foundations of the kingdom were undermined; social and economic chaos, as well as psychic and spiritual distress prevailed, as can be discerned in the prophets' words. This was the *mise en scène* for the appearance of irresponsible elements in Judean leadership; such was the fate, time and again, of vanquished states who had been burdened with such harsh conditions of surrender.

5. Bereft of experienced leadership and saddled with a puppet king, Judah soon became entangled again in international intrigue, leading up to the fifth turning point. The new king and last monarch of Judah, Zedekiah, summoned, or was forced to summon, an anti-Babylonian conference of delegates of petty kingdoms in Jerusalem in the year 594/593 BC, thus rebelling against the power which had enthroned him, a step in conflict with his own personal interest. The motivation for this plot is not clear, but it was assumed to be connected with the enthronement of the new Egyptian king Psammetich II. Yet according to a relatively recent chronology for this period (that has been widely overlooked) Psammetich II

ascended the throne already in 595 BC, *not* 594 as was previously held. It seems more likely that the intrigue (accompanied by the intensive activity of the 'false' prophets, predicting the prompt return of the exiles from Babylonia) was inspired by the serious revolt which broke out in Babylonia proper, the previous winter. Though this was immediately crushed by Nebuchadnezzar, we still hear a year later (i.e. close to the Jerusalem conference) that an important functionary of the king is on trial, accused of 'high treason' (publication by E. Weidner, *AfO* 17 [1954/56]). Thus the time may have seemed opportune for the nations of the West to rebel against Babylonia and for Judah to nourish illusory hopes for an immediate ingathering of the Judean exiles. The states represented in the Jerusalem conference —this 'mini-summit' of petty states—were Edom, Moab and Ammon in Transjordan and the cities of the Phoenician coast. Thus Judah was attempting to set up a league against Babylonia, encompassing the area of modern Jordan, Israel and the coastal plain of Lebanon.

As so often occurs in military history, this alliance of several (six) small and rather weak states was of little avail against the big power. The coalition also suffered from a serious lack of political and military cohesion, for each component state still sought to promote its own narrow interests and priorities. Thus it actually constituted no real threat to Nebuchadnezzar. Here again it would seem that Egypt subverted Judah against Babylonia, though we have no clear evidence. We do know, however, that the new Pharaoh, Psammetich II, staged an expedition to Palestine and Phoenicia in 592 BC (and *not* 591 BC) undoubtedly arousing anti-Babylonian sentiments within Judean leadership. Nevertheless, it was not until the succession of the aggressive Pharaoh Hophra (Apries) to the throne in Egypt, that open rebellion erupted against Babylonia, and with this we arrive at the sixth and final turning point.

6. When Nebuchadnezzar finally reacted in the winter of 589/588 BC, Judah found herself in a highly vulnerable position. From both a diplomatic and military point of view, Judah was left in the lurch and had to face the Babylonian might alone—'all her friends have dealt treacherously with her' (Lam. 1.2). In addition, the nation was internally divided between the 'hawks', set on total war and the 'doves', advocating appeasement and surrender. Under the circumstances, Jerusalem's resistance for as long as a year and a half was quite remarkable, the more so if we adopt the variant, more likely

Tishri chronological calculation, according to which the siege lasted for two and a half years. The rest of the kingdom had quickly been overrun, a few royal fortresses such as Lachish having taken somewhat longer to subdue. At one point prospects brightened, and the siege of Jerusalem was even temporarily lifted when the Babylonians moved to counter a rumoured Egyptian relief force; but this in the end proved abortive as the prophets Jeremiah and Ezekiel correctly foresaw.

The Babylonian army now proved its flexibility as well as superiority in military strategy. Initially deployed to quell a rebellious city, it was now obliged to change from siege warfare to open field battle (and back again; cf. I. Eph'al, in *History, Historiography*, ed. H. Tadmor and M. Weinfeld, 1983), a difficult task! The conquest of the capital city was a serious challenge for Nebuchadnezzar and so, reorganizing again, he employed his finest military commanders and the most advanced siegecraft of the day: dikes and ramps, upon which were stationed weapons such as battering rams; but it was that veteran of siege warfare, famine, that ultimately turned the tide for the population of Jerusalem, which had constantly to accept the flow of refugees from provincial towns.

Scholars have often been perplexed by the time lapse between the breaching of the walls of Jerusalem on 9 Tammuz (July 18, 586 BC according to one of the chronological systems) and the beginning of the total destruction of the city, not until a month later on 7 or 19 Ab (August 14 or 17, 586 BC). Once the enemy penetrated its walls, why was the vulnerable city not razed immediately? This delay can hardly be attributed to the fighting spirit of the city's defenders, so characteristic of the last siege of Jerusalem in the Second Temple period. Rather, the destruction of the city seems to have been postponed by the Babylonians, pending Nebuchadnezzar's final verdict concerning the city.

At that time, Nebuchadnezzar's headquarters were stationed at Riblah, in the land of Hamat, in central Syria (to the south of Kadesh on the Orontes), a distance of 350-400 km from Jerusalem, or a ten-to thirteen-day march, bearing in mind the long summer days. Upon the breaching of its northern walls, Zedekiah and his entourage stole away from the city in the south, only to be captured later near Jericho and dragged to Riblah. It was there that the Judean leadership was tried for treason and evidently then, that the fate of Jerusalem was decided by the king of Babylon. Nebuzaradan, the commander-in-chief of the Babylonian army (with some troops), was dispatched to the Judean capital to carry out his master's orders. Following the exacting biblical sources, the date 7 or 10 Ab refers to Nebuzaradan's arrival in Jerusalem (2 Kgs 25.8) rather than the city's destruction. This chain of events accords well with the lapse of time between the breaching of the walls of Jerusalem and Nebuzaradan's appearance before its gates, which sealed the fate of the city. With the fall of Jerusalem and the total destruction of the palace and the holy temple, the Davidic dynasty came to an end, and Judah was divested of its polity for generations to come.

In conclusion, this case study of Judah in its final years may serve as a universally valid paradigm for the conduct and function of a small or secondary state in a bi-polar power system. Unable to remain detached in a major confrontation between the great powers, the small or weak state must side with either of the big actors. In time of conflict, the precarious status of neutrality for a small state, particularly when it is located in the centre of the system, is practically impossible—a fact already stressed by Machiavelli. By remaining neutral, it would invariably and eventually arouse the enmity of each of the big competitors. Genuine neutrality, resting on independent strength, contains a prerequisite: the peaceful coexistence of the two big powers or the existence of a multiplicity of political entities of roughly equal power—namely, a multi-power system.

The decision, with which antagonist to side, is a crucial factor for the small state and poses a serious dilemma. In order to survive, this choice must be based on sober calculations and long-range interests. At best, Egypt was able to offer her camp-followers only short-range advantages, and proved powerless in the hour of peril. Instead of turning to powerful Babylonia, the Judeans toyed with false hopes created by the misleading image of Egypt, that led to Judah's hazardous gamble on her. On the international scene—as in Judah's case—both major powers watch the small state carefully and are ready to intervene to prevent defection to the rival camp, eventually leading to complete control and ultimate conquest.

NOTE

*This paper is based on a lecture delivered at the International Colloquy on 'Warfare throughout the Ages between Small States and Big Powers . . .', organized by the Israeli branch of the International Committee for Military History, Tel Aviv, August 1984. This study was prepared within the framework of a grant from the Fund for Basic Research administered by the Israel Academy of Sciences and Humanities, and was carried out during my term as a fellow of the Institute of Advanced Studies at the Hebrew University of Jerusalem.

BACKGROUND REFERENCES

On the historical period see:

Malamat, A., 'Josiah's Bid for Armageddon', *Journal of the Ancient Near Eastern Society* 5 (= *The Gaster Festschrift*) (1973), pp. 267-79.

—'The Twilight in Judah: In the Egyptian-Babylonian Maelstrom', *Vetus Testamentum Supplements* 28 (1975), pp. 123-45.

—'The Last Years of the Kingdom of Judah', *The Age of the Monarchies: Political History* (ed. A. Malamat; World History of the Jewish People IV, 1; Jerusalem, 1979), ch. 10, pp. 205-21, 349-53.

Bickerman, E.J., 'Nebuchadnezzar and Jerusalem', *Proceedings of the American Academy for Jewish Research*, 46-47 (1979-1980), pp. 69-85.

Migsch, *Gottes Wort über das Ende Jerusalems*, Klosterneuburg, 1981.

Cazelles, H., '587 ou 586?', *The Word of the Lord Shall Go Forth, Essays in Honor of D.N. Freedman* (Philadelphia, 1983), pp. 427-35.

Fensham, F.C., 'Nebukadnezzar in the Book of Jeremiah', *Journal of Northwest Semitic Languages* 10 (1982), pp. 53-65.

On the theoretical framework see:

Fliess, P.J., *Thucydides and the Politics of Bipolarity*, Louisiana, 1966.

Rothstein, R.L., *Alliances and Small Powers*, New York, 1968.

Rosenau, J.N. (ed.), *International Politics and Foreign Policy*, New York, 2nd edn, 1969 (esp. ch. 27 by M.A. Kaplan and ch. 30 by R.N. Rosecrance).

Handel, M.I., *Weak States in the International System*, London, 1981.

8

QṢWṢY P'H AND *PẢT MDBR*

William McKane

The disagreement about the sense of *qṣwṣy p'h* (Jer. 9.25; 25.23; 49.32) is ancient and is well-recorded in the *Thesaurus* of Wilhelm Gesenius.[1] The two possibilities which are to be entertained are (a) *abscissi extremis crinibus*, 'trimmed at the edges of the hair', and (b) *quorum regio abscissa sive separata est, id est qui remota sunt a locis habitatis*, 'whose geographical area is cut off or separated, that is, those whose places of habitation are remote'. The second sense is taken by Gesenius from the dictionary of Abu'l Walīd Marwān ibn Janāh,[2] a mediaeval Jewish lexicographer who wrote in Arabic.

The first of these two meanings of *qṣwṣy p'h* is the one which appears in the ancient versions (Septuagint, Vulgate, Peshiṭta and Targum Jonathan), and in Jerome's commentary on the book of Jeremiah.[3] There is no doubt that in all three passages the Septuagint is deriving *qṣwṣy* from *qṣṣ* 'cut' (περικειρόμενον; περικεκαρμένον; κεκραμένους), but *p'h* is paraphrased in an obscure way (τὰ κατὰ πρόσωπον αὐτοῦ; κατὰ πρόσωπον αὐτοῦ; πρὸ προσώπου αὐτῶν). The sense is not obvious, but 'what is in front of the face' could mean 'the temples', in which case the Septuagint would be recording the meaning '(the hair) on whose temples is clipped' or the like.

The matter is much clearer in the Vulgate, where *p'h*, 'edge', 'fringe', has been interpreted explicitly as 'fringes of the hair' in the rendering *qui attonsi sunt in comam* which the Douai version[4] translates as 'and all that have their hair cut round'. With this should be compared the Peshiṭta, which could be regarded as a mere transcription of the Hebrew (*qṣyṣy p't'*), except that *p't'* is used of the fringe or corner of the beard in the phrase *p't' ddqn'*,[5] so that it may be a rendering with the same intention as that of the Vulgate.

The most significant of the ancient versions is the Targum Jonathan (*w'l kl mqpy pt'*),[6] because it makes a double contribution: it elucidates 'cut' as a rounding of the fringes of the hair, and by its choice of vocabulary it connects the three Jeremiah passages with Lev. 19.27, where *tqpw* occurs with *p'h* in a verse which prohibits the rounding of the hair and the disfiguring (*tšḥyt*) of the beard. NEB translates, 'You shall not round off your hair from side to side, and you shall not shave the edge of your beard'. That the trimming or shaving of the beard is intended can be gathered from Lev. 21.5, where the phrase *p't zqnm* occurs and where *yglhw* is substituted for *tšḥyt*. Thus Targum Jonathan understands *qṣwṣy p'h* pejoratively by connecting the phrase with a kind of hair-cut or trimming of the beard which was prohibited in the book of Leviticus.

This is not how *qṣwṣy p'h* is represented in the text of KJV but this sense does appear as a marginal alternative which was preferred by the learned eighteenth-century English commentator, William Lowth,[7] who remarks, 'And 'tis probable that the precept in Levit. chap. xix 27 . . . hath reference to this custom which was a rite in several countries near Judaea, whereby they devoted themselves to the worship of some false god'. His precise comment on *qṣwṣy p'h* runs, 'The expression denotes those Arabians who cut their hair upon the forepart of the head round, and let the hair behind grow long'. This elucidation was adopted by RV ('and all that have the corners *of their hair* polled') and RSV ('and those who cut the corners of their hair') and is found generally in modern commentators (for example, Duhm,[8] Rudolph,[9] Weiser,[10] Bright,[11] Freehof[12]).

There is a reference to this style of hair-cut among the Arabs in Wellhausen[13] and Robertson Smith,[14] and the latter observes, 'The peculiar Arab tonsure is already referred to in Jer. xxv 23 RV . . . Among the Arabs the two side locks are the distinguishing mark of an immature lad'. In other words, the trimming of the side locks was associated with an initiation ceremony marking the achievement of 'maturity' (cf. Wellhausen). It will have been noticed that Lowth attaches a religious significance to this manner of cutting the hair and deduces that the prohibition in Lev. 19.27 (21.5) arises from these idolatrous associations. At this point it is appropriate to introduce the testimony of Herodotus[15] which occurs in the context of his observations about the Arabs: 'They acknowledge no other gods but Dionysius and Urania, and it is said that their hair is cut in the same way as that of Dionysius: they cut it in a circular form, shaving it around the temples'. The verbs which indicate 'cutting' (κείρεσθαι; κεκάρθαι; κείρονται) are similar to those used in the Septuagint, but the precise allusion to rounding the hair at the temples is given in the closing explication by κείρονταί δὲ περιτρόχαλα, ὑποξυρῶντες τοὺς κροτάφους.

The second of the two senses of *qṣwṣy p'h* appears in Ibn Janāh (see above) and in Rashi and Kimchi, namely, 'cut off at the extremes (of the desert)'. Rashi explains *qṣṣ* not as 'cut' but as a variant form of *qṣh*, 'to be at the end' or 'to be at the terminus'. His comment at 9.25 is *hmwqṣyn bp't mdbr*; at 25.23, *hmwqṣym bqṣh 'wth hrwḥ*, 'Those who are remote in an extreme quarter'; at 49.32, *mwqṣym mqṣh 'l qṣh hrwḥwt*, 'Remote in all the extreme quarters of the world'. The phrase which he uses at 9.25 (*p't mdbr*) is identical with the *pát mdbr* of the Ugaritic texts (see further below). This coincidence of use in mediaeval Hebrew and Ugaritic should not, however, be regarded as more than a coincidence and it should not be supposed that it has a crucial contribution to make to the elucidation of *qṣwṣy p'h*.

At Jer. 9.25 Kimchi identifies *qṣwṣy p'h* with Arab communities: they are those who live in the extreme corner, that is, who are remote in the desert. What is most remote is called *qṣh*, and *p'h* is used because *qṣh* and *p'h* are the remotest boundaries in every case. *qṣh* and *qṣṣ* are variants of the same root and are identical in sense. At 25.23 Kimchi associates *qṣwṣy* with *qṣ*, 'end', and his comment runs, 'Those who dwell at the extremity (*bqṣh*) of the world in its corner (*bp'tw*), for *hp'h* is *qṣ mdbr*'. This is reinforced by what he has to say about 49.32, 'They are *qṣwṣym* in every *p'h*, from the meaning *qṣ* 'end', for their quarter is the furthest reach (*qṣ*) and the terminus (*swp*)'.

Both Rashi and Kimchi offer a wrong lexicography of *qṣwṣy*, and their exegesis rests on this error. The equalizing of *qṣṣ* and *qṣh* is mistaken, and if this type of interpretation is to be pursued, it must be on the basis of *qṣṣ*, 'cut' or 'cut off', so that *qṣwṣy p'h* are those who are cut off (from civilization), at the edge (*p'h*) (of the world). Nevertheless, the exegetical trend which is represented by Rashi and Kimchi is not nullified by their unsound lexicography, because it can be more or less maintained on the foundation of the paraphrase of *qṣwṣy p'h* which appears in the preceding sentence. That this is a correct estimate is proved by the circumstance that the exposition of *qṣwṣy p'h* which appears in Ibn Janāh (see above) does not differ much from that of Rashi and Kimchi, although it assumes the sense 'cut' or 'cut off' for *qṣṣ*. This is clear from Ibn Janāh's equivalence for *qṣwṣy p'h*, which is *'lmnqṭ'y 'ljht*, 'those whose geographical area is cut off'. His further explication of this is *'lb'ydyn mn 'l'mrn 'y 'lmtjwlyn fy 'lṣḥry*, 'those who are remote from civilization, who wander across tracts of desert'.[16]

This interpretation of *qṣwṣy p'h* is adopted by Calvin[17] who notices *qui attonsi sunt in comam*, but dismisses it with *sed nulla ratio apparet*. At 9.25 he apparently associates *qṣwṣy* with *qṣ*, 'end', as Rashi and Kimchi had done, but at 49.32 his lexicography is explicitly *qṣṣ*, 'cut off', and this may be the foundation of KJV '*that are* in the utmost corners', which was explained by Benjamin Blayney,[18] another eighteenth-century commentator, as a reference to the inhabitants of the Arabian peninsula. This understanding of *qṣwṣy p'h* is apparently present in NEB, which has relegated 'those who clip the hair on their temples' to its footnotes, but which has translated *qṣwṣy p'h* so freely in its text that it is unclear whether its rendering is derived from *qṣṣ*, 'cut', or from a new, undisclosed lexicography. 'Haunt the fringes of the desert' (9.25; 25.23) or 'roam the fringes of the desert' (49.32) is perhaps an acceptable amplification of the sense of *qṣwṣy p'h* like Ibn Janāh's *'lmtjwlyn fy 'lṣḥry*, but it is not a translation, if *qṣwṣy* is derived from *qṣṣ*, 'cut' or 'cut off'.

Both the meanings of *p'h* which are invoked to explain *qṣwṣy p'h* are present in the Ugaritic texts: *pe̓[th]*, with the sense 'temple' or 'brow' occurs in parallelism with *pnm*, 'face', in the stichos *yshl pe̓[th]*, 'his face was lightened',[19] and *pa̓t mdbr*[20] or *pa̓t mlbr*[21] is a phrase to which no obscurity attaches and which clearly means 'fringe of the desert'. Thus *kḥsn pa̓t mdbr*,[22] which means 'like hoppers on the fringe of the desert' is entirely transparent. Does Ugaritic *pa̓t mdbr* tilt the balance towards an interpretation of *qṣwṣy p'h* which was established in mediaeval Jewish lexicography, and in the mediaeval commentaries of Rashi and Kimchi, which was adopted by Calvin and KJV and which has reappeared in a free translation in NEB? The second edition of Koehler–Baumgartner[23] gives a negative answer to this question, because although *pa̓t mdbr* is cited, the lexicography of *qṣwṣy p'h* is not swayed by it and the other sense, 'those who clip the edges of the hair', is preferred. The case is not different in the fascicle of the third edition of Koehler-Baumgartner[24] which has recently appeared. The Ugaritic evidence is certainly interesting and significant: it shows that in the second millennium BC *pảt* was used in the cultural area of Syria/Palestine of the edge or fringe of the desert. To this extent it lends support to the view that *p'h* in *qṣwṣy p'h* means 'the furthest corners of the desert' and that *qṣwṣy p'h* are those who are cut off (from civilization) at the furthest reaches (of the desert).

An examination of the contexts in which the three occurrences of *qṣwṣy p'h* appear shows that the expression is used of desert communities in each case. This is gathered at 9.25 by the circumstance that a reference to desert dwellers (*hyšbym bmdbr*) follows immediately after *qṣwṣy p'h*, and at 49.28-33 by the description of Kedar as a desert people (49.28f.). The third passage (25.23f.) refers to a group of desert communities, and since *qṣwṣy p'h hyšbym bmdbr* occurs at 9.25 (*hšknym* is substituted for *hyšbym* at 25.24), there is a suspicion that the words *w't kl mlky ʿrb w't kl mlky hʿrb*, which break the connection between *kl qṣwṣy p'h* and *hšknym bmdbr*, are an intrusion.

Moreover, the intrusive element is clearly a doublet, and the translator of the Septuagint was reading a Hebrew text which had only one of the variants and which he mistranslated (καὶ πάντας τοὺς συμμίκτους) under the influence of *w't kl hʿrb* (v. 20). καὶ πάντας τοὺς συμμίκτους does not show that he read *w't kl hʿrb* in his Hebrew *Vorlage* at v. 24 (LXX, 32.10); it is more probable that he harmonized *w't kl mlky ʿrb* or *w't kl mlky hʿrb* with his translation of *w't kl hʿrb* at v. 20. Hence it is not clear that Janzen[25] is right in supposing that the variants at v. 24 derive from *w't kl hʿrb* (v. 20) and that they have been displaced. For one thing *ʿrb* in v. 20 must mean 'a mixed population', and, if so, *mlky (h)ʿrb* is not a variant which makes any sense; for another thing *mlky (h)ʿrb* has a point at v. 24 only if *ʿrb* has a different sense from what it has at v. 20. The doublet in v. 24 is an exegetical gloss on *kl qṣwṣy p'h hšknym bmdbr*, which identifies these as Arab kings, and it has no connection with *w't kl hʿrb* (v. 20).

The conclusion of this particular discussion is that in a shorter and more original Hebrew text *hšknym bmdbr* followed immediately after *kl qṣwṣy p'h* and has been separated from it by two variants of an intervening gloss. This shows that in two of the three passages (9.25; 25.23) *qṣwṣy p'h* are immediately defined as desert dwellers, but it does not necessarily follow that *hyšbym bmdbr* or *hšknym bmdbr* is no more than an epexegesis or spelling-out of *qṣwṣy p'h*. If these expressions were merely epexegetical, the sense of *qṣwṣy p'h* would be determined as 'those who are isolated in the furthest corners (of the desert)' or the like. It is a question whether the Masoretes by inserting a *zaqeph qaton* at *p'h* (9.23) are not giving a different indication, namely, that *qṣwṣy p'h* and *hyšbym bmdbr* are independent descriptions and that *hyšbym bmdbr* is not epexegetical of *qṣwṣy p'h*.

The lexicographical judgment of Koehler–Baumgartner is probably sound, because *pa̓t mdbr* is not a sufficiently weighty piece of evidence to carry the issue against other factors which give a different indication. These are the appearance of *l' tqpw p't r'škm* at Lev. 19.27 (cf. Lev. 21.5), the insight of Targum Jonathan that the Jeremiah passages are connected with this style of hair-cut and the notice of Herodotus that the clipping or rounding of the locks at the temples by the Arabs had idolatrous associations. This explains the prohibitions at Lev. 19.27 and 21.5, and it is with this complex of ideas that *qṣwṣy p'h* in the Jeremiah passages is to be integrated. *qṣwṣy p'h* is not explicitly pejorative in these passages; it may be implicitly pejorative or merely descriptive, but, at any rate, it refers to a style of hair-cut which is prohibited in Lev. 19.27.

Finally, another consideration is the order of the word-string *w'l kl qṣwṣy p'h hyšbym bmdbr* (9.25) and *w't kl qṣwṣy p'h hšknym bmdbr* (25.23—reconstructed). If *qṣwṣy p'h* means 'those who live in the furthest recesses of the desert', *hyšbym bmdbr* or *hšknym bmdbr* is reduced to a weak tautology, although Blayney[26] avoids this conclusion by urging improbably that *qṣwṣy p'h* are those who inhabit the Arabian peninsula, while *hyšbym bmdbr* are those who live in the desert between Mesopotamia and Palestine. If the order of the phrases were reversed, it would be reasonable to think in terms of an epexegesis: *qṣwṣy p'h* would define more exactly what is intended by the preceding *hyšbym bmdbr*. As it is we have (*ex hypothesi*) a precise description followed by a general one which does not have a function, and 'Those in the deepest desert who live in the desert' is unlikely to be right.

I had the pleasure of meeting Professor Fensham when I was in Stellenbosch last year and I am happy to have the opportunity of contributing to his *Festschrift* and to be associated with all those who are honouring him by recognizing the contributions which he has made to Semitic scholarship.

NOTES

1. W. Gesenius, *Thesaurus Philologicus Criticus Linguae Hebraeae et Chaldaeae Veteris Testamenti*, II (Leipzig, 1840), p. 1087.
2. A. Neubauer (ed.), *The Book of Hebrew Roots* (Oxford, 1875; repr. Amsterdam: Philo Press, 1968), p. 559.
3. S. Reiter (ed.), *Sancti Eusebii Hieronymi in Hieremiam Prophetam* (CSEL 59, 1913), *in loc.*
4. *The Holie Bible Faithfully Translated into English Out of the Authentical Latin*, Douai, 1609.
5. J. Payne Smith (ed.), *A Compendious Syriac Dictionary* (Oxford, 1903), p. 433.
6. Cf. M. Jastrow, *A Dictionary of the Targumim, the Talmud Babli and Yerushalmi, and the Midrashic Literature* (New York, Berlin and London, 1926), p. 934.
7. W. Lowth, *A Commentary upon the Prophecy and Lamentations of Jeremiah* (London, 1718), at Jer. 9.25.
8. B. Duhm, *Das Buch Jeremia* (KHCAT; Tübingen and Leipzig, 1901), *in loc.*
9. W. Rudolph. *Jeremia* (HAT 1/12; 3rd edn; Tübingen, 1968), *in loc.*
10. A. Weiser, *Das Buch Jeremia* (ATD 20/21; 6th edn; Göttingen, 1969), *in loc.*
11. J. Bright, *Jeremiah: Introduction, Translation and Notes* (AB 21; New York, 1965), *in loc.*
12. S.B. Freehof, *Book of Jeremiah* (The Jewish Commentary for Bible Readers; New York, 1977), *in loc.*
13. J. Wellhausen, *Skizzen und Vorarbeiten*. III *Reste Arabischen Heidentums* (Berlin, 1887), p. 119.
14. W.R. Smith, *Lectures on the Religion of the Semites* (3rd edn; Edinburgh, 1927), p. 325 n. 2.
15. Book 3.8. C. Hude (ed.), *Herodoti Historiae*, Libri I-IV (3rd edn; Oxford, 1927).
16. A. Neubauer (ed.), *op. cit.*, p. 559.
17. J. Calvin, *Praelectiones in Librum Jeremia et Lamentationes* (3rd edn; Geneva, 1589), *in loc.*
18. B. Blayney, *Jeremiah and Lamentations: A New Translation with Notes critical, philological and explanatory*, Oxford, 1784.
19. 17 ii 9; G.R. Driver and J.C.L. Gibson, *Canaanite Myths and Legends* (2nd edn; Edinburgh, 1978), p. 105.
20. 14.193; 23.68 (*CML*^{2}, pp. 87, 127).
21. 12 i 35 (*CML*^{2}, p. 134).
22. 14.193 (*CML*^{2}, p. 87).

23. L. Koehler–W. Baumgartner, *Lexicon in Veteris Testamenti Libros* (2nd edn; Leiden, 1958), p. 749.
24. *Hebräisches und Aramäisches Lexikon zum Alten Testament* (3rd edn; Leiden, 1983), p. 858.
25. J.G. Janzen, *Studies in the Text of Jeremiah* (Harvard Semitic Monographs; Cambridge, Massachusetts, 1973), p. 13.
26. *Op. cit.*, at 9.25.

9

PRAYER AND SACRIFICE IN UGARIT AND ISRAEL

Patrick D. Miller, Jr

In his study of individual prayer in Sumerian[1] W.W. Hallo has demonstrated the importance of Mesopotamian hymnic and prayer material for the study of the Hebrew Psalter. In that context he also noted that the Sumerian and Akkadian texts may take prior place in this regard to the Ugaritic texts because they include many examples of types of prayers similar to those in the Psalter, whereas the Ugaritic texts that have been studied in relation to the Psalms 'are neither hymns nor prayers, and thus can only indirectly serve to illuminate the categories of Biblical psalmody as such'.[2] Hallo's claim is valid; the absence of hymnic and prayer texts from the large corpus of Ugaritic literature has often been noted. This lack exists despite the fact that the literary texts tell of prayers to the gods, and ritual texts give us much information about cultic activity.

That makes it all the more important, therefore, that the latest major publication of Ugaritic texts[3] includes a genuine prayer to the god Baal that is circumscribed by a typical ritual text (RS 24.266=KTU 1.119).[4] While one could wish for more such texts, this one does give us some insight into prayer and sacrifice at Ugarit as well as the perceived relationship of the populace to Baal.

Text

The absence of published photographs of RS 24.266 makes comment on the text somewhat provisional. The following transliteration, however, is drawn not only from the facsimile, and notes of Herdner in *Ugaritica* VII together with the transcription in KTU, but also from the very careful collation of the text by Dennis Pardee in the

Damascus Museum in 1981, using a binocular microscope to check his readings. I am greatly indebted to him for sharing his work with me but wish to absolve him of any final responsibility for either the reading of the text below or the interpretation given here.

Recto

(1) *byrḥ.ib‘lt.b͑ẙ[m.šb‘]*
(2) *š.lb‘l.r‘̊k͑t.°b͑[ ]°°°[ ]*
(3) *wbt.b‘l.ugr[t]°.š[ ]°*
(4) *‘rb.špš whl̊ m̊l̊k͑[.]b͑š̊b͑‘t*
(5) *‘šrt.yrtḥṣ̊ mlk br̊r̊*
(6) *gdlt.qdš il.°gdlt.°lb‘lm*
(7) *gdlt lǵlm.°dqtm.ẘǵ̊lt*
(8) *lǵlmtm.bt.ṯ‘y.ydbḥ*
(9) *wtnrr.b‘d.bt b‘l*
(10) *lgrt imr.°wynt.qrt*
(11) *lṯ‘.bṯmnt.°‘šrt.°ib‘lt*
(12) *alp.lmdǵ̊l b‘l.ugrt*
(13) *ůurm.ušnpt.°lydḅh*
(14) *m̊lk.bt il.npš.liš̊[ḫry]*
(15) *npš lb‘l̊[ ]*
(16) *w‘r.°l°[ ]*
(17) *°°°[ ]*

Verso

(18′) *[ ]°l̊°°° [ ]*
(19′) *°tml.yk °[ ]*
(20′) *brb‘.‘ṣrmm.bḫmš[ ]‘̊š̊r̊*
(21′) *mm.wkbd.w.š šrp̊ lb‘l̊*
(22′) *ugrt.bbt.lšb‘.tdn*
(23′) *mḥllm.‘rb.špš*
(24′) *wḥl m̊l͑k.hn šm̊n.šlm*
(25′) *b‘l.mtk.mlkm̊ ri̊šyt*
(26′) *kgr ‘z.ṯǵr̊km.°q̊rd*
(27′) *ḥmytkm.‘n̊km.l̊b͑‘l tšun*
(28′) *yb‘̊l̊m.°[ḥ̊]m̊.°t͑dy ‘z l̊ṯǵ̊rn*
(29′) *y.qrd [l]ḥ̊mytny.°ibry*
(30′) *b‘l.nšqdš.mḏr b‘l*
(31′) *nmlu [d]kr b‘l.nš[q]dš*
(32′) *ḥtp̊ b‘l̊[.n]mlu. ‘̊š̊r̊t.b͑‘l̊[.] n̊[‘]*
(33′) *šr qdš b‘l.n‘l.ntbtb[t.b‘l]*
(34′) *ntlk.wš[m‘.b]‘l̊.°l̊.°ṣlt͑.[km]*
(35′) *ẙdy.‘z lṯǵrk[m.qrd]*
(36′) *lḥmytk[m]*

Text Notes

The horizontal lines are drawn conventionally. From Herdner and from Pardee's copy it is clear they are worn and broken so that only parts of the lines remain.

Recto

Line 1: Herdner reconstructs *ḥdṯ* at the end of the line. Pardee and KTU indicate that letters are partially visible here and more likely to be read as *šbʿ*. The clearest sign is probably the last one /ʿ/.

Line 2: Several letters are too broken to read. Before the break KTU and Herdner see a /*š*/ or /*d*/. Pardee claims it is probably /*b*/and therefore a new date indicator, e.g. *bym*...

Line 3: Pardee says the word divider before /*š*/ is virtually certain, but the /*y*/ read by KTU at the end is not.

Line 12: Pardee indicates the /*ġ̊*/ of /*lmdġ̊l*/ could be /*ḫ*/, but the orientation of the sign that is visible is more suitable for /*g*/.

Line 13: The /*u*/ before /*šnpt*/ is certain according to Pardee. He says that the first letter of the line is probably /*u*/ but could be /*u*/remade into /*b*/, which is the reading in KTU. Apparently, only three vertical wedges are clear.

Line 14: Herdner restores [*l*] as the last sign. Pardee says the angle of the first wedge makes [*l*] highly improbable. He reads /*š*/, as does KTU, which restores *liš*[*ḫry*].

Verso

Line 18': Pardee maintains /*gdlt*/ cannot be reconstructed in this line as does Herdner. Nor is /*ṯn*/ visible after /*l*/ (so KTU).

Line 19': Pardee says the first sign could be /*u*/ but not /*i*/ and there is a trace of what could be /*b*/ or /*d*/ before the break.

Line 20': According to Pardee, at the end of the line /ʿ/ is very likely, /*ṣ*/ possibly, and /*r*/ only a slight trace. Herdner reads the same letters; KTU has /*s**/ and /*l**/ after /*bḫms*/.

Line 21': Pardee says the /*p*/ of /*šrp*/ is virtually certain (with Herdner, against KTU's /*t*/).

Line 28': Between /*ybʿ̊l̊m*/ and /*t̊dy*/ Pardee says there is room for two letters and that the second one is probably /*m*/. KTU has [*a*]*l** and Herdner reconstructs [*al*]. The /*l*/ before /*t̊ġ̊rn*/ is in the text, according to Pardee, although KTU reads a word divider at that place. Herdner has /*l*/ also.

Line 31': For the broken space before /*kr*/ Pardee says 'there is no way of deciding between [*b*]*kr* and [*d*]*kr* other than space available'. At the time of collation it appeared to him that the space was a bit narrow for /*d*/, but he would not insist on reading /*b*/ in the gap, although that was his inclination.

Translation

Recto

(1) In the month of *ib'lt* on the [seventh d]ay:
(2) a ram for Baal of the ranks on [. . .]
(3) and the temple of Baal of Ugar[it
(4) At the setting of the sun then they purify the king. On the seven-
(5) teenth the king washes himself pure.
(6) A cow (for) the holy ones of El; a cow for the Baals;
(7) a cow for the Lad; two ewes and a cow
(8) for the Lasses in the temple. The one who offers will sacrifice
(9) and they will consume(?) in the throne room of the temple of Baal
(10) of Ugarit, a lamb and a dove of the city
(11) for an offering. On the eighteenth of *ib'lt*:
(12) a bull for the tower of Baal of Ugarit,
(13) either a flame(?) offering or an elevated offering. Let sacrifice
(14) the king in the temple of the god a throat for Iš[ḫaray].
(15) a throat for Baal[ ]
(16) and an ass for Ba[al]
(17) . . .

Verso

(18′) . . .
(19′) [the pre]ceding day . . . [ ]
(20′) on the fourth (day) two birds; on the fifth two
(21′) birds and a liver and a ram as a fire offering for Baal
(22′) of Ugarit in the temple. On the seventh day approach
(23′) the purifiers. At the setting of the sun
(24′) then they purify the king. Here is oil of peace,
(25′) O Baal, a libation of the king. The beginning:
(26′) When a strong one has attacked your gates,
a warrior (27′) your walls,
your eyes to Baal you shall lift up:
(28′) O Baal,
if you will drive the strong one from our gates,
the warrior from our walls,
a bull, O (30′) Baal, we shall consecrate,
a vow, O Baal (31′), we shall fulfill,
(32′) a male ani[mal], O Baal, we shall consecrate,
a sacrifice, O Baal, we shall fulfill,
a libation, O Baal, we (33′) shall pour out.

To the sanctuary of Baal we shall go up,
the paths of the house of Baal (34′) we shall traverse.
So Ba[al has hea]rd your prayer.
(35′) He will drive the strong one from your ga[tes,
the warrior] (36′) from your walls.

Translation notes

Line 1: The month *ib'lt*, which is not known outside of Ugarit, is one of five month names known from the ritual texts. It is not clear when it occurs during the year (Tarragon, p. 25).

Line 2: On the likelihood that *š* in the ritual texts refers to a *male* of the flock, ram or he-goat, see Levine, 'Ugaritic Descriptive Rituals', *JCS* 17 (1963), pp. 108ff.

The *r'kt* is surely a scribal error for *'rkt*. *r'kt* is unknown while the root *'rk* is not only familiar from Hebrew and Phoenician but appears in two other places in Ugaritic, both times in relation to *b'lt*. In RS 24.249 (KTU 1.105=*Ug* V.12), 11.3-4 the collocation *b'lt 'rkm* appears, which is usually understood as a construct chain. Because of its close association with *b'lt bhtm*, 'Lady of the Houses', Xella (*TRU* I, 28) translates in that text as well as here 'Baal degli edifice', which is not impossible though not exactly what one would expect from the use of this root in Hebrew. Cazelles (*VT* 19 [1969], p. 504), de Moor (*UF* 2 [1970], p. 319), and Herdner (*Ug.* VII, p. 13) see the term as designating a type of offering, cakes or loaves of bread. Virolleaud in his publication of the text cited Hebrew *'ōrᵉkîm*, 'men of war', and was followed in this association by Fisher (*HTR* 63 [1970], pp. 488-89), who regards the final *-m* as enclitic and thus sees here a title 'Baal the Warrior'.

The association of the root with battle ranks reflects the most common usage in Hebrew and is confirmed by its other appearance in Ugaritic in RS 24.292 (= KTU 4.278=*Ug.* VII, pp. 143-44), which in its first three lines reads *'rk.*[5]*b'l/ḫlb.dt. lyt/šm'n*: 'The ranks/men of war of Baal of Ḫalab[6] who are to be summoned',[7] followed by a list of names. Here *'rk* refers to a group of males and thus cannot be either structural or edible.

Line 3: *bt b'l ugrt* presumably refers to the Baal temple at Ugarit.

Line 4: The precise character of the ritual involving the king that appears in this text twice and several times elsewhere is still not altogether clear. The expression *'rb špš wḥl mlk* is a formula as is *yrtḥṣ mlk brr*. They appear to represent a sequence of ritual acts, but they do not always appear in the same order. The word *ḥl* comes from the root *ḥl(l)*, but it can be related either to such a root meaning 'pure' in Syriac (*pael* of *ḥl*) and Akkadian or to the root *ḥll* meaning 'profane' in Hebrew. Tarragon assumes the latter and sees here a desacralization of the king (so also Xella, TRU I, 26).[8] That may well be correct. Tarragon, however, seems to assume an order of purifying followed by desacralization. That is less clear from the text. I have gone with the meaning 'pure' but regard the matter as open. The form *ḥl* is difficult. One would expect *yḥl* or *ḥll* (i.e. either N stem or D stem). This appears to be a G stem perfect or infinitive. The plural translation is derived from the reference to the *mḥllm* in 1.23′.

Line 5: The principal uncertainty here is the word *brr*, which can be either an active participle *bārir* or a passive participle *barūr*. The issue is whether it refers to the king's state, as context suggests, or the king's role as purifier, as some analogies would suggest. I would opt for the former in line with the analysis of Tarragon (pp. 79-82), i.e. the king engages in ablutions which serve to cleanse or purify him.

Line 6: *qdš il* could be understood as 'the sanctuary of El' (so Herdner) or 'consecrated for El' (so Xella). The other three uses of *gdlt* in sequence here followed by *l-* indicating one for whom the offering is set suggest that *l* should be restored before *qdš*. The pairing with *lb'lm*, 'for the baals', suggests that *qdš* also is the plural 'holy ones', either the members of the divine assembly in general or the coterie of El. The plural *b'lm* appears several times in ritual texts, and several Baals associated with particular places are named.

Line 7: *g<d>lt* is to be restored at the end of the line. *ǵlm* would seem to refer to a deity although the use of this term with reference to messenger deities of Baal or Yam and the pairing with the dual *ǵlmtm* in 1.8 would lead us to expect *glmm* and indeed there may have been a haplography. (The text shows a high degree of scribal error, e.g. *r'kt*[1.2], *wglt*[1.7], *lgrt*[1.10], *lmdgl*[1.12], etc.)

Line 8: The two *ǵlmtm* are unidentified though they may be Anat and Aṯtart. *bt* elsewhere in this text refers to the temple of Baal at Ugarit and therefore may be presumed to do so here also. It is either an adverbial accusative or there has been a haplography of the preposition *b* before *bt*. The presence of labials before and after the preposition may have caused its omission. One notes in KTU 1.105

(= Ug. VII, p. 12) the expression *šb' alpm bt.b'l. ugrt*, where the preposition is missing.

Line 9: The word *tnrr* is unknown outside of this context. Xella's proposal to relate it to Akkadian *na'arruru(m)* is doubtful. I am simply following Herdner's proposal to see it as a D stem of *nyr/nwr* with a possible meaning that fits the context, i.e. 'consume' (cf. Tarragon, p. 63).

For *'d* as 'throne' or 'throne room' see the extended analysis of J.D. Shenkel, *Biblica* 46 (1965), pp. 404-409. In one of its other appearances in Ugaritic *'d* refers to a structure in Baal's house, which is the present context also.

Line 10: Tarragon notes that *ynt* is qualified by *qrt* seven times and suggests 'il s'agirait d'un oiseau familier au paysage urbain, sorte de pigeon' (p. 35).

Line 12: In KTU 1.39.10 (= CTA 34) *š ilt mgdl* appears, which may be a reference to the *mgdl b'l ugrt*. One notes that Krt is commanded to go up on a *mgdl* to sacrifice. It is customarily assumed that this *migdal* was a part of his palace, but inasmuch as the prayer for help is to Baal, it is likely in the light of the present text that the tower was a part of the temple of Baal at Ugarit.

Line 13: For the sacrificial terms *urm* and *šnpt* see Tarragon, pp. 62-66. The former term is the least clear and is here related to Hebrew *'ûr*. The latter term is to be related to Hebrew *t^enûpâ*. It is not clear whether the verb *lydbḥ* goes with the preceding words or the next line.

Line 14: While *il* in the ritual texts often refers to El, the centrality of Baal and the house and tower of Baal suggest that the *bt il* of this line refers to Baal's temple.

The meaning of *npš* is not altogether clear. In this immediate context as well as elsewhere in the ritual texts it is doubtful that it refers to a human being. Because of its relation to *ap* in some cases, Tarragon (pp. 40-41) suggests plausibly that the *npš* that is sacrificed is a lung.

Line 19': The first word is probably *utml*, 'yesterday', 'the preceding day'.

Line 23': The *mḥllm* may be associated with the Akkadian *mullilu(m)*, 'Reiniger' (*AHw*, p. 670). The *Chicago Assyrian Dictionary* (vol. M/II, p. 189) identifies this type of figure as 'a cultic functionary' or 'a sprinkler used for ritual cleaning' especially of the king.[9]

Line 24′: On two occasions Anat pours out *šmn šlm* in a bowl and washes herself, once after her blood bath against the warriors in KTU 1.3.II.31-32 (= *Ug*. V.3.2.4). The two occasions may be related when the latter text is compared with KTU 1.3.II.31-32 and the following column a few lines further on (KTU 1.3.III.4-7=CTA 3.C.1-3).

Line 25′: There is no reason to see a deity *Mlkm* in this context. Xella reads *Mlkt*, 'regina', which makes sense but acording to Pardee is less likely than *mlkm*. The plural, 'kings', also does not fit the context, so one must assume an enclitic *-m* on the end of *mlk*.

The final word of this line, *rišyt*, may be another term of an offering, i.e. 'fresh fruits'. The other possible meaning of *rišyt*, viz. 'the beginning', has been followed here. It has been suggested by Xella (TRU I, p. 33), who sees it as a liturgical indicator.[10] Such a translation provides the needed transition into the prayer to Baal. Otherwise, the shift in the next line is too abrupt and unaccounted for.

Line 26′: *gr* is from *gwr II*, 'attack', and so may be either masculine singular participle or 3 m.s. perfect tense. The collocation of *'z* + *gr*, i.e. a strong one attacking, occurs in Hebrew in Ps. 59.4. The use of this verb here in a prayer referring to an attacking enemy should make one hesitate to emend *gûr* in Ps. 56.7, 59.4 and 140.3 to *gdd* or *grh*.

Lines 28′-29′: The first-person dual ending *-ny* on *tǵr* and *ḥmyt* is puzzling. I have no better suggestion than that of Herdner, who sees the duality as possibly referring to the deity and the people. Inasmuch as this is a prayer to 'Baal of Ugarit', such an explanation is plausible. One notes other cases of dual where one would expect plural, e.g. KTU 1.15.V.20 (= CTA 15.V.20), *b'lny*.[11]

The prayer part of this text is clearly poetic as recognized by Herdner from the beginning and as one would expect for a prayer to the deity. The lines are balanced in rhythm, length, and meaning. That is, they form primarily bicola that are 3 + 3 in meter with a syllable count averaging 10 syllables per colon (± 2); the parallelism of lines is obvious. The initial address to the deity, *yb'lm*, in line 28′ is extra-metrical (cf. *yhwh 'dnynw* of Ps. 8.1). The colon would have sixteen syllables with the vocative included, which is much too long for this poem, or indeed most cola of Ugaritic poetry. The translation of lines 26′ff. is designed to show the poetic structure.

Lines 30'-31': The idiom *ml'* + *mḏr* is equivalent to the familiar *šlm* + *ndr* of the Psalms. Indeed the Ugaritic expression makes one wonder if the expression *pl'* (piel or hiphil) + *ndr* in Hebrew (Lev. 22.21; 27.3; Num. 6.2, 15.3, 8) could be a corruption of linguistic development out of *ml' ndr*, which would be a natural expression but does not occur in Hebrew.

The broken text of the word [ ]*kr* has been the primary center of discussion in the text since Herdner first proposed to read [*b*]*kr*, i.e. 'first-born', and understand it as a human sacrifice. Xella has measured the gap carefully and believes it is too narrow for /*b*/ but would be appropriate for /*d*/.[12] Pardee tentatively came up with the opposite conclusion (private communication). The matter apparently cannot be settled palaeographically. While the example of the king of Moab's sacrifice of his first-born in the battle against Israel (2 Kgs 3.27), cited by Herdner, would make a good analogy and the possibility of a human sacrifice cannot be ruled out in a situation such as envisioned here, I am inclined to agree with Xella that *dkr* is more suitable to the immediate context, i.e. the middle of the list of sacrifices, and comparison with other ritual texts where *bkr* does not occur but *dkr* does occur (KTU 1.86.2 [= PRU V, 158.2] and KTU 1.43.6 [= CTA 33.6]).[13]

Xella has called attention to the parallelism and semantic relationships between the first four sacrifices promised. The verb *qdš* refers to the consecration of the animal, and *ml'* to the actual carrying out of the sacrifice. He suggests, therefore, that *dkr* in this context refers to the *ibr* in l. 29 and identifies the victim while *mḏr*// *ḥtp*[14] designates the offering or sacrifice.

Finally with regard to these sacrifices, Herdner, following Dupont-Sommer's suggestion, may be correct in seeing all of them as collective, and thus referring to a number of bulls, etc.

Line 33': For *'šr* referring to a libation or liquid for drinking see KTU 1.3.I.8 (= CTA 3.I.8) and for its usage in parallel with *dbḥ* see KTU 1.16.I.39-41 (= CTA 16.I.39-41). *'šr. 'šr* appears in the ritual text KTU 1.43.2 (= CTA 33.2).

Genre and Structure

One of the knotty questions confronting the interpreter of this text is its unity. That issue is a problem even for understanding the Verso by itself. The relation of Recto and Verso to each other is even more problematic and the problem is not aided by the missing part of the tablet at the end of the Recto and the beginning of the Verso that might have clarified the relationship of the two parts of the tablet. Because what is clearly the first part of the tablet, the Recto, refers to the seventeenth and eighteenth days of the month while the second part, the Verso, speaks of the fourth, fifth, and seventh days, Herdner regards the two sides as independent texts.

That may well be the case, and the repetition on both sides of the tablet of the formula for the king washing himself tends to support that view. Certainly she is correct that the Verso can hardly be read as the straightforward continuation of the ritual process described on the Recto. But there are elements that link the two sides together also. One is the very presence of the king and not only in a repetitious way. On the Verso the king also sacrifices to Baal and pours out libations. The centrality of Baal and Baal's house or temple is clear on both sides of the text. The 'house/temple of Baal' is referred to twice explicitly on the Recto and probably alluded to two more times (ll. 8 and 14). It is referred to explicitly twice on the Verso (l. 34′) and alluded to once (l. 22′). Furthermore, Baal of Ugarit is the central deity on both sides, and the prayer of the city under attack, presumably Ugarit, is to its god Baal.

Thus, while the missing portion of the tablet prohibits us from seeing clearly how the Recto may lead into the Verso, that cannot be ruled out. It may be that the Recto describes a standard ritual for the month of *ib'lt* whereas the Verso suggests modifications or special rituals appropriate particularly for a military emergency. That certainly seems to be what we have there. Sacrifice is brought or offered on successive days followed by royal purification rites and libations. The king and people are instructed in appropriate petition to Baal of Ugarit when an enemy has come up against the city. The petition is essentially a vow to sacrifice and visit the temple if the deity delivers. The Verso may be understood without the Recto, but that does not necessarily mean it should be. Some of the actions on the Recto are not unlike those of Krt when he prepares for a military expedition. (See below.)

As to genre, the text is something of a mix. Up to the prayer it is a typical example of a descriptive ritual with a narrative *yqtl* sequence, formulaic style, and a focus on the sequence of sacrifices.[15] But at l. 26′ the text changes to the style and structure of a prescriptive ritual like much of the instruction in Leviticus or Deuteronomy. In his study of Ugaritic descriptive rituals Levine not only distinguished descriptive rituals, 'descriptions of what transpired on special occasions—the sequence of sacrifices to the various gods, and the rites which accompanied them', from prescriptive rituals, 'which set down the manner in which rites were to be performed', but he also distinguished the descriptive ritual texts from those such as KTU 1.40 and 43 (= CTA 32 and 33), which are 'semi-poetic and employ characteristic features of epic style . . . liturgies meant for recitation and perhaps dramatization as part of religious rites'.[16] It is clear as one looks at both sides of the tablet that all of these features are present in this text. Prescriptive ritual is joined to descriptive; poetic epic style is attached to formulaic prose.

The poetic epic character of ll. 26′ff. is seen when one recognizes that the closest parallels in Ugaritic are found in the Krt text both in El's instruction about sacrifice to Baal before Krt's expedition, which is analogous to ll. 26′-27′, and Krt's vow to Aṯirat that he will give gold and silver if he is able to take Hurriya to his house, which is analogous to ll. 28′-34′a. These last lines, the prayer to Baal, are specifically a vow. The characteristics of the vow in Ugaritic and Israelite literature that have been laid out in an essay by Simon Parker are all present here:[17]

(1) vocative adress to the deity (l. 28′a)
(2) protasis beginning with a conditional conjunction (*hm/ʾm*) stating the condition which the deity is asked to meet (verb in *yqtl*; ll. 28′b-29′b).
(3) apodosis is first person *yqtl* (or in Hebrew a consecutive *qtl*) indicating what the one vowing promises to give when the condition is met (ll. 29′c-34′a).

More precisely the structure of ll. 26′ff. can be described as follows:

Priestly Prescription
A. Occasion—enemy attack on the city
B. Required act—prayer to the city deity

Vow
A. Address to the deity
B. Request of the deity for help (conditional clause)
C. Promise of devotion when help granted

1. Sacrifice sequence (animal consecrated → sacrifice completed)
   a. bull
   b. libation
2. Worship at the deity's temple

Announcement of divine response:
A. Prayer has been heard
B. The deity will deliver

KTU 1.119 in the context of Ugaritic and Israelite literature

The descriptive ritual part of this tablet shares many affinities with other descriptive ritual texts from Ugarit. It is also the case that it resonates with what we read in the epic texts, particularly with regard to the activity of the king. The joining of prayer with sacrifice to the gods is seen in the Aqhat tale: Danel sacrifices and then Paghat on the basis of her father's sacrifice prays for blessing before taking off on her mission to avenge her brother's death (KTU 1.19.IV.28-35=CTA 19.IV.190-97). Even more significant is the similarity between our text and components of Krt's expedition on behalf of a wife. We have already noted the structural similarity between Krt's vow and the vow of the people in the prayer to Baal. The vow of Krt is made in the sanctuary of Aṯirat. Nothing is said of sacrifice in this context though it may well have accompanied the vow.

The first part of the Krt epic is strikingly analogous to KTU 1.119. When the king is weeping because of the demise of his family and asks El for children, the god gives him instructions for purification, sacrifice, and libations (KTU 1.14.II.7-26=CTA 14.60-80). The similarity to what takes place in KTU 1.119 is not precise, but a number of elements are shared by the two texts. The king washes himself (*trtḥṣ/yrtḥṣ*). The sacrifices include lamb(s) (*imr*) and bird(s) (*'ṣr*). The king lifts his hands to heaven (cf. KTU 1.119.27'). The sacrifices are made to Baal and El, apparently to seek their support in the military adventure that lies ahead. The specific prayer of Krt is not given though one would expect it to be like prayer to Baal in the text under consideration. With reference to the instruction in KTU 1.119.12 to sacrifice 'a bull for the tower of Baal of Ugarit', that would seem to have its narrative reflex in Krt's going up to 'the top of the tower (*mgdl*)' to make his sacrifice (KTU 1.14.II.20-21; cf. 11.26-27). Such actions are consistent with what we know of the Baal temple at Ugarit, as well as the reference to the king sacrificing on a roof (*gg*) in the ritual text KTU 1.41.50=CTA 35.50. One may infer, therefore, that royal sacrifices were made on the walls or roof of the Baal temple and that royal sacrifices and prayers to secure the protection and support of Baal of Ugarit for the city and the military endeavors of the king and his army took place along the lines set forth in KTU 1.119.

KTU 1.119 in relation to Israelite prayer and ritual

The student of Ugaritic and Israelite literature is not surprised to find congruences between the two. That is no less true with regard to the prayer to Baal text than it has been of other Ugaritic texts when examined in relation to Israelite texts and practices. We have indicated the formal similarities to the vow in Israelite literature, a likeness that could be extended to other texts such as Num. 21.1-4 and Judg. 11.30-32, both of which have to do with vows to the deity in situations of military conflict, seeking God's help to defeat the enemy. The resemblances are rather sharp, even though the Ugaritic vow is in the context of ritual prescription while the biblical vows are parts of narrative reports. Not only do we have the formal and material similarity of a conditional clause asking the deity's help in overcoming the enemy and an apodosis vowing sacrifices to the deity when the help is given, but in all three cases the report is given that the deity responded. In KTU 1.119 and Num. 21.3 the texts explicitly report that Baal and Yahweh hear (*šmʿ*) the prayer and drive the enemy out (KTU 1.119) or give them over (Num. 21.3). It should be noted, further, that while the balance of evidence appears to us to weigh against reading [*b*]*kr* in l. 31′ and seeing it as a reference to human sacrifice, not only does the sacrifice of his first-born by the king of Moab to secure the deity's help against Israel (2 Kgs 3.26-27) suggest, by analogy, such an interpretation as a possibility, but both the Numbers 21 and Judges 11 texts also report dedication of human beings to the deity as the gift that is offered in return for the deity's help.

The prayer to Baal is formally a vow, but it has affinities also with the biblical laments or complaints. Indeed vow and lament belong together in the biblical Psalms, although there the vows are only reported and the laments spelled out while in KTU 1.119 it is the vow that is spelled out. The (priestly) bracket around the prayer to

Baal (ll. 26′-27′ and 35′-36′) is an important connection to the biblical laments. Before the prayer it serves to identify the *situation of crisis*, i.e. the reason for the petition; after the prayer it announces Baal's *response* and *deliverance*. The latter is especially important. It has the characteristic elements of the divine response to complaints as one often encounters them in the lament Psalms and the oracle of salvation in Deutero-Isaiah:

a. announcement that the deity has heard or will hear the prayer (*qtl* or *wyqtl* verb forms normally)
b. announcement of the deity's delivering action, i.e. he will do what the petition sought (*yqtl*).

These clear words declaring the deity's turning toward the petitioners and acting in their behalf are not always present or there may be only one element explicitly stated. At the turning point of Psalm 22 the petitioner says:

> Save me from the mouth of the lion;
> from the horns of the wild oxen you have answered me (v. 22).

Later in the Psalm the word is repeated:

> When he cried to him, he heard (v. 25).

In Psalm 28 the one praying concludes:

> Blessed be the Lord!
> for he has heard the voice of my supplications.

The double announcement that God has heard and will deliver is best seen at the end of Psalm 6:

> Depart from me, all you workers of evil;
> for the Lord has heard the sound of my weeping.
> The Lord has heard my supplication;
> the Lord accepts my prayer.
> All my enemies shall be ashamed and terrified greatly;
> they shall turn back and be put to shame in a moment (vv. 9-11).

In the oracles of salvation in Isa. 41.8-13 and 14-16 the turning of God to lamenting Israel is stated in perfect tense verbs (*qtl*) in vv. 10b and 14b followed by the spelling out of what God will do to Israel's enemies in imperfect-tense (*yqtl*) verbs.

The story of Hannah's visit to the temple at Shiloh (1 Sam. 1) is instructive when compared with KTU 1.119. While little detail is given about the ritual activity involved, the story does show clearly the interaction of *lament* and *vow*. As already indicated, the structure of Hannah's vow is the same as that in KTU 1.119, although in the former it is the vow of an individual, while in the latter case it is communal. But the narrative places the vow within the context of supplication and weeping, i.e. lament or complaint,[18] even as the vow of KTU 1.119 is described as 'prayer' (*ṣlt*).[19] The prayer is granted by the deity and that word is brought by the priest, as presumably is the case in KTU 1.119.34′-36′. One notes further that we have here a *particular* petition and vow to the deity set in the context of *regular* sacrifice ritual. There are significant differences in that Hannah's prayer is not identified as set within an actual prescribed ritual. But the fact that she takes the occasion of their regular worship and sacrifice to make a special petition suggests that a text which incorporates within descriptive ritual for *recurring* sacrificial activities (note 1 Sam. 1 is set in the context of yearly sacrifice at Shiloh) a prescription for petition to the deity for help in a particular crisis is not outside the realm of intelligibility.

As in the prayer to Baal so in the Psalms of Israel, which are or reflect the petitions that accompanied ritual in situations of distress, vow and prayer come together:

> For you, O Lord, have heard my vows (*šāmaʿtā lindārāy*);
> you have granted the wish (*'ršt* for *yršt*) of those
> that fear your name.

Sacrifice (e.g. Ps. 46.12) and going to the shrine (Ps. 22.23, 26; 122.1-4) are the critical or primary dimensions of the vows or the response to the deity's hearing of the prayer. In several respects Ps. 66.13ff. brings together features reminiscent of the vow-prayer prescribed in KTU 1.119. The 'I' of the Psalm may well be the king who responds to God for the help that has been given to the people. In the closing verses the king promises to come to God's house (*bêtekā*) with sacrifices (v. 13). The vows uttered in time of trouble will be paid (vv. 13-14). These vows are clearly sacrifices, and types of sacrifice and sacrificial victims are spelled out as in the prayer to Baal (vv. 13a, 15). Explicit declaration that God has heard (*šāmaʿ*) the prayer (*tᵉpillātî*) concludes the Psalm.

So it is that this unique text from Ugarit reminds us again of the continuities in the religious practices of peoples and groups within Syria-Palestine, continuities that neither obscure the complexity and particularity of any single unity nor are confined to the rituals of Ugarit and Israel.[20]

NOTES

1. W.W. Hallo, 'Individual Prayer in Sumerian: The Continuity of a Tradition', *JAOS* 88 (1968), pp. 71-89.
2. Hallo, p. 72.
3. *Ugaritica* VII, pp. 31-39.
4. The prayer part of the text was first published by Mlle A. Herdner in *CRAIBL* (1973), pp. 693-97.
5. KTU has *'rb* for the first word, but the photograph in *Ugaritic* VII, p. 144, clearly shows the sign for /*k*/, as Milik read it in the *editio princeps*.
6. Milik translates 'Propriétaires, notables, de Ḫalba', plutôt que "Ba'l d'Alep"'. That makes good sense and may be correct. The several occurrences of *b'l ḫlb* as a divine name, however, tip the scales in that direction.
7. On this form of *šm'* see 1 Sam. 15.4 and 23.8, as well as Milik's discussion in *Ugaritica* VII, p. 143.
8. J.M. de Tarragon, *Le culte à Ugarit* (Paris: J. Gabalda, 1980), p. 84.
9. So also Xella, *TRU*, I, pp. 32-33.
10. '*rišyt*: indico l' "inizio" della recitazione della preghiera ed è quindi una prescripzione liturgica'. B. Levine, 'Ugaritic Descriptive Rituals', *JCS* 17 (1963), p. 106, notes that rituals are not infrequently interrupted by recitations or dramatizations and that in poetic and semi-poetic texts we occasionally find instructions to the officiant.
11. See the discussion of this in H.L. Ginsberg, *The Legend of King Keret* (BASOR Supplementary Series, 2-3; New Haven: ASOR, 1946), p. 43.
12. P. Xella, 'Un testo ugaritico recente (RS 24.266, Vs. 9-19) e il "sacrificio dei primi nati"', *RSF* 6 (1978), p. 134.
13. Xella properly follows KTU in assuming a scribal error (*drk* for *dkr*) in the second example.
14. On the *ḫitpu* sacrifice see *ḫatāpu* and *ḫitpu* in CAD or *AHw* as well as Xella's discussion in *RSF* 6, p. 135.
15. Cf. Levine, p. 105.
16. Levine, p. 105.
17. S. Parker, 'The Vow in Ugaritic and Israelite Narrative Literature', *UF* 11 (1979), p. 694.

18. For linguistic and other relationships between Psalm 6 and 1 Samuel 1 see P.D. Miller, 'Trouble and Woe: Interpreting the Biblical Laments', *Interpretation* 37 (1983), pp. 32-45.

19. In his important article 'Psalms and Inscriptions of Petition and Acknowledgement', in A. Marx (ed.), *Louis Ginzberg Jubilee Volume* (New York: American Academy for Jewish Research, 1945), pp. 159-71, H.L. Ginsberg argued that *nzr* in the Bar Hadad stele should be translated 'prayed' instead of 'vowed' and cited additional evidence for Northwest Semitic texts, including biblical ones. KTU 1.119 is a good indication of the fact that the distinction and the argument are essentially unnecessary. Petition and vow belong together.

20. Ginsberg's article gives an indication of other and later examples of such continuities.

10

SECOND THOUGHTS ON EBLA AND THE OLD TESTAMENT

L.M. Muntingh

Professor F.C. Fensham has made a contribution to various aspects of Old Testament study and to the study of Semitic languages. To the best of my knowledge, he was the first to publish a scholarly article in South Africa on the spectacular discoveries at Tell Mardikh-Ebla (Fensham 1977a; cf. 1980: 154). As his former student and colleague, I thus deem it an honour to present this paper to him.

After the initial conclusions of G. Pettinato, the former epigrapher of the Italian Archaeological Mission to Syria (see e.g. Freedman 1978), concerning Ebla and the Bible, a process of re-evaluation has already started. Recently J.D. Muhly (1984) stated:

> The present controversy over Ebla and the Bible should not be seen as something new in the history of Assyriology but rather as the latest episode of an ongoing debate that has dominated the field from its inception over one hundred years ago. Various attempts have been made to 'secularize' the field and to establish Assyriology as an independent discipline, free from any direct asociations with Old Testament or biblical studies.

R. Biggs has also pointed out that archaeological discoveries often attract wide-spread publicity and popular attention: tablets that reveal a Babylonian flood story, Mari, Nuzi, Ugarit, the Dead Sea Scrolls and now Ebla. Most of the excitement about these finds, he says, can be attributed directly to a concern with the Bible and the claims that were made concerning their relevance for the Bible. He starts with the problem of *reading* the Ebla texts. He has been working with the Sumerian tablets from Abū Ṣalābīkh, a site in Iraq. These tablets are close in date to the Ebla tablets and therefore he is familiar with the difficulties and ambiguities involved in reading cuneiform writing of the mid-third millennium BC (1980: 76ff.).

Pettinato, in the meantime, has warned against the rising tendency to Pan-eblaitism like the earlier Pan-babylonism and Pan-ugaritism (1977a: 242-43; cf. Dahood 1978: 107-109). P. Matthiae, the director of the Italian Archaeological Mission to Syria, who has always been cautious to draw inferences regarding a connection between Ebla and the Bible, as is evident from his major publication, *Ebla un empero ritrovato* (1977), emphatically denies such a connection in his preface to the English edition (1980: 11).

Thus, a *Babel und Bibel* controversy, or its opposite, is futile, but the assumption that the Old Testament, which originated from the ancient Near East, has strong ties with its environment, cannot be neglected. Fensham agrees with J. Barr in so far as his criticism is directed against Arabophiles and Ugaritophiles, but then he correctly states that it is unnecessary to liquidate philology because of certain excesses of over-zealous interpreters. The only way to understand a Ugaritic text, for instance, is to use the meanings of other Semitic languages from the same stem. Philological study, he continues, has considerably advanced our knowledge of biblical Hebrew on various points, as Barr has admitted (Fensham 1971a: 53).

One point, dealing with the distinctiveness of the Bible compared with its *Umwelt*, is still to be made. A decade ago Barr, in a survey of trends and prospects in Old Testament theology, noticed a shift of emphasis in G.E. Wright's approach to the covenant: instead of its being treated as 'utterly distinct', its conformity to a common Near Eastern pattern had been defended. Barr also refers to B. Albrecktson's *History and the Gods* (1967), according to which not only the God of Israel 'acted in history', but also the gods of other nations (Barr 1974: 266-68; see, however, Lambert 1972). We shall return to the question of whether extra-biblical texts shed light on the distinctiveness of the Old Testament.

Starting from this point, I shall discuss a few matters concerning which, to my mind, the discoveries at Ebla can further our knowledge of the Old Testament and the biblical world.

I. *Eblaite and Hebrew*

The entire archive excavated at Ebla in 1974-76 contains approximately 4000 tablets, of which 1800 are complete and date from around 2600–2500 BC (Pettinato 1979a: xvii). The majority of these tablets deal with economic reports of expenses or acquisitions by the royal palace (Pettinato 1980a; Edzard 1981; Archi-Biga 1982). Other texts contain lists of various professions, animals, birds, fish, geographical names and bilingual texts with Sumerian-Eblaite lexical lists, treaties, letters and incantations. By means of the lexical lists Pettinato reconstructed the vocabulary of Ebla (Pettinato 1981a; 1982; Viganò 1984: 8-9).

Since the discovery of the tablets and the identification of the language of Ebla (Eblaite), it has been a subject of intensive study (see e.g. Cagni 1981).[1] Pettinato, who formerly estimated that 80% of the Ebla texts were written in Sumerian and 20% in Eblaite (1977a: 238), later assumed that the bilingualism was only apparent. The Sumerian terms are in reality logograms and all of them were read in Eblaite (1981b: 57). I.J. Gelb also holds that the great majority of the Ebla texts were written in Eblaite and not in Sumerian (Gelb 1981: 11, 13; cf. Viganò 1984: 12). Our sources for the study of Eblaite are limited to the bilingual lexical lists, personal and geographical names, but no narrative or literary Eblaite text is yet available. Thus we are here in more or less the same situation as with Amorite.

Regarding the classification of the language of Ebla, scholars hold two main positions (Viganò 1984: 12-13): either Eblaite is a Northwest Semitic language, or its closest linguistic relative is Old Akkadian.

a. *Northwest Semitic language*

Pettinato identified Eblaite for the first time in 1975, classified it as Northwest Semitic and called it Old-Canaanite (Pettinato 1979b). It is to be distinguished clearly from Old Akkadian and from Old Amorite, whereas on the other hand it is closely related to Ugaritic, Phoenician and Hebrew.

G. Garbini (1978; 1981: 78-79) assumes that the language of Ebla owes its peculiar character to the fact that, whereas the vocabulary has its broadest terms of comparison in Northwestern Semitic, the morphology corresponds substantially to that of Akkadian. 'The language of Ebla has now made us change this idea (viz. of Akkadian as 'Eastern' Semitic): Akkadian differs from Western Semitic as we knew it hitherto because the latter was documented only on the phase following the Amorite innovation.'

Contrary to Gelb's earlier viewpoint (1961) on the basis of onomastic and toponymic evidence that in Northern Syria and in nearby regions east of the Euphrates there are no traces of a West Semitic presence until about the end of the third millennium BC, the discoveries at Tell Mardikh testify to the presence of a West Semitic chancery language, different from Amorite, in the Sargonic period (Fronzaroli 1977a: 145-46; 1977b: 31).

In numerous publications the late M.J. Dahood related Eblaite to the Northwest Semitic languages, especially Hebrew (Martinez 1981). He was aware of scholars who considered the chronological chasm of more than a millennium separating Ebla and the Bible as a serious obstacle, but Dahood argued that Ugarit, just 85 kilometers southwest of Ebla on the coast, has been a link between the two.[2] Not only is Ugarit mentioned in the Ebla archive, but Eblaite had already shed light on some problematic Ugaritic phrases (Dahood–Pettinato 1977: 230-32; Dahood 1981c: 380-82). His approach is clear from the following statement: 'While deploring over-zealous use by biblicists of Northwest Semitic material, one should never lose to sight the centrality of Biblical Hebrew for an understanding of ancient Canaan, and a mastery of same remains the best preparation for the interpretation of the Ebla Canaanite texts' (Dahood 1978: 101 n. 81). Dahood (1981a) went even further than Pettinato by regarding Eblaite's closest kinship as being neither Ugaritic nor Phoenician, but rather late second- and first-millennium Biblical Hebrew of Palestine. To prove the close kinship, he applied seven criteria (cf. Dahood 1982: 5), and offered many illustrations of the application of his methods, hoping that gradually the great discoveries at Ugarit and Ebla would help to put more rigorous and coherent translations of the Old Testament in the hands of readers. Just as postbiblical Hebrew represents a stage in the organic life of the same culture, tradition and language, so Eblaite and Biblical Hebrew are mutually elucidating and defining because they represent successive stages of the same Canaanite language and tradition (Dahood 1982: 3, 4; see p. 18 on the 'Canaanite Connection').

Dahood's methods, already applied in relating Ugaritic to Biblical Hebrew, have not been generally accepted. He accumulated a lot of material and some of his conclusions may stand the test of time. One gets the impression, however, of a preconceived position, as if Eblaite's closest kin *should* be Biblical Hebrew.

b. *Old Akkadian and Amorite*

Gelb presents a list of twenty-six linguistic features in the form of a chart to show the relationship of Eblaite to Old Akkadian, Amorite, Ugaritic and Hebrew. According to the chart, the closest linguistic relatives of Eblaite are Old Akkadian and Amorite, with Ugaritic farther and Hebrew (Canaanite) still farther away. Furthermore, Eblaite cannot be considered an Akkadian dialect, neither can it be called Amorite, while the question whether Eblaite is to be considered a West Semitic language is not easy to answer. The whole question of what West Semitic is, Gelb says, is to be reconsidered. Gelb himself disregards all such divisions as 'Eastern' and 'Western', 'Northwestern' and 'Southwestern' Semitic languages, and simply lists, in chronological order, the eight attested Semitic languages: Akkadian, Amorite, Ugaritic, Canaanite, Aramaic, (classical) Arabic, South Arabic and Ethiopic, with their dialects. Eblaite is to be added to this list as a ninth Semitic language having the closest relationship with Old Akkadian and Amorite (Gelb 1977: 24-28; cf. 1981: 46-52).

E. Ullendorff (1978) fully agrees with Gelb that matters of linguistic relationship must be based on linguistic criteria and not on extraneous aspects such as cultural or religious ties or even on the occurrence of Old Testament personal names (e.g. Abraham, Israel, David, etc.) (cf. Gelb 1977:16). However, he regards Gelb's list of twenty-six linguistic features as, at best, preliminary, while from Gelb's own assessments there is not much to choose between Akkadian and Ugaritic. Finally, Ullendorff criticizes Gelb's avoidance of geographical terms in connection with the Semitic languages. He finds the chronological order of Gelb's eight attested Semitic languages odd, while the description of Eblaite as the ninth is highly arbitrary. Ullendorff concludes that the most urgent task is not the 'elucidation of interrelationships' but a simple, straightforward and full descriptive analysis of Eblaite. This is true, but I fear that at present Ullendorff's ideal will not easily be reached. The sources available are such that one can hardly study Eblaite without the help of cognate languages.

II. *Treaty and Covenant*

> The study of the ancient Near Eastern 'covenant' or 'treaty' has had far-reaching implications for Old Testament studies over the past decades. It has revealed more than a fundamental historico-political phenomenon, helping us to understanding afresh the relations between the Israelites and their neighbours. The covenant idea and its terminology has been shown to form the warp and woof of the fabric of ancient society. W. Zimmerli, in the latest survey of the history of Israelite religion to appear, reminds us that covenant is still the key word of Israelite faith and is best applied to the relation of the people with their God (Wiseman 1982: 311).

The structural form(ularies), and to a large extent the language, of these oath-bound covenants are common to the peoples of the ancient Near East from the fourth millennium to the Hellenistic and Roman periods. Texts from Ebla, Ras Shamra and other sites show us that they are basically 'Mesopotamian' in form and concept, and bound up with the cultural and legal traditions of that area. Valuable and penetrating studies of the covenant terminology have been done by several scholars, e.g. by D.R. Hillers and F.C. Fensham on the treaty-curses or maledictions (Wiseman, pp. 311-12; cf. Fensham 1963). In fact, in several publications Fensham contributed to the study of ancient Near Eastern treaties and covenants in relation to the Old and New Testament (Fensham 1967, 1971b).

At least ten treaties have been discovered in the archives of Ebla, of which TM.75.G.2420 seems to be the most important. Scholars differ, however, on the interpretation of the text. Pettinato holds that it is a commercial treaty, concluded between the king of Ebla and the king of Ashur (1976a: 48; 1976b: 14; 1979a: 177 No. 1859; 1981b: 103-105, 121; cf. McCarthy 1978: 34-35). A long introduction is followed by the body of the treaty, and curse formulas conclude it. 'Despite the generosity of the king of Ebla, the malediction addressed to the king of Ashur leaves no doubt about the superiority of Ebla over Ashur' (Pettinato 1981: 105).

E. Sollberger (1980: 129-31), however, reads the toponym 'Abarsal' instead of 'Ashur'. He acknowledges that he had to leave several passages in the text untranslated or simply did not understand them. 'But it should be borne in mind that the study of Eblaic is still in its infancy . . . ' (p. 132). As to the structure of the text, he agrees with Pettinato and divides it into three main parts: the preamble (lines 1-111), the clauses of the treaty (lines 112-607), and the curse formulas, normally expected at the end of a treaty (lines 608-23). The preamble seems to end with a warning about the consequences of not abiding by the agreement: 'Whomever the king curses, or the district curses, or the country curses, shall die' (lines 106-111) (Sollberger, pp. 134, 136). Lines 393-417 seem to establish Ebla's exclusive rights to the waterways trade with Abarsal. The agreement also provides for a kind of annual dues to be paid by Abarsal (Sollberger, p. 142). Sollberger (p. 147; cf. Pettinato 1981b: 105) translates the curse formulas as follows:

> All (those who)... assemble for evil (purposes) Šamas, Adad, (and)... shall cause its (that assembly's) words to perish in (its) bile. To (its) couriers who go on (their) travels, no one shall bring drinking-water nor (?) (give) shelter. And you (Abarsal) (if) you go on an evil expedition you shall be cast out.

Recently Viganò (1984: 8-9), in agreement with Pettinato, regards the text as a treaty between Ebla and Ashur and as one of the few historical texts yet found at Ebla. It is a long commercial agreement regulating trade between the two cities, which he summarizes as follows:

> It starts by listing the localities under their respective jurisdictions; then it gives regulations about trade, taking special care to avoid a double taxation of merchants. Messengers are the concern of the next section, which sets up rules that will assure their food supplies and lodging during their travels. Another important section contains regulations for the release of citizens kept in custody in the foreign city. The treaty ends with a curse in uncommon form in the name of the Sun-god, of Haddad, and of the assembly of gods.

Thus we have here a mid-third millennium witness of malediction and curses that, besides benediction, was still characteristic of much later treaties, as Fensham (1962, 1963) and others have pointed out.

A fine example of diplomatic correspondence is to be found in what is probably another treaty (TM.G.2342), namely between Ebla and the kingdom of Ḫamazi in Northern Iran, more than a thousand kilometers away. Pettinato, who studied this text (1977a: 238-42; 1979a: 169 No. 1781; 1981b: 96-98; cf. McCarthy 1979: 247-48), comments that the recurring phrase, 'you are my brother, I am your brother' (I.8–II.2, etc.) is purely Near Eastern in style, showing the constancy of certain traditions in Syria down the centuries. 'Only a very close alliance between the states will explain how the king of Ebla could turn to the king of Ḫamazi for some soldiers, in this case mercenaries.'

Does this letter (TM.75.G.2342) really prove that a treaty was concluded between Ebla and the kingdom of Ḫamazi? In structure it differs from the common treaty: a preamble and curse formulas as in TM.75.G.2420 are lacking. D.J. McCarthy (1978: 34-35) considers the latter as good evidence for the extension of the treaty tradition from Ebla into Syria in the third millennium BC, while the above-mentioned letter also uses the language and concepts of the treaties. The partners are 'brothers', aid (men or animals) is requested, and a counter-payment for it is made, with which the treaty of Asa with Damascus (1 Kgs 15.18-19) or Ahaz with Assyria (2 Kgs 16.7-9) two millennia later are to be compared. The letter also shows explicitly the role of subordinates in making a treaty (McCarthy 1979: 247-48).

Since the method and extent of diplomacy leading to the making of peace and to a full covenant relationship has been little studied either in the Old Testament or in the wider Near East, Wiseman makes such an attempt (1982: 314f.). He doubts whether McCarthy's interpretation of the first word *en-ma* as 'greeting' (= *ḥēn-ma* instead of *umma*)[4] is correct. The ten pieces of woodwork and two wooden ornaments given to the ambassador, rather than being a 'counter-payment' to the ambassador for aid requested, are more likely symbolic or token gifts similar to those given by Assyrian kings to departing dignitaries as part of the whole ritual of exchange of gifts in diplomacy. Elsewhere Wiseman criticizes McCarthy who sometimes presumes from the presence of a single term that a complete covenant relationship has been shown to exist (pp. 312-13).

This is a timely warning. On the other hand, Wiseman and other scholars give evidence that in 'covenant terminology' common words such as 'love', 'good', 'peace', etc. were used.

III. *Jurisprudence and Judges*

> Discoveries of ancient Near Eastern legal material make it clear that the legal tradition, as we also have it in the OT, started well back in the 3rd millennium BC (Fensham 1982: 682).

As a result of the discoveries at Ebla this legal tradition can be traced back to the middle of the third millennium BC. The juridical texts of Ebla concern contracts of purchase and sale and the division of goods and official loans (Pettinato 1981b: 46). In the bilingual lists the following entry appears: d i k u $_5$=*ba-da-qù da-ne-um*, 'to judge' (Pettinato 1981b: 242; 1982: 335 No. 1327).

One juridical document in the form of a letter (TM.75.G.1766) deals with a royal act according to which the king ceded to a high functionary, as a possession for a period of ten years, an agricultural property, thus immovable property. The document reads:

> Thus the king to Inkar, listen: for 10 years the king makes available and gives you the property in Baytayn that belongs to Tāb-Li'm, the inspector; I do not take it; for 10 years it is available and your residence shall be in the village; from time to time you shall reside in the village.
>
> The year in which the sacrifices are brought.

P. Fronzaroli, who studied and published this document, refers to similar documents of Ugarit, studied by G. Boyer, in which the kings appear as protagonists. The documents, formulated in a particular manner, contain the dynastic seal and the names of witnesses (Boyer 1955: 284ff). Juridical documents from Hittite Hatussas, the kudurrus of the Kassite period, Middle-Assyrian and Elamite laws of ± 1600 BC should also be compared. Now the tablet, cited above, enables us to compare the juridical institutions of the third millennium in Syria with those of the second millennium BC. Though the names of neither protagonist nor receiver are mentioned, and a dynastic seal as well as the names of witnesses are missing, the person of the king is in clear relief. This document, as well as others (e.g. TM.75.G.1430 and TM.75.G.1452), bears witness that juridical texts were stored in the archives of Ebla. The last-mentioned text (cf. Pettinato 1979a: 67-68, No. 890), dating from the time of king Ebrium, explicitly states that it deals with a 'decision of the king and a decision of the lord' (d i - k u $_5$ e n *wa* s a - MI + ŠITA$^{ki}_{x}$ d i - k u $_5$) (Fronzaroli 1979: 3-16).[5]

If Pettinato's conclusions are valid, the Old Testament 'judges' (*šôf^{e}tîm*) have their counterpart in Ebla. Fensham (1959) holds that in Akkadian (including the Mari tablets) and Ugaritic material earlier than the 13th century BC, thus pointing to a very ancient use, the stem *špṭ* was used both for 'to judge' and 'to govern', and that still applied to the Israelite 'judges'.

Pettinato argues that d i - k u $_5$, 'judge', in the Ebla texts evokes the 'judges' of the Old Testament. He relates the judges of Ebla to their counterparts in the Old Testament because in Eblaite the term 'judge' is synonymous with l u g a l, which designates a 'governor' of the kingdom (TM.75.G.1261 and *passim*), a meaning that it never bears in Mesopotamia but only in the Old Testament where the judges were also 'rulers' of the people (Pettinato 1976a: 47; 1980b: 208). The assembly of Elders consisted of notables, including the l u g a l or d i - k u $_5$ (Grégoire 1981: 387 n. 36).

In a note added to Pettinato 1980b, J.A. Soggin (1980) states that it is a well-known fact that the Hebrew term *šôpᵉṭîm* for Israel's army leaders in its pre-history period does not have a forensic function, but indicates a variety of leaders. The phenomenon is also attested by other Northwest Semitic languages (Mari, Ugaritic and Phoenician). Thus, in Biblical Hebrew *špṭ* is used with a double meaning: for the process of adjudication and to designate political and military activity.

Archi (1979a: 561; 1981a: 150-51), on the contrary, does not accept that Eblaite d i - k u $_5$ can be regarded as a counterpart of the Old Testament 'judges'. The term d i - k u $_5$ appears quite frequently in Mesopotamian administrative texts since the third millennium, but it has never been related to biblical analogies. Although it is difficult to define the exact function of the Eblaite 'judges', they were certainly officials of the palace organization, while the biblical 'judges' were some kind of functionaries of tribal organizations in pre-monarchic Israel. Furthermore, Pettinato does not provide the evidence that the Sumerogram d i - k u $_5$ is truly synonymous with l u g a l at Ebla. While Pettinato tries to relate d i k u $_5$ to a term derived from the root *špṭ*, he elsewhere cites a bilingual text (TM.75.G.10023) where d i k u $_5$=*ba-da-qù da-ne-um* but should rather consider a term derived from the root *dīn* (cf. Mari *dajānu*= d i—k u $_5$ besides *šāpiṭu*, and Ugaritic *dn* besides *ṯpṭ*).

Thus it may be that Pettinato's comparison of Eblaite d i - k u $_5$ with Old Testament 'judges' is forced. On the other hand kingship and urbanization in Ebla by the middle of the third millennium BC do not exclude the existence of tribes and tribal leaders in Mari in the eighteenth century (Kupper 1957). Ebla and Mari had strong relations (Pettinato 1977b; Archi 1981b) which will again be referred to below in connection with prophetism.

IV. *History of Religion*

The Ebla tablets also shed light on the history of ancient Near Eastern religion, of which the following aspects may be briefly mentioned.

1. *Polytheism*

The Ebla pantheon consists of about 500 divinities, including Dagan, in a pre-eminent position; Kamiš, later the principal god Chemosh of the Moabites; Rasap, later Resheph; Baal, later highly popular in Ugarit (Pettinato 1980c: 333ff.; 1980d; 1981b: 245ff.; Viganò 1984: 10-12; cf. Van Zijl 1972). While Pettinato holds that these divinities were predominantly Canaanite, Viganò states that Canaanite/Semitic deities such as the river god Balikh, ^{d}Kamiš and ^{d}Haddad played a minor role.

2. *Henotheism*

The Eblaites were essentially polytheistic, yet certain considerations such as the appellative 'lord' for Dagan (e.g. ^{d}*BE kà-na-na*, 'Lord of Canaan', thus *BE=bēlum*), the preponderance of the elements Il and Ya in the onomastica, as well as the hymn to the 'Lord of heaven and earth' suggest that the Eblaites had a quite advanced concept of the divine and were very near to henotheism, that is, the special worship of some particular divinity from among other existing deities. The 'Lord of heaven and earth' as creator is not Dagan, Rasap or Sipiš, but GOD written in capitals (Pettinato 1980c: 45-48; 1981b: 248-49). The hymn l u g a l an - k i, 'Lord of heaven and earth', reminds Pettinato of Genesis 1 (Pettinato 1977a: 231-32; 1980b: 208-23; 1981b: 244, 259-60). Archi, on the contrary, says that this is a Sumerian composition very difficult to understand, but he doubts that the similarity with Genesis 1 is self-evident (1979a: 561-62; 1981a: 151). Whatever the case may be, the relevant texts should be studied carefully.

3. *Yahweh in the Ebla texts?*

In his commentary on the book of Exodus (3.14) Fensham comments on the divine name YHWH. There are quite a variety of viewpoints as to its meaning. One has to make a clear distinction between the meaning of the name as such, and the theological implications of the name in the Old Testament. Fensham mentions three instances from outside Israel that may be related to Yahweh, the God of Israel: *yhw3* as a geographical term on an Egyptian incription found at Soleb in Nubia (cf. Herrmann 1975: 76-77), the element *yahwi-* in Amorite personal names such as Yahwi-ila (cf. Huffmon 1965: 71-73), and Eblaite personal names such as Mi-kà-yà, 'Who is like Ya (Yahweh)?' and Iš-ra-ya (Fensham 1977b: 25-26, 29).

Whether a god Ya(w) is indeed testified by the Ebla texts has been much debated in recent years. There are four main positions, depending on the reading and interpretation of the cuneiform sign NI:

a. Read by Pettinato as *ià* which, at least in some cases, e.g. in Mi-ka-yà with the alternation Mi-ka-il, is not a hycoristicon and demonstrates that at Ebla Yà has the same value as Il and points to a specific deity. The form Ya may be considered a shortened form of Yaw, as may be inferred from personal names such as Šu-mi-a-u compared with Šu-mi-a. In the personal name ^{d}ià-ra-mu, 'Ya is exalted', with the same meaning as the Biblical name Joram, the theophoric function of Ya in some personal names is evident (Pettinato 1976a: 48; 1980b: 203-205; 1980c: 43-45; 1981b: 248-49). Two cases of ^{d}*yà* in god lists from Fara have been identified (Mander 1980: 190-91). Dahood, with reference to F. Böhl (1909: 89) who considered the *-ya* at the end of personal names as probably pointing to the divine name Yahweh in the Amarna period, as well as to many Ugaritic personal names that end in -y, argues that *-yà* can be considered a divine element. Dahood related this name to biblical Yah and Yahweh and tried to square the pre-Abrahamic designation of God as Ya with biblical tradition as in Gen. 4.26 and Exod. 3.15 (Dahood 1978: 105-107; 1981a: 186-87; 1981b: 276-77).

b. Read as *ià* by Archi, who regards the ending *-ià* as a hypocoristicon. He reads the above-mentioned personal name ^{d}ià-ra-mu as AN.NI-ra-mu=il-ì-ra-mu, 'my god is exalted', a name also attested at Mari and Ugarit. The sign AN=il is, however, unusual. Archi finds in the epigraphic documentation of Ebla no element favouring the presence of Yaw, whose name is considered an archaic form of Yahweh (Archi 1979a: 556-60; 1979b; 1981a: 145-46; cf. Fronzaroli 1977b: 35).

c. H.-P. Müller, who has problems in explaining NI=*ì(a)* as a hypocoristic ending, regards NI as a fixed abbreviated form and reads *ì-li* (*ilī*), 'my god', the expression of a personal god met all over the ancient Near East (Müller 1980a: 162; 1980b: 5; 1981a: 306; 1981b: 80). The concept 'my god' as a personal god in the ancient Near East and the Old Testament is fully discussed by Vorländer (1975).

d. I.J. Gelb formerly read -NI only as *-ni* which, besides *-na*, indicates the suffix of the first person plural. Consequently, the second of the pair of personal names Iš-ra-il/Iš-ra-ni was incomprehensible to him, though it was obviously related to Hebrew 'Israel' (Gelb 1977: 20-21). Pettinato (1981b: 249) reads the second name Iš-ra-ìa. Based on later evidence from Ebla, Gelb accepts that the sign NI alone indeed has the syllabic value *ìà*; consequently one may assume that hypocoristic names ending in NI=*ìà* existed at Ebla, though every NI appearing in the final position of a name should not automatically be interpreted as the hypocoristic *-ìà*. It would even be absurd to interpret every final -NI as the hypocoristic *-ìà* (or the divine name -Ya/Yahweh) (Gelb 1981: 26-30).

Thus we have to agree with Viganò (1984: 12) that, because of the ambiguity of the cuneiform writing system, a completely decisive form in favour of the interpretation of a divine name has not yet appeared. We also have to agree with Archi (1979a: 560) who concludes: 'It seems clear that even if there were an Amorite or a more generally West Semitic god named Yahweh, he did not correspond to what Yahweh meant for Israel'. In order to determine the meaning of the divine name Yahweh for Israel, Müller (1981a) attempts to interpret the well-known Exod. 3.14 in the light of the Ebla texts. We have to realize, however, that in the Old Testament it is not the name Yahweh as such and its etymology that counts, but its theological meaning.

4. *Prophetism*

Foreign priests in Ebla belonged to the category of the *na-bi-ù-tum*, 'prophets', who came from Mari (TM.75.G.454). The term *nabi'ūtum* (pl. nom.) is derived from the root *nb'/nby*, 'to call, announce' (Pettinato 1981b: 119, 253; Gelb 1981: 31). In a bilingual vocabulary from Ebla (TM.75.G.2000, rev. VII 36) the Sumerian word *pà*, 'to speak', recite', is translated into Eblaite as *na-ba-um*, the root of the Hebrew *nābî*, 'prophet'. The Eblaite 'prophets' came from Mari, a city with which Ebla had strong relations. Tablets of the eighteenth century BC, discovered in Mari, shed early light on prophetism. While Rabe (1976) states that the question whether Israelite prophetism came from Phoenicia-Canaan or from Mesopotamia (Mari) is not indicated by the date, Dahood says that the above-mentioned evidence from Ebla points to Canaan, according to his viewpoint of Eblaite as Canaanite (Dahood 1981b: 278, 319 n. 12).

In a recent survey of Mari prophetism and a comparison with Israelite prophets, Pardee (1984: 94-95) concludes that we can, at the least, say that the choice by the God of Israel of prophets going between himself and his people was not a new or unfamiliar mode of communication. Now we know that this mode of communication already existed in Ebla in the middle of the third millennium BC.

Fensham (1975: 116-18) draws our attention to the uniqueness of Old Testament prophetism, however. While prophets did exist outside Israel, such a combination of preaching and prediction as in the Old Testament prophecies is unparallelled in the literature of the ancient Near East.

Conclusions

It seems that, as the publication and the study of Ebla texts proceed, we shall obtain a better insight into Syrian life and literature during the third millennium BC. Thousands of personal and geographical names have been discovered, some of which also appear in the Old Testament. To the study of Syro-Palestinian social structure a new chapter has been added that takes us back to the middle of the third millennium BC. When the Ebla texts, or any ancient Near Eastern texts, are related to the Old Testament, a rigid linguistic method must be followed to escape from pre-conceived ideas. Thus the ambivalent character of the Old Testament becomes evident: its ancient Near Eastern origin, and its distinctiveness in relation to it.

NOTES

1. A conference on Eblaite bilingualism was held in Naples, 1982. L. Cagni announced in *Akkadica* 39 (1984), p. 21, that the volume *Il bilinguismo a Ebla* (= Atti del convegno di Napoli del 1982) will soon be published.

2. See, for instance, Dahood's reaction to the warnings of R. Tournay and F.C. Fensham against the danger of employing second-millennium writings from Ugarit to explain first-millennium BC difficulties in the Old Testament (Dahood 1978: 110). See also Fensham ('Extra-biblical Material and the Hermeneutics of the Old Testament with special reference to the legal material of the Covenant Code', *Aspects of the Exegetical Process. OTWSA* 20 (1977) and *OTWSA* 21 (1978). *Old Testament Essays*, pp. 53-65) on the

importance of extra-biblical material to the exegesis of the Old Testament and the uniqueness of Biblical law. It is important, he says, to note that every time discoveries were made which are somehow related to the Old Testament world, a tendency to over-emphasize their importance has arisen, e.g. the Pan-babylonian school of Hugo Winckler and the so-called Pan-ugaritic school of studies (pp. 53-54).

3. S.A. Picchioni (1981a), who has studied the direction of cuneiform writing and paleography of the Ebla texts (1980, 1981b), reconstructs TM.75.G.2420 as follows, according to Sollberger's numbering of the lines: 1-269, 293-572, 573-590, 270-292 and 591-623.

4. Pettinato (1977a: 239-40; 1981b: 97-98) translates *en-ma* in I 1 and VI 3 with 'thus'. For *emma*, later *umma*, as introduction to a letter, see Von Soden 1965: 218.

5. See my paper, read at XXXI CISHAAN, 'The Conception of Ancient Syro-Palestinian Kingship in the Light of Contemporary Royal Archives with special reference to the recent discoveries at Tell Mardikh (Ebla)', published in H.I.H. Prince Takahito Mikasa (ed.), *Monarchies and Socio-religious Traditions in the Ancient Near East* (Bulletin of the Middle Eastern Culture Center in Japan, 1; Wiesbaden: Otto Harrasowitz, 1984), pp. 1-10.

BIBLIOGRAPHY

Archi, A.

1979a 'The Epigraphic Evidence from Ebla and the Old Testament', *Biblica* 60, pp. 556-66.

1979b '^{d}ià-ramu at Ebla', *Studi Eblaiti* I, pp. 45-48.

1981 'Further concerning Ebla and the Bible', *BA* 44, pp. 145-54.

1981b 'I rapporti tra Ebla e Mari', *Studi Eblaiti* IV, pp. 129-66.

Archi, A. and Biga, M.G.

1982 *Testi amministrativi di vario contenuto* (Archivio L. 2769: TM.75.G. 3000-4101) (Archivi reali di Ebla. Testi—III), Università degli studi di Roma; Missione archeologica italiana in Siria.

Barr, J.

1974 'Trends and Prospects in Biblical Theology', *JTS* 25, pp. 265-82.

Biggs, R.

1980 'The Ebla Tablets, An Interim Perspective', *BA* 43, pp. 76-87.

Böhl, F.M.Th.

1909 *Die Sprache der Amarnabriefe* (Leipziger Semitische Studien, 5/2); Leipzig: J.C. Hinrichs'sche Buchhandlung.

Boyer, G.

1955 'La place des textes d'Ugarit dans l'histoire de l'ancien droit oriental', *Le Palais Royal d'Ugarit* III (Mission de Ras Shamra, Tome VI), Paris.

Cagni, L. (ed.)

1981 *La Lingua di Ebla* (Atti del Convegno Internazionale), Napoli, 21-23 aprile 1980. Napoli: Istituto Universitario Orientale.

Dahood, M. and Pettinato, G.
1977 'Ugaritic *ršp gn* and Eblaite *rasap gunu(m)*^{ki}', *Orientalia* 46, pp. 230-32.

Dahood, M.
1978 'Ebla, Ugarit and the Old Testament', *Vetus Testamentum, Supplement* 29, pp. 81-112.
1981a 'The Linguistic Classification of Eblaite', in Cagni (1981), pp. 177-89.
1981b 'Ebla, Ugarit and the Bible', in Pettinato (1981b), pp. 271-321.
1981c Review of *Ugaritica VII*, by Abou-l-Faradj Al-Ouche, A. Caquot, J.-C. and L. Courtois and others (Leiden, 1978), in *Bibliotheca Orientalis* 38, cols. 380-83.
1982 'Eblaite and Biblical Hebrew', *CBQ* 44, pp. 1-24.

Edzard, D.O.
1981 *Verwaltungstexte verschiedenen Inhalts (aus dem Archiv L. 2769)* (Archivi reali di Ebla. Testi—II), Università degli studi di Roma. Missione archeologica italiana in Siria.

Fensham, F.C.
1959 'The Judges and Ancient Israelite Jurisprudence', *Die Ou-Testamentiese Werkgemeenskap in Suid-Afrika* (Papers read at 2nd meeting, Pretoria), pp. 15-22.
1962 'Malediction and Benediction in Ancient Near Eastern Vassal-Treaties and the Old Testament', *ZAW* 74, pp. 1-9.
1963 'Common Trends in Curses of the Near Eastern Treaties and Kudurru-inscriptions compared with Maledictions of Amos and Isaiah', *ZAW* 75, pp. 155-75.
1967 'Covenant, Promise and Expectations in the Bible', *TZ* 23, pp. 305-21.
1971a 'Problems in Connection with Translation of Ancient Texts', in I.H. Eybers and others (eds.), *De Fructu Oris Sui. Essays in honour of Adrianus van Selms* (Pretoria Oriental Series, 9; Leiden), pp. 46-57.
1971b 'The Covenant as Giving Expression to the Relationship between Old and New Testament', *Tyndale Bulletin* 22, pp. 82-94.
1975 *Wetenskap en Byblkunde*, 2nd rev. edn; Cape Town: Human & Rousseau.
1977a ''n Argeologiese Opskudding: die ontdekking by Ebla', *Ned. Geref. Teologiese Tydskrif* 18, pp. 225-29.
1977b *Exodus* (De Prediking van het Oude Testament), 2nd, enlarged edn; Nijkerk: Uitgewerij G.F. Callenbach B.V.
1980 'Die tyd van Abraham is soos kwiksilwer', *Ned. Geref. Teologiese Tydskrif 21*, pp. 140-57.
1982 'Law. I. In the Old Testament', in Douglas, J.D. (ed.), *New Bible Dictionary* (2nd edn; Leicester: Intervarsity Press), pp. 682-85.

Freedman, D.N.
1978 'The Real Story of the Ebla Tablets. Ebla and the Cities of the Plain', *BA* 41, pp. 143-64.

Fronzaroli, P.
1977a 'West Semitic Toponymy in Northern Syria in the Third Millennium BC', *JSS* 22, pp. 145-66.

1977b 'L'Interferenza Linguistica nella Siria Settentrionale del III Millennio', in *Interferenza Linguistica*, pp. 27-43. (Atti del Convegno della Societă Italiana di Glottologia. Perugia, 24 e 25 aprile 1977. Testi raccolti da R. Ajello, Giardini Editori, E. Stampatori in Pisa.)

1979 'Un atto reale di donazione dagli Archivi di Ebla (TM.75.G.1766)', *Studi Eblaiti* I, pp. 3-16.

Garbini, G.

1978 'La Lingua di Ebla', *La Parola del Passato* (Sommario del Fascicolo CLXXXI—Luglio Agosto), pp. 241-59.

1981 'Considerations on the Language of Ebla', in Cagni (1981), pp. 75-82.

Gelb, I.J.

1977 *Thoughts about Ibla: A Preliminary Evaluation* (Syro-Mesopotamian Studies, 1/1); Malibu, CA: Undena Publications.

1981 'Ebla and the Kish Civilization', in Cagni (1981), pp. 9-73.

Grégoire, J.-P.

1981 'Remarques sur quelques noms de fonction et sur l'organisation administrative dans les archives d'Ebla', in Cagni (1981), pp. 379-99.

Herrmann, S.

1975 *A History of Israel in Old Testament Times*, London: SCM.

Huffmon, H.B.

1965 *Amorite Personal Names in the Mari Texts*, Baltimore: Johns Hopkins Press.

Kupper, J.-R.

1957 *Les nomades en Mésopotamie au temps des rois de Mari* (Paris: Société d'Edition 'Les Belles Lettres').

Lambert, W.G.

1975 'Destiny and Divine Intervention in Babylon and Israel', *The Witness of Tradition, Oudtestamentische Studiën*, Leiden, pp. 65-72.

Mander, P.

1980 'Brevi considerazioni sul testo "lessicale" SF 23=SF 24 e paralleli da Abū-Ṣalābīkh', *Oriens Antiquus* 19, pp. 187-92.

Martinez, E.R.

1981 *Hebrew-Ugaritic Index II with an Eblaite Index to the writings of Mitchel J. Dahood* (Subsidia Biblica, 4); Rome: Biblical Institute Press.

Matthiae, P.

1980 *Ebla, an Empire Rediscovered*. Original title: *Ebla, un impero ritrovato* (1977), translated by C. Holme; London: Hodder & Stoughton.

McCarthy, D.J.

1978 *Treaty and Covenant* (Analecta Biblica, 21A) new edition completely rewritten; Rome: Biblical Institute Press.

1979 'Ebla, ὁρκια τεμνειν, ṭb šlm: Addenda to *Treaty and Covenant*', *Biblica* 60, pp. 247-53.

Muhly, J.D.

1984 *BA* 47, p. 29.

Müller, H.-P.

1980a 'Die Texte aus Ebla. Eine Herausforderung an die alttestamentliche Wissenschaft', *BZ* 24, pp. 161-79.

1980b 'Religionsgeschichtliche Beobachtungen zu den Texten von Ebla', *Zeitschrift des Deutschen Palästina-Vereins* 96, pp. 1-19.

1981a 'Der Jahwename und seine Deutung. Ex 3,14 im Licht der Textpublikationen aus Ebla', *Biblica* 62, pp. 305-27.

1981b 'Gab es in Ebla einen Gottesnamen Ja?', *Zeitschrift für Assyriologie und vorderasiatische Archäologie* 70, pp. 70-92.

Pardee, D.

1984 'Literary Sources for the History of Palestine and Syria. The Mari Archives', *BA* 47, pp. 88-99.

Pettinato, G.

1975 'Testi cuneiformi del 3. millennio in paleocaneneo rinvenuti nella campagna 1974 a Tell Mardikh=Ebla', *Orientalia* 44, pp. 361-74.

1976a 'The Royal Archives of Tell Mardikh-Ebla', *BA* 39, pp. 44-52.

1976b 'Carchemiš-kār-kamiš. Le prime attestazioni del III millennio', *Oriens Antiquus* 15, pp. 11-15.

1977a 'Gli archivi reali di Tell Mardikh-Ebla. Riflessioni e Prospettive', *Rivista biblica Italiana* 25, pp. 225-43.

1977b 'Relations entre les royaumes d'Ebla et de Mari au troisième millénaire d'après les archives royales de Tell Mardikh-Ebla', *Akkadica* 2, pp. 20-28.

1979a *Catalogo dei Testi Cuneiformi di Tell Mardikh-Ebla* (Materiali Epigrafici di Ebla—1), Istituto Universitario Orientale di Napoli. Seminario di studi Asiatici I; Naples.

1979b *Old Canaanite Cuneiform Texts of the Third Millennium* (Sources and Monographs on the Ancient Near East 1/7; Malibu: Undena Publications. ET Pettinato 1975.

1980a *Testi amministrativi della biblioteca L. 2769* (Parte I. Materiali epigrafici di Ebla—2), Istituto Universitario Orientale di Napoli. Seminario di Studi Asiatici. Series Maior II, Naples.

1980b 'Ebla and the Bible', *BA* 43, pp. 203-16. ET of: 'Ebla e la Bibbia', *Oriens Antiquus* 19 (1980), pp. 49-72.

1980c 'Polytheismus und Henotheismus in der Religion von Ebla', in O. Keel (ed.), *Monotheismus im Alten Israel und seiner Umwelt* (Biblische Beiträge, 14), Fribourg: Verlag Schweizerisches Katholisches Bibelwerk, pp. 31-48. German translation of: 'Politeismo ed enoteismo nella religione di Ebla. Atti del Simposio dell' AB1 su Dio nella Biblica e nella culture ad essa contemporanee e connesse', *L'Osservatore Romano*, 21 April 1978.

1980d 'Pre-Ugaritic Documentation of Ba'al', *C.H. Gordon Festschrift*, New York (ed. Gary Rendsburg).

1981a 'I vocabolari bilingui di Ebla. Problemi di traduzione e di lessicografia Sumerico-Eblaita', in Cagni (1981), pp. 241-76.

1981b *The Archives of Ebla. An Empire Inscribed in Clay* (Garden City, New York: Doubleday). ET of *Un impero inciso nell' argilla*, 1979.

1982 *Testi lessicali bilingui della biblioteca L.2769.* Parte I (Materiali epigrafici di Ebla—4), Istituto Universitario Orientale di Napoli. Seminario di Studi Asiatici. Series maior IV; Naples.

Picchioni, S.A.

1980 'La direzione della scrittura cuneiforme e gli archivi di Tell Mardikh-Ebla', *Orientalia* 49, pp. 225-51.

1981a 'Ricostruzioni segmentale del testo storico TM.75.G.2420', *Oriens Antiquus* 20, pp. 187-90.

1981b 'Osservazioni sulla paleografia e sulla cronologia dei testi di Ebla', in Cagni (1981), pp. 109-20.

Rabe, V.W.
1976 'Origins of Prophecy', *BASOR* 221, pp. 125-28.

Soggin, J.A.
1980 'Observations on the Root *špṭ* and the Term *šôpĕṭîm* in Biblical Hebrew', *BA* 43, p. 208.

Sollberger, E.
1980 'The So-called Treaty between Ebla and "Ashur"', *Studi Eblaiti* 3, pp. 129-55.

Ullendorff, E.
1978 Review of Gelb, I.J.: *Thoughts about Ibla: A Preliminary Evaluation* (1977), *JSS* 23, pp. 151-54.

Van Zijl, P.J.
1972 *Baal. A Study of Texts in Connection with Baal in the Ugaritic Epics* (Alter Orient und Altes Testament, 10), Kevelaer: Butzon & Bercker.

Viganò, L.
1984 'Literary Sources for the History of Palestine and Syria. The Ebla Tablets' (revised and edited by Dennis Pardee), *BA* 47, pp. 6-16.

Von Soden, W.
1965 *Akkadisches Handwörterbuch*, I. Wiesbaden: Otto Harrassowitz.

Vorländer, H.
1975 *Mein Gott. Die Vorstellungen vom persönlichen Gott im Alten Orient und im Alten Testament* (Alter Orient und Altes Testament, 23), Kevelaer: Butzon & Bercker.

Wiseman, D.J.
1982 '"Is it Peace?"—Covenant and Diplomacy', *Vetus Testamentum* 32, pp. 311-26.

11

PA'AM AS A MEASURE OF LENGTH IN 1 KINGS 7.4 AND KAI 80.1

M.J. Mulder

As a contribution to the *Festschrift* of my dear colleague Professor Fensham, I should like to call attention to an exegetical problem I came across while working on the difficult chapters 1 Kings 6 and 7. As is well known, 1 Kgs 7.1-12 describes the building of Solomon's palace for which vv. 2-5 give the plan of the 'House of the Forest of Lebanon'.[1] Verse 4 tells something about the illumination of this house by means of three rows of window-frames, the *šequpîm*.[2] In the second half of the verse, *meḥezā*, only found here and in the following verse, means 'window' or 'opening for light'.[3] Now it is said: *ûmeḥezā 'el-meḥezā šāloš pe'āmîm*. First of all we will introduce a rather arbitrary selection of translations of especially the last two words. Next, we will give our proposal for translation. Finally we will discuss briefly KAI 80.1.

1. LXX translates as follows: ... καὶ χώρα ἐπὶ χώραν τρισσῶς. The word χώρα means 'space'[4] and τρισσῶς means 'threefold'. The Pešiṭta reads: *wmqblyn* (*sc.*: *'ksdr'*[*pl.*]) *ḥd lḥd tlt zbnyn*, '(balconies) set one agaist another in three tiers (?, or: times)'. The Targum has roughly the same translation: *wḥzy lqbyl ḥzy tlt zmnyn*. The translation of the Vulgate is in our case of no importance.

More recent translators are going in the same direction as the older ones just mentioned. For example KJV: 'and light *was* against light *in* three ranks'.[5] Luther translates vv. 4ff. as follows: 'VND waren Fenster gegen die drey riegen gegen ander vber/ drey gegen drey/ vnd waren in jren pfosten vierecket'[6]; RSV: 'and window opposite window in three tiers'; NEB 'and window corresponded to window at three levels'; GNB (TEV) (v. 4): 'in each of the two side walls there were three rows of windows'.

We find similar translations in most French versions, e.g. that of L. Segond (v. 4): 'Il y avait trois étages, à chacun desquels se trouvaient des fenêtres les unes vis-à-vis des autres'; La Bible de Jérusalem[7]: 'se faisant vis-à-vis trois fois'; Traduction Œcuménique de la Bible: 'chaque fenêtre de ces trois rangées faisait face à une autre fenêtre'.[8] Only the translation of the Bibliothèque de la Pléïade published by É. Dhorme reads: 'fenêtre vers fenêtre, tous les trois pas'. In an annotation to this translation the translator points out: 'Nous rendons par "trois pas", d'après le sens étymologique, l'hébreu *shâlosh pe'âmîm*, qui généralement signifie "trois fois". Il s'agit de trois rangées de fenêtres superposées et se faisant face d'un mur à l'autre'.

The German versions as well are in line with most of the translations mentioned hitherto: that of P. Riessler and R. Storr: 'und so war eine dreifache Lichtöffnung einander gegenüber'; that of H. Torczyner: 'und zwar Durchblick zu Durchblick dreimal'; that of V. Hamp, M. Stenzel and J. Kürzinger: 'Fenster gab es in drei Reihen, und zwar eines gegenüber dem andern'. The 'Revidierte Fassung der Übersetzung Martin Luthers' (1964) reads: 'und Fenster waren einander gegenüber dreimal'; the Zürcher Bibel: 'Lichtöffnung gegenüber Lichtöffnung, dreimal'; and the translation of M. Buber and F. Rosenzweig: 'Durchblick gegen Durchblick, dreimal'. Even the translation of the Bible 'in Afrikaans' renders: 'en oop venster teenoor oop venster, drie maal'.[9]

Also in the commentaries one finds, on the whole, the same translations. O. Thenius (2nd edn, 1873); A. Klostermann (1887); I. Benzinger (1899); R. Kittel (1900); A. Šanda (1911); C. van Gelderen (2nd edn, 1937)[10]; I.W. Slotki (1950); J.A. Montgomery and H.S. Gehman (1951); A. van den Born (1958); M. Noth (1968); E. Würthwein (1977) and M. Rehm (1979), to mention only a few, are all going in the same direction: 'dreimal' or 'in triplicate' or the like.[11] Others, e.g. C.F. Keil (2nd edn, 1876); C.F. Burney (1903); A.B. Ehrlich (1914) or J. Gray (2nd edn, 1970) pay no attention at all to this question of translation.

2. Sixteen times the expression *šālôš pᵉʿāmîm* appears in the Old

Testament: Exod. 23.17; 34.23f.; Num. 24.10; Deut. 16.16; Judg. 16.15; 1 Sam. 20.41; 1 Kgs 7.4f.; 9.25; 17.21; 2 Kgs 13.18f., 25; Ezek. 41.6; 2 Chron. 8.13; and once we find the expression *pa'amayim šālôš* (Job 33.29).[12] Lipiński is of the opinion that on the whole *šālôš p^e'āmîm* can be translated by 'efficacement'. On some occasions its meaning is 'three times' (e.g. Exod. 23.17; 34.23f.; Deut. 16.16: three times a year there will be a pilgrim-feast). In our case Lipiński points out that the windows were 'disposées vis-à-vis *šlš p'mym*, c'est-à-dire "trois fois" ou "tous les trois pas", d'après le sens étymologique de *p'm*'.[13] At this point Lipiński agrees with the above-mentioned opinion of Dhorme in his annotation to his translation in the Bibliothèque de la Pléïade.

It is exactly this 'etymological' meaning of *p'm* we accept as the basis of our translation of the words under discussion. The translation of v. 4 runs as follows: 'There were three rows of window-frames of which the light-openings were each at a distance of three yards'.

Of the 118 times we find the word *pa'am* in the Old Testament, its meaning is about 100 times 'time' ('occurrence').[14] Sometimes its meaning is 'foot' (of man), e.g. Cant. 7.2; 2 Kgs 19.24//Isa. 37.25; (of God), e.g. Ps. 85.14; or 'step', e.g. Judg. 5.28; Isa. 26.6, etc. In one case the translation of the word is 'anvil' (Isa. 41.7).[15]

As a measure of length the 'foot' appears in Israel's environment,[16] but we do not encounter it in the literature of the Old Testament.[17] A usual measure of length was the 'cubit' (*'ammâ*), the smaller measures the 'span' (*zeret*), 'palm' or 'handbreadth' (*ṭôpaḥ*) and 'fingerbreadth' (*'eṣba'*).[18] E. Stern in a readable article on measures and weights wonders why the 'foot', a common linear measure with the peoples in Israel's neighbourhood, and even in Hellenistic and later times in Israel itself, was not mentioned in the Old Testament.[19] In our view, however, Dhorme and Lipiński have shown the right way in translating *pa'am* with *pas*. In our verses *pa'am* clearly is a measure of length, which may possibly indicate a 'foot', but better still, a 'pace' or 'yard', the distance covered by the foot in a single step. According to our verse there were in the 'House of the Forest of Lebanon' three rows of window-frames in which were at regular intervals, light-openings at a distance of three paces. We reject the opinions of most commentators that there were storeys with rooms around this house.[20] With Noth we presume the last five words of v. 5 to be a gloss (dittography).[21]

3. The translation of *pa'am* in some cases with 'pace' or 'yard' may possibly also shed some light on a Punic inscription, published by H. Donner and W. Röllig in KAI 80.[22] The beginning of this inscription reads: *ḥds wp'l 'yt hmṭbḥ z dl p'mn 'śrt h'šm 'š 'l hmqdšm* . . . In the translation of Donner and Röllig: 'Diese Schlachtopferstelle mit Füßen erneuerten und stellten her die zehn Männer, die über das Heiligtum (gesetzt waren)'.[23] It is not very clear what is meant by the words 'with feet'.[24] A much better translation in our opinion would be: 'This slaughtering-place of ten yards restored and made the men who were in charge of the sanctuary . . .' This meaning of *pa'am* fits well into the context of this inscription, and may be a further proof of the fact that this word could be a measure of length in Hebrew and other Northwest Semitic languages.

NOTES

1. M.J. Mulder, 'Einige Bemerkungen zur Beschreibung des Libanonwaldhauses in I Reg 7,2f.', *ZAW* 88 (1976), pp. 99-105.

2. Cf. K. Möhlenbrink, *Der Tempel Salomos* (Stuttgart, 1932), pp. 128f.; KBL, p. 1009; Th. A. Busink, *Der Tempel von Jerusalem*, I (Leiden, 1970), pp. 193-97.

3. HAL, p. 538.

4. H.G. Liddell and R. Scott, *A Greek-English Lexicon* (Oxford, 1968), *s.v.*; cf. I. Fr. Schleusner, *Novus Thesaurus Philologico-Criticus . . . Veteris Testamenti*, V (Lipsiae, 1821), p. 552, and otherwise O. Thenius, *Die Bücher der Könige* (2nd edn; Leipzig, 1873), p. 89.

5. Cf. e.g. also the Dutch 'Statenvertaling': 'dat het eene venster was over het andere venster in drie orden'.

6. D. Martin Luther, *Die gantze Heilige Schrifft Deudsch* (Wittenberg, 1545; Darmstadt: Wissenschaftliche Buchgesellschaft, 1972).

7. Nouvelle édition entièrement revue et augmentée (Paris, 1979).

8. In v. 5 this translation reads: 'aux trois rangées de fenêtres'.

9. We will mention here some modern Dutch translations: Leidse Vertaling: 'en drie rijen latwerk, raam tegenover raam, driemaal'; Petrus Canisius-vertaling: 'De vensters lagen in drie rijen recht boven elkaar"; Nieuwe Vertaling van het Nederlands Bijbelgenootschap: 'en driemaal een open venster tegenover een open venster'; Willibrord-vertaling: 'In het gebouw waren drie rijen vensters aangebracht en deze vensters lagen recht boven elkaar'; Groot-Nieuws-Bijbel: 'Het had drie rijen dakvensters, telkens drie lichtopeningen naast elkaar'. The new Frisian translation (1978) reads: 'Ek wiene der trije rigen finsters, iepening foar iepening oer, trijerisom'.

10. Cf. C. van Gelderen, 'Der Salomonische Palastbau (zu I Reg. 7, 1-12)', *AfO* 6 (1930/31), pp. 101f.

11. Cf. B. Stade, 'Der Text des Berichtes über Salomos Bauten. 1 Kö. 5–7', *ZAW* 3 (1883), pp. 151ff.; Busink, *Tempel*, pp. 135ff.

12. E. Lipiński, 'Trois Hébraïsmes oubliés ou méconnus', *RivStudOr* 44 (1970), pp. 93, 98ff.

13. Lipiński, *loc. cit.*, p. 93.

14. HAL, p. 897; E. Jenni, *THAT*, II, p. 378; cf. also W. von Soden, 'Zum hebräischen Wörterbuch', *UF* 13 (1981), p. 163 n. 17.

15. But see C. Westermann, *Das Buch Jesaja* (ATD, 19; Göttingen, 1966), p. 56, and K. Elliger, *Deuterojesaja*, I (BK XI/1; Neukirchen-Vluyn, 1978), pp. 129ff.

16. I. Benzinger, *Hebräische Archäologie* (3rd edn; Leipzig, 1927), pp. 190ff.; W. von Soden, *AHw*, *s.v. šēpu(m)* 15, p. 1215.

17. We meet *pesa'* once, in 1 Sam. 20.3; cf. *psy'h*: S. Krauss, *Talmudische Archäologie*, II (Leipzig, 1911), p. 391 n. 9, and also *ṣa'ad* in 2 Sam. 6.13.

18. G. Schmitt, 'Maße', in *Biblisches Reallexikon* (ed. K. Galling; 2nd edn; Tübingen, 1977), p. 204; cf. also A.-G. Barrois, *Manuel d'Archéologie Biblique*, II (Paris, 1953), pp. 244-47; R. de Vaux, *Les Institutions de l'Ancien Testament*, I (Paris, 1958), pp. 299-302; O.R. Sellers, 'Measures of Length', in *The Interpreter's Dictionary of the Bible* IV pp. 836ff.

19. In *Encyclopedia Biblica*, IV (Jerusalem: Institutum Bialik and Museum Antiquitatum Iudaicarum ad Universitatem Hebraicam Hierosolymitanam pertinens, 1962), p. 849; W.L. Bevan, in *A Dictionary of the Bible*, III (2nd edn; ed. Sir William Smith; London, 1893), p. 1736, wrote already: 'It will be observed in the sequel that the Hebrews restricted themselves to the forearm, to the exclusion of the foot and also of the pace, as a proper measure of length'.

20. See my article, mentioned in note 1.

21. M. Noth, *Könige*, I (BK IX/1; Neukirchen-Vluyn, 1968), p. 131: 'danach liegt textkritisch die Annahme einer versehentlichen Wiederholung außerordentlich nahe'.

22. H. Donner and W. Röllig, *Kanaanäische und Aramäische Inschriften*, I (Wiesbaden, 1962); II and III (*ibid.*, 1964). KAI 80=CIS, I, p. 175.

23. KAI II, p. 98. G.A. Cooke, *A Text-Book of North-Semitic Inscriptions* (Oxford, 1903), p. 130, translates: 'The Decemvirs in charge of the sanctuaries renovated and made this slaughter-house (?) ? steps: which was in the year of the s[uffetes . . .] . . .'

24. See note of the editors of KAI, II, p. 98; cf. DISO, *s.v.* $p'm^I$, p. 232, 'dans CIS i 175[1] pieds d' une boucherie . . .'

12

PSALM 132 AND COVENANT THEOLOGY

Philip Nel

The formulation of the title indicates a delimitation of the subject-matter. Not all aspects of the so-called covenant theology will be dealt with here—only those relevant to our theme. The discussion of Psalm 132 will also be scaled down to the fundamental questions surrounding its basic theme, i.e.

a. How should we understand the relation between the foundation of Zion as the cultic centre and the election of the dynasty of David as an eternal dynasty?
b. Does the doctrinal character of Psalm 132 exemplify the *hieros logos* of the ark sanctuary in Jerusalem to the same extent as 2 Sam. 6 and 7?
c. Do we find clear-cut evidence of a typical Deuteronomistic theology in Psalm 132?
d. Is Psalm 132 reminiscent of an early Jerusalem theology which has nothing in common with a covenant theology?

In this article I intend to substantiate a further possibility for the understanding of the theological framework of Psalm 132, namely that a covenant theology, different from and older than that of the Deuteronomistic tradition, is intertwined with the Jerusalem theology in Psalm 132.

Psalm 132 is a perfect example of a symmetrically constructed poem, both in line-pattern and in conceptual strategy. Almost every line exhibits a perfect binary and semantically corresponding pair.[1] A structural analysis of Psalm 132[2] further reveals a significant symmetry of two almost complete poems in Psalm 132. The two poems have a distinctly strophic character which can be presented thus:

Poem A	*Poem B*
vv. 1-5	vv. 11-12
vv. 6-8	vv. 13-14
vv. 9-10	vv. 15-18[3]

Both poems start off with a David-Yahweh polarity and both conclude with the same polarity. This polarity is explicated by means of the *hieros logos* of the Zion cult in the first poem. In vv. 1-5 one finds David's promise to etablish a מקום (abode) for Yahweh.

The interjection הנה (v. 6) indicates a dramatic shift in focus. The symbolic and ceremonial search for the ark (vv. 6-8) already constitutes the execution of David's promise.[4] Yahweh is then invited, in the form of an old 'Ladespruch',[5] to take possession of his dwelling place (מנוחה, v. 8). As a direct consequence of the newly created cultic order, the wish is expressed that its functionaries should execute their duty in צדק (righteousness, v. 9). A special prayer of blessing (v. 10) for David, the anointed king, forms the conclusion of the first poem.

Verse 10 not only forms the conclusion of the first poem, but simultaneously serves as the logical transition to the following poem (B). The opening call (זכר) in v. 1 is now answered by the action of Yahweh (v. 11). The promise of David is echoed by the promise (שבע) of Yahweh introducing the second poem. The David-Yahweh polarity of the first poem is thus taken a step further. Although two distinct units are demarcated in Psalm 132, the introduction of the second poem stresses the symbiosis of the two. It is therefore impossible to separate them altogether. Moreover, from the following discussion it should become evident that the second poem is perfectly superimposed on the first. This symmetry can be represented as follows:

Foundation of Zion as cultic centre		*Election of the dynasty of David*
Promise of David	→	Promise of Yahweh
vv. 1-2 David's promise		v. 11a Yahweh's promise
vv. 3-5 citation		vv. 11b-12 citation
Foundation of Zion as cultic centre	→	Acceptance of Zion

vv. 6-7 ceremonial prelude		v. 13 historical prelude
v. 8 invitation to מנוחה		v. 14 acceptance of מנוחה
Consequences (wishes)	→	Consequences (promises)
		v. 15 for whole community
v. 9 for cultic personnel		v. 16 for cultic personnel
v. 10 for David		vv. 17-18 for dynasty of David

Verses 1-5 (A) and 11-12 (B)

The David-Yahweh polarity figures in the beginning of both A and B. In A one encounters the promise of David to establish a dwelling place for Yahweh. Yahweh's promise in B on the other hand entails the election of the Davidic dynasty.

Verses 6-8 (A) and 13-14 (B)

Section A unmistakably recalls (by cultic recitation) the historical events of the ark's return to Jerusalem[6] (cf. 2 Sam. 6). The newly erected dwelling place of Yahweh is designated as his משכנה (v. 7) and מנוחה (v. 8). Yahweh is also invited to take possession of his abode (v. 8).[7]

The prelude of B (v. 13) equally tries to manifest a historical fact by the indicative statement that Yahweh has chosen Zion. This conviction is further enhanced by the direct acceptance of Zion by Yahweh as his מנוחה.

The historical re-installation of the Ark in Jerusalem, actualized by cultic commemoration[8] in Psalm 132, is sanctioned by the Zion theology as Yahweh's 'desire' and 'choice'.

Verses 9-10 (A) and 15-18 (B)

Verses 9-10 express the consequences, in the form of wishes (prayers), of the establishment of Zion as the cultic centre. Verses 15-18 can equally be regarded as the consequences, expressed in promises, of the election and acceptance of Zion as Yahweh's מנוחה (resting-place). The climax of both A and B is reached through the development of the David-Yahweh polarity, which forms the keystone of the entire Psalm.

The interpretation of Psalm 132 is closely linked with its supposed date, which varies from the early Israelite[9] period to the Greek[10] period.

F.M. Cross maintains that vv. 1-5 and 11-12 (together with a missing strophe [!]) constitute the oldest poem which presumably should have its Sitz im Leben in the covenant renewal festival. The dogma of obedience is claimed to be its theological centre. Cross further claims that vv. 6-10 and 13-18 are reminiscent of the dogma of election. The latter also appears to be in conflict with the dogma of obedience. The cultic context is that of the New Year festival. Definite traces of Deuteronomistic influences are to be seen, and one should therefore consider a much later date for vv. 6-10 and 13-18.[11] Cross expressly recognizes the two prominent aspects of Psalm 132, but he fails to observe the symmetry between the two poems without conflicting ideologies existing between them.

It has become *communis opinio* that Psalm 132 exhibits features of an old Zion theology, which have, however, undergone fundamental re-interpretation from the perspective of the Deuteronomist or the Deuteronomistic tradition.[12] This assumption is mainly derived from two arguments, *viz*.:

a. The election of the dynasty of David is inherently part of the theological core of the Deuteronomist;
b. The covenant (ברית) in v. 12 refers to the Davidic covenant which is equally part and parcel of the theologumena of the Deuteronomist.

H.J. Kraus holds the opinion that the election of the Davidids is part of the *hieros logos* of the 'königliches Sionsfest'.[13] The theological context of Psalm 132 is thus the same as that of Nathan's prophecy in 2 Sam. 7.4ff. and is in fact constructed in accordance with it. Although N. Poulssen maintains a critical position over against Kraus's *hieros logos* of the festival of Zion, he nevertheless argues in favour of a development of the 'König-Tempel-Bekenntnis'[14] from the Nathan prophecy.

The text of 2 Sam. 7 tends to be always in the centre of controversies! Notwithstanding the complexities of the text of 2 Sam. 7, and without denying the intricacies attending the tradition complexes[15] in that chapter, the basic differences between 2 Sam. 7 and Psalm 132 must be articulated. H. Gese has convincingly shown that 2 Sam. 7 cannot possibly be the conceptual framework of Psalm 132.[16] He also considers it most likely that 1 Chron. 17 represents a more authentic rendering of the events of 2 Sam. 7. The overriding conceptual context of 2 Sam. 7 is undeniably that of the Deuteronomist. It is essential to notice that 2 Sam. 7 is not concerned with the foundation of the cult of Zion, but concentrates on the building of the temple. David is not rejected because of his efforts to establish the cult in Zion. He is, however, forbidden by Nathan to build the temple. What is being rejected, is the idea that the initiative to build a house for Yahweh originated with David. The Deuteronomist wants to emphasize that everything has its origin solely in the initiative of Yahweh. Yahweh also does not protest (through Nathan) against a permanent dwelling place as such—that would surely contradict his own promise (cf. 2 Sam. 7.13). The text of 2 Sam. 7 is intended to convince the reader beyond doubt that Yahweh has initiated the building of the temple and that the election of the dynasty of David originates from His autonomy.[17]

My own analysis and interpretation of Psalm 132 underscores Gese's viewpoint that it primarily concerns the establishment of the cult of Zion and not the building of the temple (as is the case in 2 Sam. 7).[18]

From the symmetry of the two poems of Psalm 132 as well as from the conceptual stategy employed in the whole Psalm, it may be concluded that the election of the dynasty of David (vv. 11-18) is the direct result of David's establishment of the ark-cult in Jerusalem (vv. 1-10). This clearly contradicts the theological presupposition of 2 Sam. 7, in which such a high premium is put on the sole initiative of Yahweh (cf. vv 8-16). Psalm 132 cannot, therefore, be a derivative of an already existing text of 2 Sam. 7, but vice versa! The contents of the Psalm are, therefore, reminiscent of a theology distinct from and older than that of 2 Sam. 7.[19] The theology of Psalm 132 is, therefore, also not typically Deuteronomistic.

The occurrence of ברית (v. 12) in the Psalm still requires attention. From the discussion above it should be clear that ברית cannot refer to the Davidic covenant in accordance with the theology of the Deuteronomist.[20]

Gese interprets ברית as a direct reference to the Davidic covenant. 'Ps. 132 gibt in seiner einfachen Art die ursprüngliche Verbindung der beiden Akte, Überführung der Lade auf den Zion und Bund mit David wieder.'[21]

E. Kutsch, in consequence, virtually denies any possibility that ברית could designate a covenantal relationship between two parties with mutual obligations in a period prior to that of the Deuteronomist.[22] He translates ברית in v. 12 with 'Zusage'[23] which already shows familiarity with Deuteronomistic theology. Even if one accepted the translation of Kutsch, it still does not justify his interpretation of ברית as a mere self-imposed obligation by Yahweh. The overriding structural feature in Psalm 132 is the David-Yahweh polarity. The instance of ברית in this polarity already implies mutuality. The conditional clause of v. 12 has not attracted the attention it deserves from Kutsch. The interpretation of the conditional clause in this instance is impossible without any indication of mutual obligation.

Another possibility still exists: ברית in v. 12 does not exclusively refer to the Davidic covenant. Parallel to the promise of David (vv. 1-5), Yahweh makes an oath to David (v. 11) concerning the election of David's dynasty. The oath is further explicated by a conditional clause: 'If your sons observe my ברית, the stipulations that I have taught them, their sons too shall succeed you on the throne for evermore'. If ברית directly refers to the oath of v. 11, then one has a clear case of a *contradictio in terminis*, because the condition (אם שמר . . .) of the oath cannot be the oath itself. The observance (שמר) of 'my stipulations' (עדתי) would then also make no sense. ברית must, therefore, be interpreted from the context of Psalm 132 itself.

It has already been pointed out that the election of the dynasty of David (a totally new concept in Israel) is motivated by the establishment of the ark-cult in Jerusalem by David. This coalescence must not be viewed as a chronological process in our Psalm, but rather as a logical explanation from a particular theological point of view. The stratagems employed in this Psalm to sanction the new community, united under the elected Davidid, are mainly directed towards the constitutive features of the amphictyonic Israel in the pre-monarchical period.[24]

Yahweh, is, therefore, deliberately associated with the patriarchal tradition (אביר יעקב,[25] vv. 2 and 5). The bringing of the Ark to Jerusalem also demonstrates the continuity and re-establishment of amphictyonic Israel. The occurrence of ברית in v. 12 indicates that Psalm 132 presupposes an existing covenantal relationship between Israel and Yahweh.[26] This covenant does not merely imply a promissory character, but is essentially conditional in character.[27]

The connotation of ברית (v. 12) can only be determined from the context of the first poem (vv. 1-10) of Psalm 132 and not from v. 11 as such. The conditional character of v. 12 makes it impossible to maintain an unconditional covenantal relation. McCarthy minimizes this conditional statement: 'the condition imposed on the permanence of the dynasty is not very serious. In fact it is unreal. If Zion must endure, so must the dynasty linked with it.'[28] It seems reasonable, therefore, to assume that the ark as represented in vv. 1-10 was not only a palladium for the warrior-God, but was already associated with the conditional covenantal relation between Yahweh and Israel.[29] Notwithstanding the fact that the election of the Davidids resulted from the establishment of the ark-cult in Jerusalem, the realization of this election of the Davidids, as representative of the new amphictyonic Israel, is not totally unconditional. The guarantee of continuity is the observance of Yahweh's covenant by the Davidids.

If this assumption is accepted, it calls for a revaluation of those passages (e.g. Exod. 19–34) in which the ark is associated with the covenant and which are normally ascribed to the theologumena of the Deuteronomist. There is considerable reason to believe that the stipulations (law) and the idea of a covenant existed in essential harmony in early Israelite periods.[30]

Conclusion

Psalm 132 can be typified as a royal Psalm in which one aspect of the royal ideology, i.e. the relation between the establishment of the cult in Zion and the election of the dynasty of David, receives special illumination. Psalm 132 is reminiscent of an early form of Jerusalem theology which differs from the typical Deuteronomistic theology. Psalm 132 points to a pre-Deuteronomistic theological core which endeavours to achieve harmony between the election of the dynasty of David (the new element) and the constitutive features of pre-monarchical Israel. The re-installation of the ark as symbol of the conditional covenant between Yahweh and Israel (of which the Davidids became representatives) bridges the gap. The theology of Psalm 132 could, therefore, be described as covenant theology.

NOTES

1. Cf. J.L. Kugel, *The Idea of Biblical Poetry (Parallelism and its History)* (Yale, 1981), p. 68.

2. Cf. P.J. Nel, *Studiebrief* 5 (Research Project of the U.O.F.S.; Bloemfontein, 1984), pp. 4-28.

3. My analysis differs from those of F.M. Cross, *Canaanite Myth and Hebrew Epic* (Cambridge, 1973), pp. 94-97, 232-38, 244-46 and 251; C.A. Briggs, *Psalms*, II (ICC, 1960), pp. 470ff.; C.B. Houk, 'Psalm 132: Literary Integrity and Syllable-word Structures', *JSOT* 6 (1978), pp. 41-48; and T.E. Fretheim, 'Psalm 132: A Form-Critical Study', *JBL* 86 (1967), pp. 293-300.

4. Cf. S. Mowinckel, *The Psalms in Israel's Worship*, I (trans. by D.R. Ap-Thomas; Oxford, 1967), p. 176.

5. Cf. H. Gese, 'Der Davidsbund und Zionserwählung', in *Vom Sinai zum Zion* (München, 1974), p. 118; and H. Gunkel, *Die Psalmen* (HK 2/2; Göttingen, 1926), p. 566.

6. Cf. H.-J. Kraus, *Psalmen* II (BK; Neukirchen-Vluyn, 1978), pp. 878ff.; L. Sabourin, *The Psalms: Their Origin and Meaning* (New York, 1974), pp. 365f.; S. Mowinckel, *op. cit.*, pp. 176ff.; and H. Gese, *op. cit.*, pp. 119f.

7. I have preferred a closer linkage of v. 8 with vv. 6-7 than with vv. 9-10 in view of the following considerations: a. The cultic call or invitation (cf. also 2 Chron. 6.41-42) in v. 8 results from the previous ceremonial events (vv. 6-7); b. The imperative of v. 8 is essentially different from the implicit imperatives of vv. 9-10; c. the 3rd f.s. suffix in v. 6 as well as the lexical item 'footstool' (v. 7) anticipate the explicit mentioning of the ark in v. 8.

8. Cf. H. Gunkel, *op. cit.*, p. 568.

9. Cf. e.g. F.M. Cross, *loc. cit.*; J. Bright, *Covenant and Promise* (London, 1977), p. 64; and M. Dahood, *Psalms* III (The Anchor Bible; New York, 1970), pp. 241ff.

10. Cf. e.g. C.A. Briggs, *op. cit.*, pp. 470ff.; and A. Johnson, 'The Psalms', in *The Old Testament and Modern Study* (ed. H.H. Rowley; Oxford, 1952), p. 168.

11. Cross's reconstruction of Psalm 132 is as follows: Original poem: vv. 1-5 + 11-12 + missing strophe. Adaptation: vv. 6-10 + 13-18.

12. Cf. L. Perlitt, *Bundestheologie im Alten Testament* (WMANT; Neukirchen-Vluyn, 1969), pp. 51ff.; H.-J. Kraus, *Theologie der Psalmen* (BK; Neukirchen-Vluyn, 1979), pp. 65 and 139-50; E. Kutsch, *Verheissung und Gesetz* (BZAW, 131; Berlin, 1972), pp. 52 and 116-18; G. Fohrer, *Geschichte der israelitischen Religion* (Berlin, 1969), p. 302; R. Smend, *Die Bundesformel* (ThS, 68; Zürich, 1962), pp. 11ff. and 19ff.; L. Rost, Sinaibund und Davidbund, *ThLZ* 72 (1947), pp. 129-34; and N. Poulssen, *König und Tempel im Glaubenszeugnis des Alten Testaments* (SBM, 3; Stuttgart, 1967), pp. 130f. and 140f.

13. H.-J. Kraus, *Psalmen*, p. 882, and *Gottesdienst in Israel* (Munich, 1962), pp. 215f.

14. N. Poulssen, *op. cit.*, pp. 66, 72 and 132. Cf. also the reservation on the concept of the *hieros logos* put forward by A.F. Campbell, *The Ark Narrative* (SBL Dissertation Series; Missoula, 1975), pp. 197ff. and 249f.

15. Cf. e.g. R. Schmitt, *Zelt und Lade als Thema alttestamentlicher Wissenschaft* (Gütersloh, 1972), pp. 299ff.; N. Poulssen, *op. cit.*, pp. 50ff. and H.-J. Kraus, *Gottesdienst*, pp. 212f.

16. H. Gese, *op. cit.*, pp. 122-29.

17. A thorough study of the traditional backgrounds of Nathan and Zadok will surely shed more light on the stratagems employed in 2 Sam. 7, by means of which the building of the temple is associated with David (cf. e.g.

1 Chron. 21 and 2 Chron. 3.11), but in such a way that he never becomes the initiator. Obvious affinities with Solomon are to be seen.

18. H. Gese, *op. cit.*, p. 119.

19. *Ibid.*, p. 129.

20. Cf. note 12.

21. H. Gese, *op. cit.*, p. 121.

22. E. Kutsch, *op. cit.*, p. 52.

23. *Ibid.*, pp. 116-18.

24. Cf. e.g. H.-J. Kraus, *Gottesdienst*, pp. 213f.; L. Rost, *Die Überlieferung von der Thronnachfolge Davids* (BWANT 111/6; Stuttgart, 1926), pp. 4ff.; H. Gese, *op. cit.*, pp. 115ff.; A.H.J. Gunneweg, 'Sinaibund und Davidsbund', *VT* 10 (1960), pp. 338-40; and J. Bright, *op. cit.*, p. 53.

25. Cf. the discussion of this concept by F. Stolz, *Jahwehs und Israels Kriege* (AThANT, 60; Zürich, 1972), pp. 33ff.

26. F.C. Fensham, 'Covenant, Promise and Expectation', *ThZ* 23 (1967), pp. 305-22, maintains a similar view, although he bases it on quite different grounds. He actually tries to understand the history of Israel from a synthesis of the various covenants (Abraham, Moses and David).

27. R.E. Clements, *Abraham and David* (Studies in Biblical Theology, 2/5; London, 1967), pp. 47ff., concentrates on the connection between the Davidic and Abraham covenants. The character of the Davidic covenant is typified as promissory. H.D. Preuss, *Jahweglaube und Zukunftserwartung* (BWANT, 87; Stuttgart, 1968), pp. 62-70, on the other hand, suggests a close linkage between the Abraham covenant and the Sinai covenant. If one accepted this view, one has to reconsider Clements's viewpoint. D.J. McCarthy, *Old Testament Covenant* (Oxford, 1972), pp. 58f., correctly points out that the relation between the Mosaic and the Davidic covenant still needs further clarification. He has, however, severe doubts about any meaningful relation between the two.

28. McCarthy, *op. cit.*, p. 51.

29. Cf. also J. Bright, *op. cit.*, p. 64.

30. Cf. e.g. R. Smend, *Die Entstehung des Alten Testaments* (Stuttgart, 1978), pp. 66ff.; W. Zimmerli, *Grundriss der alttestamentlichen Theologie* (Stuttgart, 1975), p. 45 (vs. E. Gerstenberger, *JBL* 84, 1965), pp. 38-51 and J. Bright, *op. cit.*, pp. 43ff.

13

A THIRD MASCULINE SINGULAR *TAQTUL* IN BIBLICAL HEBREW?

Antoon Schoors

While studying the language of Koheleth, I faced the problem of the form *t*[e]*yagg*[e]*'ennû* in Koh. 10.15: the preformative *t* suggests a feminine form, although the subject *'āmāl* is masculine. A number of solutions have been proposed, the easiest of which is to state that the construction 'shews the inattention to the agreement of genders, numbers, etc.'[1] M. Thilo simply states that *'āmāl* is constructed as feminine, whereas N.H. Tur Sinai changes the preformative into *yod*.[2] A very drastic emendation has been put forward by A.B. Ehrlich and adopted by some critics: they read *'*[a]*mal hakk*[e]*sîl mātay y*[e]*yagg*[e]*'ennû*, 'the work of the fool, when does it weary him?'[3] This emendation is purely conjectural and should only be accepted as a last resort.

But could we not justify the reading of the MT as a 3rd m. sg. *taqtul*? This question made me investigate again the problem of 3rd m. sg. *taqtul* in Biblical Hebrew. I would like to present the results of that research as a modest contribution to this *Festschrift*, offered to Professor F.C. Fensham, whom I esteem very highly as a competent scholar and a generous colleague.

In Ugaritic, the preformative *t* seems sometimes to have the force of a third-person masculine singular. In his *Ugaritic Textbook*, C.H. Gordon mentions only that *t*- often displaces *y*- in 3rd du. and pl.[4] But there are possible instances of the same phenomenon in the singular, e.g. UT 75 II 55 (KTU 1.12.II.54) *wtkms hd*, 'and Hadad was prostrate', and 1 Aqht 36 (KTU 1.19.I.36) *tmz' kst dnil*, 'Danel tears his garb'. However, C.H. Gordon and J. Aistleitner, followed by others, consider the forms *tkms* and *tmz'* as tD, a reflexive conjugation, which would leave us with a perfect tense.[5] In 1 Aqht 36, *tmz'* can be parsed as a passive impf. 3rd f. sg., with *kst* as the subject,[6] and the original editor of the text, C. Virolleaud, reads it as an active impf. 3rd f. sg. with *pǵt* as the subject.[7] L.R. Fisher and F.B. Knutson have added another example of this phenomenon, which they find in RS 24.245 (KTU 1.101) line 5: *rišh. tply*, rendered as 'His head is wonderful'. This translation, however, is more than doubtful, since the meaning of *tply* is not clear at all.[8] In sum, the evidence for a 3rd m. sg. *taqtul* in Ugaritic is far from conclusive and it is even rather negative.

N.M. Sarna, when trying to parse Job 18.14-15 *w^{e}taṣ'idēhû* and *tiškôn*, and 20.9 *t^{e}šûrennû* as 3rd m. sg. forms, referred to three examples from the Amarna letters: *ti-di-nu* (EA 71.5; 86.4), *ta-az-ra-ḫi* (143.27-28) and *ti-ra-am* (323.22).[9] But the first form is jussive plural, the second probably feminine, having *^{d}šamaš* as subject, and the last seems to be a noun, as has been convincingly demonstrated by W.L. Moran.[10] As to Job 18.14-15 and 20.9, the texts are rather complicated and other parsings are quite possible: *taṣ'idēhû* (18.14) seems to be 3rd f. sg. with an indefinite subject 'it'[11] and the same applies to *tiškôn* (v. 15),[12] unless we read with M. Dahood *mabbēl*, 'flame', as a feminine subject instead of *mibb^{e}lî*.[13] In Job 20.9 the ancient versions and the majority of modern critics consider *m^{e}qômô*, which is masculine, as the subject of *t^{e}šûrennû*. This certainly is the easiest way to read the verse, and if it is correct, then we have here either a textual corruption or a 3rd m. sg. *taqtul*. But it remains possible to take *'ayin* as the subject of the verbs in the verse, *m^{e}qômô* then being an accusative.[14]

In an article on the subject of 3rd m. sg. *t-*, H.J. van Dijk produces a few instances from the Ahiram inscription and Punic texts.[15] As to the former, it reads *tḥtsp ḥṭr. . . thtpk ks'* (KAI 1.2). If *ks'* and *ḥṭr* are masculine, the reference is well chosen. According to H. Donner–W. Röllig, both nouns are here feminine as they are in Ugaritic and Akkadian.[16] This statement should be qualified: in Ugaritic *ḥṭr* is unknown, whereas *ksu* seems to be feminine in UT.51.V. 108 (KTU 1.4.V.46) *t'db ksu*;[17] in Akkadian there is no indication that *ḫuṭāru* is fem. (a feminine form *ḫuṭartu* does exist) but *kussû* is generally fem.[18] As to the Punic instances, all of them can be explained in different ways, since in *tšmḥ ql' brk'* (RES 337), *šm' ql' tbrk'* (Costa 17), and *tšm' qlm* (KAI 77.3-4), none of the forms with *t*- preformative has *ql*, 'voice', as subject.[19] Thus the comparative base for accepting a 3rd m. sg. *t*- preformative is very narrow and does not provide us with one single example that is absolutely sure.

Van Dijk adduces some nine instances of this form from the Hebrew Bible: Isa. 42.20; 53.10; Ezek. 12.25; Ps. 42.2; Isa. 7.20; Hab. 1.14; Ps. 10.13, 15 and Koh. 10.15, with which we opened this paper. None of them can stand the test. Isa. 42.20 *tišmōr*; Hab. 1.14 *ta'ăšeh*; Ps. 10.13 *tidrōš* and 15 *timṣā'* are all second person.[20] Isa. 53.10 *tāśîm* can also be second person unless the text is corrupt.[21] Ezek. 12.25 *timmāšēk* is 3rd fem. *pro neutro*; Ps. 42.2 *ta'ᵃrōg* is 3rd fem. with *'ayyelet* as subject (MT *'ayyāl* originated by haplography), and Isa. 7.20 *tispeh* is 3rd fem. with *ta'ar* as subject.[22] Van Dijk himself has some doubts about Deut. 32.14 *tišteh*, 'which in the context looks like a third masculine singular'. A third person admittedly fits the context better, but a second person remains quite possible.[23] B. Pennacchini tends to accept here a 3rd m. sg. *taqtul*.[24]

More recently M. Dahood came up with thirty more examples of this form.[25] Some of them involve a textual emendation, which in all of the instances is superfluous. In Gen. 49.24 he reads *wattᵉšōbēb 'êtān*, 'The Perennial restored', instead of MT *wattēšeb bᵉ'êtān*, but MT makes good sense, as may appear from the translation in TOB 'mais son arc demeure ferme'. Ezek. 26.11 *tērēd* is changed into *tōrīd* and the sentence is translated as follows: 'and your strong pillars he will bring down to the ground'; this parsing is in accordance with LXX, Syr and Tg; however, more than once plural nouns, referring to animals or objects, have a verbal predicate in 3rd fem. sg., especially when they are in a construct state connected with a singular noun,[26] so that Ezek. 26.11b can be rendered thus: 'your mighty pillars will fall to the ground' (RSV).[27] The reading *timse*, which Dahood suggests to replace MT *temes* in Ps. 58.9, is out of the question; *temes* is an internal object of *yahᵃlōk*: 'Like the snail which dissolves into slime' (RSV). In Job 16.7 Dahood reads *hāšēm wattᵉkal* for MT *hᵃšimmôtā kol*, translating the verse thus: 'But now he has overcome me, he has laid waste and annihilated my family'. MT *hᵃšimmôtā* is consistent with *wattiqmᵉṭēnî* in v. 8. RSV has the third person for both verbs, but TOB offers an acceptable rendering of MT: 'Mais c'est que maintenant il m'a poussé à bout: Oui, tu as ravagé tout mon entourage, [8] tu m'as creusé des rides . . .' The text is probably corrupt. Also in Job 34.26 an emendation of *taḥat* to *tāḥīt* is superfluous. M.H. Pope translates the verse as follows: 'As criminals he strikes them down . . .' with the comment: 'Literally "among criminals" or "in the place of/for criminals", the preposition *taḥat*, "under", having the sense of "among" or "in the place of"'.[28]

Others of Dahood's examples are based on grammatical or syntactical misunderstandings. Thus in Isa. 32.13, *taʿaleh* is 3rd fem. sg. with *'admat 'ammî* as subject; in Hos. 5.9, *'eprayim*, the subject of *tihyeh*, is fem., being the name of a region; the same applies to *kûš* as the subject of *tāriṣ* in Ps. 68.32; in Hab. 3.4, the subject of *tihyeh* is *nōgah*, which elsewhere does not occur in syntagmas that would indicate its gender: could it not be feminine like *'ēš*, 'fire'?[29] Other feminine subjects are *rištô* for *tilkᵉdô* in Ps. 35.8, *šemeš* for *tizraḥ* in Ps. 104.22,[30] *rûaḥ* for *wattᵉrômēm* in Ps. 107.25[31] and *rā'â* for *tāmûš* (qerē) in Prov. 17.13. A number of *taqtul* forms can be parsed as second person; thus *ûtᵉkônēn* in Ps. 7.10; *tāšet* in Ps. 104.20; *taršîa'* in Job 34.17; *tᵉšûrennû* in Job 35.14; *tarbeh* in Prov. 6.35; *tiqrā'* in Lam. 2.22.[32] In Ps. 68.15, *tašlēg* can be parsed as an impersonal 3rd fem. sg. Isa. 57.3 *mᵉnā'ēp wattizneh* doubtlessly conceals *mᵉnā'epet wᵉzōnâ* (BHS).[33] Sometimes it is difficult to make a definite choice between two possibilities: in Ps. 48.8 we could read *kᵉrûaḥ qādîm tᵉšabbēr*, parsing *tᵉšabbēr* as an asyndetic relative clause which goes with *rûaḥ*, but a reading *tiššābēr*, with *'oniyôt* as the subject cannot be excluded.[34] Lam. 3.17 *wattiznaḥ* can be parsed as a second person or revocalized as a niphal 3rd fem. sg. *wattizzānaḥ*, the subject of which is *napšî*.[35] In Isa. 38.13 the situation is very complicated and no satisfactory solution has been found to the problems which beset the interpreter of this verse. The masculine *taqtul* suggested by Dahood is *tašlîmēnî*. Verse 13b is a dittographic repetition of v. 12bβ. But there the difficulties are not diminished: the verbs are first person *qippadtî*, third person *yᵉbaṣṣᵉ'ēnî* and the *tašlîmēnî* under consideration. The parallelism seems to favour Dahood's proposal, but a second person remains possible, the more so since v. 14 has an imperative, addressed to Adonai. Verse 12b can be translated as follows: 'like a weaver I have rolled up my life; one cuts me off from the loom: from day to night thou dost bring me to an end'.[36] BHS, R.B.Y. Scott and H. Wildberger read the three verbs as second person.[37] A similar approach is possible with respect to Ps. 41.3, where *'al-tittᵉnēhû* seems to be a third person according to the context, and so it has been rendered by LXX, Sym and Syr,[38] but again a second person cannot be excluded, as may appear from Dahood's own commentary:

'Do not put him into the maw of his Foe!'[39] Isa. 35.9 *timmāṣē'* may be a 3rd m. sg. if *p^erîṣ* is the subject (cf. 1QIsa[a] *ymṣ'*); however, the form can be parsed as feminine with an implicit reference to *ḥayyâ*, since the composed subject is *p^erîṣ ḥayyôt*, or the consonantal text allows a second person qal *lō' timṣā'*, 'you will not find'. Concerning Ps. 49.20 *tābô'*, most commentators agree that it should be a third person and therefore emend it to *yābô'*.[40] But a 3rd fem. sg. can be accounted for with *napšô* (v. 19) as the subject,[41] and in his commentary, Dahood even saves a second person: 'And though they praise you when you prosper, you will enter the circle of your fathers'.[42] This rendering, however, involves an unacceptable analysis of the suffix of *'^abôtāyw*, 'reading, with no change of consonants, *'ăbōtī*, the oblique plural as in Ugaritic, and attaching the final *waw* to the next word'.[43]

After having discussed some of the aforementioned instances, B. Pennacchini puts forward another text where *taqtul* 3rd m. sg. would occur: Isa. 27.8 *t^erîbennâ*.[44] It must be admitted that a verb in the second person is quite isolated here, in a context where the other verbs are third person: *hikkāhû* (v. 7) and *hāgâ* (v. 8). But this verse is so difficult and its functioning in the context so obscure that one can hardly decide which parsing should be preferred.[45]

In sum, the evidence for the existence of a 3rd m. sg. *taqtul* in Northwest Semitic is very scarce and never beyond doubt. Particularly in Biblical Hebrew, all instances alleged so far are capable of alternative explanations. Thus the parsing of Koh. 10.15 *t^eyagg^e'ennû* as a 3rd masc. *taqtul*, as suggested by H.J. van Dijk and C.F. Whitley,[46] is founded on a narrow and rather shaky base. Therefore it seems preferable to suppose a textual corruption or to accept that *'āmāl* is feminine here.[47]

NOTES

1. Thus C.D. Ginsburg, *Coheleth* (London, 1861), p. 440.
2. M. Thilo, *Der Prediger Salomo* (Bonn, 1923), p. 40; cf. F. Delitzsch, *Hoheslied und Koheleth* (Leipzig, 1875), p. 372; N.H. Tur Sinai, *P^ešûṭô šel miqrā'*, IV, 2 (Jerusalem, 1968), p. 174.
3. Cf. A.B. Ehrlich, *Randglossen*', VII, p. 99; BHK; BHS; H.W. Hertzberg, *Der Prediger* (KAT, 17/4; Gütersloh, 1963), p. 193; K. Galling, *Der Prediger* (HbAT, 1/18; Tübingen, 1969), p. 116; A. Lauha, *Kohelet* (BKAT, 19; Neukirchen-Vluyn, 1978), p. 190.
4. C.H. Gordon, *UT*, §9.14.

5. Cf. *UT*, §19.1258; J. Aistleitner, *WUS*, nos. 1330 and 1538. Cf. A. Caquot–M. Sznycer–A. Herdner, *Textes ougaritiques* (Littératures anciennes du Proche-Orient, 7; Paris, 1974), pp. 349-50 and 444; G.R. Driver, *CML*, pp. 59 and 145; and for 75.II.55: C. Virolleaud, *Syria* 16 (1935), p. 265; J. Montgomery, *JAOS* 56 (1936), p. 231; J.C.L. Gibson, *CML* (2nd edn), p. 149; G. del Olmo Lete, *Mitos y leyendas de Canaan* (Madrid, 1981), p. 566. According to J. Sanmartín, *UF* 10 (1978), p. 355, *tkms* is a noun of the *tqtl* type.

6. M. Dijkstra–J.C. de Moor, *UF* 7 (1975), p. 201; cf. R. de Vaux, *RB* 46 (1937), p. 447; G. del Olmo Lete, *Mitos y leyendas*, p. 576.

7. C. Virolleaud, *La légende phénicienne de Danel* (Paris, 1936), pp. 142-44; cf. J.C.L. Gibson, *CML* (2nd edn), p. 114.

8. Cf. L.R. Fisher–F.B. Knutson, *JBL* 28 (1969), p. 159; *RSP* II, p. 134. M. Dahood, *Or* 48 (1979), p. 98, agrees to this parsing of *tply* as 3rd m. sg. of *ply*, a by-form of *pl'*. But Fisher and Knutson have been criticized by M.H. Pope, *Song of Songs* (AB, 7C; Garden City, 1977), p. 512; S.E. Loewenstamm, *Bib* 59 (1978), p. 112. C. Virolleaud, *Ug* V, p. 558, leaves *tply* untranslated with the comment: 'Ces deux mots désignent sans doute quelque phénomène atmosphérique'. B. Margulis, *ZAW* 86 (1974), pp. 5-6, syntactically separates *tply* from *rišh*. J.C. Moor, *UF* 1 (1969), pp. 180-81, and M. Dietrich–O. Loretz–J. Sanmartín, *UF* 7 (1975), pp. 534-35, take *ṭly* as subject; the former translates: 'Ṭallayu made his head wonderful', whereas the latter have: 'Seinen Kopf sondert Ṭly aus'. This meaning of the clause is undoubtedly the most consistent in the context of the tablet. Cf. E. Lipiński, *UF* 3 (1971), pp. 82 and 84: 'Sur sa tête se distingue Ṭalay' (*tply* is N. impf. 3rd fem. sg.).

9. N.M. Sarna, 'The Mythological Background of Job 18', *JBL* 82 (1963), pp. 317-18.

10. W.L. Moran, '**taqtul*—Third Masculine Singular?', *Bib* 45 (1964), pp. 80-82.

11. Cf. C. Epping–J.T. Nelis, *Job* (BOT, 7A; Roermond, 1968), p. 89; F. Horst, *Hiob* (BKAT, 16; Neukirchen-Vluyn, 1968), p. 273.

12. F. Horst, *loc. cit.*

13. M. Dahood, *Bib* 38 (1957), pp. 312-13; C. Epping–J.T. Nelis, *loc. cit.*; M.H. Pope, *Job* (AB, 15; Garden City, 1965), p. 126.

14. E.g. M. Buber, *Die Schriftwerke verdeutscht* (Köln, 1962), p. 305: 'das Auge mustert ihn und nimmer wieder, nie mehr gewahrts ihn an seinem Platz'. Cf. also NEB.

15. H.J. van Dijk, 'Does Third Masculine Singular **taqtul* exist in Hebrew?', *VT* 19 (1969), pp. 440-47.

16. *KAI* II, p. 5.

17. J.C.L. Gibson, *CML* (2nd edn), p. 61, translates this clause by 'they made ready a seat'. This certainly does not improve on G.R. Driver's former edition, which has 'a seat was made ready' (p. 99); *ksu*, ending with *u*, is

undoubtedly the subject and *t'db* is consequently to be parsed as passive 3rd sg. The fact that Akk. *kussû* is generally feminine makes it highly probable that Ug. *ksu* is feminine too.

18. Cf. *AHw*, pp. 362; 515; *GAG*, §60d.

19. Cf. *KAI* II, pp. 95; 100; 116.

20. Isa. 42.20: cf. A. Schoors, *I am God your Saviour* (SVT, 24; Leiden, 1973), p. 201: *tišmōr* follows after *ra'îtā* (K). Hab. 1.14: cf. RSV; NEB. Ps. 10.13: cf. M. Dahood, *Psalms* I (AB, 16; Garden City, 1966), p. 60: 'You will not requite'; LXX and Syr have 3rd sg. Ps. 10.15: cf. M. Dahood, *op. cit.*, p. 61: 'Can't you find his wickedness?'; RSV; NEB; LXX has εὑρεθῇ.

21. Cf. TOB; possibly to be read **met śām 'āšām napšô*: cf. M. Dahood, *CBQ* 22 (1960), p. 406; or *napšô* can be the subject: cf. C.R. North, *The Second Isaiah* (Oxford, 1967), p. 232.

22. Ezek. 12.25: cf. W. Zimmerli, *Ezechiel* (BKAT, 13; Neukirchen-Vluyn, 1969), p. 275. In v. 28 the same form occurs with the plural *d^ebāray* as subject; GK, §145 k offers a list of 3rd fem. sg. verb forms that have a plural subject. Ps. 42.2: cf. BHS; M. Dahood, *Psalms* I, p. 255; lg. *k^e'ayyelet 'ārōg* (infin. absol.). Isa. 7.20: cf. G. Fohrer, *Das Buch Jesaja*, I (Zürich, 1966), p. 119; RSV; NEB.

23. LXX ἔπιον (B ἔπιεν) and Vg *biberet* are facilitating readings. Cf. TOB; G. von Rad, *Das fünfte Buch Mose* (ATD, 8; Göttingen, 1968), p. 137; S.R. Driver, *Deuteronomy* (ICC; Edinburgh, 1902), p. 360.

24. B. Pennacchini, *Euntes Docete* 33 (1980), pp. 189-92.

25. M. Dahood, 'Third Masculine Singular with Preformative *t*- in Northwest Semitic', *Or* 48 (1979), pp. 97-106.

26. Cf. GK, §145 k; Joüon, §150 i; W. Zimmerli, *op. cit.*, p. 609.

27. B. Pennacchini, *Euntes Docete* 33 (1980), pp. 180-88, is in doubt whether to follow Dahood or to accept the parsing we adopt here.

28. M.H. Pope, *Job*, pp. 222 and 225; cf. TOB.

29. Cf. BDB, p. 618.

30. NEB parses it as second person.

31. Cf. M. Dahood, *Psalms* III (AB, 17A; Garden City, 1970), p. 79: 'a storm which lifted high his waves'; H.J. Kraus, *Psalmen* (BKAT, 15; Neukirchen-Vluyn, 1966), p. 735.

32. Ps. 7.10: cf. M. Dahood, *Psalms* I, p. 40; H.J. Kraus, *op. cit.*, pp. 53-54. Ps. 104.20: cf. NEB; H.J. Kraus, *op. cit.*, p. 707; Syr has third person. Job 34.17: cf. TOB; RSV; M.H. Pope, *Job*, p. 222; 2 MSS have *yaršîa'*. Job 35.14: cf. TOB; RSV; M.H. Pope, *op. cit.*, p. 227. Prov. 6.35: cf. TOB, RSV; O. Plöger, *Sprüche Salomos* (BKAT, 17; Neukirchen-Vluyn, 1984), p. 68. Lam. 2.22: cf. TOB; RSV; H.J. Kraus, *Klagelieder* (BKAT, 20; Neukirchen-Vluyn, 1960), p. 37; LXX^AB has ἐκάλεσεν.

33. LXX μοιχῶν καὶ πόρνης; Vg *adulteri et fornicariae* reflect *m^enā'ēp* and *zōnâ*; J.L. McKenzie, *Second Isaiah* (AB, 20; Garden City, 1968), p. 156, and G. Fohrer, *Das Buch Jesaja*, III (Zürich, 1964), p. 194, adopt this reading.

C. Westermann, *Das Buch Jesaja. Kap. 40–66* (ATD, 19; Göttingen 1966), p. 256 follows BHS.

34. Cf. BHS for the first possibility. The second has been put forward by M. Dahood himself in *Psalms* I, p. 292. Cf. B. Pennacchini, *Euntes Docete* 33 (1980), pp. 193-97.

35. Vg: *repulsa est*, followed by RSV; second person: cf. TOB; H.J. Kraus, *op. cit.*, p. 53. LXX ἀπώσατο, which seems to support Dahood, is a *lectio facilitans*.

36. Cf. A. Schoors, *Jesaja* (BOT, 9; Roermond, 1972), p. 215.

37. R.B.Y. Scott, *Isaiah* (The Interpreter's Bible, V; Nashville, 1956), p. 375; H. Wildberger, *Jesaja* (BKAT, 10/3; Neukirchen-Vluyn, 1982), p. 1443. G. Fohrer, *Das Buch Jesaja* 2 (Zürich, 1967), p. 190, reads the three verbs as third person.

38. LXX: καὶ μὴ παραδώῃ; Syr: *wl' nšlmywhy*.

39. M. Dahood, *Psalms* I, p. 248; J. van der Ploeg, *Psalmen* (BOT, 7; Roermond, 1974), p. 256; TOB. H.J. Kraus, *Psalmen*, p. 311, reads third person emending the text.

40. Cf. BHS; TOB; NEB; RSV; H.J. Kraus, *op. cit.* p. 364.

41. J. van der Ploeg, *op. cit.*, p. 306.

42. M. Dahood, *op. cit.*, p. 296.

43. M. Dahood, *op. cit.*, p. 303.

44. B. Pennacchini, 'Alcuni nuovi esempi della forma taqtul', *Euntes Docete* 33 (1980), pp. 177-98, esp. 197-98.

45. H. Wildberger, *Jesaja*, p. 1014: 'Bei der Unmöglichkeit, zu einer sicheren Deutung des Zusammenhangs zu kommen, ist kein wirklich fundiertes Urteil möglich'. Cf. A. Schoors, *Jesaja*, p. 162.

46. C.F. Whitley, *Koheleth. His Language and Thought* (BZAW, 145; Berlin, 1979), pp. 87-88.

47. Cf. BDB, p. 765. This would be the only instance; in Pss. 7.17; 140.10; Job 5.6, *'āmāl* is masculine.

14

ANCIENT ISRAEL: AN ATTEMPT AT A SOCIAL AND ECONOMIC ANALYSIS OF THE AVAILABLE DATA

J.A. Soggin

I

A study on the economic and social world of Ancient Israel (and I shall be dealing mostly with the monarchical period, i.e. the first half of the first millennium BC, from the tenth to the sixth centuries BC) is notoriously a most difficult task. Any attempt at reconstruction, any research on its political implications and impact, clashes with the almost total absence of economic and administrative texts.

1. As is well known, the opposite is the case in Mesopotamia, be it the two major kingdoms or the city-states of Mari and Nuzi or in Syria where we deal with the city-states of Ebla, Ugarit and Alalaḫ. Here relevant textual finds have been made, and many of these are economic and administrative texts. So, if we succeed, for example, in establishing how much a farmer, a craftsman or a merchant paid the state in taxes, be it in kind or otherwise, or what sums were taken to the temple in tithes, it is not difficult in most cases to ascertain the quantity, the quality and the value of their products and thus draw conclusions about the social and economic situation in general.

2. But in Israel the contrary seems to be the case. For the Southern Kingdom, Judah, nothing has so far been preserved of the archives of the temple and the royal palace, and we have practically no hope whatsoever that at least parts of the archives may be discovered. Therefore our only source remains the Hebrew Bible, but as this is a work with essentially religious aims, it has little interest in economics and sociology as such. Where the northern part of Israel is concerned, we are in a slightly better position. A few Biblical texts and non-biblical materials give us at least some information. So we hear that during the united kingdom under Solomon, the country

was divided into twelve districts whose main task it was to provide for the maintenance of the court and the temple in Jerusalem (1 Kgs 4.7-19). It should further be noticed that all this refers only to Israel, the North.

We are also told that the major source of manpower was forced labour, to which all Israel again (here also quite likely only the North) was subjected, without any discrimination between nationality, religion or race[1] (1 Kgs 5.27, cf. Josephus *Ant.* 8.58). In the parallel text 2 Chron. 2.16, the levy of forced labour was supposed to have been limited to the conquered Canaanites, and this is confirmed by 1 Kgs 9.15a, 20-22 (LXX 10.22a-c), 2 Chron. 8.7-10; but here we are obviously dealing with later embellishments of the tradition by a redactor, a later phase of the Dtr., who proved to be a true *laudator temporis acti.* These embellishments ignore in fact the complex composition of the empire, where also the Canaanite city-states and their populations had quite probably been incorporated mostly in a peaceful way, probably through treaties. It further does not take into consideration that the main cause of the secession of the North at Solomon's death was, according to the sources, the exploitation of the North by the South. The same texts offer us also a picture of Solomon's commercial enterprises, by sea and by land. To the superficial reader the texts show a great quantity of wealth flowing into the royal treasury, although a more critical study makes it quite clear that most of these enterprises were rather not so much assets as liabilities to the crown, and therefore also causes of economic crises.

3. And from the *ostraca* from Samaria, which should tentatively be dated to the beginning of the second half of the eighth century BC, we can deduce, according to an older but authoritative interpretation,[2] that they were more or less forwarding notes, for delivery to the court of taxes similar to those of the former Solomonic districts. Paradoxically, therefore, a fiscal system considered as unfair, and which appears for this reason to have been one of the main causes of the disruption of the empire, seems to have still been fully operating a few decades before the end of the Northern Kingdom!

4. Again in the kingdom of Israel a few decades before its end we find, in the Bible, another economic text (2 Kgs 15.17-22) which tells us that king Menahem (c. 747 or 746-727 BC) paid to king Tiglath Pileser III of Assyria (744-727 BC) in 738 (according to the Assyrian annals, *ANET*, p. 283) the considerable sum of 1000 talents of silver,

as a token of submission. The texts inform us further that the Israelite king had no difficulty in gathering the sum. He did so by taxing 'all the men of wealth' fifty shekels a person.[3] This shows us that a most prosperous class of landowners existed in Israel. On the other hand, there could be reason to doubt these figures, as there is simply no way to verify their accuracy and some may consider the sum and the number of prosperous people too high. But all commentaries agree that we are dealing here with an abstract from the annals of the court or with an older Dtr. text.[4] Further, we know of at least two other cases in which considerable sums were paid to Assyrian kings by Syrian and Palestinian rulers: the tribute of Mari', king of Damascus, to Adad-nirari III in 806 and that by Hezekiah to Sennacherib in 701 (*ANET*, pp. 281f. and 288).

But concerning all other aspects of the transaction we are left in the dark, e.g. whether these landowners lived on their land or were absentees; or what the conditions were under which their wage earners lived. Were they day labourers and shepherds, or even tenant farmers? Certainly, if we pay heed to the social invectives of the prophets of the eighth century, conditions must be rated from poor to rather bad. But further deductions from those invectives, and especially attempts to translate them into figures and statistical data, appear arbitrary.[5]

II

These fundamental obstacles have prompted many scholars to attempt to reconstruct the social and economic structures of ancient Israel by referring to domain assumptions and to models from nearby countries. These models are obviously hypothetical, and I shall here try to deal with some of the more recent and important ones.

1. The subtitle of a recent North American work on Israel's tribes at the time of the settlement,[6] by the Marxist author N.K. Gottwald, calls itself nothing less than 'A Sociology of the Religion of Liberated Israel', an entity which he identifies with Israel after the settlement in Canaan. Unfortunately, this 'Liberated Israel' exists mostly in the author's imagination and seems to have more to do with the conditions, considered unsatisfactory, in the USA at the present time than with facts of ancient Israel. This is simply because, the sources being what they are, it is impossible to write a sociology of ancient Israel, be it of the religion or of anything else. What seems, however,

to be necessary, and here Gottwald is right, is a re-orientation of archaeological investigation in a more sociological sense.

2. A second work, a doctoral dissertation presented at the Humboldt University in Berlin, GDR, after a most useful analysis of semi-nomadism and of class structures within and around ancient Syria and Palestine, tries to apply these data to ancient Israelite society before the monarchy.[7] But we know little or nothing from the written sources about this society, as already argued.[8] Fully valid, however, is his criticism of the various contemporary hypotheses and models for Israel's settlement.

3. Not much different, it seems to me, should be our judgment on parts of a recent, otherwise notable contribution on 'Palestine in Transition' from the Late Bronze Age to Iron I.[9] Again: as we do not really know anything definite apart from the available written sources, the birth of Israel, when it settled in Palestine, remains for all present research hidden in darkness,[10] apart from the traditions recorded by the Hebrew Bible. Any systematic comparison with peasants' revolts or similar references to ethnic movements, refugees and social upheavals, will never go beyond the realm of hypothesis, whether brilliant or otherwise.

4. If we now want to make a short excursion into Judaism during the time of Jesus, things often seem not so very different there either. It is in this field that a decade ago a few works were produced, the theme of which was a 'materialistic' or in some sense political reading of the Gospels. The main contribution was by Fernando Belo,[11] a Portuguese scholar active in France, who left this undertaking a few years later to devote himself to other fields of research. Also in this field, however, the scholar lacks adequate written sources dealing with economic and social problems, without which his work can hardly be well-founded.[12]

III

Let us now turn towards the settlement of Israel in Palestine[13] as an example of what can be ascertained from our sources, and what cannot. 'Settlement', incidentally, is a neutral term, far better than the traditional 'conquest', as was already argued a decade ago by R. de Vaux. Now, we have to state here immediately, even if it may offend some, that the Biblical texts referring to this fundamental event (and we lack any other kind of text) are all, without exception, practically unsuitable for the use of the historian. The only data we can use stem from archaeological excavations, provided we do remember something archaeologists always tell us, viz. that excavations without adequate epigraphic finds or existing texts are mute.

Now the picture which archaeology offers us seems to exclude, in any case, the violent immigration of foreign elements, especially by semi-nomads.[14] This is the unquestionable result of the data produced by the finds made in the last ten or twenty years (data which have been only partially published in scattered places). A first, although limited, synthesis towards a global appreciation of the phenomenon seems to me that made by Diethelm Conrad of Marburg, which I have attached as Appendix I to my *History of Israel* (London: SCM, 1984).

1. The transition period from LB to Iron I was a very disturbed one in the whole eastern Mediterranean region, including Syria and the Aegean. Ancient towns were destroyed, new people settled in the territories, amongst them the Ammonites, the Edomites and the Moabites in Transjordan, the Aramaeans in Syria, Israel and the Philistines in Canaan. The Philistines actually gave the region one of its names, Palestine, attested as early as Herodotus (second half of the fifth century BC). These factors are quite sufficient to postulate great political unrest and disruption of trade and widespread destruction on which only economic instability and therefore a crisis could follow. Now, while Palestinian archaeology, during its first century, concentrated rather on cities and tended to connect their destruction with the Israelite 'conquest' (and this explains the particular interest in the narratives about Jericho, 'Ai, Hazor, 'Arad and others), the trend during recent decades has been rather to survey broad regions in search of variations in their settlement pattern, where such exist.

In course of this, a most interesting phenomenon has been noticed: during the transition from LB to Iron I, while most of the old city-states of the coasts and the plains remained in existence, on the highlands and in the marginal steppes, where city-states have always been very few, many new settlements came into being, most of them unfortified and therefore presumably peaceful. But the most interesting feature is that these villages (for villages these settlements were indeed) were anything but technically backward, as one might reasonably have expected them to be if their inhabitants had been nomads in the process of becoming settled (cf. what is happening nowadays in Israel, Jordan and the Arabian peninsula where Bedouin groups are being installed). The buildings testify to a considerable technical capability and they are provided with sophisticated installations not only for preserving rain water in cisterns, but also for filtering it. Paved roads and agricultural terraces bear witness to settlers who came from a civilized context and were familiar with hill and mountain farming. Further, the new settlers seem to have moved from west to east, more rarely from north to south, so that their starting point *must* have been the territories of the city-states, from where they moved to the highlands and the steppes. Also, these factors make it highly improbable that we are dealing with the sedentarization of semi-nomads, as was maintained from the 1930s to the 1960s in Germany by A. Alt and M. Noth, on the basis of the data then available, and accepted by many up to this day. They have seen rightly, however, where the settlement took place and that it must have been mostly peaceful. The origin of the city-states, from where the settlers must have come as farmers, sustains the recent theses by G.E. Mendenhall and N.K. Gottwald in the USA, who see the settlement as the result of the farmers' revolt against the authority of the city-states, but on the condition that it was not an active revolt, a violent one, but rather a flight. They fled from the economic misery, due to internecine struggles and overtaxation, and went to lands that had become habitable for man and cattle because of the discovery of techniques of preserving water in cisterns during the dry season.

2. At present we have no conclusive evidence at all that ancient Israel grew out of these settlements. But it seems to be a reasonable working hypothesis to assume it. However, as archaeology under such circumstances is mute, as we have seen, we do not know much about the social and political structures of the settlements which have recently been compared to African 'segmentary' societies, although it seems likely that out of them grew those entities that eventually became Israel and Judah, probably worshipping the same God Yhwh. Economically they seem to have operated on the basis of agriculture and shepherding, with the village as permanent base, as still happens in some mountain regions of southern Europe and in Africa. But if this should be true, the tradition that the core of Israel was made up of groups of people who had immigrated from countries far away remains extremely doubtful. It reminds us much more of the migration of Aeneas in the lore of Imperial Rome (where these

traditions had a clear socio-political function: legitimizing the ascent of the *Gens Julia* to the throne, thus replacing the ancient republican structures), than of any known connection with historical fact. And it would be a most interesting undertaking, although a very difficult one, to try and ascertain what political and social and eventually legitimizing functions the traditions of the Patriarchs and the legends of the Exodus, the Conquest and the Judges had within the later structures of the people of Israel.

NOTES

*For reading and correcting my English typescript I wish to thank Mrs Barbara Bishop, of the English-speaking Methodist Church in Rome.

1. For details I must refer to my *History of Israel* (London: SCM, 1984), ch. 4, §5.

2. For the main texts see *KAI*, pp. 183ff. The thesis referred to has been proposed by M. Noth, 'Das Krongut der israelitischen Könige und seine Verwaltung, 2. Die samarischen Ostraka', *ZDPV* 50 (1927), pp. 219-29 (*Aufsätze* [1971], pp. 164-72). According to Y. Yadin, 'Recipients or Owners. A Note on the Samaria Ostraka', *IEJ* 9 (1959), pp. 184-87, and A. F. Rainey, 'Administration in Ugarit and the Samaria Ostraca', *IEJ* 12 (1962), pp. 62-66 and 'The Samaria Ostraka in the Light of Fresh Evidence', *PEQ* 99 (1967), pp. 32-41, we are dealing here with gifts by the crown to officials and other persons. These positions, although different, do not seem mutually exclusive.

3. The ordinary talent, Heb. *kikkār*, weighed 34.373 kilos and contained 3,000 shekels, weighing 11.424 grammes each; the royal talent, used for taxation, contained 3,600 shekels. Therefore the number of owners taxed must have been 60,000.

4. Cf. the commentaries by C.F. Burney, *Notes on the Hebrew Text of Kings*, Oxford, 1903; S. Garofalo, *Il libro dei Re*, Torino, 1951; J.A. Montgomery-H.S. Gehman, *The Book of Kings* (ICC), Edinburgh, 1951; J. Gray, *I and & II Kings* (OTL), 2nd edn, London and Philadelphia, 1970; E. Würthwein, *Die Bücher der Könige*, II (ATD), Göttingen, 1984, all *ad loc.*

5. Many are the works on the social message of Israel's prophets, a problem with which we cannot deal here.

6. N.K. Gottwald, *The Tribes of Yahweh. A Sociology of the Religion of Liberated Israel, 1250-1050*, Maryknoll and London, 1979-80; cf. my review, *Bib* 62 (1981), pp. 583-590. Gottwald's teacher, G.E. Mendenhall, from whom the thesis of the peasants' revolt originates, has recently dissociated himself from his pupil; cf. 'Ancient Hypenated History', *Palestine in Transition* (see note 9), pp. 91-103.

7. W. Thiel, *Die soziale Entwicklung Israels in vorstaatlicher Zeit*, Berlin DDR, 1980.

8. Particularly open to question appears the comparison between Israel's ancestors and ancient Near Eastern semi-nomads, who earned their lives as itinerant shepherds. In fact our texts never depict the Patriarchs or the Exodus generation as semi-nomads, but, if anything at all, as migrants. The difference between these two categories seems obvious: itinerant shepherding is a mode of production and exists to this day in many regions (southern Europe, Africa); and the condition of the migrant is temporary and ceases as soon as the group or the individual has reached his goal.

9. D.N. Freedman–D.F. Graf (eds.), *Palestine in Transition*, Sheffield, 1983. The following essays are devoted to Israel: N.K. Gottwald, 'Early Israel and the Canaanite Economic System', pp. 25-37; L.M. Chaney, 'Ancient Palestinian Peasant Movements and the Formation of pre-Monarchic Israel', pp. 39-90; and the article quoted above in n. 6.

10. The problem is correctly stated in an article by M. Liverani, 'Le "origini" d'Israele—progetto irrealizzabile di ricerca etnogenetica', *RiBib* 28 (1980), pp. 9-32.

11. F. Belo, *Lecture matérialiste de l'évangile de Marc*, Paris, 1974.

12. It is hardly by chance that Belo and his followers did not work on original data: these were taken from the classical work by J. Jeremias, *Jerusalem zur Zeit Jesu*, Göttingen and Berlin, 1923; 3rd edn, 1963.

13. For more details I must again refer to my *History* (cited in note 1), ch. 7, §§6ff. and App. I by Diethelm Conrad.

14. For details, see again my *History*, ch. 8.

15

STRUCTURAL LINGUISTICS AND TEXTUAL CRITICISM*

J.B. van Zijl

There seems to be enough evidence that a number of textual-critical variants in the Old Testament can be explained as resulting from a confusion of closely related sounds in the process of hearing. Here we are interested in variant readings of this kind and in their relation to the internal structure of masoretic Hebrew. For very often such textual-critical variants are discussed ad hoc, or a consonantal shift is described in isolation. One must however look at a fair number of examples in order to detect regularities in the distributional relations among them. For the purpose of this study the corpus of data is the Hebrew text of the book of Job. From the two critical editions of *Codex Leningradensis*, viz. *Biblia Hebraica* edited by Kittel (K) and *Biblia Hebraica Stuttgartensia* (S), a number of variant readings which seemed linguistically significant were collected. These are variants which evidently arise from a confusion of speech sounds rather than from letter-shapes. From more than a hundred such variants fifty examples were chosen for a sample illustration. The basis of most of them is either a manuscript variant reading or variants supported by one or more of the ancient Versions. By way of exception, interesting suggestions by Beer (K) or Gerleman (S) are included. In order to present the material in a systematic way a hint by Gleason (1970: 275) was acted on, to arrange the examples according to 'suspicious pairs', that is pairs of sounds which seem phonetically similar. The following abbreviations indicate the distributional positions of the sounds under discussion: P=pre-root position; I=initial root position; M=medial root position; F=final root position; A=post-root position. The K/S following a reference refer to the source of the example.

[*b*]:[*p*]	M	14.18KS; 28.11K
[*d*:[*t*]	M	30.15KS
	F	39.22KS
[ʿ]:[*ḥ*]	I	24.12K
	M	29.7K
[*z*]:[*ṣ*]	M	30.13KS
[*d*]:[*z*]	I	17.1KS
[*t*]:[*ṭ*]	M	9.12KS
[*b*]:[*v*]	P	22.16KS
[*b*]:[*m*]	P	3.11K; 5.19K; 5.12KS; 12.12S; 23.12KS; 39.25K
	I	24.12KS
	F	7.15KS; 9.8KS; 34.14K
[*m*]:[*n*]	P	37.16K
	I	28.11K
	M	22.17KS; 30.3S
	F	39.3KS
[*r*]:[*l*]	M	6.25KS; 15.8K; 16.3K; 19.20S; 36.29K
[ʿ]:[*h*]	F	4.2K; 8.21KS; 12.23KS; 26.9K
[*h*]:[*ḥ*]	I	15.20K; 19.3KS
	A	30.12KS
[*s*]:[*ṣ*]	F	30.13K
[*s*]:[*ś*]	F	6.14K
[*s*]:[*š*]	I	1.10KS; 9.17KS; 34.37S; 36.18KS
	M	4.2K
	F	5.2KS
[*ś*]:[*š*]	I	12.23KS; 23.7K; 36.24K
	F	28.11K; 34.14K

Certain of these 'pairs' and some individual references will now be discussed in more detail.

[*b*]:[*p*]

It is easy to confuse [*b*] and [*p*] because the only difference between them is that [*b*] is voiced and [*p*] is voiceless. Similarly voice is the basis of distinction, and possible confusion, in the pairs [*d*]:[*t*], [ʿ]:[*ḥ*] and [*z*]:[*ṣ*]. According to Blommerde the [*b*] and [*p*] are subject to reciprocal interchange in all the Semitic languages. He mentions relevant literature as well as a few possible implications of this interchange for the book of Job (Blommerde 1969: 5f.). In the case of Early Standard Aramaic this has been taken as a dialectal distinction: cf. e.g. *nbš* in the Sfîre inscription I lines 36, 37 for *npš*, 'soul' (Greenfield 1978: 94).

[*d*]:[*t*]
At 39.22 a few MSS and the Syriac support a reading *paḥat* for *paḥad*. These two words are often used together in the Old Testament: cf. Isa. 24.17, 18; Jer. 48.43, 44; Lam. 3.47. Both the meanings 'ditch' and 'fear' suit the context here; and if, as may well be, the voiced/voiceless contrast were neutralized in word-final position so that the words seemed the same, it would be impossible to tell which was originally meant.

[*d*]:[*z*]
The verb *zā'ak* occurs in the Old Testament only at 17.1, whereas the form *dā'ak* is well-attested, and so a number of MSS have that form at this point. Confusion on the graphic level can be ruled out. The interchange of these two related sounds is well-known in Northwest Semitic as an accepted shift between Hebrew and Aramaic. This is a possible example of a dialectal variant.

[*t*]:[*ṭ*]
The verb *ḥātap* is only found in 9.12 against the form *ḥāṭap* which occurs three times elsewhere in the old Testament. A few MSS have the form *ḥāṭap* here. It is not uncommon to find emphatic sounds interchanging with their non-emphatic counterparts, see e.g. at 30.13 and compare *ḳtl* for *ḳṭl* in the Aramaic Sfire inscription III lines 11, 18 (2x) and 21 where the form is the same as the Arabic *ḳtl*. The reference in BDB (369a) to another Arabic word does not seem justified.

[*b*]:[*m*]
S.R. Driver noticed in his research on the Hebrew text of the books of Samuel that the letters *beth* and *mem* were interchanged in many parts of the Septugint and he explained this as a confusion in writing of these letters in a particular form of the square script which he

described as 'a transitional alphabet . . . of a type not greatly differing from that of Kefr-Bircim' (Driver 1890: lxv). Even here in the book of Job he explains the interchange as a confusion of letters in writing (Driver 1977: II, 32, 323). No doubt as a result of Ugaritic studies, a number of authors like Sarna (1959), W. Chomsky (1970), Schmuttermayr (1971) and Zevit (1975) have drawn attention to a phenomenon akin to that observed by Driver and already recognized by Saadia Gaon in the tenth century, viz. that the prepositions *b* and *m(in)* sometimes interchange in the language of the Old Testament. For Driver in 1890 this interchange was a clear instance of confusion in writing. Now that we know that this interchange is also common in a number of other Semitic languages (see Schmuttermayr 1971: 30-40 and Zevit 1975: 104-110, and cf. Arabic *Bekka* for *Mekka* [Wright 1962: II, 227]), and admitting that there could have been some accidental confusion in some form of the square script, an appeal to a confusion in writing is not enough to explain this phenomenon. Also, to discuss this only as an interchange of prepositions is not without problems. More prepositions interchange than the two or three usually discussed. Further, to think only in terms of an interchange of prepositions leads to too much preoccupation with meaning. A meaning is given to each preposition and then from our Indo-Germanic use of the prepositions the interchange is discussed. So in the case of Amos 6.6 the *beth* makes sense to a French reader who will use '*dans*', but not to a German who uses '*aus*' (Schmuttermayr 1971: 48). Method dictates that we cannot use meaning to determine meaning. From the above sample two conclusions may be drawn: first, that this interchange is one of a number of comparable interchanges, and second, that this interchange is not restricted to pre-root position, although the frequency here is quite high. This is also found in other positions. It should be noted that Driver did not restrict his examples to *beth* and *mem* as prepositions (1890: lxviii). In masoretic Hebrew /*b*/ and /*m*/distinguish meaning. Compare the minimal pairs:

/*bānā*/ 'he built'—/*mānā*/ 'he counted'
/*nišba'*/ 'he swore'—/*nišma'*/ 'it was heard'
/*'āb*/ 'thickness'—/*'am*/ 'people' (Cantineau 1950: 86).

But because they are phonetically so similar, being distinguished only by the oral/nasal contrast, they are often confused or interchanged even to a point of a non-contrastive distribution. This seems to happen in some instances in the pre-root position; see especially 5.19, 21; 12.12; 39.25. Compare further *nāṣal b* (5.19) with *nāṣal m*(*n*) (10.7) and *'akal m*(*n*) (31.17) with *'akal b* (21.25). From later (Mishnaic) Hebrew an interesting example of this 'partitive' *beth* is found in *Ber*. 1.1, where the best MSS read *'akal b*. The parallellism in the chiastic sentence of 7.14 is also of interest. Only here is *ḥtt* construed with *b*, otherwise always with *m*(*n*) (Sarna 1959: 313). It is noteworthy that most of the ancient Versions did not contrast meaning here: the Septuagint each time uses the dative case; the Vulgate *per . . . per*, the Syriac *b . . . b* while the Targum and Saadia Gaon follow the Hebrew literally (Beer 1897: 47).

[*m*]:[*n*]

The only occurrence of a form *miplā'ōt* in the Old Testament is at 37.16, while there are many examples of *niplā'ōt*. Although noun-forms can be formed in Hebrew by a prefix *mem*, it is also possible to explain the variant in the context phonetically, i.e. the [*n*] became [*m*] under influence of the preceding [*b*], thus a case of partial progressive assimilation.

[*r*]:[*l*]

It is fascinating to observe the behaviour of [*r*]-like sounds and [*l*]-like sounds in both ancient and modern languages. Middle-Egyptian had no [*l*] sound while Isi-Xhosa has no [*r*] sound in its original inventory of phonemes. These two sounds are very close to each other and were in fact confused, although on the graphic level they could not be mixed up. In our sample the interchange is restricted to a medial root position. In masoretic Hebrew /*r*/ and /*l*/ distinguish meaning, cf.

> /*reḥem*/ 'womb'—/*leḥem*/ 'bread'
> /*kārā*/ 'he dug'—/*kālā*/ 'it is finished'
> /*kōr*/ 'a wheat measure'—/*kōl*/ 'all' (Cantineau: 91).

Exchanging the [*r*] for [*l*] in 6.25, as the Targum and one MS (Ken 150) suggest, makes, according to Driver, for a better translation: 'How pleasant are words of uprightness' (Driver 1977: I, 66 and II, 43; cf. Ps. 119.103) instead of 'How forceful . . .' Also at 16.3 the Targum and Saadia Gaon favour a root *mlṣ* for *mrṣ* (Beer 1897: 99). It seems as if the editor of S (Gerleman) rightly takes advantage of the possibility of this interchange when he suggests at 19.20 a root *mrṭ* meaning 'to devour' for *mlṭ*. For the noun *miprāś* at 36.29 there is a variant reading *miplāś* which is like the word used in 37.16a where we have an expression in form—a question and meaning—very much like 36.29. One can conclude that *miprāś* and *miplāś* then are two forms of one word. According to BDB (814a) this has been suggested by Budde.

[ʾ]:[*h*]
In the examples the interchange is restricted to a final root position. Only at 26.9 is a change of meaning implied. Otherwise it is a matter of variant spellings.

[*h*]:[*ḥ*]
In the Phoenician Old Hebrew script the symbols for these two sounds could hardly be confused. In the square script the graphs representing the two sounds differ slightly.

[*s*]:[*ṣ*]
In 30.13 we have the only occurrence of the verb *nātas* in the Old Testament as against a number of examples of *nātaṣ* and *nātaš*. So some MSS have *nātaṣ* here (Beer 1897: 194). It is probable that the emphatic [*ṣ*] was changed under influence of the non-emphatic [*t*] to [*s*], a form of assimilation. At 4.10 there is another variant for the verb under discussion, viz. *ntʿ* (cf. Ps. 58.7). In the book of Job one must reckon with a bilingual Hebrew-Aramaic situation, and the development of [*ṣ*] to [ʿ] between these two languages is common knowledge. Now Driver sees this form as a clerical error and not as an Aramaism, first because acording to him *ntʿ* is not known in the sense of 'to be dashed out', and second, no Arabic *ntḍ* is known (Driver 1977: II, 24). Against Driver one can say that such a form can be explained on the basis of analogy or even phonetically (Jakobson 1971: I, 519; see also Wagner 1966: 85). In any case, in the book of Job there are three forms of one verb: *nātaṣ* (19.10), *nātas* (30.13) and *nātaʿ* (4.10).

[*s*]:[*ś*]
According to Cantineau (1950: 89) /*s*/ was earlier confused with /*ś*/. Here only in the medial root position is a difference of meaning marked. In all the other cases we have spelling variants.

[ś]:[š]
In each instance here change of meaning is implied. It should also be noted that not only do we have closely related sounds which can be confused on hearing, but also on the graphic level the difference between the two symbols is minimal.

Even from this very limited sample comparable patterns of interchange can be observed in the book of Job and certain variant readings accounted for. A clear trend emerges: two closely related sounds of which one can be substituted for the other, usually changing the meaning of the word, but also in some cases apparently functioning only as a variant form of the word with no change in meaning. This trend has implications for the textual criticism of the Old Testament as well as for the lexicon of masoretic Hebrew. Throughout the discussion of the material, which was in general phonetic terms, one was aware of the almost insurmountable methodological problem, that in the case of a corpus which is an ancient transmitted text, the final test for segment substitutability, viz. the action of the native speaker (Harris 1957: 31) could not be applied. This means that we do not know how the consonants were expressed, that we cannot apply phonetics or distinguish allophones or recognize dialects (Richter 1978: 6, 7). The way out of this impasse is to rely on reconstruction (Harris 1941: 147). Thus, to confirm or reject the tendencies noted in the sample, the book of Job will have to be subjected to a graphemic analysis as a first stage in the process of reconstruction. In this way one may hopefully arrive at a statement of 'those rigorous criteria by which Biblical textual corruption may be diagnosed' (Schramm 1964: 65).

NOTE

*Mr C.D. Jeffery read the first draft of this paper and I am grateful for his constructive remarks.

BIBLIOGRAPHY

Beer, G.
1897 *Der Text des Buches Hiob* (Marburg).
Blommerde, A.C.M.
1969 *Northwest Semitic Grammar and Job* (Rome).

Brown, F. & Driver, S.R. & Briggs, C.A.
1972 *A Hebrew and English Lexicon of the Old Testament* (Oxford)

Cantineau, J.
1950 'Essai d'une phonologie de l'hébreu biblique', in *Bulletin de la Société de Linguistique de Paris*, pp. 82-122.

Chomsky, W.
1970 'The Ambiguity of the Prefixed Prepositions מ, ל, ב in the Bible', *The Jewish Quarterly Review* n.s. 61, pp. 87-89.

Driver, S.R.
1890 *Notes on the Hebrew Text of the Books of Samuel* (Oxford).
1977 *A Critical and Exegetical Commentary on the Book of Job* (Edinburgh).

Gleason, H.A.
1970 *An Introduction to Descriptive Linguistics* (London).

Greenfield, J.
1978 'The Dialects of Early Aramaic', in *Journal of Near Eastern Studies* 37, pp. 93-99.

Harris, Z.S.
1941 'Linguistic Structure of Hebrew', in *Journal of the American Oriental Society* 61, pp. 143-67.
1957 *Methods in Structural Linguistics* (Chicago)

Jakobson, R.
1971 'Mufaxxama—The "Emphatic" Phonemes in Arabic', *Selected Writings* 1, pp. 510-22.

Richter, W.
1978 *Grundlagen einer althebräischen Grammatik* (München).

Sarna, N.M.
1959 'The Interchange of the Prepositions Beth and Min in Biblical Hebrew', *JBL* 78, pp. 310-16.

Schmuttermayr, G.
1971 'Ambivalenz und Aspektdifferenz—Bemerkungen zu den hebräischen Präpositionen ב, ל und מן', *Biblische Zeitschrift* n.s. 15, pp. 29-51.

Schramm, G.M.
1964 *The Graphemes of Tiberian Hebrew* (University of California Publications Near Eastern Studies, 2; Berkeley and Los Angeles).

Wagner, M.
1966 *Die lexikalischen und grammatikalischen Aramäismen im alttestamentlichen Hebräisch* (Berlin).

Wright, W.
1962 *A Grammar of the Arabic Language* (Cambridge).

Zevit, Z.
1975 'The So-called Interchangeability of the Prepositions b, l, and m(n) in Northwest Semitic', *Columbia University, Journal of the Ancient Near Eastern Society*, pp. 103-112.

16

JOB AND ITS MESOPOTAMIAN PARALLELS— A TYPOLOGICAL ANALYSIS

Moshe Weinfeld

I

It is our contention here that the Sumerian composition published by Kramer in 1955 under the title 'Man and his God: a Sumerian Variation on the "Job" Motif'[1] and the poem of the 'righteous sufferer' (*Ludlul bēl nēmeqi*)[2] are not just stories about a righteous sufferer, as is the story about Job in the book of Job, but actually reflect liturgies of thanksgiving of the sufferer to his god for having saved him from destruction. Thanksgiving gives the opportunity to recount the events surrounding the troubles and the deliverance from them. Unlike the story in Job which tells us about the sufferer in the third person, the sufferer in the above-mentioned Mesopotamian 'Job' compositions speaks about himself in the first person,[3] and, what is most decisive, the compositions open with praise to God and finish with it. In this repect they resemble the Psalms of Thanksgiving in the Bible, where the man who proclaims his thanks to God recounts his troubles in the past in order to present before the masses the salvation brought by God.[4]

Thus the Sumerian poem opens with the words: 'Let man utter constantly the exaltedness of his god . . .' Afterwards we find the sufferer describing his troubles, physical as well as social, and delivering a thanksgiving hymn (see note 3 and the reference to J. Klein there). Finally we are informed that the god saved the man from his afflictions and sent to him the watching spirit and guardian or his tutelary genius (the *maškim* and ^{d}*lama*, ll. 128-129). At the end of this composition we read as in the beginning: 'The [man utters] constantly the exaltedness of his God'.

A similar pattern may be discerned in the Akkadian poem *Ludlul bēl nēmeqi*. The poem opens with the words which serve as the title of the work: 'I will praise the lord of wisdom... whose anger is irresistible... but whose heart is merciful'.[5] Then comes the description in the first person of the misfortunes which befell him, in spite of his innocence. This is followed by three revelations which predict his recovery. Then he tells about his delivery and restoration to health, praises Marduk for this, and describes his entrance into the temple of Esagil, and how he passed the various gates of the temple[6] while prostrating himself and presenting offerings and gifts. He also appeases the protecting genius and the guardian spirit.[7] The poem ends, as von Soden has seen,[8] with the exhortation: 'Mortals, as many as they are, give praise to Marduk'.

The pattern reflected in these creations reminds us of the Thanksgiving Psalms in the Bible. Thus, for example, Ps. 34 opens with the verse 'I will bless the Lord constantly, praise of Him will be ever in my mouth', which resembles the opening clauses of the Mesopotamian compositions discussed here. Then comes the description of his troubles and deliverance:

> I turned to the Lord and he responded,... he saved me from all my terrors... The angel of the Lord camps around those who fear Him and rescues them...

The angel here is the protecting spirit which occurs prominently, as we have seen, in the Mesopotamian 'Job' compositions. The angel's departure signifies trouble while his return means restoration.[9]

The pattern of *Ludlul* is reflected in the descriptions of God's saving of the sick and afflicted in Job 33 in the reaction of Elihu to Job. Elihu describes here the suffering man who is close to death and, as in *Ludlul*, appears here as crossing the infernal river: the שלח in Job 33.18[10] and the river Ḫubur in *Ludlul* (IV.71; cf. *Theodicy* 17). All the elements found in *Ludlul*—the terrifying disease, which brings the sufferer close to the pit, the dream revelations, the protecting angel and the thanksgiving—are represented here. Let us read some of the verses:

> Why do you plead your case with him (i.e. God)?
> God may speak in one way or another and one does not perceive it.
> In a dream, a vision of the night...
> to spare his soul from the pit,

his life from crossing the channel (שלח) . . .
his soul draws near the pit . . . unless he have by him an angel (*ml'k*), a mediator (*mlyṣ*) to tell of man's uprightness . . . he prays to God and accepts him . . . he announces to men his salvation . . . he sings before men, and says: . . . 'he saved my soul from the pit' . . . all these God does twice or thrice with a man to turn back his soul from the pit, to light him with the light of life
(vv. 13ff).

The text from Ugarit about the righteous sufferer published by J. Nougayrol in *Ugaritica* V, pp. 267f., also speaks about the righteous man who was close to the pit and was saved, and therefore praised Marduk, his saviour.[11]

Saving from the pit in order to see the light of life is a basic motif in the Mesopotamian 'Job literature' as well as in the Israelite Psalmodic literature. Thus we read in *Ludlul*, 'The Babylonian saw how Marduk restores to life . . . who thought that he would see the sun?' (IV.29-31).

Similarly we read in Hezekiah's prayer (Isa. 38.9-20): 'I said I shall no longer see the Lord in the land of living. . . but you saved my life from the pit'. In this prayer we also find the metaphor of the devouring lion (v. 13)[12] attested in *Ludlul* III (commentary)[13] and there is a reference there to *dreaming* before recovery (v. 16). ותחלימני והחיני should be translated—in my opinion—'*make me dream* and restore me to health' (חלם as recovery is not attested elsewhere).[14] Hezekiah promises to proclaim thanks and play songs in the House of the Lord after recovery (Isa. 38.11ff.); this is to be compared with the Sumerian letter prayers to the gods by ailing kings.[15]

The description of the suffering found in the two Mesopotamian works discussed here is also very similar to that of the Psalmodic literature and the poetic passages in he book of Job. The similarity is reflected mainly in two major motifs: (1) the sufferer feels a social outcast; (2) the depiction of the physical suffering.

1. Thus the sufferer in the 'Sumerian Job' complains: 'My companion says not a true word to me, my friend gives the lie to my righteous word; the man of deceit has conspired (?) against me . . . I, the wise, why am I bound to the ignorant youths?' (lines 35-42).

In the poem of the righteous sufferer: 'my city frowns on me as an enemy . . . my friend has become foe, my companion has become a wretch and devil . . . my intimate friend has brought my life into danger, my slave has publicly cursed me in the assembly . . . my family treats me as an alien' (I.82-92).

Similarly we read in a Sumerian letter prayer of a scribe to Enki: 'My acquaintance does not approach me, speaks never a word with me, my friend will not take counsel with me, will not put my mind at rest'.[16]

Such complaints are amply attested in the poetic part of Job and in the individual laments in the Psalmodic literature. Thus we find in Job 19.12ff.:

> My kin have abandoned me, my acquaintances are alienated from me
> My relatives and intimates have deserted me,
> the inmates of my house have forgotten me.
> My slave girls treat me as a stranger,
> to them I have become alien.
> I call my slave but he doesn't answer,
> though I entreat him humbly.
> My breath is offensive to my wife . . .
> Young boys despise me. I rise up and they revile me.

Similarly we read in Ps. 31.12ff:

> I am scorned by all my enemies,
> I have become the butt of my neighbours,
> a horror to my friends.
> Those who see me on the street avoid me,
> I am put out of mind like the dead.
> I am like an object given up for lost.
> I hear the whispering of many, a terror on every side . . .

Similar descriptions are found in Pss. 38.12ff.; 35.13f.; 88.9, 19; Jer. 12.6; 20.10.

2. Physical suffering is also described in identical terms in the Mesopotamian and Biblical laments. Thus we read in the 'Sumerian Job'—next to the description of social misfortunes—the following complaints:

> Tears, laments, anguish and depression are lodged within me.
> Suffering overwhelms me like one who does nothing but weep.
> The demon . . . carries off my breath of life.
> The malignant sickness bathes in my body . . . (69ff.)

and in the Poem of the Righteous Sufferer (*Ludlul bēl nēmeqi*):

> As for me, exhausted, a windstorm is driving me,
> a debilitating disease is let loose upon me . . .

> an evil wind has blown from the horizon;
> [they struck] my head, they enveloped my skull,
> my face is gloomy, my eyes flow;
> they have wrenched my neck muscles and made my neck limp;
> they struck my chest . . . they affected my flesh and made me shake.
> Through not eating my looks have become strange,
> my flesh is flaccid . . . my bones look separated and are covered with my skin, my flesh is inflamed . . .
> my afflictions are grievous, my wound is severe (II.49ff.).

Identical descriptions are found in the poetic part of Job and in the Psalmodic laments. Similar to the sentence which opens the section of the physical calamities in *Ludlul* II.49 we read in Job 9.17f.:

> He has blown upon me with the tempest
> and multiplied my wound without cause;
> he would not let me draw my breath,
> but would sate me with bitterness.

In this case the interpretation of the verse gains support from the Mesopotamian work. The words בשערה ישופני have been understood by some as 'crush me for a hair' but this has no basis. As Tur Sinai saw[17] the verb ישופני comes from the root נשף 'blow', and שערה 'tempest' with *śin*, instead of *samekh*, is attested in the book of Job (27.21) and in other places in the Bible (Isa. 28.2; Nah. 1.3). At any rate the fact that in *Ludlul* the list of afflictions is opened by the metaphor of a driving tempest supports our interpretation of Job 9.17.

Elaborate lists of physical afflictions like those of *Ludlul* are found in the Psalms. Thus we read in Ps. 38.3f:

> There is no soundness in my flesh because of your rage, no wholeness in my bones because of my sin . . . my wounds stink and fester . . . am all bent and bowed. I walk about in gloom all day long for my sinews are full of fever; there is not a sound spot in my body . . . my mind reels, my strength fails me, my eyes too have lost their lustre.

Compare Pss. 22.15f.; 31.10.; 32.3; 102.5f.; Lam. 3.4; etc.

It seems that these topoi are rooted in the type of individual prayer which is known to us from Mesopotamia, beginning with the third millennium BCE, and from there spreading to Syria and Palestine. The basic elements of the 'Job literature' in Mesopotamia have then more affinities with the individual complaint in the Psalmodic literature than with the Job story.

II

On the other hand the Mesopotamian work which resembles typologically the poems of Job is the so-called Babylonian *Theodicy*.[18] As the poetic part of Job in the Bible, so the *Theodicy* deals with the problem of the suffering of the righteous in the form of dialogue between the sufferer and his friend. The similarity between the two texts may be presented as follows:

1. In both works the sufferer deplores the success of the evildoer and the failure of the righteous while the friend justifies God's ways and supports the case of divine retribution. Thus the sufferer in the Theodicy says:

> Those who neglect the god go the way of prosperity while those who pray to the goddess are impoverished and dispossessed (ll. 70-71).

Similarly we hear Job complaining:

> Why do the wicked go on living, grow old, and yet rich!
> their progeny secure with them . . . no scourge of God upon them
> (21.7-9).

Contrary to this the friend argues in the *Theodicy*:

> Unless you seek the will of God, what luck have you?
> he that bears his god's yoke never lacks food . . .
> seek the kind spirit of God (239ff.)

Similar ideas are found in the answer of the friend in the book of Job:

> Yield to him (to God), submit; thereby good will come to you . . . take his word to your heart . . . then shall you delight in Shaddai (22.21ff.).

2. The sufferer and his friend address each other as wise men though disagreeing profoundly. Thus the sufferer in the *Theodicy* says to the friend:

> My friend, your mind is a well whose source never fails . . .
> I will ask you a question, etc. (23f.).

Job similarly addresses his friends and says:

> No doubt you are gentry and absolute wisdom is yours (12.2).[19]

The friend, on the other hand, is surprised by the fact that the sufferer who is a wise man utters worthless and irrational words.

The friend in the *Theodicy* says to the sufferer:

> Your reason is like that of a mad man.
> You make your words diffuse and irrational (35-36).

Eliphaz the friend of Job opens his address in a similar manner:

> Would a wise man speak with such folly,
> fill his belly with delusion,
> argue with useless talk with words utterly worthless? (15.2-3).

3. In both works, *Theodicy* and Job as well, the sufferer is accused of blasphemy. The sufferer claims wisdom but this causes arrogance and hence subversion of faith.

Thus in *Theodicy* the friend says:

> My fellow, holder of knowledge . . .
> you have forsaken truth and you despise god's designs (78-79).

> O wise one, O savant, who masters knowledge,
> in your anguish you blaspheme the god (254-55).

and Job 15.2f.:

> Would a wise man speak with such folly . . .
> argue with useless talk with words utterly worthless?
> You even subvert religion and deprecate devotion towards God . . .
> your own mouth condemns you—not I.
> Your own lips testify against you.

4. Furthermore the wisdom which the sufferer professes to possess makes him forget that as a human being he will never understand the divine mind and that his arguments against God are worthless. Thus, in the passage just quoted from the *Theodicy*, the blasphemy uttered by the alleged wise stands next to the idea about the incomprehensibility of the divine mind:

> The divine mind like the centre of the heavens is remote,
> knowledge of it is difficult, people do not know it (ll. 256-57).

Similarly we read in Job 11.2ff. in the words of the friend:

Shall your babblings silence men? Shall you mock and none rebuke you?
You say my doctrine is pure . . .
but would that God may speak . . .
he would tell you the secrets of wisdom . . .
Can you fathom the depth of God . . . the heights of heaven—
what can you do? Deeper than Sheol, how can you know?

5. In both works the negative confession contains moral and not cultic sins, in contrast to *Ludlul* where cultic sins prevail.

The sufferer in *Ludlul* refers to sins like: not making libations to his god, not invoking god at table, not prostrating oneself and praying, neglecting holy days, despising divine rites, etc. (I.12ff.); compare the Sumerian prayer of the sufferer to Enki: 'I have not been negligent toward the name by which you are called . . . I did not plunder your offerings at the festivals to which I go regularly' (Hallo, *JAOS* 88 [1968], p. 85).

In contrast with *Ludlul* and the Sumerian prayer just quoted we hear in the *Theodicy* about *moral* sins:

I have trodden the square of my city unobtrusively,
my voice was not raised, my speech was kept low.
I did not raise my head but looked at the ground (ll. 291ff.).

Similarly in the oath of innocence in Job 31 no cultic sins are mentioned but mainly moral-religious transgressions, such as theft, adultery, oppression of the weak, confidence in wealth, not helping the poor, the widow and the orphan, rejoicing at the foe's misfortune, etc. Furthermore the beginning of the list of sins in Job 31 resembles the quoted passage from the *Theodicy*. Here we read:

Have I walked with worthless men
or my feet hurried to deceit . . .
If my feet have strayed from their course,
my heart followed my eyes . . . (vv. 5-7).

A similar type of moral confession is found in Ps. 131:

O Lord, my heart is not proud
nor my look haughty,
I do not aspire to great things
or to what is beyond me (v. 1).[20]

It is true, the *Theodicy* lacks the literary-philosophical dimension which marks the poetry of the book of Job. The confrontation of the sufferer with God is altogether missing in the *Theodicy*, and thus no revelation and divine response as found in Job could be expected there. However, what may be learned from the *Theodicy* is that theoretical discussions about the problem of the sufferings of the righteous were prevalent in Mesopotamia as well as in ancient Israel, and that there are even typological affinities between them. We ought not to speak about direct influences. What can be stated is that philosophical discussions about individual retribution were common in the ancient Near East in the first millennium BCE and it is even possible that the Arameans (compare the Aramean background of Job) were a dominant factor in the diffusion of this type of literature.

NOTES

1. S.N. Kramer, *VTS* 3 (1955), pp. 170-82. Jacob Klein is preparing a new edition of this poem; see his article, '"Personal God" and Individual Prayer in Sumerian Religion', *AfO* Beiheft 19, 1982 (=1981) (ed. by H. Hunger and H. Hirsch), pp. 295-306.

2. W.G. Lambert, *Babylonian Wisdom Literature* (Oxford, 1960), pp. 51-62.

3. The poem 'Man and his God' contains a prologue (lines 1-20) and an epilogue (lines 117-131) in which the poet refers to the sufferer in the third person, but the major part of the poem consists of a story of the afflicted man who utters the prayer of complaint and sings a thanksgiving hymn in the first person, the latter in accordance with the new readings of J. Klein in his above-mentioned article (p. 298).

4. Cf. H.L. Ginsberg, 'Psalms and Inscriptions of Petition and Acknowledgement', *Louis Ginsberg Jubilee Volume* (New York, 1945), pp. 159-71. Cf. my discussion of Psalms of individual complaints in my article 'Literary Creativity', *The World History of the Jewish People* (The Age of the Monarchies: Culture and Society, Vol. V; ed. A. Malamat; Jerusalem, 1979), pp. 62-63.

5. The beginning was identified by E. Leichty, *Orientalia* n.s. 28 (1959), pp. 361-63.

6. IV.76-90 (pp. 60-61). Compare the thanksgiving hymn in Ps. 118.19-20.

> The Lord punished me severely, but did not hand me over to death.
> Open the gates of victory/righteousness (*ṣdq*) for me
> that I may enter them and praise the Lord.
> This is the gateway to the Lord—
> the victorious/righteous (*ṣdyqym*) shall enter through it.

7. 'The protecting genius and guardian spirit (*šēdu lamassu*) . . . I made their hearts glow' (IV.96-97).

8. *Mitteilungen der Deutschen Orient-Gesellschaft* 96 (1965), p. 51 n. 5.

9. Compare the new text which completes the first tablet of the poem of the 'Righteous Sufferer' (*Ludlul bēl nēmeqi*). Here we read: 'the *lamassu* and *šedu*-spirits move away' (line 15). Cf. D.J. Wiseman, *Anatolian Studies* 30 (1980), pp. 101ff.

10. Cf. M. Tsevat, 'The Canaanite God *Šälah*', *VT* 4 (1954), pp. 41-49.

11. The praise starts in line 25 (p. 268) and goes on until the end.

12. Cf. Ps. 22.22: 'save me from the mouth of the lion'.

13. Cf. *BWL*, p. 56 line 9: 'It was Marduk who put a muzzle on the mouth of the lion who was eating me'.

14. In Job 39.4 יחלמו בניהם means 'their sons will get mature/sane'; compare the antonym: שוטה (= insane) vs. חלום (= sane) in Tosefta, *Terumot* 1.3.

15. Cf. W.W. Hallo, 'The Royal Correspondence of Larsa: I. A Sumerian Prototype for the Prayer of Hezekiah?', *Kramer Anniversary Volume, Cuneiform Studies in Honor of Samuel Noah Kramer* (ed. B. Eichler; 1976), pp. 209-24; see also *idem*, 'The Expansion of Cuneiform Literature', *Jubilee Volume of the American Academy for Jewish Research Proceedings*, Vols. 46-47 (1979-1980), pp. 307-22.

16. Cf. W.W. Hallo, 'Individual Prayer in Sumerian: the Continuity of a Tradition', *Essays in Memory of E.A. Speiser* (ed. W.W. Hallo), *JAOS* 88 (1968), p. 86, ll. 27-28. Compare also in a hymn for the Queen of Nippur:

> the family kept distance . . . and did not come near . . . his city shunned him, his people stood aloof from him; he used to walk bent outside his city . . .

(W.G. Lambert, 'The Hymn to the Queen of Nippur', *Zikir Šumin, Assyriological Studies Presented to F.R. Kraus* [Leiden, 1982], pp. 194-95, lines 11-15).

17. N.H. Tur-Sinai (Torczyner), *The Book of Job, A New Commentary* (1957), *ad loc.*

18. W.G. Lambert, *BWL*, pp. 63ff.

19. Read תמות from the verb תמם with Tur-Sinai (see note 17) and rendered accordingly by the NEB.

20. Cf. my article, 'Instructions for Temple Visitors in the Bible and in Ancient Egypt', *Egyptological Studies*, ed. S. Israelit-Groll (Scripta Hierosolymitana 28 (1982), pp. 236ff.

17

THE PERIODICITY OF THE *MĒŠARUM* AGAIN

Hannes Olivier

I

Ever since the publication of Kraus's *Ein Edikt des Königs Ammi-Ṣaduqa von Babylon* in 1958, the relationship between the Old Babylonian *mēšarum*-edicts and the Old Testament laws of the *šᵉmiṭṭâ*, the *dᵉrôr* and the *yôbēl* has been an important item on the agenda of studies dealing with the legal, social and administrative institutions of ancient Israel.[1] In line with his interest in the legal and social position of the less-privileged in the Ancient East,[2] Professor Fensham also has devoted some attention to this subject in a rather unfamiliar essay.[3] In this he correctly argues that the Old Testament concept of social justice is deeply embedded in the common ancient Near Eastern ideology regarding the duties of the kings, and is not the mere result of religious and moral reflection. Although the *mēšarum*-edict provides a new dimension of and an important view on the social and legal institutions of ancient Israel, he refrains from drawing any direct parallels between the *mēšarum* and the relevant laws because the differences involved are simply too many.

II

The periodicity of the *mēšarum*-acts serves as one of the major reasons why some scholars still attempt to relate this Old Babylonian practice to the Old Testament institutions of *šᵉmiṭṭâ* and *dᵉrôr*.[4] The periodicity, i.e. the regular recurrence of *mēšarum*-acts at fixed intervals, is a matter raised by Landsberger, observing that precisely seven years had elapsed between the two different *mēšarum*-enactments of Samsuiluna.[5] Almost simultaneously Finkelstein postulated his arguments for the regular recurrence of the *mēšarum*-acts. According to Finkelstein, 'the most suggestive analogy is of course that offered by the provisions of the biblical jubilee year (Lev. 25.8ff.) and by the Deuteronomic version of the prescriptions of the Sabbatical year (Deut. 15). But apart from this analogy, the inner logic of the situation—once the recurrent character of the *misharum* is established, as it now is for the Old Babylonian period at least—requires the further presupposition that enactments of this type had to recur *at fairly regular or predictable intervals*' (his italics).[6]

He further argues that if this were not the case, 'there would have occurred a drying-up of the sources of credit and a virtual paralysis of economic activity every few years' (p. 245). Finkelstein's idea is however based upon his conception of the Old Babylonian economic system, a model which Komoróczy so aptly describes as 'in sehr starkem Masse "amerikanisch"'.[7]

Kraus collected and arranged in chronological order all the different instances which refer directly or indirectly to such *mēšarum*-edicts.[8] These were later supplemented by Edzard.[9] Dating from the 25th century until the 17th century BC, it would seem that after the Old Babylonian period the *mēšarum*-practice was discontinued though some of its features remained prevalent in the later pratices of *kidinnūtū*[10] and of the Neo-Assyrian royal decrees of *andurārum*.[11] Evidently *mēšarum*-edicts were issued from time to time. During the Old Babylonian period it is referred to in year-formulae, contracts, letters, etc., showing it to have had some real effect in, for example, the drafting of contracts.[12]

III

The question whether it is possible to establish any fixed intervals between the different *mēšarum*-enactments is really an academic one, because the textual evidence shows no regular recurrent pattern comparable to the seven-year cycle of ancient Israel's laws of *š^emiṭṭâ* and *d^erôr*. Apart from the fact that a *mēšarum* each year would have been completely senseless, Komoróczy argues that since different numbers of years had elapsed between the various *mēšarum*-enactments, numbers of which no common factor can be established, any interval shorter than five to seven years is logically ruled out.

> Es liegt die Folgerung auf der Hand: Die *mīšarum*-Erlässe wurden recht oft, jedoch stets in unregelmässigen, nicht voraussehbaren

> Zeitabständen veröffentlicht. Diese Irregularität scheint mir gerade ihr wesentlichstes Merkmal zu sein.[13]

The regular recurrence of the *mēšarum*-acts would certainly have destroyed its very purpose, namely to correct the existing economic disorder.[14] Just as the death of a king which led to the promulgation of his successor's *mēšarum* in his first regnal year was generally unforeseen, so also were any subsequent decrees involving such redress of economic disorder.[15] The system of *mēšarum*-acts could only function properly if the edicts were unexpectedly announced.[16]

IV

The question of the *mēšarum*'s periodicity is inseparably connected with the question of its contents and of its intended effectiveness. Judging from contemporary administrative and business documents, it is clear that the *mēšarum* did have an effect upon the prevailing economic conditions, and that it is not to be regarded as a mere product of the literary imagination of the scribes.[17] The Edict of Ammiṣaduqa contains the only complete verbatim copy of such a *mēšarum*-act.[18] Its contents show it to be a very specific document, accurately formulated, designed to intervene in the existing economic situation by means of an extraordinary complex of administrative regulations, consisting of, among other things, the remission of certain public taxes and arrears, as well as the cancellation of private loans of a certain kind to certain people. Its contents create, in fact, the impression of a carefully worked-out 'budget', although some pronouncements of a more general character were included, obviously to add to Ammiṣaduqa's public image as a *šar mēšarim*.[19] Hence the Edict must be understood as a collection of economic measures designed to alleviate or to modify a particular distressing economic situation.[20] The Edict is very specific concerning the people who were to benefit from the *mēšarum* and which particular areas were to be affected. The remission of taxes directed to the rent-payers of the palace and other fiefholding groups was subjected to very strict limitations,[21] e.g. their taxes consisting of a proportion of the crop to be paid *in natura* to the palace, were not *in toto* remitted, but only the proportion required for their own consumption and the quantity needed as seed-corn. The remainder destined for selling was, however, not covered. Moreover, this remission was confined to only Babylon and its vicinity, thereby excluding the rest of the country.

All other stipulations regarding the remission of obligations concern only the arrears thereupon. Thus the 'normal' tax obligations remained while the tenant-farmers were only relieved from the burden of accumulated arrears owed to the palace.

The stipulations regarding the cancellation of debts in the private sector were also subjected to strict limitations, e.g. they concern only private debts involving non-commercial loans; in other words, loans without any objective of profitmaking, hence loans of necessity which bear interest. Further, the *mēšarum* concerns only those debts of which the date of refund had not expired on 2 Addar 11 Amiditana 37 (§5). Otherwise debtors would have been in the position of delaying the repayment of their debts in view of an impending *mēšarum*. While most of the remissions were granted at the expense of the palace, the cancellation of debts was at the expense of the creditors. To compensate for their losses, the king made certain concessions to the merchant, *šusikku* and inn-keeper.

All these measures point to a thorough assessment of the country's contemporary economic condition. The different provisions were based upon these specific 'facts'. The effects of the various remissions and concessions upon the economy as a whole seem to have been calculated beforehand and were reckoned to have been sufficient for an improvement temporarily, acting like a 'compression valve'.[22] The economic 'policy' of the palace aimed at removing those obstacles ('désordre économique') in the way of higher production of staple commodities and at keeping the small farmers content and productive. The special concessions concerning the cultivation of new land (§19) and also those concerning the business enterprise of independent merchants (§ 10) add to the impression that Ammiṣaduqa's edict was motivated by very specific considerations and circumstances.

The contents of the edict thus show that it is highly unlikely that the provisions of different *mēšarum*-enactments would have been the same. Even if the same groups of people were to benefit, the particular *area* where these remissions and concessions were applicable might have been different, or the exceptions limiting the effects thereof.

V

Komoróczy's argument, namely that the *mēšarum*-acts need to have occurred unexpectedly and at irregular intervals if they were to have any effect (contra Finkelstein), can be supported. Even if clever merchants became aware of an impending *mēšarum* and thus took action to avoid its effects, they hardly would have known its contents. The people would have expected a *mēšarum* to be promulgated by a new king in his first regnal year as it was customary for Old Babylonian kings, but the particular area or groups of tax-payers to profit from it would have remained secret until its promulgation. Thus, to have any real effect the *mēšarum*'s announcement must have been unexpected and its contents must have been unpredictable. A comparison of the Edicts of Ammiṣaduqa and Samsuiluna (Si 507)[24] shows a remarkable similarity in phraseology, contents and arrangements of subject-matter. Hence it would be logical to question the *mēšarum*'s effectiveness, because it made use of such an apparently well-known standard text. One should, however, bear in mind that the text of Si 507, dating almost a century earlier, is very fragmentary. Only 14 of the approximate 255 lines are legible. Lines 11-17 (A) are similar to lines 5-11, and rev. 1-7 (B) almost the exact equivalent of lines 200-205 of the Edict of Ammiṣaduqa. Although the groups of people to be exempted from tax-obligations are more or less the same in both, it should be pointed out that in the Edict of Ammiṣaduqa §2 is a preliminary and general statement which is worked out in specific details in §§10-19.[25] It is precisely those details which explain the intended effects of the *mēšarum* that are lacking in Si 507. B, like §21, contains the exception to the regulation regarding the release of debt-slaves, thus maintaining the *status quo* of house-born slaves (cf. LH).[26] Since §§20-22 take up subjects not mentioned earlier in the Edict, Lemche correctly regards them as supplementary.

VI

The contents of and intention behind the Old Babylonian *mēšarum*-edicts show them to have envisaged immediate relief for certain groups of people from overburdening (tax-)obligations and from accumulated arrears. The mere fact that areas such as Babylon and the province of Suhum were granted special concessions shows that the *mēšarum* was not meant to be of general and universal character. The decree of Ammiṣaduqa was necessary to alleviate the untenable social and economic conditions in certain areas which could cause serious economic disorder,[27] or even the total collapse of the economy under too great a weight of private debts.[28] Complicated calculations must have been made beforehand to create maximum effect at minimum expense for the palace. Its success depended upon its unexpectedness, both in terms of its announcement and in terms of its contents.

When the king issued a *mēšarum*-decree he hardly acted out of compassion towards the poor and underprivileged. His interest concerned economic stability and growth by which the palace eventually would profit more. It is conceivable that he would couch his *mēšarum*-decree in the traditional phraseology extolling his virtues as a just king (*šar mēšarim*). The king's adhering to the eternal cosmic truths (*kittu ú mēšaru*)[29] is, however, a literary *topos* and, as such, not a characteristic feature of the *mēšarum*-edict. In the royal ideology of the ancient Near East one does find some common characteristics pertaining to the social responsibility of kings towards the under-privileged, as Fensham has pointed out. It is methodologically unsound and factually impossible to draw any direct parallels between the Old Babylonian *mēšarum* and the Old Testament institutions of *š^emiṭṭâ* and *d^erôr*;[30] in any case, definitely not on the ground of the alleged recurrent character of the *mēšarum* at fixed intervals.

NOTES

1. For a recent survey compare N.P. Lemche, '*Andurārum* and *Mīšarum*: Comments on the Problem of Social Edicts and their Application in the Ancient Near East', *JNES* 38 (1979), pp. 11-22; *idem*, 'The Manumission of Slaves—The Fallow Year—The Sabbatical Year—The Jobel Year', *VT* 26 (1976), pp. 38-59; W. Schottroff, 'Zum alttestamentlichen Recht', *VuF* 22 (1977), pp. 3-29, esp. p. 17; J.P.J. Olivier, 'The Old Babylonian mēšarum-Edict and the Old Testament', unpublished D.Litt. dissertation, University of Stellenbosch; R. Hentschke, 'Erwägungen zur israelitischen Rechtsgeschichte', *Theologia Viatorum* 10 (1965/66), pp. 108-33, esp. pp. 118f.; D.J. Wiseman, 'Law and Order in Old Testament Times', *Vox Evangelica* 8 (1973), pp. 5-21; M. Weinfeld, '"Justice and Righteousness" in Ancient Israel against the Background of "Social Reforms" in the Ancient Near East', in H.-J. Nissen and J. Renger (eds.), *Mesopotamien und seine Nachbarn. Politische und kulturelle Wechselbeziehungen im Alten Vorderasien vom 4. bis 1. Jahrtausend v. Chr.* (= XXV Rencontre Assyriologique Internationale, Berlin, 1982), pp. 491-519; D.O. Edzard '"Soziale Reformen" im Zweistromland bis ca 1600 v. Chr.: Realität oder literarischer Topos', in J. Harmatta

and G. Komoróczy (eds.), *Wirtschaft und Gesellschaft im Alten Vorderasien* (1976), pp. 145-56.

2. F.C. Fensham, 'Widow, Orphan and the Poor in Ancient Near Eastern Legal and Wisdom Literature', *JNES* 21 (1962), pp. 129-39.

3. F.C. Fensham, 'Geregtigheid in die Boek Miga en Parallelle uit die Ou Nabye Ooste', *Tydskrif vir Geesteswetenskappe* 7 (1967), pp. 416-25.

4. Cf. the viewpoints of Wiseman, Weinfeld and A. van Selms, 'The Year of the Jubilee, in and outside the Pentateuch', *OTWSA 17-18* (1974/75), pp. 74-85; J.B. Alexander, 'A Babylonian Year of Jubilee?', *JBL* 57 (1938), pp. 75f.; J. Levy, 'The Biblical Institution of D^{e}ROR in the Light of Accadian Documents', *Eretz-Israel* 5 (1938), pp. 21-31; H. Gevaryahu, 'The Announcement of Freedom in Jerusalem by Nehemia in comparison with *Mesharum* and Social Reform in the Ancient World' [Hebrew], *Festschrift Abraham Katz* (1969), pp. 354-87; N. Sarna, 'Zedekiah's Emancipation of Slaves and the Sabbatical Year', in H.A. Hoffner (ed.), *Orient and Occident. Essays presented to Cyrus H. Gordon on the Occasion of his Sixty-Fifth Birthday* (= *AOAT*, 22; 1973), pp. 143-49; M. Silver, *Prophets and Markets. The Political Economy of Ancient Israel* (1983), pp. 233f.

5. B. Landsberger and S.I. Feigin, 'The Date List of the Babylonian King Samsu-ditana', *JNES* 14 (1955), p. 145; Kraus, *Edikt*, pp. 225f. for a discussion of *TCL* 17 no. 76 referring to the first *mēšarum*-act of Samsuiluna. Cf. F.M. Th. de Liagre Böhl, 'Ein Brief des Königs Samsuiluna von Babylon', *BO* 8 (1951), pp. 50-56; *ANET*, p. 625; Olivier, pp. 171f. The second *mēšarum*-enactment is alluded to in Si 507 published by Kraus, 'Ein Edikt des Königs Samsu-iluna von Babylon', *Assyriological Studies* 16 (1965), pp. 225-31. Cf. H. Petschow, 'Neufunde zur keilschriftlichen Rechtssammlungen', *Zeitschrift Savigny-Stiftung für Rechtsgeschichte* (Rom. Abt.) 85 (1968), pp. 26-29; Olivier, pp. 173-77.

6. J.J. Finkelstein, 'Some New Misharum Material and its Implications', *Assyriological Studies* 16 (1965), pp. 233-46 esp. pp. 243f.

7. G. Komoróczy, 'Zur Frage der Periodizität der altbabylonischen Mišarum-Erlässe', in *Societies and Languages of the Ancient Near East. Studies in Honour of I.M. Diakonoff* (1982), pp. 196-205, esp. p. 197.

8. Kraus, *Edikt*, pp. 224-37; *AS* 16 (1965), pp. 229-31; *idem*, 'Akkadische Wörter und Ausdrücke, XII', *RA* 73 (1979), pp. 51-62.

9. Edzard, pp. 146-47.

10. W.F. Leemans, '*Kidinnu*, un symbole de droit divin babylonien', in M. David *et al.* (eds), *Symbolae ad jus et historiam antiquitatis pertinentes Julio Christiano Van Oven Dedicatae* (1946), pp. 36-61.

11. Cf. Lemche, *JNES* 38 (1979), pp. 15-21; *CAD* A/2, pp. 115f.

12. One of the most noticeable 'proofs' of the effect of the *mēšarum* is KU III no. 745=BE VI/I no. 103, discussed by M. Schorr, *Urkunden des altbabylonischen Zivil- und Prozessrechts* (= VAB 5; 1913), no. 273. Cf.

Olivier, pp. 178-83; *idem*, 'The Effectiveness of the Old Babylonian Mēšarum Decree', *JNSL* 12 (1984), pp. 107-13.

13. Komoróczy, p. 198. Apart from Ammiṣaduqa's *mēšarum* in his first full regnal year he also had issued a *mēšarum* in his tenth year (cf. A. Ungnad, *s.v.* Datenliste, *RLA* 2 [1938], no. 258; VAB 5 no. 273) and most probably also one in his fourteenth year, assuming the rather uncertain reading *warki mēšarum iššaknu* in MAH 16376 from Sippar, dated Ammiṣaduqa 14 (cf. L. Matouš, 'Erlässe altbabylonischer Könige', *BO* 16 [1959], p. 95 n. 16). This would imply an interval of only four years between two such *mēšarum*-acts.

14. J. Bottéro, 'Désordre économique et annulation des dettes en Mésopotamie l'époque paléo-babylonienne', *JESHO* 4 (1961), pp. 114-64, esp. pp. 151f.

15. *CAD* M/II *s.v.* *mēšaru* (pp. 116f.); *AHw*, *s.v.* *mī/ēšaru(m)* (p. 659).

16. Komoróczy, p. 199.

17. Olivier, pp. 131-34. Cf. H. Klengel, *Hammurapi von Babylon und seine Zeit* (1978), pp. 216-22.

18. The existence of such a practice was already widely accepted by Assyriologists at the beginning of this century. Langdon's publication of BM 78259 (S. Langdon, 'A Fragment of the Hammurapi Code', *PSBA* 36 [1914], pp. 100-106) was followed by Schorr's elaborate study of this 'Seisachthie' (M. Schorr, *Eine babylonische Seisachthie aus dem Anfang der Kassitenzeit* (SHAW, Phil.-hist. Kl., 1915) which he designates 'ein Dekret über Aufhebung von Schuldverpflichtungen innerhalb bestimmter Grenzen'. It was, however, the text Ni 632, published by Kraus in 1958, that really stimulated the interest in the subject of royal *mēšarum*-decrees. Another copy of the text of the edict (BM 80289) containing the beginning and almost all of the lacunae of Ni 632, was published by J.J. Finkelstein, 'The Edict of Ammiṣaduqa: A New Text', *RA* 63 (1969), pp. 45-64. Recently Kraus has suggested a new reading, re. lines 97, 102, 103 (F.R. Kraus, 'Der Palast, Produzent und Unternehmer im Königreiche Babylon nach Hammurabi (ca. 1750-1600 v. Chr.)', in E. Lipiński (ed.), *State and Temple Economy in the Ancient Near East* (= Orientalia Lovaniensia Analecta, 5; 1979), pp. 423-34, esp. p. 427.

19. B.A. van Proosdij, 'Šar Mēšarim. Titre des rois Babyloniens comme législateurs', in *Symbolae Van Oven* (1946), pp. 29-35 (cf. above, n. 10).

20. Cf. Kraus, *Edikt*, pp. 189-90: 'eine Sammlung von Vorschriften sozialen Charakters . . . dazu bestimmt, gewisse vorwiegend wirtschaftliche Misstände meist vorübergehend zu beseitigen oder zu lindern'. *CAD*, M/II defines it as an officially promulgated legislative act designed to remedy certain economic malfunctions.

21. Olivier, pp. 120f.

22. F.R. Kraus, 'Ein zentrales Problem des altmesopotamischen Rechtes: Was ist der Codex Hammu-rabi?', *Genava* 8 (1960), p. 296.

23. Kraus, 'Der Palast, Produzent und Unternehmer . . . ', in E. Lipiński (ed.), p. 432 (above, n. 18).

24. Kraus, *AS* 16 (1965), pp. 225-32.
25. Lemche, *JNES* 38 (1979), pp. 11-13; Olivier, pp. 60-101.
26. H. Petschow, *s.v.* Gesetze, *RLA* 3 (1966), p. 274.
27. Bottéro, pp. 152f., argues that these concessions were granted only to those people and areas where the situation had become completely unbearable and showed no signs of possible recovery. Cf. H. Klengel, 'Einige Bemerkungen zur sozialökonomischen Entwicklung in der alt-babylonischen Zeit', in J. Harmatta and G. Komoróczy (eds.) (1976), pp. 249-57, esp. p. 254.
28. Wiseman, *Vox Evangelica* 8 (1973), p. 11.
29. P. Koschaker, 'Randnotizen zu neueren keilschriftlichen Rechtsurkunden', *ZA* 43 (1936), pp. 196-232, esp. pp. 219f.; B. Landsberger, 'Die babylonischen Termini für Gesetz und Recht', in *Symbolae ad iura Orientis Antiqui pertinentes Paulo Koschaker dedicatae* (1939), pp. 219-34; H. Cazelles, 'De l'idéologie royale', *JANES* 5 (1973), pp. 59-73. Cf. J.P.J. Olivier, 'The Sceptre of Justice and Ps. 45.7b', *JNSL* 7 (1979), pp. 45-54, esp. pp. 50f.
30. Cf. Weinfeld, pp. 497-99.

This paper was completed before Kraus's new edition of the Edict of Ammiṣaduqa became available to the author. Cf. F.R. Kraus, *Königliche Verfügungen in altbabylonischer Zeit* (SD XI) (1984).

18

ZION AS PRIMEVAL STONE IN ZECHARIAH 3 AND 4

Adam S. van der Woude

There are many enigmatic passages in Proto-Zechariah, but few of them have given rise to such a variety of views as Zech. 3.9, 4.7 and 4.10. In each of these texts mention is made of a stone (*'eben*) which throughout the ages has been a stumbling-block to both translators and commentators. In the following pages we want to propose a fresh interpretation of the named texts. It is a pleasure to contribute these lines to the present *Festschrift*, dedicated to a good friend and a meritorious scholar who in the last decades has made his mark by clarifying the ancient Near Eastern impact on the biblical world.

Before broaching the intricate questions posed by the texts just mentioned, a few remarks on the literary, critical and historical problems of Zechariah 3 and 4 seem to be in order. Many scholars consider ch. 3 as a later addition to the original series of seven visions revealed to the prophet in the night preceding the 24th day of the 11th month of Darius's second regnal year, i.e. February 15th, 519 (cf. Zech. 1.7-8).[1] We subscribe to this view. The so-called fourth vision differs considerably from the others. In it the usual introductory formula, 'I looked up (again) and saw, and behold . . . ', is missing. We do not find mysterious persons or things calling for an inquiry by the prophet and an explanation by the *angelus interpres*. Zechariah deliberately interferes in the scene (v. 5). The interpreting angel himself is not missing (we consider him as identical with the angel of the Lord, mentioned in ch. 3 and in the first night vision),[2] but the term 'the angel who talked with me' does not occur. Rudolph's contention that these formal divergences are due to the unique character of the fourth vision is unconvincing.[3]

That ch. 3 does not belong originally to the other visions is corroborated by its contents as well. Verse 7 suggests that the reconstruction of the temple is in its final stage and v. 8 harks back to the promise about the Branch given to the high priest Joshua in 6.11ff.[4] On the strength of these facts we may confidently state that ch. 3 dates to about 515, not to 519. There are in our opinion no compelling reasons for dividing the chapter into two independent literary units (v. 1-7 and 8-10).[5]

Since Wellhausen the literary unity of ch. 4 has been contested by almost all commentators. The text of the original vision is said to cover vv. 1-6aα and 10b-14 (excluding v. 12) only. The remaining verses are held to be a small collection of prophetic sayings added later to the main text. This generally received opinion however raises more questions than it solves. Apart from the fact that nobody has ever given a satisfying answer to the problem where vv. 6aβ-10a stood originally if this section does not belong to the vision (at the end of ch. 3, or at the end of ch. 4, or in the margin of ch. 4),[6] the process of reducing the vision to vv. 1-6aα, 10b-11 and 13-14 leaves us with a revelation which is interpreted just in part, because in that case only the lamps and the olives are explained. Proclamation of weal and foretelling of future salvation, which are typical features of all other visions, would be almost lacking if we had to cut out vv. 6aβ-10a from the text. This seems to be inconceivable just in case of a vision which originally formed the centre of the series of seven. But there are more serious objections to be made against the prevailing view which leads to a fragmentation of the chapter into independent literary units. In his dissertation, W.A.M. Beuken[7] has convincingly argued that sentences like 'This is a word of YHWH for Zerubbabel' (v. 6), elsewhere in the Old Testament refer to a preceding divine revelation and never introduce separate prophetic sayings; cf. Isa. 16.13; 37.22 (= 2 Kgs 19.21); 2 Kgs 9.36; 15.12; Judg. 3.20. We cannot, therefore, avoid the conclusion that vv. 6aβ-7 are a continuation of preceding verses and that the so-called prophecies of vv. 6aβff. are an integral part of the vision. On the other hand, the alleged original transition from v. 6aα to v. 10b is not as smooth as has been suggested. The precise wording of the explanatory formula used by the interpreting angel in answer to questions posed by Zechariah about the meaning of the persons and things revealed to him in the visions in all instances begins with the demonstrative pronouns *'ēlleh* or *zō't* (cf. 1.10; 2.2, 4; 5.3, 6, 8), even when a numeral is used (cf. 6.5). If v. 10b were the sequel of v. 6aα, we would expect *'ēlleh šeba'* (or: *šib'â*)[8] *'ênê yhwh*, 'These are the seven eyes of the Lord', instead of *šib'â 'ēlleh 'ênê yhwh*, 'These seven are the eyes of the Lord'.

Yet another point requires consideration. It is generally thought that the words, 'Then you shall know that the Lord Almighty has sent me (to you)', which occur four times in Proto-Zechariah (2.13, 15; 4.9; 6.15), must be understood as a formula used by the prophet to stress his divine commission which would be authenticated by future events,[9] or as a formula which was added to his prophecies at a time when some had begun to question the authenticity of Zechariah's claims.[10] In our opinion, these words should be attributed neither to the prophet nor to a later redactor, but to the interpreting angel. If we leave Zech. 2.12 unaltered, the words 'He (= YHWH) has sent me after *kābōd* to the nations that plunder you', cannot have been said by Zechariah, because he was never sent to the nations.[11] They rather mean that the Lord had sent the interpreting angel (the same as the angel of the Lord) to secure the wealth of the nations that had hitherto spoiled his people.[12] In that case the formula 'Then you shall know that the Lord Almighty has sent me', which concludes vv. 12f., must be assigned to the *angelus interpres*. This implies that the said formula should be ascribed to this angel in the other three texts (2.15; 4.9; 6.15) as well. The conclusion is corroborated by the text of Zech. 4.8-9. In v. 9b the singular *w^{e}yāda'tā*, 'then you shall know', is unintelligible if spoken by the prophet, since in that case an antecedent is lacking to which the singular could refer. On the supposition however that the interpreting angel is the spokesman in vv. 8-9, the passage is perfectly clear, because in that case Zechariah is the person addressed. The usual emendation of *w^{e}yāda'tā* into *wîyda'tem* (plural) is unwarranted.[13] But if the interpreting angel acts as a spokesman in vv. 8-9, there is no reason to doubt that the same goes for vv. 6aβ-7 and 10a. In conclusion, vv. 6aβ-10a form an integral part of the vision, in which first of all the lamp-stand is explained as the temple mountain (v. 7), then the 'bowl' on top of it as the temple building (vv. 8-9), then the lamps as the eyes of the Lord (v. 10), and finally the olives as the two 'sons of the fresh oil' (v. 14), who should not, as is usually thought, be identified with Joshua and Zerubbabel, but with the expected messianic king and high priest of 6.13. Since there is no reason to deny that ch. 4 belongs to the original series of the seven visions, it must be dated to February 519 (cf. 1.7).

These conclusions pave the way for a reconsideration of the texts dealing with the *'eben*. Because ch. 4 antedates ch. 3, it is desirable to treat first Zech. 4.7 and 4.10.

The wording of Zech. 4.7 raises a number of problems, but no compelling reasons can be adduced for altering the text handed down to us. Even *har haggādôl* can be retained on the strength of Gesenius–Kautzsch, *Grammar*, §126x (perhaps the article before *har* is lacking for euphonic reasons; cf. Ps. 104.18).

Fresh light is thrown on the words *mī 'attâ har haggādôl* by the Phoenician inscription KAI 13, line 2, which runs as follows: *my 't kl 'dm 'š tpq 'yt 'rn z*, 'Whoever you are, each man, who shall open this sarcophagus'. Similarly, we can translate Zech. 4.7a thus: 'Whatever you are, great mountain, in the eyes of Zerubbabel (you shall be) like a plain'.[14] The great mountain is neither the temple ruin[15] nor the destroying mountain of Chaldaean world power (cf. Jer. 51.25)[16] nor a symbol for Zechariah's adversaries (cf. Isa. 41.15)[17] or for accumulating difficulties during the reconstruction of the temple.[18] What we have before us is a general statement: no mountain, however great and impressive, can ultimately venture to compete with Zion!

That this is meant, is intimated by v. 7b. Traditional exegesis finds here a certain stone brought out by Zerubbabel, whilst the attendants acclaim: Grace, grace to it! It is noteworthy however that many manuscripts of the Septuagint read ἐξοίσω, 'I shall bring out', instead of 'he shall bring out' in the Hebrew text, thus taking YHWH as the subject of the verbal form (cf. v. 6). The enigmatic stone, called *hā'eben hārō'šâ* in the masoretic text, has been interpreted in quite different ways already in the ancient versions, but the Septuagint, the Vulgate and the Peshitta concur in considering *t^ešu'ôt* not as a derivative from *š'h* 'to roar', but from *šwh*, 'to be equal' (LXX: ἰσότητα; V: *exaequabit*; S: *ršwywt'*, 'dignitas').[19] This remarkable unanimity opens a hitherto untrodden avenue as far as the modern interpretation of the text is concerned and induces us to explain *t^ešu'ôt* not in the sense of 'joyous acclamations' but as 'splendour', by assuming a semantic development from 'equality' via 'worth' to 'splendour' (cf. Hebrew *yāqar*, 'be valued', 'be precious', and *y^eqār*, 'precious thing' 'splendour', and Aram. *šᵉwā*, 'to be equal', 'to be worth'). We can translate therefore: 'Splendour of grace shall be the grace given to it'.

Petitjean[20] has proposed to interpret *hā'eben hārō'šâ* as the foundation stone of the temple by referring to Mesopotamian festivities during the founding of a sanctuary. This interpretation must be refuted since it would carry us back to 537 (cf. Ezr. 3.8ff.), about two decades earlier than the revelation of the night visions. As pointed out above, v. 7 can no longer be severed from the contents of the fifth vision revealed to Zechariah in February 519. Other commentators think of a top stone,[21] but apart from the fact that ancient Near Eastern literature fails to provide us with an example of the dedication of a facing-brick, the flat roof of the temple tells against this interpretation. It is therefore most unlikely that we have to explain *hārō'šâ* as a locative ('to the top') or as an adverbial accusative ('as the top'), let alone as an adjective with feminine ending ('the top stone').[22] In our opinion *rō'šâ* is an (archaic?) equivalent of *ri'šâ*, 'beginning' (Ezek. 36.11) and of *rē'šît*, 'beginning', and should be considered as an apposition to *'eben*. The stone Beginning constitutes the primeval stone from which the creation of the world commenced. Mount Zion is described as the navel of the earth and as its mythological centre. The wording resorts to the old and well-known ancient Near Eastern and Egyptian cosmological idea of the *Urhügel* which arose from the waters of chaos as the starting-point of creation. We find this conception in connection with Mount Zion even in rabbinic literature. Rudolph has once more pointed to the tradition about the *'eben šᵉtiyyâ*, 'the stone of foundation',[23] which according to Mishnah *Yoma* 5.2 rose three fingers high above its surroundings in the Holy of Holies and on which the high priest used to place the incense on the Day of Atonement (cf. Lev. 16.12f.). According to the *gemara* of the Babylonian Talmud (fol. 54b), this stone is the primeval stone from which God created the world.

Zech. 4.7 apparently draws on pre-exilic Zion theology, though in an eschatological setting, and reminds us by means of the words 'Splendour of grace shall be the grace given to it' of Ps. 48.3 which praises the holy mountain thus: 'Beautiful in elevation, the joy of all the earth is mount Zion, in the far north, the city of the great King'.

On the strength of all this, we finally propose to derive the hiphil of *yāṣā'* not from *yāṣā'*, 'to go out', but from *yāṣā'*, 'to shine', 'to be radiant' (cf. Arab. *waḍu'a*),[24] and to take YHWH as its subject. The following translation of Zech. 4.7 is suggested:

> Whatever you are, great mountain,
> in the eyes of Zerubbabel (you shall be) like a plain,
> when He makes radiant the stone Beginning.
> Splendid[25] grace shall be the grace given to it.

We are also put to great difficulties in trying to interpret Zech. 4.10. As indicated above, we can no longer share the opinion of the vast majority of scholars who consider v. 10a to belong to a prophetic saying, whereas v. 10b (as the continuation of v. 6aα) would be an integral part of the fifth vision. Our own position forces us to read v. 10b directly after v. 10a, thus to look at the whole verse as a unity.

Zech. 4.10 counteracts the disheartening voices already heard by Haggai at the beginning of the temple reconstruction activities (cf. Hag. 2.3-5), which disparaged the 'day of small things'. The verse is introduced by *kî*, in this case apparently as affirmative interjection ('truly'), followed by *mî*, which in our opinion functions as an interrogative (who?) rather than as an indefinite pronoun (*quicunque*): 'Truly, who would despise the day of small things . . . ?' It is true that the division of v. 10 into two parts (the first belonging to a prophetic saying, the second to the vision) has forced commentators to assume that the subject of the verbal forms *śāmeḥû* and *rā'û* must be an indefinite *mî*, since v. 10a (up to *beyad zerubbābel*) does not provide them with another subject. Keil,[26] however, pointed out already that we cannot find in the Old Testament clear instances of the connection of an indefinite *mî* with a consecutive perfect. From a material point of view, it should be stressed that we can hardly imagine why those people who were disparaging the reconstruction of the sanctuary would rejoice when they saw Zerubbabel holding a plummet (so the traditional explanation) or even a separate stone which allegedly marked the completion of the temple (so many modern commentators), quite apart from the fact that nothing is known to us about a dedication of a top stone. Even the completion of the temple, unimpressive as it was, could scarcely silence the discouraging and depreciating criticisms of those people who from the outset (cf. Hag. 2.3) had been derogatory about the rebuilding activities. It is hardly conceivable that Zerubbabel was so directly involved in the reconstruction of the sanctuary that he himself handled a plummet, as suggested by the Septuagint, Aquila, the Vulgate, the Targum, and modern versions.

The interpretation of *hā'eben habbᵉdîl* in the sense of a separate stone is no more convincing. Apart from the fact that a top stone as dedication stone is unknown to ancient Near Eastern men, a feminine *habbᵉdîlâ* instead of *habbᵉdîl* would be necessary in that case.[27] Corresponding to what we have seen in Zech. 4.7, *habbᵉdîl* should be considered as an apposition to *hā'eben*. Again we come across the primeval stone which is Mount Zion, called here 'Separation', because the primeval mountain separated cosmos from chaos for the first time (cf. also Gen. 1.6). If this is the right interpretation of the stone, the criticizing despisers of the small things cannot possibly be the subject of 'rejoice' and 'see'. Why would they be pleased to see Zion under the authority of Zerubbabel? There is no other possibility left than to take 'these seven' as the subject of the verbal forms. Admittedly, they are mentioned far away from the verbal forms, but this construction of the sentence is not impossible from a grammatical point of view[28] and may be explained by the specific stress laid on 'these seven' and the explanation subsequently given to them at the end of v. 10. Symbolized by the lamps of the menorah, they are 'the eyes of the Lord ranging over the whole earth' in order to 'show his might in behalf of those whose heart is blameless toward Him' (2 Chron. 16.9). The people's disheartening criticisms are discredited by the gracious assistance of the Lord's celestial servants. Our verse seems to hark back to the promise of v. 6. In conclusion, Zech. 4.10 can be translated thus:

> Truly, who wants to despise the day of the small things,
> whilst are pleased to see the stone Separation
> under the authority of Zerubbabel these seven?
> They are the eyes of the Lord ranging over the whole earth.

Zech. 3.9, the last text to be dealt with, is also a *crux interpretum*. As stated above, we should not consider Zech. 3.8-10 as a self-contained prophecy spoken by Zechariah, nor as a collection of prophetic sayings.[29] Nothing speaks against the literary unity of ch. 3. Of course, one cannot deny that v. 8 introduces a new theme, but the call on Joshua and his colleagues to listen to a divine promise does not as such mark a separate literary unit, as can be seen from Gen. 27.43, Exod. 18.19, Deut. 6.3 and Jer. 34.4. The high priest and his colleagues are invited to hear because they are the 'men of the omen' that the Lord would bring his servant, the Branch (v. 8b). The expression 'men of the omen' is difficult to explain,[30] but we infer that 'men' has here the connotation of 'watchers' as in the case of the 'men of the cave' in Josh. 10.18. The omen referred to is the messianic crown which according to Zech. 6.11b was offered to Joshua[31] about four years before and which was to be kept in the sanctuary until the promised messianic king would arrive (Zech. 6.14).

The contents of the message for Joshua and his colleagues are formulated in v. 9. It refers to a stone handed over[32] to the high priest on which seven eyes are resting. Also in this case the stone has been interpreted in various ways. Some scholars have identified it with the foundation stone of the temple,[33] others with its top stone.[34] Wellhausen[35] thought of a gem stone for the diadem of the expected messianic king, Gressmann[36] suggested a seal with Zerubbabel's name. More recently, scholars seem to prefer the identification with a gem for the turban of the high priest, in which case the seven eyes are interpreted as seven facets of the stone or as seven letters engraved on it (*qdš lyhw*: 'Holy to the Lord', cf. Exod. 28.36). Schmidt[37] identified the stone with the temple rock, Chary[38] thought of a symbol for the temple and Rudolph[39] pointed to the *'eben šᵉtiyyâ* of Mishnah *Yoma* 5.2 (see above).

Once again a foundation stone or a top stone is unlikely for the reasons given above. At first sight, one might be inclined to think of a gem for the high priest's turban because v. 9b seems to speak about an engraving (cf. Exod. 28.36). But a closer inspection of our verse casts doubt on the traditional interpretation (see below) and even if v. 9b would speak of an engraving of a gem stone, the meaning of *'eben* would be different from that in 4.7 and 4.10. Schmidt's interpretation however is in accordance with these verses.

That we have to think of the temple mountain also in this case is not only intimated by 4.7 and 4.10, but by the wording of v. 9 as well. The expression *'eben 'aḥat* does not mean 'one stone' (which would be senseless in this connection) but 'the first stone', i.e. the primeval stone, cf. *yôm 'eḥād*, 'the first day', in Gen. 1.5.[40] The words *hinnᵉnî mᵉpatteāḥ pittuḥāh* are usually translated by 'I will engrave its engraving', but the Septuagint has *idou egō orussō bothron*, 'Behold, I will sink its well'. In our opinion, this interpretation is to be preferred, not only on the strength of Zech. 13.1, 14.8, Ezek. 47.1ff. and Joel 4.18, but also because v. 9c speaks of a flood which will wipe away[41] the burden of sin from 'that domain',[42] i.e. the temple mountain. In any case, nothing seems to contradict the identification of the *'eben* with Mount Zion. Since the temple building reached its completion by 515, the terrain is put at Joshua's disposal because he has to function there as high priest (cf. v. 7).[43]

Our proposal to identify the *'eben* of 3.9, 4.7 and 4.10 with the holy mountain should not come as a surprise. In Zechariah's visions mythological language is regularly used: cf. 1.8; 2.9; 6.1. Pre-exilic Zion theology provided the starting point for its application in an eschatological setting, as far as *'eben* is concerned. This mythological background explains the use of 'stone' instead of 'rock' or 'mountain' in the visions of the prophet.

NOTES

1. J. Ridderbos, *De kleine profeten* III (Korte Verklaring; 2nd edn; Kampen, 1952); M. Bič, *Die Nachtgesichte des Sacharja* (Biblische Studien, 42; Neukirchen, 1964); J.C. Baldwin, *Haggai-Zechariah-Malachi* (Tyndale Old Testament Commentaries; London, 1972); and W. Rudolph, *Haggai-Sacharja 1–8-Sacharja 9–14-Maleachi* (KAT 13/4; Gütersloh, 1976), consider ch. 3 as an integral part of the original night visions of Zechariah.

2. That 'the man among the myrtles' (Zech. 1.10) must be identified with 'the angel of the Lord', is intimated by Zech. 1.11 which speaks about the angel of the Lord standing among the myrtles. That this angel is the same person as the interpreting angel of 1.9 etc. is probable already on the strength of the fact that the angel who intervened on behalf of Jerusalem and the cities of Judah (1.12) is apparently identical with the one who was comforted by God (1.13), although he is called 'the angel who talked with me' in the last verse. Decisive for the identification of 'the angel of the Lord' and the interpreting angel is, however, that according to 1.10 'the man among the myrtles' (the same as the angel of the Lord; cf. 1.11) did not belong to the horsemen who ranged through the world. In the reverse case, the angel of the Lord/the man among the myrtles would not have been in need of a report. The question of the prophet: 'What are these, sir?', in the sense of: 'What mean these, sir?', implies that the angel of the Lord did not belong to them, because otherwise the prophet would also have asked about the significance of the man among the myrtles. The difficulty is solved if the man among the myrtles, the angel who talked to the prophet, and the angel of the Lord are one and the same figure. On the problem of the identification see also Chr.

Jeremias, *Die Nachtgesichte des Sacharja* (FRLANT, 117; Göttingen, 1977), who finds two persons, although he admits: 'Man wird allerdings die noch weitergehende Möglichkeit nicht gänzlich ausschliessen können, dass hinter 1,7ff. ursprünglich eine Textfassung stand, in der nur von *einer* Gestalt, dem *'îš*, die Rede war...' (p. 86).

3. Cf. Chr. Jeremias, *op. cit.* (n. 2), pp. 201ff., for a comprehensive refutation of this view.

4. For our own interpretation of 6.11b see n. 31.

5. The literary unity of the chapter is defended e.g. by K. Marti, *Das Dodekapropheton* (KHC 13; Tübingen, 1904); H.G. Mitchell, *Haggai and Zechariah* (ICC; Edinburgh, 1912; 2nd edn, 1961); E. Sellin, *Das Zwölfprophetenbuch* (KAT 12; Leipzig, 1929/1930); J. Ridderbos, *op. cit.* (n. 1); G. Smit, *De kleine profeten* III (Tekst en Uitleg; Groningen-Den Haag-Batavia, 1934); M. Delcor (-A. Deissler), *Les petits prophètes* II (La Sainte Bible, Pirot–Clamer VIII; Paris, 1964). T. Chary, *Aggée–Zacharie–Malachie* (Sources Bibliques; Paris, 1969), pp. 78ff., places v. 9a, b after v. 7 and considers vv. 8, 9c and 10 as a separate prophecy. S. Amsler in S. Amsler–A. Lacocque–R. Vuilleumier, *Aggée–Zacharie–Malachie* (Commentaire de l'Ancien Testament, XIc), pp. 83ff., finds three prophecies: vv. 8, 9 and 10.

6. W. Nowack, *Die kleinen Propheten* (HK 3/4; 3rd edn; Göttingen, 1922), p. 321, places the section between 3.7 and 3.8; but D. Deden, *De kleine profeten* (BOT; Roermond-Maaseik, 1953-1956), pp. 334f., speaks of a promise for Zerubbabel added to the fifth vision. Marti, *op. cit.* (n. 5), pp. 412f., considers the section as 'eine Beigabe entweder zu 3.9 oder zu 4.14'. Sellin, *op. cit.* (n. 5), p. 502, considers the possibility of an addition originally written in the margin of the text.

7. W.A.M. Beuken, *Haggai–Sacharja 1–8* (Studia Semitica Neerlandica, 10; Assen, 1967), pp. 261ff.

8. On the use of the feminine form of the cardinal number, cf. Zech. 3.9.

9. Cf. K. Marti, 'Der Zweifel an der prophetischen Sendung Sacharjas', *Festschrift für J. Wellhausen* (BZAW, 27; Giessen, 1914), pp. 279-94.

10. Some scholars consider the text as a late redactional addition in defence of the prophet at a time when his prophecies failed to be fulfilled (Marti; K. Elliger, *Das Buch der zwölf kleinen Propheten* 2 (ATD 25/2; 5th edn; Göttingen, 1964); others reckon with a secondary redaction by the prophet himself (Sellin; F. Horst, in T.H. Robinson–F. Horst, *Die zwölf kleinen Propheten* (HAT 1/14; 3rd edn; Tübingen, 1964).

11. As pointed out already by T.C. Vriezen, 'Two Old Cruces', *OTS* 5 (1948), pp. 88-91.

12. Cf. Hag. 2.7; Rev. 21.24.

13. Although it must be admitted that the Peshiṭta, the Vulgate, the Targum and a number of Hebrew manuscripts have the plural form, this is

most certainly the *lectio facilior*, due to the following *ᵃlêkem*.

14. For the *comparatio decurtata* cf. Gesenius-Kautzsch, *Grammar*, §118r.

15. As suggested by K. Galling, *Studien zur Geschichte Israels im persischen Zeitalter* (Tübingen, 1964), p. 141.

16. So L.G. Rignell, *Die Nachtgesichte des Sacharja* (Lund, 1950), and E. Sellin, 'Noch einmal der Stein des Sacharja', *ZAW* 48 (1942/43), p. 70.

17. K. Elliger, *op. cit.* (n. 10), thinks of the Samaritans in particular.

18. So the majority of commentators.

19. Cf. also *nāweh*, 'fine', 'lovely', next to *nā'eh*, and Job 30.22, where *tšwh*=*tᵉšū'â*, 'storm'.

20. A. Petitjean, *Les oracles du Proto-Zacharie* (Etudes Bibliques; Paris-Louvain, 1969), pp. 247ff.

21. Rudolph, *op. cit.* (n. 1), prefers 'Schlussstein' or 'Scheitelstein'.

22. Cf. E. Lipiński, *VT* 20 (1970), pp. 30ff.

23. *Op. cit.* (n. 1), pp. 101f., although in connection with the stone of 3.9.

24. For this meaning of *yāṣā'* cf. G.R. Driver, *Biblica* 32 (1951), p. 190; S. Esh, *VT* 4 (1954), pp. 306-307; M. Dahood, *Biblica* 46 (1965), p. 321; 47 (1966), p. 416.

25. This translation seems to be possible on the strength of Gesenius-Kautzsch, *Grammar*, §132c.

26. C. Keil, *Biblischer Commentar über die zwölf kleinen Propheten* (3rd edn; Leipzig, 1888), p. 569.

27. Rudolph (*op. cit.* [n. 1], p. 111) proposes the infin. abs. hiphil *habdēl*.

28. Cf. Gesenius-Kautzsch, *Grammar*, §142f.

29. Cf. n. 5.

30. J. Wellhausen (*Die kleinen Propheten übersetzt und erklärt* [Berlin, 3rd edn, 1898; 4th edn, 1963], p. 181) already stated: 'In wie fern sie Vorzeichen des kommenden Königs sind, ist nicht ganz deutlich'. Mitchell, *op. cit.* (n. 5), p. 156, proposed to find the omen in the names of the priests, cf. Isa. 8.18. But we do not know their names and it is unlikely that they *in toto* referred to the future. That the re-established priesthood of Jerusalem were the men of the omen because their very existence warranted the advent of the messianic king (cf. Chary, Amsler), is scarcely convincing.

31. Since *śîm 'al*, not *śîm bᵉ*, is the usual expression for 'to put on', and the Akkadian expression *šakānu ina rēši N.N.* signifies 'to put at the disposal of somebody' (cf. *AHw*, pp. 973f.), we propose the following translation: 'And you shall hand (it) over to Joshua . . .' It is not that the high priest is crowned, but he receives the messianic crown as an omen of the advent of the expected king.

32. For the meaning of *nātan lipnê* cf. Deut. 1.21; 2.36.

33. E.g. Petitjean, *op. cit.* (n. 20), pp. 179ff.

34. E.g. Marti, *op. cit.* (n. 5), p. 411 ('Schlussstein').
35. *Op.cit.* (n. 30), p. 181.
36. H. Gressmann, *Der Messias* (Göttingen, 1919), pp. 258-62.
37. H. Schmidt, *ZAW* 54 (1936), pp. 54-57.
38. *Op.cit.* (n. 5), p. 80.
39. *Op.cit.* (n. 1), p. 101.
40. For other such instances of this use as an ordinal cf. *HAL*, p. 30.
41. The transitive use of the qal of *mūš* is not attested elsewhere in the Old Testament. Perhaps we should read *w^{e}maššōtī* (from *māšaš*; cf. Akk. *mašāšu*), 'I shall wipe'.
42. The demonstrative pronoun *hahî'* seems to refer to the stone of v. 9a.
43. Cf. 3.7.

19

SATZGRENZEN BEI PENDENSKONSTRUKTIONEN—DER PENDENSSATZ

Walter Groß

Die für jede syntaktische Analyse grundlegende Bestimmung der Satzgrenzen wird in den Grammatiken gar nicht oder unzureichend thematisiert; im besondern gilt das für den vielgestaltigen Grenzfall der Pendenskonstruktionen. Im folgenden diskutiere ich hierzu einige Gesichtspunkte am Beispiel der pendierenden direkten Objekte.[1]

(1)	(a)	Ex 33,17:	*gam 'at ha=dabar ha=zā̈ 'ăšr dibbarta 'i'śā̈*
	(b)	Gen 39,22:	*w·='ăt kul 'ăšr 'ōśīm šam hū(') hayā 'ōśā̈*
	(c)	Gen 41,25:	*'ăt 'ăšr ha='ilōhīm 'ōśā̈ higgīd l·= PR'H*
(2)	(a)	1 Kön 20,34:	*ha='arīm 'ăšr laqaḥ 'ab=ī mi[n]='it 'abī=ka 'ašīb*
	(b)	Num 22,17	*w·=kul 'ăšr tō(')mar il-a=y 'i'śā̈*
	(c)	Gen 41,55:	*'ăšr yō(')mar la=kim ta'śū*

Die Belege unterstreichen eine bekannte Tatsache: Die Setzung des *'at* bei verbalem Prädikat vorausgehenden direkten Objekten ist fakultativ, seien diese durch eine Nominalgruppe oder durch einen Satz (Objektsatz) repräsentiert; vgl. die Fälle je identischer Struktur und Determination: (1a—2a); (1b—2b); (1c—2c). Niemand würde behaupten, in (2a-c) seien die dem Verb vorausgehenden Elemente im Gegensatz zu (1a-c) gar keine Objekte, es seien vielmehr 'absolut' gesetzte Substantive bzw. nominalisierte *'ăšr*-Sätze. Sie gelten nach einhelliger Beurteilung als direkte Objekte, die lediglich auf der

Oberflächenstruktur nicht durch *'at* als solche gekennzeichnet sind. Daß es sich um direkte Objekte handelt, konnte der althebräische Sprecher/Hörer erkennen aus (a) Ersetzungsproben mit *'at* + *Substantiv*, (b) dem Kontext, (c) der Bedeutung der Sätze. Die Setzung des *'at* ist bei vorausgehendem Objekt auch dann fakultativ, wenn dieses Objekt pendiert, d.h. zusätzlich pronominal aufgenommen wird; vgl. die Belege identischer Struktur und Determination: (3a—4a); (3b—4b); (3c—4c).

(3) (a) Num 22,20: *'ak 'at ha=dabar 'ȧšr ʾ·dabbir 'il-ē=ka 'ōt=ō ta'śā̄*
(b) Ri 11,24: *w·='ȧt kul 'ȧšr hôrīš YHWH . . . mi[n]=panē=nū 'ōt=ō nīraš*
(c) Num 23,12: *hȧ=lō(') 'ȧt 'ȧšr yaśîm YHWH b·=pī=y 'ōt=ō 'išmur l· =dabbir*

(4) (a) Num 22,38: *ha=dabar 'ȧšr yaśīm 'ilōhīm b·=pī=y 'ōt=ō ʾ·dabbir*
(b) Num 23,26: *kul 'ȧšr y dabbir YHWH 'ōt=ō 'i'śā̄*
(c) Num 24,13: *'ȧšr y dabbir YHWH 'ōt=ō ʾ·dabbir*

(5) Dtn 4,3: *kul ha='īš 'ȧšr halak 'aḥȧrẹ ba'l P'WR hišmīd=ō*

Um die voranstehenden Elemente in (4) als direkte Objekte zu identifizieren, konnte der Althebräer dieselben Instrumente verwenden wie bei (2). Wie bei (1) + (2) besteht der Unterschied zwischen (3) und (4) nur für die Oberflächenstruktur oder, falls uns nicht mehr faßbare Differenzierungen der Intonation etc. hinzugetreten sein sollten, nur für uns, nicht bezüglich der syntaktischen Tiefenstruktur.[2] Auf Grund der parallelen Erscheinungen im Verhältnis von (1) zu (2) besteht keine Berechtigung, zwischen (3) und (4) folgendermaßen zu unterscheiden: In (3) steht das Objekt voran und wird anschließend im *selben* Satz pronominal *aufgenommen*; in (4) steht ein Element 'absolut', *pendierend* voran, erst die pronominale Aufnahme im *zugehörigen* Satz zeigt, daß es darin als Objekt fungiert.[3] In (3) wie (4) pendiert das direkte Objekt, in (3) zeigt lediglich *'at* beim Pendens bereits an, was in (4) erst durch die Aufnahme im zugehörigen Satz verdeutlicht wird, daß das Pendens nämlich im zugehörigen Satz die syntaktische Rolle des direkten Objekts spielt.

(1) und (2) werden übereinstimmend analysiert: *direktes Objekt* + (*Subjekt*) + *Verb*. Wie aber sind (3) und (4) zu analysieren? Masora

gibt keinen Hinweis; bei (1) + (2) wie bei (3) + (4) steht überwiegend der schwache Trenner *Tipḥa* vor dem Verb bzw. vor der pronominalen Aufnahme. Sie unterschiedlich zu analysieren, wurde soeben abgelehnt: (3) = *I* (*ohne interne Satzgrenze?*): *direktes Objekt* + *Aufnahme des direkten Objekts* + (*Subjekt*) + *Verb*; (4) = II (*mit Satzgrenze nach Pendens?*): *Pendens* + *direktes Objekt* (*referenzidentisch mit Pendens*) + (*Subjekt*) + *Verb*. (3) und (4) sind gemeinsam nach I oder nach II zu analysieren. Analyse I muß annehmen, daß dasselbe Objekt im selben Satz zweimal vertreten sein kann. Analyse II muß für die Belege (3) annehmen, daß die Rektion des Verbs (auf der Oberflächenstruktur) nicht nur semantisch, sondern auch syntaktisch über die Satzgrenze auf ein vorausgehendes nicht-satzhaftes Element hinausreicht. Dies scheint die schwierigere Annahme zu sein, wenngleich das Hebräische nicht überall stringent zwischen satzhaften und nicht-satzhaften Einheiten unterscheidet.[4] Noch weniger leuchtet Analyse II bei den Belegen der Struktur (5) ein; *kul ha='īš . . . hišmīd =ō* YHWH: Beide abgetrennte Größen sind zufriedenstellende hebräische Sätze.

Ob man zwischen pendierendem Objekt und zugehörigem Satz eine Satzgrenze annimmt oder nicht, jedenfalls ist festzustellen, daß die Trennung/Verbindung zwischen beiden Elementen sehr unterschiedlich sein kann.

(6)	Num 14,31:	*wᵉ=ṭapp=kim 'ăšr 'ămartim la=baz yihyă wᵉ=hibē(')tī 'ōt=am*
(7)	1 Kön 13,11:	*'at ha=dàbarīm 'ăšr dibbir 'il ha=malk wa=y sappᵉrū=m*
(8)	Num 23,3:	*wᵉ=dàbar mah yar'-i=nī wᵉ=higgadtī la=k*
(9)	Num 4,26:	*wᵉ='ăt kul 'ăšr yi'[ ]aśă la=him wᵉ='abadū*
(10)	1 Sam 30,22:	*kī 'im 'īš 'at 'išt=ō wᵉ='at ban-a(y)=w wᵉ=yinhàgū*

Bei Beleg (6) liegt die Annahme einer Satzgrenze nach 'absolut' vorausstehendem Pendens auf den ersten Blick vor allem deshalb nahe, weil der zugehörige Satz mit *wᵉ*=qaṭal beginnt und *wᵉ*=/*wa*= vor finitem Verb häufigstes Kriterium für Beginn eines Satzes ist.[5] Beleg (7)[6] jedoch—die Entsprechung mit *'at* vor dem Pendens—läßt diese Analyse wieder zweifelhaft erscheinen: durch *'at* wird das Pendens der Rektion des folgenden Verbs unterworfen. (6) und (7) sind somit syntaktisch gleichartig zu analysieren. Gründe für eine Satzgrenze nach dem Pendens (Satzweiser *wa*=, pronominales direktes Objekt in diesem Satz) und Gründe dagegen (*'at* vor dem pendierenden direkten Objekt) stehen bei Beleg (7) gegeneinander. Für eine Satzgrenze kann auch nicht die Analogie der Objektsätze herangezogen werden, denn (1) voranstehende Objektsätze schließen asyndetisch an den zugehörigen folgenden übergeordneten Satz an;[7] (2) Objektsätze sind die satzhafte Realisierung des Objekts des übergeordneten Satzes, sie unterliegen direkt der Rektion des Verbs im übergeordneten Satz; daher ist das Objekt in diesem nicht zusätzlich auch noch pronominal vertreten; (3) die pendierenden Objekte in (6) und (7) sind keine Sätze.

In den bisher diskutierten Beispielen waren die zugehörigen Sätze auch ohne ihr Pendens syntaktisch vollständig.[8] Anders ist dies in den folgenden Belegen. Dadurch verstärkt sich die syntaktische Klammer zwischen Pendens und zugehörigem Satz, obgleich dieser durch *w*= eröffnet wird. In (8) pendiert das direkte Objekt, es wird aber im zugehörigen Satz nicht aufgenommen. Der Satz *w=higgadtī la=k* ist weder syntaktisch vollständig noch semantisch verständlich; man muß wissen, daß *dābar mah yar'-i=nī* das zugehörige Objekt ist, obgleich nicht einmal *'at* es als solches kennzeichnet und der folgende Satz mit *w*= beginnt. Zwar kennt das Hebräische die stilistische Regel, daß ein direktes Objekt, das zwei koordinierten Sätzen gemeinsam ist, nur beim ersten Verb (gelegentlich nur beim zweiten Verb) genannt werden muß. Aber in Num 23,3 geht ja *w=higgadtī* gar kein Satz, kein Verb mit zugehörigem direktem Objekt voraus, sondern nur das Element, das Objekt dieses durch *w*= angeschlossenen Verbs ist.

Noch deutlicher präsentiert sich in der Oberflächenstruktur das Problem bei (9), dem entsprechenden Satztyp mit *'at* vor dem pendierenden Objekt. Dem Satz *w='abadū* ist nicht anzusehen, daß *'BD* hier nicht—mit abweichender Bedeutung—ohne Komplement, sondern als zweiwertiges Verb mit direktem Objekt konstruiert ist und die entsprechenden semantischen Nuancen besitzt; andererseits erklärt nur die Rektion von 'BD das *'at* vor *kul*. Im Fall von (8) und (9) ergeben nur Pendens zusammen mit folgendem Satz den Bauplan des Satzes mit zwei- bzw. dreiwertigem Verb; ohne *w*= vor dem Verb wären es vollständige, wohlgeformte Sätze,[9] einzig dieses *w*= trennt das Verb von seinem zugehörigen vorausgehenden direkten Objekt.

Am schwierigsten schließlich ist Beleg (10): Subjekt und durch *'at* bezeichnetes direktes Objekt pendieren gemeinsam vor dem zugehörigen mit *w*= eingeführten Verb, ohne daß das Objekt bei diesem pronominal aufgenommen wird.[10] Nicht nur die Valenzbeziehungen von *w·=yinhágū* bleiben semantisch und syntaktisch unklar, es sei denn man ergänze die vorausgehenden pendierenden Subjekt + Objekt, sondern auch die syntaktische Beziehung zwischen *'īš* und *'at 'išt=ō* bleibt völlig dunkel, sofern sie nicht durch die Valenzen des Verbs *w·=yinhágū* erhellt wird.

Hier sprechen Gründe für und gegen eine Satzgrenze nach dem Pendens. Zumindest für den heutigen Betrachter, dem Informationen über Intonation, Sprechpausen etc. fehlen,[11] vielleicht auch für den damaligen Sprecher werden in diesen Fällen die Satzgrenzen unklar, gerät die scharfe Trennung zwischen nicht-satzhaftem Element: Pendens und zugehörigem Satz ins Fließen. Andererseits liegt hier keine unpräzise, gar ungrammatische Redeweise vor; nach Ausweis vor allem der poetischen Belege gehören Pendenskonstruktionen zu den regelhaften Ausdrücken, die besondere stilistische Effekte erzielen.[12] Soweit die Grammatiken nicht nur von isolierender Vorausstellung des Pendens etc. sprechen, sondern auf die Frage der Satzgrenzen bzw. der Satzart eingehen, begegnen vornehmlich die Termini 'zusammengesetzter Satz' bzw. 'zusammengesetzter Nominalsatz'. Kautzsch nennt die Pendenskonstruktion 'zusammengesetzter Satz' und definiert: 'Ein zusammengesetzter Satz entsteht durch die Nebeneinanderstellung eines (allzeit vorangehenden . . .) Subjekts und a) eines selbständigen Nominalsatzes . . . b) eines selbständigen Verbalsatzes'.[13] Diese Bezeichnung ist nicht nur zu weit, da z.B. Brockelmann in seiner Syntax[14] unter dieser Sammelüberschrift im dritten Buch alle Satzgefüge einschließlich der Konjunktionalsätze behandelt, sie ist auch falsch oder zumindest mißverständlich. In allen oben diskutierten Belegen ging nicht das Subjekt, sondern das Objekt pendierend voraus. Verwendet man Subjekt dagegen, wie hier von Kautzsch vorausgesetzt, nicht als syntaktische, sondern als semantische Größe, so wird man bezüglich unserer Belege zu so eigenartigen Formulierungen gezwungen, wie Meyer sie in seiner Syntax vorlegt: 'Darüber hinaus kann ein Objekt synt. als Subjekt gelten'.[15] In Beleg (10) pendieren sogar mehrere Satzteile, die nicht gemeinsam als Subjekt bestimmt werden können. Meyer reiht die Pendenskonstruktionen unter die 'zusammengesetzten Nominalsätze' ein.[16] Zu den bereits erhobenen Einwänden tritt hier der weitere, daß diese Benennung bezüglich sämtlicher obiger Belege pendierender Objekte, die alle Verbalsätzen zugeordnet sind, und angesichts der Tatsache, daß nur Verbalsätze, nicht aber Nominalsätze

Objekte bei sich haben können,[17] die Übernahme der Kategorien der arabischen Nationalgrammatik voraussetzt; in dieser Konzeption gibt es aber überhaupt keine Verbalsätze mit vorausstehendem Subjekt; die von vielen Hebraisten zu Recht als Verbalsätze aufgefaßten Sätze der Typen *x-qaṭal* und *x-yiqṭol* müssen dann ebenfalls als 'zusammengesetzte Nominalsätze' analysiert werden.[18] Damit wird diese Bezeichnung zu weit und ist nicht mehr in der Lage, speziell die Pendenskonstruktionen auszugrenzen.

Ich schlage vor, die Verbindung von pendierendem Element und zugehörigem Satz als *'Pendenssatz'* zu bezeichnen. Der Pendenssatz hat die syntaktischen Besonderheiten, daß (a) in ihm dasselbe referenzidentische Syntagma zweimal—in der Regel einmal lexematisch, einmal pronominal—vorkommen kann und daß (b) *wa=/ w·=yiqṭol* bzw. *w·=qaṭal* nicht am Satzanfang stehen. Da diese Verbformen zusammen mit dem 'Satzweiser' *w·=/wa=* dennoch entsprechend ihrer sonstigen Funktion den Satzanfang bezeichnen, hat der Pendenssatz in diesen Fällen von seiner äußeren Form her zwei Anfänge, d.h. die erste Position des Satzes als herausragende Tonstelle ist verdoppelt. Deswegen wird der Pendenssatz oft gewählt, wenn eine zusätzliche Betonung am Satzanfang erreicht werden soll.[19] Das pendierende Element ist zwar eine eigene Äußerungseinheit,[20] aber auf der Ebene der Sätze keine eigene syntaktische Einheit. Das Pendens ist ein—wenn auch unterschiedlich stark desintegriertes—Syntagma des Pendenssatzes. Ob innerhalb der Größe Pendenssatz bei manchen Beleggruppen—z.B. den Pendentia mit zugehörigem Satz mit *w·=/wa= + Verb*—zusätzlich eine untergeordnete Satzgrenze anzunehmen ist, kann zunächst offen bleiben; die Beispiele (8)—(10) raten davon ab. Die Konstituierung der syntaktischen Größe 'Pendenssatz' mag dazu helfen, seine sehr differenzierten Realisierungen schärfer zu erfassen und ihn auf seine syntaktischen wie stilistischen Eigenheiten zu untersuchen.

ANMERKUNGEN

1. Eine Untersuchung der althebräischen Pendenskonstruktionen insgesamt hoffe ich in Kürze vorzulegen: *Die Pendens Konstruktion im Biblischen Hebräisch. Studien zum althebräischen Satz* I (ATS 27), St. Attilien, 1987. Bei anderen Untergruppen, z.B. den pendierenden Zeitangaben, stellen sich die Fragen abweichend, die in diesem Beitrag genannten Gesichtspunkte bewähren sich aber differenziert auch dort.

2. Das gilt unabhängig davon, ob die pronominale Aufnahme vor—vgl. (3) und (4)—oder nach—vgl. (5)—dem Verb steht.

3. So unterscheidet z.B. KÖNIG in seiner Syntax, 438f §340 g+h; 442 §341 c-e. KROPAT, 60, weiß sogar, in welchem Kasus das pendierende Element steht: im Nominativ. Dafür faßt KÖNIG, 445 §341 o, Belege der Art von (7) als 'ausgeprägten Accusativus absolutus' auf. Wie in zahlreichen wissenschaftlichen Abhandlungen zur hebräischen Syntax wird hier ganz selbstverständlich von den Kasus-Sprachen her gedacht und formuliert. (Vgl. zu Nominativus absolutus und Accusativus absolutus im Bereich der indogermanischen Kasus-Sprachen HAVERS. Er behandelt ausführlich den 'isoliertemphatischen Nominativ' und führt dann S. 248 zum Beleg mit vorausstehendem Akkusativ: *columellam ferream, quae in miliario stat, eam recte stare oportet* aus: 'Hier könnte auch der emph. Nom. stehen mit Einrenkung durch das folgende eam, und der Unterschied besteht nur darin, daß in obiger Stelle das Substantiv schon bewußtermaßen als Bestandteil in den Satz eingefügt ist'.) Das Hebräische ist aber keine Kasus-Sprache, seine Oberflächenstruktur im nominalen Bereich ist sehr viel weniger und mit anderen Mitteln differenziert. Die willkürliche Einführung von Nominativ und Akkusativ in die Beschreibung der hebräischen Pendenskonstruktionen bereitet nur zusätzliche Probleme. Wir können für das Hebräische feststellen: Das pendierende Element hat entweder und überwiegend kein sprachliches Anzeichen oder aber doch ein syntaktisches Funktionswort (z.B. *'at* bei manchen pendierenden Objekten; *b*ᵉ=/*k*ᵉ= bei fast allen pendierenden Zeitangaben) bei sich; das verdeutlicht, welche Rolle es im zugehörigen Satz—dort in der Regel, aber z.B. bei pendierenden Zeitangaben fast nie durch pronominale/lexematische Aufnahme angezeigt—spielt.

4. Vgl. die koordinierte Weiterführung von Partizip oder nebensatzersetzender Präpositionalverbindung mit Inf. constr. durch syndetische Verbalsätze.

5. Vgl. RICHTER, 7f.50, der seine bereits mehrfach vorgeschlagene Bezeichnung von *w*ᵉ=/wa= als 'Satzweiser' begründet.

6. 1 Kön 13,11 unterliegt allerdings (nicht allzu schwerwiegenden) text- wie literarkritischen Bedenken. Außerdem läßt sich die weniger wahrscheinliche Auffassung nicht ausschließen, das Objekt von *wa=ysappir: 'at kul ha=ma'śā* werde durch asyndetisches *'at ha=dåbarīm* expliziert und nach diesem langen direkten Objekt habe *wa=ysappirū=m* resümierende Funktion (vgl. dazu GROSS 1978, 106 n 19); das würde zur Informationsarmut des zweiten Satzes passen; dann läge keine Pendenskonstruktion vor. Vgl. jedoch 1 Kön 15,13; wohl auch Num 17,3; 2 Kön 24,16.

7. Vgl. (1c), (2c). Andernfalls pendiert eben der ganze Objektsatz.

8. Semantisch allerdings ergab sich die Füllung des pronominalen Objekts nur aus seiner Referenzidentität mit dem pendierenden lexematischen Objekt.

9. Allerdings müßte bei identischer Verbfunktion dann das jeweilige Verb in Präfixkonjugation statt in Suffixkonjugation gebildet sein.

10. STOEBE, 504, zieht zwar nach Ausweis seiner Übersetzung *kī 'im 'īš 'at 'išt=ō* als Objekt zu *lō(') nittin*. Doch bereitet *'īš* dieser Deutung große Probleme; auch setzt Masora den stärksten Trenner nach *hiṣṣalnū*. So hat denn KÖNIG in seiner Syntax, indem er im Index S. 650 zur Stelle auf §372f verwies, *kī 'im* hier als 'Satzverbindung' und 'Conjunction', somit das Folgende als Satz gedeutet (wie schon LXX). Entsprechend hat DRIVER, 154 §125, den Beleg unter die Pendensbeispiele eingereiht. Vgl. auch MCCARTER, 430, und z.B. die Übersetzung von STOLZ, 178: 'Nur seine Frau und seine Kinder soll ein jeder abholen und dann gehen'.

11. Die Intonation der althebräischen Sätze ist leider unbekannt. Auch die masoretischen Akzente können, soweit sie überhaupt syntaktische Strukturen berücksichtigen bzw. anzeigen, natürlich nur die viel jüngere Vortragstechnik der Zeit, der sie entstammen, bezeugen; dennoch sind sie wertvoll. BRAVMANN, 58 n 3, stellt differenzierte Thesen zur Intonation von Pendenskonstruktionen im Althebräischen auf, verrät aber nicht, woraus er sie ermittelt (vielleicht aus Parallelen in modernen arabischen Dialekten?).

12. Vgl. GESENIUS-KAUTZSCH, 479 n 4.

13. Vgl. GESENIUS-KAUTZSCH, 479 §143.

14. BROCKELMANN, 130ff.

15. MEYER, 14 §92.4 b.

16. MEYER, 13f §92.4. So auch MICHEL, 179ff §28. Selbst IRSIGLER, der durch seine Monographien von (1977) und (1984), speziell durch die Erarbeitung der Kategorien 'erweiterter Satz' und 'Satzbund', sehr zur Verfeinerung der Analyse von Satzgrenzen und Satzverbindungen beigetragen hat, verwendet diesen Terminus; vgl. IRSIGLER 1984, 218 und öfter zu Ps 73,28a; allerdings enthält sein Beleg auch nur nominale/pronominale Elemente.

17. Auch Partizipialsätze können direkte Objekte haben. Aus diesem Grund und wegen der Einbeziehung der Partizipialsätze in das System der hebräischen Verbalfunktionen trenne ich die Partizipialsätze von den Nominalsätzen ab und betrachte sie als eigene Satzgruppe, die den Verbalsätzen nähersteht als den Nominalsätzen; vg. GROSS 1975; 1982, 61f. 67f.

18. Vgl. MEYER 14 §92.4 b; MICHEL, 179ff §28.

19. Bei den pendierenden Zeitangaben z.B. ist freilich fraglich, ob, bzw. oft vom Kontext ausgeschlossen, daß diese selbst überhaupt den Ton tragen. In diesen Fällen erweist sich daher BROCKELMANNs, 123 §123f, Bezeichnung der pendierenden Zeitangaben als 'dominierende Vorstellung' (in Anlehnung an WUNDTs Völkerpsychologie) als besonders ungeeignet. Zeitbestimmungen treten im Hebräischen generell, also auch, wo sie unbetont sind, gern an die Spitze des Satzes bzw. Satzgefüges (vgl. BLOCH, 54). Ihre Voranstellung in Pendens-Konstruktionen beweist daher noch nicht ihre Betonung. Vielmehr

dient hier die Pendens-Konstruktion dazu, der unbetonten Zeitangabe ihre übliche Erststellung zu belassen und dennoch durch die Fortsetzung der Formulierung mit *w=/wa=* + *Verb* dem Verb im Pendenssatz eine zusätzliche Erststellung mit Betonung zu sichern. Die syntaktische und semantische Funktion pendierender Zeitangaben trifft BLAU, 22f, sehr gut mit dem—allerdings zu weiten—Terminus 'sentence adverbial'.

20. Zum Terminus Äußerungseinheit vgl. SCHWEIZER, 23 und *passim*. Die Konsequenzen der Tatsache, daß ich nicht Äußerungseinheiten, sondern Sätze untersuche, seien an der unterschiedlichen Behandlung von Jes 42,1 verdeutlicht. SCHWEIZER, 32ff, lehnt es ab, die Partikel *hin* zum ersten Satz zu ziehen, da sie kontextbezogen ist und auch für den zweiten Satz gilt (das kann ich als syntaktisches Argument nicht anerkennen; Satzbezug und Kontextbezug können demselben Lexem zugleich zukommen, da mit Satz und Kontext zwei verschiedene Ebenen im Blick sind; ich betrachte daher mit den Kommentaren und Versionen *hin 'abd=ī* als präsentierenden Nominalsatz). Er isoliert sie vielmehr als erste Äußerungseinheit. Die verbleibende Fügung *'abd=ī 'itmuk b=ō* versteht er als 'casus pendens' und löst sie entsprechend in zwei Äußerungseinheiten auf (1: das Pendens; 2: der Verbalsatz). Da ich hingegen *hin 'abd=ī* als Nominalsatz ansehe, ordne ich Jes 42,1 nicht unter den Pendensbelegen ein. Auch sehe ich keinen Grund, mit SCHWEIZER zu leugnen, daß in 42,1 zwei asyndetische Attributsätze auch ausdrucksformal vorliegen. Bei *'itmuk b=ō* sprechen asyndetischer Anschluß an das Beziehungswort, Verb an erster Position und pronominale Aufnahme für diese Bestimmung. Bezüglich *raṣātā napš=ī* scheint es mir sehr fraglich, ob ohne Bezug zu *'abd=ī* ein im Kontext befriedigender 'kompletter' Satz (auch nur unter Rücksicht der Bedeutung des Verbs und der daraus resultierenden Valenzen) vorliegt. Da *RṢY* unter anderem präpositionales Objekt mit *b·=* bei sich haben kann, genügt die Annahme einer double-duty-Funktion des *b=ō* nach *'itmuk*, um den pronominalen Rückbezug zu ergänzen. So ist durchaus damit zu rechnen, daß nach SCHWEIZERs Analyseansatz ein anderes Belegkorpus von Pendens-Konstruktionen aus dem AT erhoben würde. Der kurze Vergleich scheint mir zu verdeutlichen, daß Textsegmentierungen nach Äußerungseinheiten und nach Sätzen verschiedenen Kriterien folgen und nicht ganz einfach aufeinander bezogen werden können; sicher ist dies nicht so möglich, daß man die Äußerungseinheiten danach befragt, ob sie phrastische oder aphrastische Größen sind. Denn auch die 'phrastischen' Größen werden in SCHWEIZERs Methode anders, mit anderen Satzgrenzen konstituiert, wie seine Behandlung der Partikel *hin* erweist. Dessen ungeachtet kann SCHWEIZER mit seinem Ansatz die rhetorische und kommunikative Funktion vieler Pendens-Konstruktionen einleuchtend beschreiben. Vgl. S. 31.

Zitierte Literatur

Blau, J., *An Adverbial Construction in Hebrew and Arabic. Sentence Adverbials in Frontal Position Separated from the Rest of the Sentence*, IASHP 6/1 (Jerusalem, 1977).

Bloch, A., *Vers und Sprache im Altarabischen. Metrische und syntaktische Untersuchungen* (Acta Tropica Suppl. 5), Basel, 1946.

Bravmann, M.M., *Studies in Arabic and General Syntax* (PIFAO—TAEI XI), Kairo 1953.

Brockelmann, C., *Hebräische Syntax*, Neukirchen, 1956.

Driver, S.R., *A Treatise on the Use of the Tenses in Hebrew and Some Other Syntactical Questions*, Oxford, ^{3}1892.

Gross, W., 'Das nicht substantivierte Partizip als Prädikat im Relativsatz hebräischer Prosa', *JNWSL* 4 (1975), 25-47.

—'Bundeszeichen und Bundesschluß in der Priesterschrift', *TrThZ* 87 (1978), 98-115.

—'OTTO RÖSSLER und die Diskussion um das althebräische Verbalsystem', *BN* 18 (1982), 28-78.

Havers, W., 'Der sog. "Nominativus pendens"', *IGF* 43 (1926), 207-57.

Irsigler, H., *Gottesgericht und Jahwetag. Die Komposition Zef 1,1–2,3, untersucht auf der Grundlage der Literarkritik des Zefanjabuches* (ATS 3), St. Ottilien, 1977.

—*Psalm 73—Monolog eines Weisen. Text, Programm, Struktur* (ATS 20), St. Ottilien, 1984.

Kautzsch, E., *Wilhelm Gesenius' Hebräische Grammatik völlig umgearbeitet*, Leipzig, ^{28}1909.

König, F.E., *Historisch-kritisches Lehrgebäude der hebräischen Sprache mit comparativer Berücksichtigung des Semitischen überhaupt*. Zweite Hälfte 2. (Schluss-)Theil. Syntax; Leipzig, 1897.

Kropat, A., *Die Syntax des Autors der Chronik verglichen mit der seiner Quellen. Ein Beitrag zur historischen Syntax des Hebräischen* (BZAW 16), Gießen 1909.

McCarter, P.K., Jr, *I Samuel. A New Translation with Introduction, Notes & Commentary* (ANCB, 8), Garden City, New York, 1980.

Meyer, R., *Hebräische Grammatik II: Satzlehre* (SG 5765), Berlin/New York, 1972.

Michel, D., *Tempora und Satzstellung in den Psalmen* (AET 1), Bonn, 1960.

Richter, W., *Grundlagen einer althebräischen Grammatik*. B. Die Beschreibungsebenen. III. Der Satz (Satztheorie) (ATS 13), St. Ottilien, 1980.

Schweizer, H., *Metaphorische Grammatik. Wege zur Integration von Grammatik und Textinterpretation in der Exegese* (ATS 15), St. Ottilien 1981.

Stoebe, H.J., *Das erste Buch Samuelis* (KAT VIII.1), Gütersloh 1973.

Stolz, F., *Das erste und zweite Buch Samuel* (ZBK.AT 9), Zürich, 1981.

Wundt, W., *Völkerpsychologie. Eine Untersuchung der Entwicklungsgesetze von Sprache, Mythus und Sitte*. Bd. 2: Die Sprache. Teil 2; Leipzig, 1912.

20

NOTES ON THE DATES IN THE BOOK OF HAGGAI

P.A. Verhoef

The Israelitic and Near Eastern chronology is an intriguing and fascinating topic, and at the same time a vexing problem. It is not our intention to discuss this comprehensive subject as such.[1] The purpose of this article in honour of my friend and colleague, Professor F.C. Fensham, is to draw attention to some relevant facts concerning the dates in the book of Haggai. The emphasis in the heading of the article is on the word 'Notes'.

The 'Notes' concern the occurrences, the structure, the occasion, the purpose and significance of the dates in the book of Haggai.

In the book of Haggai we have the remarkable fact that each of the four comparatively short oracles is introduced by a precise date (1.1; 2.1, 10, 20; cf. 1.15; 2.18). In general the dates in the prophetic literature are confined to the superscriptions to collections of prophecies (cf. Isa. 1.1; Jer. 1.1, 3; Hos. 1.1; Amos 1.1; Mic. 1.1; Zeph. 1.1; cf. also Isa. 24.1; 27.1; 32.1; 33.1; 34.1, etc.).[2]

We agree with the view that there are no reasons to doubt the historicity and authenticity of the dates, which were attached to the prophecies of Haggai probably from the very beginning.[3]

It has proven possible with the help of evidence from a vast number of Babylonian texts, and from new moon tables calculated from astronomical data, to synchronize the old lunar calendar with the Julian calendar, with accurate results.[4] J.G. Baldwin[5] provides an appropriate table with the dates given in Haggai and Zechariah, together with their equivalents. In Haggai's case it amounts to the following:

1. The first day of the sixth month (1.1) is equivalent to 29 August.
2. The twenty-fourth day of the same month (1.15) = 21 September.

3. The twenty-first day of the seventh month (2.1) = 17 October.
4. The twenty-fourth day of the ninth month (2.10, 20) = 18 December.

It is evident that Haggai's ministry really was of short duration. All his messages were delivered within a period of fifteen weeks during the second year of Darius I (521–486 BC), i.e. from August until December in the year 520 BC.[6]

The *structure* of the dates amounts to the following:

1.1	:	year-month-day
1.15	:	day-month-(year)
2.1	:	(year)-month-day
2.10	:	day-month-year
2.18	:	day-month
2.20	:	day-month

In the Old Testament the sequence of year-month-day is the most frequent, while the inverted sequence of day-month-year is found also in Num. 1.1; Ezra 6.15; Zech. 1.7. Alternative datings are: year-day-month (Zech. 7.1), month-year-day (Exod. 40.17), and month-day-year (2 Kgs 25.8; Jer. 52.13). By far the most common manner of dating is a reference to the day and the month (45 instances), followed by a reversed indication of the month and the day (19 instances). In a number of cases the explanation for the specific sequence is apparent: when a month is introduced for the first time, the general order is month and day, but the opposite order is followed when the narrative is continued (see Exod. 12.18; Lev. 23.5, 6; 23.24, 27-39; Num. 28.16, 17-25, etc). This obvious rule, however, is not consistently applied.

Because my colleague's field of interest is the Semitic languages and the Near Eastern literature, I have compared the chronological references especially in the Assyrian-Babylonian historical texts.

In the earlier texts hardly any reference was made to the precise date of an event. The authors were content with a vague indication 'at that time'. In the *Annalistic Reports* we have mostly a reference to the regnal year of the kings or officials concerned, and in a few instances an indication of the month and the day: 'In the month Aiaru, the thirteenth day, I departed' (*ANET*, p. 277); 'in the month of Addar, a favourable month, on the eighth day, the day of the Nebo festival'. In the Babylonian Empire and its successors, the years were named after the reigning king, with an indication of the month and the day of a certain event: 'The first year of Nergalushazib: In the month of Tammuz, the sixteenth day. . . . ' etc. (*op.cit.*, p. 302).

In the literature of this period two main chronologies were applied. 1. The year-month-day chronology is found when historic events need a precise date, such as referred to in the example just given and also in the following instance: 'In the year of (eponym) Daian-Ashur, in the month Aiaru, the fourteenth day, I departed from Nineveh' (*ANET*, p. 278). 2. The day-month-year chronology was generally used in decrees which required a precise date, for instance: 'On the twentieth of Markeshvan, year seventeen of King Darius II' (*ANET*, pp. 491, 492).

In the Assyrian-Babylonian literature the more comprehensive dating was generally restricted to the period of the Neo-Babylonian and Persian Empires (cf. *ANET*, pp. 301, 302, 303, 305f.).

This very brief summary of my investigation is sufficient to establish the fact of Israel's participation in the cultural and literary heritage of the ancient Near East.

The *occasions* to which the dates in the book of Haggai refer are significant on their own, although they are differently assessed.

The first day of the (sixth) month (1.1) was the day of the New Moon[7] in the lunar calendar, and as such was observed as a festival occasion. 'On the first of every month' a burnt offering was presented to the Lord (Num. 28.11). At Israel's appointed feasts and New Moon festivals, they had to sound the trumpets over their offerings, being times of rejoicing (Num. 10.10; Ps. 81.4(3)). The New Moon festivals were associated with the Sabbaths in a number of texts (2 Kgs 4.23; Isa. 66.23; Ezek. 45.17; 46.1, 3; Ps. 81.4(3); Neh. 10.34(33); 1 Chron. 2.3(4); 8.13; 31.3; compare also Num. 28.14; Ezek. 46.6; Ezra 3.5).

On this significant day, a day of worship and rejoicing (Num. 10.10), the word of the Lord came to the civil and religious leaders of the post-exilic congregation (Hag. 1.1, 2).

The occasion of the second date, that of 1.15 is obliterated by the textual and contextual problems concerning this verse.[8] Traditionally 1.15 was regarded as a unit and combined with the following passage to form the first verse of ch. 2 (so LXX, Latina, Vulgate and Peshitta). The consensus of modern opinion, however, is that the double dating of this verse suggests a division between v. 15a and 15b–2.1, and that the usual order of year-month-day, when reference is made to the kingship of Darius, endorses this division. When this division is effected, another major problem arises, namely that the date of 1.15a requires a context, which seems to have been lost, or must be provided by relocating 2.15-19 (or 2.15-23) here.[9] An additional reason to regard 1.15a as secondary is because it is alleged that a date usually introduces a prophecy, and generally does not conclude it.[10] Moreover, according to many scholars the number of the month ('the sixth') is suspect. The definite article with the preposition *b^{e}* in *baššišši* is deemed impossible after *laḥodeš*, 'the month'.[11]

It is not necessary to enter into a discussion of these and similar objections against the authenticity and unity of v. 15. The unity can be maintained by attributing a double duty to the phrase, *in the second year of King Darius* (v. 15b). This phrase simultaneously concludes the preceding series of day-month-year, and introduces the following series of year-month-day. The phrases in question, therefore, can be rendered as follows: '(It happened) on the twenty-fourth day of the sixth month in the second year of King Darius. (In the second year of King Darius) on the twenty-first day of the seventh month . . . ' (cf. *Notes* on the TEV-translation, NIV and *Groot Nieuws Bijbel*).

The date in 1.15: *on the twenty-fourth day of the sixth month*, that is on 21 September 520 BC, implies a lapse of time between the command to rebuild the temple (1.1-11) and the actual commencement of the work. This delay could have been caused by a variety of circumstances.[12] The fact, however, is that when the work officially began, it was necessary to mark it with the mention of a specific date. This would also explain the positioning of the date, not at the beginning of the prophecy or statement, as was customary (1.1, 15b–2.1, 10; cf. Zech. 1.1; 7.1), but at the end. Van der Woude[13] rightly suggests as an additional reason for the present position of the date that it forms an *inclusio* with 1.1: between the first (1.1) and the twenty-fourth (1.15) day of the same month something actually happened.

According to this explanation the date in question marks a significant event: the official commencement of work on the temple.

The occasion of the third date (2.1) is of paramount importance. The word of the Lord came through the prophet Haggai *on the twenty-first day of the seventh month*.

The seventh month is Tišri, also called Ethanim (1 Kgs 8.2), and corresponds with our September-October. The twenty-first day of this month coincides approximately with 17 October. According to the current calendar this was an important day in the Feast of Tabernacles. This Feast began on the fifteenth day of the month and lasted for seven days. The twenty-first day, therefore, was the seventh day of the Feast (cf. Lev. 23.33-43; Num. 29.12-39; Deut. 16.13-15; Ezek. 45.24). According to Chary it was also *the last day* ('le dernier jour') of the great Feast of Tabernacles (p. 25).

Because no specific reference is made in this passage to the Feast, some scholars (e.g. Keil) are inclined to deem the Feast irrelevant as part of the scenario of this prophecy. The fact, however, remains that the allusion to 'this house' (v. 3; cf. 1.4), suggests Haggai's presence in the temple site, thus in the cultic centre of the day's festivals, which presupposes a festive occasion. As a matter of fact, in no other month was the attention of the people more directed to the glory of 'the former house' (cf. 1 Kgs 8.2),[14] and during no other feast were they reminded more of the future than on this Feast of Tabernacles, heralding as it did the new (civil) year.[15]

The precise date in 2.10 and 2.20: *the twenty-fourth day of the ninth month*, the equivalent of 18 December, is nowhere mentioned in the calendar of Israel's feasts as a special remembrance day.[16] T. André's[17] assumption that because of the sacrifices performed in v. 14, this day originally was considered to be a feast day is, however, arbitrary, because no scriptural evidence can be offered to establish this point of view.

The significance of this day is, rather, that it was precisely three months since work on the temple began (1.15), and a little more than two months since Haggai's previous sermon (2.1). According to 2.18 the foundation of the Lord's temple was laid on this day, marking the actual beginning of work on the temple itself.[18] This festive occasion, therefore, might have provided the incentive for Haggai to pronounce this prophecy.

The *purpose* and *significance* of the dates in the book of Haggai must be seen in the context of the purpose of dates in general.

In the historical narratives of the Old Testament (and of ancient Near Eastern literature as such) the dating of events serves both to clarify their sequence and to emphasize their reality in time and space.[19]

In the prophetic literature[20] the purpose of a precise date is not only to establish the historic reality of the occasion on which the prophecy was pronounced, but especially to emphasize the authenticity of the prophetic message.[21]

Although the first component of our definition concerning the historicity of the occasion is valid, it must not be overestimated. The real purpose of a precise date is, for instance, over-emphasized when some scholars consider the book of Haggai originally to have been a part of a major chronological narrative concerning the rebuilding of the temple, accompanied by the messages of the prophet.[22] This point of view does not take into account (1) that the factual data in the book of Haggai is insufficient to be regarded as an abstract of an original work, and (2) that nothing is known about the so-called chronicle of the rebuilding of the temple.[23]

The second component of our definition concerning the authenticity of a prophecy is of paramount importance to evaluate the purpose and significance of the precise dates. Apart from the relative relationship between the dated event and the accompanying word of the prophet (cf. Isa. 6.1; 7.1-14; 14.28; 20.1), the emphasis is rather on the authenticity of the proclaimed message, also for future reference (cf. Isa. 8.1-4; 30.8). Koole[24] rightly pointed out that such prophetic utterances, in the form of a written record, not only required witnesses, but also a precise date, thereby to enhance the validity of the prophetic word. The same applies to the dates in Haggai.

The historical data concerning the rebuilding of the temple is important, but secondary.The dates rather concern the guaranteed character of the messages and the promises that were expressed with regard to the rebuilding of the temple. Their purpose, therefore, was to affirm beyond any doubt that the rebuilding of the temple was not humanly inspired, but was a 'work' which originated with God.

This conclusion is borne out by the exegesis of the relevant dates. In 1.1 the most significant component is the formula of revelation: *The word of the Lord came*. This is connected, *inter alia*, with the adverbial definition of time: *In the second year of King Darius, on the first day of the sixth month*. The date's purpose, therefore, is to establish the fact and the significance of the revealed word of God.

The purpose of the date in 1.15 was, as we have said, to mark the official beginning of work on the temple, as the leaders' and people's response to the command of the Lord. Here we have both components of our previous definition: the date establishes the historic reality of the event, and it underscores the validity of the divine command. The first named component is incidentally emphasized by the word *baššišši*, 'on the sixth', which is generally regarded to be a gloss. On the contrary, this word can be explained to be in the absolute state (cf. GKC, par. 134c) emphasizing the fact that the beginning of the work on the temple really happened in the *sixth* month, and not in the 'seventh' (2.1), or on the twenty-fourth day of the 'ninth' month (2.10).

The date in 2.10 again serves the double purpose of establishing the historicity and significance of the festive occasion of the laying of the foundation (2.18), and of vindicating the prophetic message. On that day the word of the Lord came to[25] the prophet Haggai.

The same applies to the date introducing the last of the series of Haggai's messages (2.20-23). This prophecy was on the same day as that addressed to the people in the previous section (2.10-19), which was identified in 2.18 as the day on which the 'foundation' of the Lord's temple was laid. We may, therefore, assume that the two prophecies had a bearing upon one another. Perhaps in a twofold manner. First, they were pronounced on the same festive occasion, the actual and official commencement of work on the temple, and second, both reflect the contours of God's blessing on his Day, thereby providing the guarantee for the revealed word of God.

Considering the purpose and significance of the *date* of our colleague's sixtieth anniversary, we are reminded of the word of the psalmist: 'But I trust in you, O Lord; I say You are my God. *My times are in your hands*' (Ps. 31.15, 16) (EVV vv. 14, 15).

NOTES

1. Cf. e.g. van Goudoever, *Biblical Calendars* (Leiden, 1959); J. Finegan, *Light from the Ancient Past* (2nd edn, Princeton, 1959); S. van Mierlo, *De oude kalender bij de Hebreëen en zijn verband met de lijdensweek* (Kampen, 1963); E. Bickerman, *Chronology of the Ancient World* (1968).

2. Cf. D.J. Wiseman, *The New Bible Commentary* (revised; London: IVP, 1970). For a thorough discussion of the dates in the prophetic literature, see W.A.M. Beuken, *Haggai–Sacharja 1–8. Studien zur Überlieferungsgeschichte der frühnachexilischen Prophetie* (Assen, 1967), pp. 21-26. He asserts that the older pre-exilic prophets are without dates for separate prophecies. This form of dating really started with the autobiographical call narrative of Isa. 6.1. Cf. also N. Habel, 'The Form and Significance of the Call Narratives', *ZAW* 77 (1965), pp. 297-324.

3. So A.S. van der Woude, *Haggai, Maleachi* (POT; Nijkerk, 1982). See also Beuken, *op.cit.*, pp. 25f., whose investigation into the dates of the

prophetic literature led him to the conclusion that there are no reasons for denying the authenticity of the dates in Haggai (and Zechariah). The only exception among scholars in this regard is P.R. Ackroyd, 'Studies in the Book of Haggai', *JJS* 2 (1951), pp. 171-73.

4. Cf. R.A. Parker and W.H. Dubberstein, *Babylonian Chronology 626 BC–AD 75* (Brown University Press, 1956); V. Coucke, 'Chronology', *DBS*, I, col. 1271.

5. *Haggai-Zechariah-Malachi* (Tyndale Old Testament Commentaries; London, 1972), p. 29.

6. This date concerns the 'regnal year' not the 'accession year'; cf. P.R. Ackroyd, 'Two Old Testament Problems of the Early Persian Period', *JNES* 17 (1958), and K.M. Beyse, *Serubbabel und die Königserwartungen der Propheten Haggai und Sacharja* (Berlin-Stuttgart, 1972), p. 10.

7. In Haggai the Hebrew word for 'month', *ḥōdeš*, is derived from a root *ḥādaš* meaning 'New'. *Ḥōdeš*, denoting the 'new' appearance or crescent of the moon, is translated respectively as *month* and *New Moon*. On the distinction between *ḥōdeš* and *yērāḥ* as indications of the month cf. S. van Mierlo, *op.cit*., p. 25.

8. I have dealt with these problems in a commentary on Haggai and Malachi in the series NICOT.

9. I.H. Eybers interestingly sided with the majority of scholars in relocating 2.15-23 after 1.15, considering 2.14 as originally the last verse in the prophecies of Haggai. See his article 'The Rebuilding of the Temple according to Haggai and Zechariah', *Studies in Old Testament Prophecy* (OTWSA, 1970/71), pp. 15-26.

10. So for instance T. Chary, *Aggée-Zacharie* (Sources Bibliques; Paris, 1969), pp. 23f.

11. So e.g. J.L. Koole, *Haggai* (COT; Kampen, 1967).

12. See the interesting considerations offered by J.G. Baldwin, *op.cit*.

13. *Op.cit*, p. 38.

14. An additional motivation for regarding this day as a festive occasion was the remembrance that on the seventh month, so many years ago, Solomon had dedicated the glorious temple with its sacred objects (1 Kgs 8.2).

15. So rightly van der Woude, *op.cit*.

16. Two references to the twenty-fourth of the month, viz. Neh. 9.1 and Dan. 10.4, are an important indication of the establishing of the beginning of the new year in respectively the Old Israelitic and the New Babylonian Calendars. Cf. J. Van Goudoever, *op.cit*., p. 37. The twenty-fourth of the eleventh month is mentioned in Zech. 1.7.

17. *Le Prophète Aggée* (Paris, 1895).

18. We need not enter into the interesting problem when the work on the rebuilding of the temple actually and officially started, and how the laying of

the foundation (2.18) ought to be explained. This exegetical problem is irrelevant for the purpose of this article.

19. So correctly J.B. Payne, in *The Zondervan P.E.B.*, Vol. I, p. 829.

20. Cf. Beuken, *op.cit.*, pp. 21-26. Also W. Zimmerli, *Ezechiel* I (BK; Neukirchen-Vluyn, 1969), pp. 12-23, etc.

21. So rightly Koole, *op.cit.*

22. See A. Klostermann, *Geschichte des Volkes Israels* (1896), pp. 212ff., and many scholars, e.g. Sellin, Deden. Cf. also J.W. Rothstein, *Die Genealogie des Königs Jojachin und seiner Nachkommen* (1902).

23. So Koole, *op.cit.*, p. 6.

24. *Op.cit.*, pp. 6f.

25. The preposition *'el* is used in 2.10 and 20, but elsewhere the compound preposition *b^eyad* (1.1, 3; 2.1) is employed. In the fragments from the cave of Murabba'at *'el* is read instead of *b^eyad* in 2.1. The difference in meaning between the prepositions is exegetically irrelevant: the reception (*'el*) and communication (*b^eyad*) of the revelation as components of the prophetical office are simultaneously applicable. The word received is meant to be communicated, according to the very definition of prophecy.

21

DIE EINHEIT VON SACHARJA 8,1-8

Siegfried Mittmann

In der Sicht der neueren kritischen Forschung lösen sich die beiden Schlußkapitel des Überlieferungskomplexes Sach. 1–8 in eine Vielzahl kürzerer und fast schon fragmentarisch kurzer Worte auf. Das ist ein auffälliger Befund, auffällig auch im Vergleich zu den vorausgehenden Kapiteln, wo größere Einheiten bei entsprechend geringerer Gesamtzahl überwiegen und ihrer sieben sich sogar zu einer übergreifenden Komposition, dem Zyklus der sogenannten Nachtgesichte, zusammenschließen. Fünf der rund zehn Worte, die man in Kap. 7–8 gewöhnlich konstatiert, stehen in konzentrierter Dichte beieinander in 8,1-8, deutlich jeweils voneinander abgesetzt durch die prophetische Botenformel 'So spricht Jahwe Zebaoth', so daß es in der Tat zunächst den Anschein hat, als handle es sich um 'eine lose Zusammenstellung selbständiger Sprüche'.[1] Doch trügt dieser vordergründige Eindruck; denn bei genauerem Hinsehen offenbart das Stück eine kompositionelle und inhaltliche Geschlossenheit, wie sie ein sekundär zusammengestelltes Florilegium niemals gewinnen kann. Zudem ist in zwei Fällen die behauptete Selbständigkeit ganz unwahrscheinlich. Schon wegen seiner Kürze, mehr aber noch wegen des andeutend allgemeinen Charakters seiner Aussage kann V. 2 schwerlich als isoliertes Heilswort verkündet worden sein. V. 2 stimmt fast wörtlich überein mit 1,14; dort aber ist das Wort in das erste Nachtgesicht eingebettet, das ihm Kontur und Hintergrund verleiht. Vollends kann bei V. 6 von Eigenständigkeit nicht gut die Rede sein, weil der vermeintliche Spruch aus sich selbst heraus gar nicht verständlich ist. Das Wunderbare, von dem V. 6 spricht, mußte ohne konkretisierenden Kontext selbst dem zeitgenössischen Adressaten ein undeutlicher Begriff bleiben. Die stereotype Wiederholung der Einleitungsformel ist deshalb als stilistisch-rhetorisches Mittel zu werten, das, wie schon Hieronymus sah,[2] den jeweiligen Aussagen autoritativen Nachdruck verleiht, indem es ihre göttliche Provenienz unterstreicht, das aber auch, formal betrachtet, Struktursignale setzt. Darüber hinaus wird sich zeigen, daß die Stilform der repetierten und gliedernden Redeeinleitung ihr zeitgenössisches Vorbild hat.

Die folgenden Ausführungen wollen, zunächst in analytischer Entfaltung Schritt für Schritt am Text entlang und dann in einer zusammenfassenden Gesamtschau, den Nachweis führen, daß Sach. 8,1-8 nicht ein Konglomerat von fünf ursprünglich selbständigen Sprüchen, sondern ein kunstvoll aus fünf Strophen gefügtes Gedicht ist. Vorangestellt sind Text und Übersetzung, in einer an zwei Stellen konjizierten Form, die später zu begründen ist, und einer der poetischen Struktur entsprechenden Anordnung.

(1) *way^{e}hī d^{e}bar-Yhwh ṣ^{e}bā'ōt lēmōr*

A (2) *kō 'āmar Yhwh ṣ^{e}bā'ōt*
qinnētī l^{e}ṣiyyōn qin'ā g^{e}dōlā 4 + 4
w^{e}ḥēmā g^{e}dōlā qinnētī lāh

Ba (3) *kō 'āmar Yhwh <ṣ^{e}bā'ōt>*
šabtī 'äl-ṣiyyōn 3 + 3
w^{e}šākantī b^{e}tōk y^{e}rūšālayim
w^{e}niqr^{e}'ā y^{e}rūšālayim 'īr-hā'ämāt 3 + 3
w^{e}har-Yhwh ṣ^{e}bā'ōt har haqqōdäš

b (4) *kō 'āmar Yhwh ṣ^{e}bā'ōt*
'ōd yēš^{e}bū z^{e}qēnīm ūz^{e}qēnōt 3 + 2
birḥōbōt y^{e}rūšālayim
w^{e}'iš miš'antō b^{e}yādō 3 + 2
mērōb yāmīm
(5) *ūr^{e}ḥōbōt hā'īr yimmāl^{e}'ū* 3 + 2
y^{e}lādīm wīlādōt
m^{e}śaḥ^{a}qīm birḥōbōtähā 3 + 2 (2 + 2)
(6aβ) *bayyāmim hāhēm*

Ca (6aαb) *kō'āmar Yhwh ṣ^{e}bā'ōt*
kī yippālē' b^{e}'ēnē 3 + 3
š^{e}'ērīt hā'ām hazzä
gam-b^{e}'ēnay yippālē' 3 + 3
n^{e}'ūm Yhwh ṣ^{e}bā'ōt

b (7) *kō 'āmar Yhwh ṣ^{e}bā'ōt*
hinnī mōšī^{a}' 'ät-'ammī 3 + 2
mē'äräṣ mizrāḥ
ūmē'äräṣ m^{e}bō' haššāmäš 3 + 2
(8) *w^{e}hēbētī 'ōtām*
w^{e}šāk^{e}nū b^{e}tōk y^{e}rūšālayim 3 + 2
w^{e}hāyū-lī l^{e}'ām
wa^{xa}nī 'ähyä lāhäm lēlōhīm 3 + 2
b^{ä}'ämät ūbiṣdāqā

(1) Und es erging das Wort Jahwe Zebaoths:

A (2) So hat Jahwe Zebaoth gesprochen:
Ich eifere für Zion mit großem Eifer,
und mit großem Ingrimm eifere ich für es.

Ba (3) So hat Jahwe Zebaoth gesprochen:
Ich kehre zurück nach Zion
und werde wohnen inmitten Jerusalems,
und Jerusalem wird heißen 'Stadt der Treue'
und der Berg Jahwe Zebaoths 'Berg der Heiligkeit'.

b (4) So hat Jahwe Zebaoth gesprochen:
Noch werden sitzen Greise und Greisinnen
auf den Plätzen Jerusalems,
ein jeder seinen Stock in seiner Hand
ob der Menge an Tagen.
(5) Und die Plätze der Stadt werden voll sein
von Knaben und Mädchen,
die spielen auf ihren Plätzen
(6aβ) in jenen Tagen.

Ca (6aα) So hat Jahwe Zebaoth gesprochen:
Wenn es zu wunderbar ist in den Augen
des Restes dieses Volkes,
ist's auch zu wunderbar in meinen Augen?
—Spruch Jahwe Zebaoths.

b (7) So hat Jahwe Zebaoth gesprochen:
Siehe ich helfe meinem Volk
aus dem Lande des Aufgangs
und aus dem Lande des Untergangs der Sonne
und bringe sie heim.
Und sie werden inmitten Jerusalems wohnen
und werden mir Volk sein,
ich aber werde ihnen Gott sein
in Treue und Gerechtigkeit.

I

Die Eingangsstrophe (V. 2) ist in ihrem poetischen Kern ein synonymer Parallelismus membrorum, synonym bis in den Wortlaut hinein, bei gleicher Satzstruktur der Stichen, doch chiastischer Zuordnung der Satzhälften bzw. Halbstichen. Diese Anordnung bringt die beiden adverbialen Bestimmungen 'mit großem Eifer'—'mit großem Grimm' in eine unmittelbare Opposition und so die Wechselbegriffe *qin'ā* und *ḥēmā*, die einzigen in diesem Vers, in eine zentrale Position. Die beiden Begriffe meinen nur partiell dasselbe, bringen vielmehr, einander ergänzend, unterschiedliche Nuancen zur Geltung. *ḥēmā* drückt gegenüber *qin'ā* eine affektive Steigerung aus, hat aber auch eine andere Zielrichtung. *qin'ā* zeigt in Gebrauch und Bedeutung eine gewisse Ambivalenz. Als inneres Objekt mit *qinnē'* zu einer figura etymologica verbunden, meint es hier den leidenschaftlichen Eifer, mit dem Jahwe für den Zion und sein Heil eintritt. Dabei darf freilich eine negative Komponente, die dem Wort von Hause aus innewohnt, nicht überhört werden. Das 'Eifern' richtet sich explizit oder unausgesprochen gegen einen Konkurrenten, der den Eifernden oder dessen Schützling in einem exklusiven Anspruch oder Recht beeinträchtigt; und so ist denn meistens der Zorneseifer, von der menschlichen Eifersucht bis zum göttlichen Gerichtszorn, im Blick.

Josua empfand nach Num. 11,29 Eifersucht für Mose, dessen charismatische Sonderstellung er durch die Verteilung des prophetischen Geistes auf einen größeren Personenkreis angetastet sah. 'In seinem Eifer für Israel und Juda', d.h. für die ethnisch-religiöse Integrität des Gottesvolkes, suchte Saul die fremdstämmigen Gibeoniten zu vernichten (2.Sam. 21,2). Pinchas 'eiferte für seinen Gott' (Num. 25,13), indem er den Israeliten, der sich in 'ehebrecherischem' Verhalten gegenüber Jahwe (25,1) mit einer Moabitin einließ, mitsamt der fremden Frau durchbohrte, um 'seinen Gott gegen die Konkurrenz fremder Götter zu schützen'.[3] 'Heftig geeifert für Jahwe, den Gott Zebaoth' (1.Kön. 19,10.14) hatte Elia in seinem Kampf gegen das abtrünnige Israel und seine Verführer. Ähnlich bekundete Jehu in Samaria mit der Ausrottung der Baalsdiener und der sie tragenden Ahab-Sippe seinen 'Eifer für Jahwe' (2.Kön. 10,16). Mit der Heilsabsicht, 'das Geschick Jakobs' zu 'wenden' und sich 'des ganzen Hauses Israel' zu 'erbarmen', will Jahwe 'für seinen heiligen Namen eifern' (Ez. 39,25), wobei im Hintergrund die feindlichen Völker stehen, aus deren Mitte und Länder Jahwe sein Volk sammeln und vor deren Augen er sich mit dieser Manifestation seiner Herrschafts- und Gerichtsmacht heiligt (V. 27). In die Nähe von Sach. 1,14; 8,2 führt Joel 2,18 'Und Jahwe eiferte für sein Land und empfand Mitleid mit seinem Volk'. Hier ist nicht Jahwe selbst das Zielobjekt seines Eiferns, sondern 'sein Land', wie bei Sacharja der Zion und Jerusalem. Zugleich verstärkt sich die Heilstendenz des göttlichen Eifers, der nun in die Nähe des göttlichen Mitleids rückt. Dennoch war es für die Wahl des Ausdrucks *qn'* wohl nicht ohne Bedeutung, daß das Heil sich durch die Vertreibung der feindlichen

Macht des 'Nördlichen'—was immer diese ist—verwirklichte.

Auch in Sach. 1,14 hat das Eifern diese positive Ausrichtung. Das negative Moment kommt gesondert zur Geltung, in dem nachfolgenden Satz, der dem Eifer für Jerusalem den Zorn *qäṣäp* über die feindlichen Völker gegenüberstellt. Ähnlich verhält es sich offenbar in 8,2, wo *ḥēmā* den *qäṣäp* analogen Gegenbegriff zu *qin'ā* bildet.

Der isolierte Vers hat eine programmatische Funktion; er ist die Einleitung, die im folgenden entfaltet wird. In welcher Richtung, zeigt die geballte Häufung des verbalen (2mal) und nominalen Eiferbegriffs: das Heil Jerusalems steht voll im Blick, das korrespondierende Völkergericht tritt in den Hintergrund, wird durch *ḥēmā* nur noch eben angedeutet.

Die nächste poetische Einheit (V. 3aβγb), ein Doppelvers, greift das Stichwort 'Zion' auf und behandelt das künftige Verhältnis zwischen Jahwe und Jerusalem. Der erste Vers beschreibt Jahwes Hinwendung zur Stadt, in zwei syntaktisch gleichlautenden Stichen, die—nacheinander und einander ergänzend—die Bewegung und ihr Ziel erfassen: Jahwe kehrt zurück zum Zion und nimmt Wohnung inmitten von Jerusalem, d.h. auf dem Zion. In chiastischer Umkehrung der Ortsangaben sagt der Parallelvers V. 3b, was dies für die Stellung der Stadt und des Tempelberges bedeutet. Sie erhalten einen neuen, appellativischen Namen und bekommen damit einen neuen Status und eine neue Qualität. Der Gottesberg heißt nun 'Berg der Heiligkeit', weil er durch die Präsenz Jahwes geheiligt ist; und 'Stadt der Treue' heißt Jerusalem, weil es ein sichtbares Zeichen der verläßlichen Treue ist, die Jahwe mit der neuerlichen Hinwendung zu seiner Stadt unter Beweis stellt. Die göttliche Treue also ist *'ämāt*, nicht etwa die Treue, Wahrhaftigkeit, Verläßlichkeit der Stadt, wie fast durchweg zu lesen ist.[4] Die beiden Verse bilden, wie schon die formale Klammer des Chiasmus zeigt, eine enge Aussageeinheit. Das Nif'al *niqr^{e}'ā* ist eine Art passivum divinum, insofern nämlich, als das, was sich in der Neubenennung an Jerusalem vollzieht, seinen Grund in dem vorausgenannten Handeln Jahwes hat, nicht in einem Verhalten oder einer immanenten Qualität der Namensträger. So wenig die Heiligkeit des Tempelberges diesem selbst entspringt, so wenig ist 'Treue' ein Prädikat, das der bislang ungetreuen Stadt für den Zeitpunkt der Wiederkehr Jahwes schon zugesprochen oder für die fernere Zukunft bei ihr ohne weiteres vorausgesetzt werden kann. Den letzten Zweifel an der vorgetragenen Bedeutung des Begriffs behebt der weitere Zusammenhang. Zum einen taucht *'ämāt* in V. 8

wieder auf, in einem Kontext, der auf V. 3 zurückgreift; und hier ist das Wort eindeutig auf Jahwes Verhalten bezogen. Zum andern ist von der gedanklichen Gesamtkonzeption her eine Aussage über Jerusalems künftiges Verhalten in V. 3 noch nicht am Platze; denn die Auswirkungen, welche die Gegenwart Jahwes auf das Leben der Stadt haben wird, thematisiert erst der folgende Abschnitt.

Mit Jahwes Gegenwart—das ist die Botschaft dieses Abschnitts (V. 4-5.6aβ)—wird neues Leben in Jerusalem einkehren, neue Lebenskraft, die hohes Alter garantiert, und neue Lebensfülle in Gestalt zahlreicher Nachkommenschaft. Der erstgenannte Aspekt ist Gegenstand der ersten beiden Verse, zwei Fünfern, die einander, wie üblich bei diesem Metrum, im Sinne des Parallelismus versuum ergänzen. Der erste Vers zeichnet den allgemeinen Rahmen: alte Männer und Frauen sitzen auf den Plätzen von Jerusalem. Der zweite Vers setzt dem Bild ein signifikantes Detail auf: ein stützender Stab in eines jeden Hand als Zeichen hohen Alters. Der zweite Vers steigert zugleich die Aussage: alte Menschen—und alle hochbetagt. Dabei ist zu bedenken, daß bei der damals durchschnittlichen Lebenserwartung von nicht einmal 50 Jahren[5] ein 'biblisches' Alter, wie es hier vorausgesetzt wird, die Ausnahme bildete und daher, ganz anders als im künftigen Jerusalem, das Straßenbild nicht bestimmend mitprägte.

Aber die Alten bilden auch im neuen Jerusalem die naturgegebene Minderheit; die Plätze füllt das junge Leben, der Kindernachwuchs. So der dritte poetische Vers (V. 5a), der den ersten (V. 4aβγ) inhaltlich teils antithetisch und in formaler Hinsicht chiastisch parallelisiert: 'die Plätze der Stadt ... Knaben und Mädchen', 'Greise und Greisinnen ... auf den Plätzen Jerusalems'. Die Analogie erstreckt sich auch auf die jeweiligen Parallelverse 4b und 5b; denn V. 5b nennt gleichfalls ein Moment, das die hiesige Altersgruppe, die Kinder, kennzeichnet: ihr Spiel (*m*^{e}*śaḥ*^{a}*qīm*) auf den Plätzen, das außerdem einen fröhlich bewegten Kontrast zur Reihe der würdig dasitzenden Alten bildet. Doch steht noch mehr hinter dieser Aussage. Nach Jer. 30,19 werden 'Dank und Laut der Lachenden (*m*^{e}*śaḥ*^{a}*qīm*)' aus dem wiedererrichteten Jerusalem erschallen; und Jer. 31,4 zufolge darf die von Jahwe wiedererbaute 'Jungfrau Israel' sich erneut mit ihren 'Handpauken schmücken und ausziehen im Reigen der Fröhlichen (*m*^{e}*śaḥ*^{a}*qīm*)'. Ebendiese Freude ist es, die auch im Treiben der Kinder zum Ausdruck kommt. Um die Idylle dieses Bildes voll und richtig zu würdigen, ist mitzuhören, was im Hintergrund an dunklen Tönen anklingt. Der in Sach. 8,4f. geschilderte Heilszustand ist das lichte Kehrbild der Schreckenszenen, wie sie etwa die 'Klagelieder' beschwören; und möglicherweise ist Sach. 8,4f. eine direkte Antwort auf Threni 2 und 4. Mehrfach wird hier das grauenvolle Schicksal der Kinder in der Hungersnot der Katastrophe von 587 v. Chr. beschrieben (2,11f.19f.; 4,3-6.11). Sie 'verschmachten auf den Plätzen der Stadt' (2,11), während 'die Alten der Tochter Zion' stumm am Boden sitzen und sich, mit dem Trauerschurz umgürtet, Staub auf ihr Haupt streuen (2,10). Andere, 'Knabe und Greis', hat das Todesgeschick schon ereilt; hingemordet liegen sie in den Straßen am Boden (2,21; ähnlich Jer. 9,20; 49,26 von Damaskus, 50,30 von Babel). Wenn nicht unmittelbar auf Threni 2 und 4 angespielt wird, so doch gewiß auf entsprechende Klagemotive der öffentlichen Bußfeiern, die zum Gedenken an den Untergang Jerusalems veranstaltet wurden und auf die ja Sacharja explizit Bezug nimmt (7,1-3; 7,4-14; 8,18f.). Ort der allgemeinen Totenklage aber waren die 'Plätze' (Jer. 15,3; 48,38; Am. 5,16). Sie, auf denen bisher Tod und Trauer herrschten, werden sich in der verheißenen Heilszeit in Stätten des Lebens, der Lebenskraft, -fülle und -freude verwandeln. Aus diesen Bezügen[6] erklärt sich die leitmotivische Rolle, die der Begriff *r^eḥōb* in diesem Abschnitt spielt.

Ein Problem ist bei dieser Betrachtung noch außer Acht geblieben: V. 5b fehlt zu einem vollen Vers (im poetischen Sinne) der zweite Stichos. Angesichts der aufgezeigten Symmetrie des Aufbaus und speziell auch wegen des Parallelismus versuum im vorausgehenden 'synthetischen', also in sich nicht parallel gegliederten Fünfer V. 5a kann dies nicht Absicht sein, auch wenn inhaltlich das Wesentliche mit dem ersten Halbvers gesagt sein sollte. Man muß also mit einem Ausfall rechnen, der aber, wie ich meine, reparabel ist. Auffälligerweise hat der erste Vers der nachfolgenden Einheit am Ende mit *bayyāmīm hāhēm* einen metrischen Überschuß, der zudem mit seinem ferndeiktisch in die Zukunft weisenden *hāhēm* inhaltlich nicht zu den gegenwartsbezogenen Aussagen im voranstehenden und nachfolgenden Teile paßt. Dagegen ergänzt die Floskel auf das beste den V. 5b. Das abschließende *bayyāmīm hāhēm* bildet einen Gleichklang mit *yāmīm* am Ende des vorausgehenden Verspaares und das sachliche Gegenstück zu dem den ganzen Abschnitt einleitenden *'ōd*, womit sich die schon beobachtete Analogie zu dem ersten Verspaar (V. 4) nur fortsetzen würde. Der Ausfall ist schwer zu erklären, aber deshalb doch nicht undenkbar. Anlaß der falschen Einbeziehung war vielleicht die Ähnlichkeit der jeweils vorausgehenden Buchstabenfolgen (*-tyh* und *hzh*), zumal dann, wenn diese, etwa am Zeilenende, unmittelbar untereinander standen.

Von der lichten Zukunft lenkt der nächste Abschnitt (V. 6aα) den Blick zurück in die immer noch trübe Gegenwart, er nun wieder in zwei Doppeldreiern, die zwar in sich 'synthetisch' durchlaufen, miteinander aber einen antithetischen Parallelismus ergeben. Die Vorderstichen stellen die konträren Ansichten vom unmöglich Wunderhaften bzw. der nicht wunderhaften Möglichkeit einer Sache einander gegenüber, wobei die Frageform, in die der Komplex syntaktisch gefaßt ist, eine weitgehend gleichlautende Formulierung erlaubt. Deren chiastische Anordnung unterstreicht den Gegensatz und verleiht zugleich dem Wort *yippālē'* im zweiten Fall ein hervorhebendes Achtergewicht. Die hinteren Stichen konfrontieren die Subjekte der jeweiligen Sicht, den 'Rest dieses Volkes' und 'Jahwe Zebaoth'. Die ausleitende Formel 'Spruch Jahwe Zebaoths' ist hier keineswegs, wie sonst so oft, eine bloße Floskel. Sie nimmt die wiederholte Einleitungsformel 'So spricht Jahwe Zebaoth', die in diesem Kontext, wie wir sehen werden, eine besondere Funktion hat, respondierend auf und verstärkt ihre Tendenz, bezeichnenderweise dort, wo es um Jahwes Macht und Glaubwürdigkeit geht.

Die Sache, die je nach Standort allzu oder gar nicht wunderhaft sein soll, wird nicht genannt, ergibt sich zum Teil aber von selbst aus dem, was vorausgeht. Doch nur zum Teil; denn formal wie inhaltlich ist dieses Verspaar vor allem auf das Folgende hin ausgerichtet. Es ist, nicht anders als der formgleiche V. 2, der einleitende Vorspann der nachfolgenden größeren Einheit. Das zeigen vor allem das verbindende Leitwort 'Volk' und die Bezugnahme auf den 'Rest dieses Volkes', die in und um Jerusalem zurückgebliebene Restgemeinde, der im folgenden die mit dem Ehrentitel 'mein Volk' apostrophierte Gola gegenübergestellt wird.

Der letzte Abschnitt gleicht im Aufbau ganz dem dritten. Auch er besteht aus vier Versen im Qinametrum, von denen je zwei sich zu einem Parallelismus versuum zusammenschließen. Die Aussage entfaltet sich somit auch hier in zwei Schritten.

Das erste Verspaar (v.7aβb.8aα) verheißt in chiastischer Anordnung der Stichen die Rückführung der Gola. Die inneren Glieder des Chiasmus deuten mit ihren geographischen Umstandsbestimmungen die Totalität des Vorgangs an: von Osten und von Westen her, aus Babylonien ebenso wie aus Ägypten, wird die Rückkehr erfolgen. Sie ist, wie das erste Wort, der betonte Selbsthinweis *hin^{e}nī* sogleich heraus- und klarstellt, das alleinige Werk Jahwes, das durch die äußeren Glieder des Chiasmus in zweifacher Hinsicht und damit wiederum umfassend charakterisiert wird. Zunächst als Herausführung, als neuer Exodus. Die heilsgeschichtliche Dimension dieses Geschehens bringt das Wort *mōšī^{a}‘* zum Ausdruck. '*hôšîa‘* ist der häufigste soteriologische terminus in religiösen Kontexten', insbesondere der exilisch-nachexilischen Zeit; sein Subjekt 'ist fast ohne Ausnahme JHWH, oder sein ernannter Stellvertreter'.[7] In den erzählenden Büchern des Alten Testaments bezeichnet das Wort überwiegend Handlungen des göttlichen Eingreifens in die Geschichte Israels, angefangen bei der Errettung am Schilfmeer (Ex. 14,30 'an diesem Tage half Jahwe Israel aus der Hand der Ägypter'). Nicht zufällig stehen von den 100 Belegen der Wurzel, die die prophetischen Bücher insgesamt aufweisen, 56 bei Deuterojesaja, dem Propheten des neuen Auszugs. Soteriologisch ausgerichtet ist hier auch der Gegenbegriff *hēbētī* im letzten Stichos, der dem Exodus die Heimkehr der Verbannten gegenüberstellt. Ohne Ortsbestimmung sonst etwa von der Heimkehr des Heeres gebraucht (Num. 27,17; 2.Sam. 5,2//1.Chron. 11,2), ist *bō’* im Hif'il wie im Qal 'seit dem Deuteronomium heilsgeschichtliches Motiv- und Leitwort'[8] für die Hineinführung bzw. das Hineinkommen in das Land der Väter und ihrer Verheißung.

Das letzte, in sich wiederum chiastisch gegliederte Verspaar (V. 8aβb) schildert Ziel und Vollendung des göttlichen Heilsweges und -werkes. Der erste Stichos 'und sie werden inmitten von Jerusalem wohnen' nennt das örtliche Ziel, ist aber mehr als eine bloße Ortsangabe, wie der zweifellos beabsichtigte Gleichklang mit der Selbstaussage Jahwes 'und ich werde inmitten von Jerusalem wohnen' V. 3 zeigt: die Heimgeführten werden in der Wohnstatt Jahwes Wohnung nehmen. Das darin angedeutete Verhältnis explizieren die beiden nachfolgenden Stichen, die eine Variante der sogenannten Bundesformel darstellen, der Bundesformel in ihrer zu einer reziproken Doppelformel entwickelten Spätgestalt. In dieser Spätform, deren 'Aussagekern' etwa 'Israel, Jahwes Volk; Jahwe, Israels Gott' lautet,[9] erscheint sie fast nur in Gottesreden, und zwar mit zweifacher Aussagerichtung: 'im Blick auf die Zukunft als Verheißung, im Rückblick auf Auszugs- und Mosezeit als Forderung'.[10] Doch besteht hier ein innerer Zusammenhang; das künftige Verhältnis zwischen Gott und Volk ist eine Erneuerung des alten Gottesverhältnisses. Das zeigt der Schlußstichos, der die zweite Verheißung der Bundesformel qualifiziert, und zwar in doppelter Hinsicht. Gottes künftiges Verhältnis zu seinem Volke ist bestimmt und getragen von *'ämät* und *ṣ^{e}dāqā*, zum einen also von verläßlicher Treue, die sich in der Wiederbegründung der einstigen Beziehung bewährt und darum weiterhin bewähren wird, zum anderen von einem Tun, das eine heilvolle Lebensordnung schafft und erhält,[11] wie sie die dritte Strophe für das künftige Jerusalem entwirft.

II

Der analytische Gang durch den Text hat mehr oder weniger deutlich auch schon die Sach-, Sprach- und Strukturzusammenhänge sichtbar werden lassen, die das Ganze durchziehen, in sich verklammern und so als Einheit erweisen. Das Stück ist, von den Redeeinleitungen abgesehen, ein poetisches Gebilde, stilistisch kunstvoll gefügt und ausgewogen im Aufbau, wenn man die Umstellung von V. 6aβ gelten läßt. Es besteht aus einer Einleitung in Gestalt eines Doppelvierers (A) und dem Korpus (B-C), gegliedert in vier Strophen, die sich aus zwei Versen im Metrum des Doppeldreiers oder vier Versen im Qinametrum zusammensetzen und einander im Wechsel von Kurz- und Langstrophen folgen. Die Strophen bilden zugleich Sinnabschnitte, die als solche markant auch durch die Redeeinführungen voneinander abgesetzt sind. In ihrer nivellierenden Stereotypie verschleiern diese freilich die Tatsache, daß je zwei Strophen des Korpus sich zu einer übergeordneten Einheit zusammenschließen.

Der Einleitungsvers (A) schlägt das Generalthema an, das im folgenden dann entfaltet wird: Jahwes großer Zorneseifer um den Zion. Die folgende Strophe (Ba) formuliert als Verheißung die erste und grundlegende Konsequenz dieses göttlichen Eiferns. Jahwe wird wieder Wohnung nehmen in Jerusalem, und Jerusalem wird durch diesen Akt der Treue Jahwes wieder in den Rang und Status einer Gottesstadt erhoben werden. Die nächste Strophe (Bb) schildert die heilvollen Auswirkungen dieses Geschehens auf die Stadt als Lebensraum und Lebensgemeinschaft. Mit Jahwes Wiederkehr kehrt neue Lebenskraft und -fülle nach Jerusalem zurück. Die dritte Strophe des Korpus (Ca), deren formale Übereinstimmung mit der ersten (Ba) noch durch das gemeinsame Gottesprädikat 'Zebaoth' im Endstichos unterstrichen wird, stellt eine Frage, die an die vorausgehende Strophe unmittelbar anknüpft und in der nachfolgenden ihre Antwort findet—die Frage, wie sich das Wunder der Wiederbelebung Jerusalems vollziehen soll. Der Zweifel, der in dieser Frage steckt, geht aus von dem 'Rest dieses Volkes', der im Land zurückgebliebenen Restgemeinde, die in ihrer dezimierten Existenz die ihr verheißene Fülle nicht begreifen kann. Ihr stellt die folgende und letzte Strophe (Cb) die Gola gegenüber, die Gemeinde des neuen Exodus, der Jahwe den Ehrentitel 'mein Volk' verleiht, in dem zugleich eine Spitze gegen 'dieses Volk da', das kleingläubige Volk von Jerusalem, enthalten ist. Noch deutlicher aber ist der Bogen, den die Schlußstrophe zurück zur Anfangsstrophe des Korpus (Ba) schlägt, um ihre Aussage und die des ganzen Gedichtes zum Ziele zu führen. Jahwes Rückkehr nach Jerusalem korrespondiert mit der Rückführung und Heimkehr des Volkes; und inmitten der Stadt, in der er selber Wohnung nimmt, wird er das Volk auch wohnen lassen. Mit der Wohngemeinschaft wird eine neue Lebensgemeinschaft begründet, genauer gesagt, die alte Lebensgemeinschaft zwischen Jahwe und seinem Volke neu begründet. Begründet in *'ämät*, in einem Akt der Treue Gottes, womit nun vollends deutlich wird, warum Jerusalem 'die Stadt der Treue' (V. 3) heißen soll. Wie *'ämät* die erste Strophe des Korpus wieder anklingen läßt, so *ṣ*^{e}*dāqā* die zweite; denn in dem neuen Leben, das sie für Jerusalem verheißt, verwirklicht sich Jahwes 'Gerechtigkeit'. Um sie in dieser Weise zu verwirklichen, will Jahwe seinem Volke Gott sein.

Ein ganzes Geflecht formaler und inhaltlicher Bezüge umspannt und verspannt somit die fünf Worte und schließt sie zusammen zu einer festgefügten Kompositions- und Aussageeinheit. Sie wird nur scheinbar durch die mehrfache Folge der prophetischen Botenformel 'So spricht Jahwe Zebaoth' gestört; diese Formel ist vielmehr ein integrierender Bestandteil des Gedichtes und seiner Botschaft. Das zeigt sich äußerlich schon an den mit ihr korrespondierenden Elementen des poetischen Kernbestandes, an der ausleitenden Wendung *n*^{e}*ūm Yhwh* V. 6 und an dem in V. 3 und V. 6 wiederaufgenommenen Gottesprädikat 'Zebaoth'. Die eingangs angedeutete Meinung des Hieronymus, durch das jedesmal davorgesetzte 'So spricht Jahwe Zebaoth' würden die schier unglaublich großen Verheißungen dieses Wortes Stück für Stück als unverfälschtes Gotteswort beglaubigt, weist zwar in die richtige Richtung, beantwortet aber noch nicht alle Fragen, vor allem nicht die Frage nach dem Warum der Häufung an dieser Stelle. In solch kompakter Dichte tritt die Botenformel oder eine analoge Redeeinführung sonst ja niemals auf im Alten Testament. Die Erklärung kommt von außen, von einem Textbereich der zeitgenössischen Umwelt, der unserem Wort auch sachlich nicht ganz fern steht. Jenes Phänomen begegnet nämlich auch in den achämenidischen Königsinschriften, zum ersten Male in der großen Inschrift Darius' I. am Felsen von Behistūn, die zum formprägenden Vorbild wurde. Die Inschrift, eine babylonisch-elamisch-altpersische Trilingue, berichtet über die Niederwerfung der großen Aufstandsbewegung zu Anfang der Regierungszeit Darius' I. (522-486 v.Chr.) und muß in einer 'vorläufigen Endform' 520 oder 519 v.Chr. angebracht worden sein.[12] Gleichzeitig wurde sie im ganzen Reich verbreitet; davon zeugen die Funde einer babylonischen Fassung in Babel und eines Papyrus mit einer aramäischen Version auf der Nilinsel Elephantine.[13] Der Text setzt sich zusammen aus 76 Abschnitten, die unterschiedlich lang sind und bisweilen nur aus einem knappen Satz bestehen. Was nun dabei im Blick auf unseren Text von Belang ist: Bis auf den Anfangssatz geht jedem dieser Sinnabschnitte, auch dem kürzesten, die stereotype Einleitung 'Es kündet Darius der König' voraus. Das führt zu der Frage, ob nicht Sach. 8,1-8 diese—wohl generell die königlichen Verlautbarungen kennzeichnende—Stilform kopiert, ja, ob nicht dem Propheten dabei das in Palästina propagierte Pendant der großen Behistūn-Inschrift vor Augen stand. Wie sehr und in welcher Weise ihn der mit der Konsolidierung der Herrschaft Darius' I. eingetretene Zustand und seine Konsequenzen für Juda bewegten, zeigt deutlich genug das erste der ihm im Februar 519 zuteilgewordenen 'Nachtgesichte': 'die ganze Erde sitzt in Ruhe da' (1,11), in einer Art Friedhofsruhe, in der sich nichts mehr bewegt, so daß in Juda die verzweifelte Frage aufbricht, wie lange Jahwe 'Jerusalem und den Städten Judas', die nun schon 70 Jahre unter seinem Fluchwort stehen, sein Erbarmen noch verweigern will (1,12). Jahwes Antwort beginnt mit dem Satz 'Ich eifere um Jerusalem und den Zion mit großem Eifer' (1,14b) und besteht in dem Programm der sieben nächtlichen Visionen, die in einer wechselnden Folge transzendenter Bilder den radikalen Wandel der Welt im Zuge der Rückkehr Jahwes zum Zion und der weltweiten Durchsetzung seiner βασιλεία verheißen.[14] Die Nähe zu Sach. 8,1-8 ist schon wegen der wörtlichen Übereinstimmung zwischen 1,14b und dem programmatischen Eingangssatz 8,2a 'und ich eifere um den Zion mit großem Eifer' nicht zu übersehen. Der Horizont ist in 8,1-8 freilich enger gezogen. Nicht die ganze Erde steht im Blick, sondern nur die begrenzte Welt der jüdischen Gemeinde des Heimatlandes und der Diaspora. Auch die Sprache ist eine andere, von wirklichkeitsnaher Sachlichkeit bestimmt und streng gebunden in der Form. Sach. 8,1-8 ist eben kein Visionsbericht, sondern trägt ungeachtet seines visionären Gehalts den Charakter einer königlichen Proklamation. Und vielleicht ist dieses Wort so etwas wie eine Gegenproklamation zur großen Behistūn-Inschrift, die an sein Volk gerichtete Antwort Jahwes auf den universalen Herrschaftsanspruch Darius des Großen und seines Gottes Ahuramazda, in dessen Namen der persische König die Völkerwelt regiert.[15] Aber wie immer es sich damit verhalten mag—daß Sach. 8,1-8 den Stil der achämenidischen Königsproklamationen imitiert, kann angesichts der auffälligen Übereinstimmung, die hier besteht, wohl nicht bezweifelt werden.

ANMERKUNGEN

1. O. Eißfeldt, *Einleitung in das Alte Testament* (Tübingen, ^{3}1964), 583, mit Bezug auf Sach. 8,1-17.

2. *Comm. in Zachariam Prophetam*, MPL 25, 1466: *Per singula verba atque sententias quibus Israeli prospera et pro rerum magnitudine pene incredibilia promittuntur, propheta proponit: Haec dixit Dominus omnipotens, alio sermone loquens: Ne putetis mea esse quae spondeo, et quasi homini non credatis: Dei sunt promissa quae replico*. 'Bei den einzelnen Worten und Sätzen, in denen Israel Glück und bei der Größe der Dinge fast Unglaubliches verheißen wird, setzt der Prophet jedesmal davor: "Das spricht der allmächtige Herr", mit anderen Worten: "Meinet nicht, es seien meine Worte, und glaubt mir nicht, als ob ich Menschenwort rede; nein, Gottes Verheißung ist es, die ich wiedergebe."' Übersetzung nach W. Rudolph, *Haggai—Sacharja 1-8—Sacharja 9-14—Maleachi* (Kommentar zum Alten Testament, XIII 4; Gütersloh, 1976), 146 (hier die Belegstelle aus MPL 25 fälschlich mit 'Sp. 1538' angegeben).

3. H. Brongers, 'Der Eifer des Herrn Zebaoth', *VT* 13 (1963), [269-84] 274.

4. Anders nur, soweit ich sehe, W. Rudolph, *op. cit.*, 147, mit dem richtigen Argument, daß hier 'nur vom Verhalten Jahwes die Rede ist'.—Zum Begriff *'ämät* allgemein vgl. (A.) Jepsen, *'āman*, in: G.J. Botterweck—H. Ringgren (Hg.), *Theologisches Wörterbuch zum Alten Testament* [künftig *TWAT*], I (Stuttgart-Berlin-Köln-Mainz, 1973), [313-48] 333-41; H. Wildberger, 'אמן *'mn* fest, sicher', in: E. Jenni—C. Westermann (Hg.), *Theologisches Handwörterbuch zum Alten Testament*, I (München-Zürich, ^{3}1978), [177-209] 201-208.

5. Vgl. H.W. Wolff, *Anthropologie des Alten Testaments* (München, 1983), 178 (Lit.).

6. Auf sie machte A. Petitjean (*Les oracles du Proto-Zacharie* [Etudes bibliques; Paris-Louvain, 1969], 372f.) aufmerksam.

7. (H.-J.) Fabry, 'ישע *js*'', *TWAT* III (1982), [1035-43] 1040.

8. (H.D.) Preuß, 'בוא', *TWAT* I (1973), [536-68] 547.

9. L. Perlitt, *Bundestheologie im Alten Testament* (WMANT 36; Neukirchen-Vluyn, 1969), 106.

10. *Op. cit.*, 109.

11. Zu diesem Begriff vgl. S. Mittmann, 'Aufbau und Einheit des Danklieds Psalm 23', *ZThK* 77 (1980), [1-23] 8 und die dort angegebene Literatur.

12. Vgl. R. Borger, *Die Chronologie des Darius-Denkmals am Behistun-Felsen* (Nachrichten der Akademie der Wissenschaften in Göttingen, I. Phil.-hist. Klasse, Jahrgang 1982, Nr. 3; Göttingen, 1982), [103-132] 112. Bei Borger teilweise noch nicht vermerkte Neuausgabe der babylonischen und aramäischen Version: Elizabeth N. von Voigtlander, *The Bisutun Inscription of Darius the Great. Babylonian Version* (Corpus Inscriptionum Iranicarum, Part I: Inscriptions of Ancient Iran, Vol. II: *The Babylonian Versions of the Achaemenean Inscriptions, Texts I*, London, 1978); J.C. Greenfield–B. Porten, *The Bisuntun Inscription of Darius the Great. Aramaic Version* (Corpus Inscriptionum Iranicarum, Part I, Vol. V: *The Aramaic Versions of the Achaemenean Inscriptions, Texts I*, London, 1982).

13. Vgl. Borger, *op. cit.*, 111 mit Literaturhinweisen.

14. Vgl. dazu H. Gese, 'Anfang und Ende der Apokalyptik, dargestellt am Sacharjabuch', in: *Vom Sinai zum Zion. Alttestamentliche Beiträge zur biblischen Theologie* (Beiträge zur evangelischen Theologie, 64; München, 1974), 202-30.

15. Dies bringt vor allem der Vorspann der Memorialinschriften zur Geltung; vgl. dazu K. Koch, 'Weltordnung und Reichsidee im alten Iran', in: P. Frei–K. Koch, *Reichsidee und Reichsorganisation im Perserreich* (Orbis Biblicus et Orientalis, 55; Freiburg/Schweiz-Göttingen, 1984), 55ff.

22

COMPUTER-ASSISTED METHODS AND THE TEXT AND LANGUAGE OF THE OLD TESTAMENT—AN OVERVIEW

Walter T. Claassen

During the past two decades—and especially during the past few years—more and more references to the application of computers to the study of the Bible and the languages and cultures of the ancient Near East have appeared in the scholarly literature. This new accent came to the fore at a relatively late stage of the academic career of Professor Charles Fensham—and yet his wide scholarly perspective enabled him to assume a positive attitude towards these new possibilities. He soon encouraged projects in the Department of Semitic Languages involving the use of computers and computer-assisted methods and he displays an optimism as to the results which can be obtained.

1. *Limitations of the present survey*

It is the purpose of this article to give a *survey* of the types of computer or 'electronic data processing' (EDP) applications to the study of the text and language of the Old Testament, to identify some *basic developments* and to draw a few *perspectives* as to what can be *expected* from research in this field. Within the limited scope of this article, it is by no means possible to give a comprehensive and exhaustive overview of all projects undertaken recently, or those presently being undertaken. That would require the scope of a monograph. What is more important, is to be able to judge the value and importance of a fast-developing approach and of projects and publications resulting from it.

The need for more intensive applications of computer processing to the processes of *text preparation, editing and publication* (both with regard to the publication of critical editions and for the purpose of regular scholarly publication), is too obvious to merit discussion in this overview. It should be clear that computerized methods could be harnessed much more effectively to speed up the process of publication, to shorten the information float (i.e. the time data spends in the information channel between author and reader), to reduce the needless waste of time of scholars proofreading at both manuscript and printing stages, etc.

2. *Hindrances in assessing the value of computer applications*

Many references to computer applications in the study of the Old Testament are of such a kind that the average Old Testament scholar can only with difficulty distinguish the *basic trends* in the development of this new perspective. Various *factors* contribute to this state of affairs:

2.1. Many projects are only announced (or sometimes only envisaged) and there is no continuity in reporting the different stages of a project or the final results obtained.

2.2. Many research reports are presented to local research authorities in the form of unpublished reports, research memoranda and working documents only—sometimes owing to the fact that the rapid development of computer facilities renders previous approaches obsolete within a very short time and opens up new channels and ways of approach.[1]

2.3. Owing to the negative attitudes vis-à-vis computer applications of many editors of scholarly journals in the field, and of many colleagues pursuing more traditional methods, progressive scholars doing research in this field have found it necessary to present their research results in journals[2] and multi-authored works not normally encountered in the field of Old Testament studies. Likewise, research results are often presented at conferences dedicated to computer applications, rather than at gatherings of scholars active in the field of Old Testament studies.

2.4. It has become difficult to distinguish between fact and fiction in the reportage of projects and results, especially in the general news media. Many reports have been highly sensational, concentrating on matters such as authorship and basing their findings on dubious grounds. Scholars with a sound background of exegetical practice sometimes had every reason to suspect the methodological basis of such results.

2.5. It is very often extremely difficult to obtain detailed information on current projects and on the nature of alliances between various academic institutions. Data has become an asset and to justify the costs involved in building up a comprehensive data base, a spirit of collegial cooperation is sometimes sacrificed by scholars in favour of the desire to gain an edge in having at their disposal a unique collection of data. Until a collection reaches a point of saturation, information on future plans is seldom made available. (Cf. Weil, 1984, pp. 3, 19 on this problem.)

2.6. It is not always clear to scholars that many publications or research tools used regularly by them have been based upon or are the results of computer applications. This applies especially to word lists and concordances.[3] Computer applications are then regarded as out of line with regard to normal and traditional applications.

2.7. Computer-orientated projects often imply a completely *different course of research* from that applicable to traditional research projects. A scholar will, for example, spend considerable time apparently not producing many concrete research results, but in fact building up a data base which will in the long run allow a new phase of research activity or will allow questions to be answered more explicitly and much more efficiently.[4]

2.8. Perhaps the most limiting factor in assessing the real or the potential value of computer applications is the (sometimes only apparent) *lack of worthwhile results* obtained from approaches of this kind. Many interesting new results and research tools have been promised over a period of already more than two decades, but most of these have either not materialized or proved to be not as usable or as revolutionary as expected, at least not to the extent of replacing the older and reliable works of reference. Many factors are responsible for this state of affairs (cf. e.g. 2.7 above), but the apparent discrepancy between expectations and concrete results has been interpreted by many scholars as an indication of the bankruptcy of computer-assisted methods.

3. *The scope and nature of computer applications to the study of the Old Testament text and language*

In describing the nature and activities of computer applications to the field of Old Testament studies, one could proceed from various points of view, e.g.

—application fields
—methods applied to the data
—results obtained
—the sociological or logistic structure of computer applications

All of these perspectives merit the attention of scholars interested in determining the impact and possibilities of computer applications to this field of study, but it proves to be the most effective way to approach the totality of activities from the point of view of application fields.

3.1. *Applications to the text and language of the Old Testament*

By far the larger number of computer applications relevant to the study of the Old Testament have as their object the text—which is typically a very wide and comprehensive designation for

a. textual criticism,
b. the study of the language of the Old Testament, and
c. the use of the former in an attempt to come to results with regard to the study of the Old Testament as literature, i.e. questions such as literary sources, literary unity, authorship.

This spectrum of applications to the text will now be treated, starting with the last named area.

3.1.1. *Literary questions*

Typically, the research activities in the three fields mentioned are closely interwoven, especially those in connection with (b) and (c). To many scholars the real motive—or one of the most important motives—for EDP applications to the language (as grammar), proves to be the need of obtaining criteria for reaching literary conclusions.[5] The term 'style' then typically functions as the bridge between the grammatical 'formal criteria' and literary postulates and claims. Likewise, the results gained by scholars mainly interested in matters of grammar are often eagerly absorbed by others mainly interested in literary and exegetical questions. Many scholars are, of course, more cautious in keeping the different applications separate from each other.[6]

Approaches by which it is attempted to make a direct transition from quantitative-linguistic data to literary matters have earned a particularly bad reputation amongst theologians—especially owing to the sensational reportage of such 'findings' in the general media. Thus, for example, scholars profess to have 'proved' the unity of the book of Isaiah on the basis of statistical information gained from computer analysis (Radday, 1973), and the conclusion is reached that 'the Documentary Hypothesis in Genesis should either be rejected or at least thoroughly revised' (Radday *et al.*, 1982, p. 481).

Proponents of this approach often find it necessary to reply upon criteria which would otherwise not have been considered the most important or the only criteria for literary analysis. Radday explicitly dissociates himself from the loosely defined term 'style' (as often used in exegetical argumentation), and opts for criteria which are countable and 'lie beyond the writer's conscious control' (Radday *et al.*, 1982, p. 468). Such criteria are, for example, word length, the definite article, the conjunctive and consecutive waw, and the transition between word categories (*loc. cit.*).[7]

The research results of followers of this approach have had very little impact on mainstream exegetical scholarship and have convinced very few serious scholars. Amongst the many reasons, the following might be singled out:[8]

3.1.1.1. The naive conception that the text corpus is a mystic puzzle[9] which can be solved in some wondrous way or other by merely performing a set of calculations on items beyond the writer's conscious control, thereby completely ignoring those grammatical factors which are, in fact, under his conscious control.

3.1.1.2. The one-sided conception that questions such as literary composition, authorship, etc. can be settled conclusively by taking into account one aspect only. Instead of following a methodological particularism, the results from statistical analysis should be integrated into a comprehensive methodological approach.

If computer-based methods are to be of any value to the literary study of the Old Testament, they should provide the *tools* necessary to reach well-considered conclusions with due allowance for traditional philological, linguistic and exegetical approaches. Many of the over-enthusiastic or completely negative attitudes towards the use of computers in Old Testament studies have had their origin in the unacceptable approaches discussed above. It is in the best interests of scholarship that these approaches be replaced by others in which the results of computer methods are integrated into accepted research patterns. We need a better grasp on syntactic structures, formulaic patterns and the like, i.e. on those elements functioning in accepted research patterns (cf. Hardmeier, 1970, pp. 180-81).

3.1.2. *The field of textual criticism*

With regard to the *textual criticism of the Old Testament*, the use of EDP has been much less contentious. Perhaps the sheer volume of data to be handled in an intelligent and flexible way contributed to the fact that computer methods have become more acceptable in this field—although not enough use by far is being made of such methods, and it is hardly realized that very large and comprehensive data bases have to be constructed in order to reach the desired results.

The following projects on the level of textual criticism demonstrate the tremendous potential of computer access to the data:

a. G.E. Weil finds computerized methods the only way to keep track of the rich variety of aspects included in the Massorah, i.e. the traditional philological commentary accompanying the sacred Hebrew text.[10] In the CATAB[11] data base, large volumes of information on Hebrew manuscripts, variant readings and paleographic data, as well as on various early translations, have been brought together in a computer data-base, enabling analyses and findings which would otherwise have been impossible.[12]

b. The logistic problem experienced by the textual critic who wishes to establish whether a variant reading in an early translation really reflects a different *Vorlage*, or is merely due to a translation technique of the translator, has nowhere come to the fore as clearly as in the study of the Septuagint.

A series of questions on the interrelationship of words and grammatical constructions within the LXX as a whole, for a particular translator and in the relation between LXX and Masoretic text have to be answered before any postulate on a varying *Vorlage* can be made. This logistic deadlock has led to the formation of the *Tools for Septuagint Studies* project, jointly undertaken by the University of Philadelphia, Pennsylvania, and the Hebrew University.[13] The study of the Septuagint and the use of the Septuagint in Old Testament textual criticism will in future be nearly unthinkable without recourse to this data base.[14]

c. At the *Centre*: *Bible et Informatique* at the *Abbaye de Maredsous*, Belgium, a large collection of texts of the Bible and the ancient translations has been built up. A *Concordantia Polyglotta*, i.e. an exhaustive analytical and multilingual index of the Bible in various languages, was announced (Vervenne, 1981, pp. 54, 61), but unfortunately did not materialize, owing to exorbitant publication costs. The material available at this centre could be of high value for textual criticism.

The value of EDP for purposes of textual criticism is indeed very promising. The final decisions will, of course, have to be taken by the scholar himself, but a new generation of tools for textual criticism holds the only viable possibility for this type of research.[15]

3.1.3. *The language of the Old Testament*

By far the most applications of EDP have been in the field of the study of the Hebrew language itself. These studies can be grouped into various categories, viz.

a. *Basic research tools*, e.g. word-lists and concordances, e.g. the various computer-generated concordances in the series *The Computer Bible*.[16]
b. *More advanced research tools*, in which the intention is to provide more than a sorted list of passages, mostly arranged according to lexical criteria. In some of these studies lists are provided of passages meeting certain lexical, semantic and content criteria, enabling the exegete and scholar of Biblical Hebrew to do further research on these selections.[17]
c. *Individual studies*, in the form of monographs or articles, in which use was made of EDP.[18]

Several individual scholars or teams have, during the past two decades, begun doing research on EDP applications to Biblical Hebrew as a language. Four centres have been prominent, owing either to the large collections of data available, or to the number of publications issued from research undertaken there:

— *Centre d'Analyse et du Traitement automatique de la Bible (CATAB)*, Université Jean-Moulin, Lyon III[19]

— *Centre*: *Informatique et Bible*, Abbaye de Maredsous, Belgium[20]

— *Dept. of Near Eastern Studies*, University of Michigan[21]

— *Werkgroep Informatica*, Faculty of Theology, Free University, Amsterdam.[22]

Several other centres[23] have sprung up during the past few years, and even more individuals have started working on limited or comprehensive text corpora.

It is important to take note of the various *motivations* for making use of EDP, or of the *underlying presuppositions* determining the various approaches. The following list is by no means comprehensive and, furthermore, it exhibits a large degree of overlap between the various categories, sometimes due to terminological variation.

The following can be described as *research motifs* or *underlying presuppositions*:

a. The *volumes of data to be handled*, be it
— the complexity of the Masorah[24] or
— the complex interrelationship of semantic, structural and literary considerations.[25]

b. *Discontent with traditional concordances*, because they
— do not give proper access to particles and other utility words (Weil, 1964/65, p. 116),
— do not allow the study of syntactic structures,[26]
— can only with difficulty be used to correlate the passages in one lexical table with those in another, in order to determine co-occurrences,[27]
— do not provide the perspectives needed for structural and thematic analyses of a text as a whole.[28]

c. The view that research on Hebrew grammar should be *more comprehensive* and less selective and subjective.[29]

d. The perspective that the computer could or should act as *a heuristic*[30] *mechanism*, i.e. a means of uncovering words, constructions, passages of patterns which exhibit a particular selection of criteria. This perspective is motivated by various considerations, viz.: (i) There are no fluent speakers or informants available to us and the only alternative is the complex process of comparing one passage and its context with another, in order to get access, be it artificially and by approximation only, to the language competence of the fluent speaker of Biblical Hebrew.[31] (ii) The complex interrelationship of semantic, syntactic and structural factors can only be uncovered[32] and presented intelligently[33] through the use of EDP.

The above-mentioned considerations—and many others—have prompted various scholars to turn to computer-orientated solutions for problems experienced in the text or, more generally, to look for fresh areas of investigation which would only be possible through the availability of such modern methods. Many publications—or unpublished memoranda (cf. 2.2 above)—have appeared and various tools have been made available, e.g. in the series *The Computer Bible* and *Instrumenta Biblica*.[34]

It is doubtful whether this new generation of computer-generated concordances does in fact constitute much of a help to scholars and does give access to the typical questions asked by the grammarian or exegete.[35] Data is indeed arranged in various ways, providing new possibilities for access to the materials, and the selections of passages displaying certain grammatical criteria[36] are extremely helpful to scholars particularly interested in those grammatical phenomena. The main problem, however, is that these lists or concordances are not interactive.[37] To supply only predefined lists is not in line with the typical research patterns of scholars, where there is a close interaction of various activities, contextual and grammatical, syntagmatic and paradigmatic, semantic and syntactic. Typical exegetical and grammatical research consists of a dynamic alternation of approaches to the data, with the possibility of testing hypotheses on smaller or larger collections of data, meeting certain criteria.

Instead of *static* and pre-determined lists of frequency, collections of passages, etc., we need a means of *dynamic access* to the rich variety of textual materials. The tools produced up to now testify to an interesting experimental and pioneering approach to the data.

However, the technology has in the meantime developed to a point where interactive and dynamic systems are being developed for many application fields. A dynamic and interactive grammatical concordance is within reach of modern scholarship.[38]

With regard to the study of the Greek New Testament we are in fact already in a much better position. Apart from the many static lists which have been published in, for example, *The Computer Bible*, scholars can make use of GRAMCORD—a system which (as the acronym suggests) fulfills the functions of a grammatical concordance to the New Testament text, i.e. for the grammatical study of the Greek text it presents those possibilities which a traditional concordance (e.g. that of Lisowsky) provides for the lexicographical study of the Old Testament.[39] It is, for example, possible to obtain a listing of any morphologically dependent construction the user might wish to define (including restrictions such as morphological agreement, word order, and positioning), or even to produce a graphic representation of grammatical phenomena. The package can run on a variety of mainframe computers, as well as on certain microcomputers.

Future developments in the provision of tools for grammatical and exegetical study will have to follow the trend towards more interactive and dynamic systems. Such a development will be completely in line with the development of computer applications, in general, to other application fields. In fact, the development towards powerful micro-computer data base systems could even provide much more sophisticated possibilities than the linear approach reflected by GRAMCORD, for example.[40]

It is important that scholars should reflect clearly and methodologically on the demands typical user needs place on a dynamic and interactive system.[41] It is not enough merely to tabulate the traditional descriptive fields associated with grammatical analysis or to provide a variety of new frequency tables. The demands of modern exegetical science (i.e. including linguistic and literary aspects) require from us to obtain a completely new and innovative grasp on the textual materials, and to obtain answers to questions which would up to now have been unimaginable.

4. *Summary and Conclusion*

There is amongst many scholars a growing dissatisfaction with many traditional approaches to the text of the Old Testament, and especially with the traditional tools for text-critical, grammatical and exegetical study. True, many scholars have still not recognized that we have reached a position of stalemate with regard to certain critical issues in this field. Fortunately many scholars—not only of the younger generation—have started asking critical questions as to the future of research in Old Testament and ancient Near Eastern Studies, viz. questions as to how the information overload can be handled, how better access can be gained to the data, what the shape of research in this field will be a few decades from now, and how we should adapt to these changes, etc.

The crisis of scholarship is voiced very clearly by a no less eminent and knowledgeable scholar than Franz Rosenthal, emeritus professor of Yale University. In a significant lecture, 'Die Krise der Orientalistik', he states that nobody can control even one of the traditional disciplines of ancient Near Eastern studies as a whole or even to a larger extent, and he expresses the hope that the development of modern technology will come to our aid before our civilization and our scholarship are overwhelmed by the available data (Rosenthal, 1983, p. 18).

It is important that more scholars should actively experiment with the application of EDP to the text of the Old Testament and that they should try to harness the unimaginable possibilities of modern computer and information technology to a field characterized—in an exponential way—by an information (or data) overload.[42] There are indications that interesting developments will characterize the grammatical, textual and exegetical work of scholars in Old Testament (or Biblical) Studies in years to come.

NOTES

1. In bibliographic circles this type of literature is described as 'grey literature'. Thus, for example, many studies of H. Van Dyke Parunak are (or have been for some time) only available as unpublished research memoranda.

2. E.g. *Computers and the Humanities, Association for Literary and Linguistic Computing Bulletin, Revue* (L.A.S.L.A.). For a comprehensive bibliography until 1981, cf. Vanhove-Romanik (1981).

3. E.g. Whitaker (1972), Even-Shoshan (1981).

4. This is, of course, also the case with larger non-computer-orientated

projects, but it is then easier to describe to the general scholar exactly what is taking place in the research process.

5. E.g. Radday *et al.* (1982), Radday (1973). The approach of Radday *et al.* is clearly summarized in their own words: 'It combines four disciplines: the problem is Biblical, the angle investigated is the linguistic, the method is supplied by statistics, and computer science is instrumental' (1982, p. 467). The approach is further described as 'fully objective' (*loc. cit.*). It should be clear that in these approaches the linguistic material is only investigated in order to reach conclusions on literary matters.

6. E.g. Hardmeier (1970, pp. 177-82), who identifies useful and necessary applications in the fields of grammar (esp. syntax), style and authorship, and literary analysis *without* confusing different application fields with each other and making the one completely subservient to the other. Weil, likewise, approached his data base from a comprehensive perspective of applications on various levels (1984), although he is also interested in approaching literary matters through external statistical criteria (e.g. Weil, 1979, pp. 61ff.; Weil & Chenique, 1967). (Cf. further the discussion in 3.1.)

7. Roughly the same criteria are used by Chenique (1967). (Cf. the review by De Wouters & Cazelles, 1968, p. 563.)

8. Portnoy & Petersen (1984) have also identified unacceptable practices in the statistical methods of Radday and his colleagues.

9. If the intention were to understand the mystic-mathematical exegesis in certain rabbinic circles, such a mechanistic approach would of course be perfectly acceptable (cf. Weil & Chenique, 1964, p. 364).

10. Cf. Weil (1964/65, p. 116), Weil & Chenique (1964, pp. 365-66), Weil (1982, 1984).

11. *Centre d'Analyse et du Traitement Automatique de la Bible*, Université Jean-Moulin, Lyon III.

12. Cf. Weil (1984) and the *Concordance de la Cantillation* (Weil *et al.*, 1978).

13. Under the joint leadership of R.A. Kraft and E. Tov respectively.

14. Cf. Kraft & Tov (1981). This project has subsequently been described in various publications by Kraft and Tov. Cf. further the reference given by Cook in his contribution to this volume.

15. Cf. further the contribution of Cook in this volume. At the Dept. of Semitic Languages of the University of Stellenbosch, Dr Johann Cook has started research concerning the development of a concordance on the Peshitta, in cooperation with the Peshitta-Institute, Leiden. Computerized methods are used in this project.

16. Eds. J.A. Baird & D.N. Freedman, Biblical Research Associates, Wooster, Ohio. Since 1971 more than 20 volumes have already been published.

17. E.g. Talstra (1981a), Postma *et al.* (1983). In various volumes of *The Computer Bible* selections of passages for further study have been presented.

18. The titles are too numerous to list here; to cite two examples: Talstra (1981a), F.I. Andersen in his commentary on *Hosea* (Anchor Bible).

19. Cf. 3.1.2a above.

20. Cf. Maredsous (1981) and Vervenne (1981), as well as various contributions to volumes of *Interface*, published by the Centre: Informatique et Bible.

21. Cf. the various publications of Parunak mentioned in the bibliography, especially (1982b).

22. Cf. Talstra (1980), Postma *et al.* (1983), and the various other contributions by Talstra.

23. At the Dept. of Semitic Languages, University of Stellenbosch, the author is working on the development of an interactive data base for the study of Biblical Hebrew. This project goes back to research undertaken at the Dept. of Old Testament (Catholic Theology) of the University of Tübingen during 1983. Many valuable perspectives were gained from discussions with Professor Walter Gross. Much appreciated financial assistance was provided by the Alexander von Humboldt Stiftung. Cf. note 15 on the work in connection with a concordance to the Peshitta.

24. Cf. Weil (1964/65, p. 116) and 3.1.2a above.

25. Cf. Lowery (1982, p. 1), Parunak (1981b). Parunak (1981b, p. 22) convincingly argues that the paucity of data (i.e. the limited corpus of texts) itself suggests that we should do more with the texts themselves; when the semantic information is exploited properly, the paucity turns into an abundance of data which can only be handled by EDP.

26. Weil (1964/65, p. 116), Talstra (1980, p. 124), Hardmeier (1970, pp. 178-79).

27. Hardmeier (1970, p. 180), Talstra (1980, p. 125). Cf. below for progress already made in connection with Greek.

28. Classical concordances are quite useful for certain needs of lexicographers or grammarians interested in morphology, but unfortunately they focus mainly on the individual word or phrase. Scholars working in structural analysis, content analysis, rhetorical criticism and redactional history, however, sometimes wish to gain perspectives on the overall structure of the entire text—and in this respect the classical concordance leaves something to be desired. Cf. Parunak (1979, 1981a).

29. Morris & James (1980, pp. x-xii). Radday *et al.* (1982, p. 468) are unhappy with the term 'style' as used in exegesis, because it is used rather loosely, mostly ill-defined and subject to personal taste. (Cf. 3.1.1. for Radday's 'more objective' alternatives for the study of literary materials.)

30. The word 'heuristic' is in this connection used differently from its typical use in circles of philosophy and artificial intelligence.

31. Cf. Parunak (1981b)—with the significant title 'Interrogating a Dead Language'. In much the same way we use comparative philology to explain a word (etc.) on the strength of its occurrence in another language, the

meaning of a construction can be elucidated better with reference to all other occurrences in other (similar or different) passages. Hardmeier stresses the need for a 'vollständige und systematische Überblick über analoge Satzstrukturen' as an alternative to 'Zufallsbeobachtungen' (1970, p. 179).

32. Cf. Lowery (1982, p. 1), Talstra (1980, p. 123). Hardmeier expresses the need for a systematic investigation into the characteristic sentence types or structures associated with certain *Gattungen* (1970, p. 181). Cf. also Morris & James (1980, p. xii) on the hope of opening up 'fresh avenues of investigation'.

33. Very often it is attempted to give a graphic representation, or visual image, of the vocabulary density in a particular text (e.g. Parunak, 1981a) or of the semantic relationships underlying certain categories of words (e.g. Parunak, 1979, 1981b). Such a mapping or graphic representation is then reached on the basis of statistical calculations. Basic to this approach is the desire to uncover relationships which would otherwise have gone unnoticed, owing either to the complexity of the interrelationship of various sets of data, or to the typical human limitations which sometimes defy a clear perspective. Parunak himself speaks of 'pictorial concordances'.

34. Cf. e.g. Radday (1971), Morris & James (1980), Postma *et al.* (1983).

35. In the general preface to one of the first volumes of *The Computer Bible* the scientific objective of the series is formulated as follows: '... to assemble vast amounts of critical data so as to make them *immediately available* in organized form, and at the same time to reduce substantially the element of subjectivity in our work' (Radday, 1971, p. i). The importance of 'massively-based searches for patterns' (p. ii) is grossly overestimated, putting the accent on quantitative rather than qualitative matters.

36. E.g. Postma *et al.* (1983), Morris & James (1980).

37. Cf. the critical discussion of the various volumes by Talstra (1980, pp. 125-27).

38. Cf. note 23 above, on the research along these lines undertaken by the present author.

39. Cf. Miller (1978, 1979). Unfortunately many scholars in Greek or New Testament studies are completely unaware of the existence of this magnificent package, the use of which is limited, more or less, to the imagination of the scholar. For details on subscription, contact Paul A. Miller, Project GRAMCORD.

40. An attempt has been made to apply the principles and mechanism of GRAMCORD to the study of Hebrew (Parunak, 1981c), but an approach on the basis of modern data base systems could be more flexible and promising. Cf. note 23 above.

41. Important work in this connection has been done by Talstra (1980, p. 124) and Hardmeier (1970, pp. 179-82). Cf. also the contributions of Parunak cited in the bibliography. These matters will be discussed in more detail at the 'Colloque: "Bible et informatique"', to take place at Louvain-la-

Neuve, 2-4 September 1985 and organized by the Centre Informatique et Bible, Maredsous.

42. This service cannot be merely rendered by computer specialists at the request of Old Testament scholars. On the contrary, the EDP expertise should be consciously developed and fostered *within* the subject field. Such a new generation of 'hybrid scholars', combining subject expertise with computer and information technology from the perspective and from the needs experienced in the subject field itself, is presently emerging. They could help to form the transition to a phase of research where EDP will be but a normal extension of the scholar's approach and his ability—if they are accommodated, encouraged and recognized properly. (Cf. further Raben & Burton, 1981, esp. pp. 248ff.) This development is already recognized in, amongst others, the following publications: Abercrombie (1984), Kraft (1984a, 1984b, 1984c).

BIBLIOGRAPHY

Abercrombie, J.R.
1984 *Computer Programs for Literary Analysis*. Philadelphia: University of Pennsylvania Press.

Bee, R.E.
1973 'The Use of Statistical Methods in Old Testament Studies', *VT* 23 (1973), pp. 257-72.

Chenique, F.
1967 'Principes et méthodes de l'Etude de la Bible Massorétique sur les calculateurs électroniques—Exemples des ordinateurs IBM 1134, Honeywell H 200, IBM 1401' (Thèse, Université de Strasbourg, 1967).

Claassen, W.T.
1984 'On Coping with Information', in *Information Management in the Forestry Industry* (Symposium held in Stellenbosch, November 1984).

De Wouters, H. & H. Cazelles
1968 Review of F. Chenique . . . (1967), *VT* 18 (1968), pp. 562-64.

Even-Shoshan, A.
1981 *A New Concordance of the Torah, Nebiim and Ketubim* (Hebr.), Jerusalem: Kirjat Sepher.

Hardmeier, C.
1970 'Die Verwendung von elektronischen Datenverarbeitungsanlagen in der alttestamentlichen Wissenschaft', *ZAW* 82 (1970), pp. 175-85.

Kraft, R.A.
1984a 'In Quest of Computer Literacy', *Council on the Study of Religion Bulletin* 15/2 (1984), pp. 41-45.
1984b 'Computer Research for Religious Studies', *Council on the Study of Religion Bulletin* 15/4 (1984), pp. 127-29.
1984c 'Computer Assisted Research for Religious Studies', *Council on the Study of Religion Bulletin* 15/5 (1984), pp. 158-60.

Kraft, R.A. & E. Tov
1981 'Computer Assisted Tools for Septuagint Studies', *Bulletin of the IOSCS* 14 (1981), pp. 22-33.

Lowery, K.E.
1982 'Toward a Discourse Grammar of Biblical Hebrew: Methods for Data Manipulation'. (Unpublished research Memorandum, 4 December 1982).

Maredsous
1981 *Centre Informatique et Bible*. Maredsous, 1981.

Miller, P.A.
1978 'Project GRAMCORD: A Grammatical Concordance Package Program for the Greek New Testament' (Unpublished memorandum, issued by Project Gramcord).
1979 *GRAMCORD Reference Manual* (Version 19.1). Published by Project Gramcord.

Morris, P.M.K. & E.B. James
1980 *A Critical Word Book of the Pentateuch* (The Computer Bible XVII), Wooster: Biblical Research Associates, Inc.

Parunak, H. van Dyke
1979 'Beating Concordances into Picturebooks' (Research Memorandum UM 79-3).
1981a 'Prolegomena to Pictorial Concordances', *Computers in the Humanities* 15 (1981), pp. 15-36.
1981b 'Interrogating a Dead Language, Computer-assisted Semantic Analysis' (A Paper presented to the Symposium on Biblical Studies and the Computer, Ann Arbor, MI, 22 February 1980) (Unpublished Research Memorandum UM 80-2).
1981c 'Hebrew and Syntax Addenda to the GRAMCORD Reference Manual' (Unpublished research memorandum UM 81-5).
1982a 'Data Base Design for Biblical Texts', in R.W. Bailey (ed.), *Computing in the Humanities*, The Hague: North-Holland Publishing Company, pp. 149-61.
1982b 'Texts of the Michigan Project for Computer Assisted Biblical Studies' (Unpublished research memorandum UM 82-2, 10 June 1982).

Portnoy, S.L. & D.L. Petersen
1984 'Biblical Texts and Statistical Analysis: Zechariah and Beyond', *JBL* 103 (1984), pp. 11-21.

Postma, F., E. Talstra & M. Vervenne
1983 *Exodus. Materials in Automatic Text Processing* [2 parts] (Instrumenta Biblica 1), Amsterdam: VW Boekhandel and Turnhout: Brepols.

Raben, J. & S.K. Burton
1981 'Information Systems and Services in the Arts and Humanities', *Annual Review of Information Science and Technology* 16 (1981), pp. 247-66.

Radday, Y.T.
1971 *An Analytic Linguistic Concordance to the Book of Isaiah* (The Computer Bible II), Wooster.
1973 *The Unity of Isaiah in the Light of Statistical Linguistics, with a Contribution by D. Wickmann*, Hildesheim: Gerstenberg.

Radday, Y.T., *et al.*
1982 'Genesis, Wellhausen and the Computer', *ZAW* 94 (1982), pp. 467-81.

Rosenthal, F.

1983 'Die Krise der Orientalistik', in *XXI. Deutscher Orientalistentag vom 24. bis 29. März 1980 in Berlin. Vorträge* (Zeitschrift der Deutschen Morgenländischen Gesellschaft, Suppl. V.; ed. F. Steppart); Wiesbaden: F. Steiner, pp. 10-21.

Talstra, E.

1980 'Exegesis and the Computer Science: Questions for the Text and Questions for the Computer', *BiOr* 37 (1980), pp. 121-28.

1981a 'The Use of Ken in Biblical Hebrew. A Case Study in Automatic Text Processing', *OTS* 21 (1981), pp. 228-39.

Talstra, E. *et al.*

1981a *Deuterojesaja. Proeve van automatische tekstverwerking ten dienste van de exegese*, Amsterdam (2nd edn) (met F. Postma en H.A. van Zwet)

Vanhove-Romanik, C.

1981 'A Bibliography of Bible and Computer', in *Centre: Informatique et Bible*, Maredsous, pp. 87-164.

Vervenne, M.

1981 'Computers and Literature. An Application in the Field of Biblical Sciences', in *Centre: Informatique et Bible*, Maredsous, pp. 52-86.

Weil, G.E.

1964/65 'Methodologie de la codification des textes sémitiques servant aux recherches de linguistique quantitative sur ordinateur', *Bulletin d'information de l'Institut de Recherche et d'Histoire des Textes* 13 (1964/65), pp. 115-33.

1979 'Analyse automatique quantifiée en critique textuelle biblique. Limite des analyses statistiques', in Z. Malachi (ed.), *Proceedings of the International Conference on Literary and Linguistic Computing* (Tel Aviv: Katz Research Institute), pp. 55-96.

1984 'La Bible Massorétique face au Golem. Problèmes méthodologiques, epistémologiques et éthiques posés par les études automatisées' (Paper presented at the 'Colloquium on the Transformation of Biblical Research in the XIXth and XXth Centuries', presented by the Israel Academy of Sciences and Humanities and the European Science Foundation, in Jerusalem, 10-13 September 1984).

Weil, G.E., *et al.*

1978 *Concordance de la Cantillation du Pentateuque et des Cinq Megillot* (Documentation de la Bible 1), Nancy: Centre d'Analyse . . ., 1978.

Weil, G.E. & F. Chenique

1964 'Prolegomènes à l'utilisation des méthodes de statistique linguistique pour l'étude historique et philologique de la Bible hébraïque et de ses paraphrases', *VT* 14 (1964), pp. 344-66.

Whitaker, R.E.

1972 *A Concordance to the Ugaritic Literature*, Cambridge, Mass.: Harvard University Press.

BIBLIOGRAPHY F. CHARLES FENSHAM

Compiled by W.T. Claassen

The following is a *select bibliography* of the writings of Prof. Frank Charles Fensham up to 1985. Scholarly writings in Afrikaans have been included in this list.

The following items are, for reasons of space, not included in this select bibliography:

(a) Reviews of scholarly publications (more than 140).
(b) Popular articles on the Bible and the ancient Near East in newspapers, magazines and (general) journals (more than 150).
(c) Entries in encyclopaedias and dictionaries (both South African and international) (more than 250).
(d) Popular articles on themes not related to the Bible and the ancient Near East.

A. *List of Abbreviations*

The abbreviations generally used in the subject fields are also followed here (cf. for example the lists of abbreviations of *Die Religion in Geschichte und Gegenwart* (3rd edn) and of other standard works of reference). The following abbreviations represent periodicals (etc.) not normally included in such standard lists.

GV —*Die Gereformeerde Vaandel*
OTWSA —*Proceedings of the Ou-Testamentiese Werkgemeenskap of South Africa*
TG —*Tydskrif vir Geesteswetenskappe*
TL —*Tydskrif vir Letterkunde*

B. *Books and Monographs*

1. *Is Israel nog die Uitverkore Volk?*, Cape Town: N.G. Kerk-Uitgewers, 1955, pp. 25.
2. *Die Messias kom!*, Cape Town: N.G. Kerk-Uitgewers, 1957, pp. 110.
3. *Die Brief aan die Hebreërs*, Cape Town: N.G. Kerk-Uitgewers, 1962, pp. xv + 191.

4. *Wetenskap en Bybelkunde*, Cape Town: Human en Rousseau, 1964, pp. 134. Second revised edition, 1975, pp. 196.
5. *Die boodskap van Johannes vir ons tyd*, Cape Town: N.G. Kerk-Uitgewers, 1964, pp. 64.
6. *Kultuur in die tyd van die Bybel*, Johannesburg: S.A.B.C., 1965, pp. 26.
7. *'n Ondersoek na die Geskiedenis van die Interpretasie van die Hebreeuse Poësie*, Stellenbosch: U.S. Annals, 1966, pp. 23.
8. *Heersers van die Ou Nabye Ooste*, Cape Town: Tafelberg-Uitgewers, 1970, pp. 143.
9. *Exodus*, Nijkerk: Callenbach, 1970, pp. 256. (Commentary in the Dutch series *De prediking van het Oude Testament*.) Second revised edition, 1977, pp. 262. Third impression, 1984.
10. *'n Beknopte Ugaritiese Grammatika*, Stellenbosch: U.S. Annals, 1970, pp. 31.
11. *Die Veelkleurige Kleed*, Cape Town: Tafelberg-Uitgewers, 1971, pp. 124.
12. *Reisgids vir Israel*, Cape Town: Tafelberg-Uitgewers, 1976, pp. 105.
13. *Die Dooie See-Rolle en die Bybel*, Cape Town: Tafelberg-Uitgewers, 1976, pp. 105.
14. Co-author in the *Bybel met Verklarende Aantekeninge*, I, 1958, pp. 493-542 and II, 1958, pp. 2025-53.
15. Co-author with A. Nel, *Palestina, die Heilige Land*, Cape Town: H.A.U.M., 1965, pp. 178.
16. Co-author with J.P. Oberholzer and J.L. Helberg, *Bybelse Aardrykskunde, Oudheidkunde en Opgrawings*, 1966, pp. 434 (responsible for pp. 1-109). Reprint 1969.
17. Co-author with J.P. Oberholzer, *Bybelse Aardrykskunde, Oudheidkunde en Opgrawings*, 1972, pp. 437 (responsible for pp. 1-116 and 311-437).
18. Translation (from German) of G.S. Wegener, *In die Begin was die Woord*, 1961, pp. 258. Second impression 1971.
19. *Die Dooie See-Rolle en die Bybel*, Cape Town: Tafelberg-Uitgewers, 1980, pp. iii + 105 (second impression).
20. *Die Brief aan die Hebreërs*, Cape Town: N.G. Kerk-Uitgewers, 1981, pp. 144 (second revised edition).
21. Co-author with D.N. Pienaar, *Geskiedenis van ou Israel*, Pretoria: Academica, 1982, pp. 222.
22. *Exoda*, 1982, pp. 111 (Commentary on Exodus in Sotho).
23. *The Books of Ezra and Nehemiah* (New International Commentaries on the Old Testament), 1982, pp. 288.

C. *Articles in Scholarly Journals*

1. 'Aparche in die Skrif', *Die Studiekring* 1 (1951), pp. 6-9.
2. 'Bybelstudie—Nahum', *Die Studiekring* 1 (1951), pp. 32-37.
3. 'Gog en die *LXX*', *Die Studiekring* 1 (1951), pp. 37-38.
4. 'Sodom en Gomorra en die Jesaja-rolle', *Die Studiekring* 1 (1951).
5. 'Verklaringsmetodes van Openbaring', *GV*, March 1954, pp. 34-45.
6. 'Genesis 41:40—A Note', *ET*, June 1957.
7. 'The Preposition B in Isaiah 27:13', *EQ* 29 (1957).
8. 'Geskiedskrywing van die Ou Testament', *GV*, Sept. 1957.
9. 'The Shaving of Samson—A Note on Judg. 16:19', *EQ* 31 (1959).
10. 'New Light on Exodus 21:6 and 22:7 from the Laws of Eshnunna', *JBL* 78 (1959), pp. 160-61.
11. 'The Stem HTL in Biblical Hebrew', *VT* 6 (1959), pp. 310-11.
12. 'Die Vier Evangelies en die Qumrân-geskrifte', *GV*, 1959, pp. 13-19.
13. 'Thunder-Stones in Ugaritic', *JNES* 18 (1959), pp. 273-74.
14. 'The Judges and Ancient Israelite Jurisprudence', *OTWSA*, 1960, pp. 15-22.
15. 'Enkele Aspekte van die Voortgang van die Goddelike Openbaring in die Vroegste Ou-Testamentiese Geskiedenis', *NGTT* 1 (1960), pp. 53-61.
16. 'The Treaty between Solomon and Hiram and the Alalakh-Tablets', *JBL* 79 (1960), pp. 59-60.
17. 'Exodus XXI 18-19 in the Light of Hittite Law, par. 10', *VT* 10 (1960), pp. 333-35.
18. 'Die Waarde van die Koptiese Tekste van Nag' Hammadi vir die Nuwe Testament en die Ou Christendom', *NGTT* 1 (1960), pp. 24-32.
19. 'The Legal Background of Mt. VI 12', *NT* 4 (1960), pp. 1-2.
20. 'Ps. 68:32 in the light of the recently discovered Ugaritic Tablets', *JNES* 19 (1960), pp. 292-93.
21. 'A Few Aspects of Legal Practices in Samuel in comparison with Legal Material from the Ancient Near East', *OTWSA* 1961, pp. 18-27.
22. 'In hoever het Israel ontleen aan sy Buurkulture?', *NGTT* 2 (1961), pp. 103-12.
23. 'Shamgar Ben 'Anath', *JNES* 20 (1961), pp. 197-98.
24. 'Die Letterkundige Skoonheid van die Bybel', *TL* 11 (1961), pp. 26-37.
25. 'The Bible as History', *NGTT* 3 (1961), pp. 301-10.
26. 'The Possibility of the Presence of Casuistic Legal Material at the Making of the Covenant at Sinai', *PEQ* 93 (1961), pp. 143-46.
27. 'Malediction and Benediction in Ancient Near Eastern Vassal Treaties and the Old Testament', *ZAW* 74 (1962), pp. 1-9.
28. 'A Cappadocian Parallel to Hebrew Kutonet', *VT* 12 (1962), pp. 196-98.

29. 'Salt as Curse in the Old Testament and the Ancient Near East', *BA* 25 (1962), pp. 48-50.
30. 'Nuutste Ontdekkings by die Dooie See', *NGTT* 3 (1962), pp. 429-32.
31. ' 'D in Exodus XXII 12', *VT* 12 (1962), pp. 337-39.
32. 'Widow, Orphan and the Poor in Ancient Near Eastern Legal and Wisdom Literature', *JNES* 21 (1962), pp. 129-39.
33. 'Die Keret-Epos van die Ou Kanaäniete', *TL* 12 (1962), pp. 17-24.
34. 'Clauses of Protection in Hittite Vassal-Treaties and the Old Testament', *VT* 13 (1963), pp. 133-43.
35. 'Common Trends in Curses of the Near Eastern Treaties and Kudurru-Inscriptions compared with Maledictions of Amos and Isaiah', *ZAW* 75 (1963), pp. 155-75.
36. 'The Wild Ass in the Aramaean Treaty between Bar-Ga'ayah and Mati'el', *JNES* 22 (1963), pp. 185-86.
37. 'Psalm 29 and Ugarit', *OTWSA* [1963], 1964, pp. 84-99.
38. 'Abraham in a New Perspective', *NGTT* 3 (1963), pp. 222-29.
39. 'Die Ou-Testamentiese Wetenskap in die Moderne Tyd', *TG* 3 (1963), pp. 202-208.
40. 'Die Poësie van die ou Hebreërs', *TL* 2 (1964), pp. 19-28.
41. '"Camp" in the New Testament and Milhamah', *RdQ* 4 (1964), pp. 557-62.
42. 'Die Bybel in die Lig van die Nuutste Ontdekkings', *NGTT* 5 (1964), pp. 251-54.
43. 'The Treaty between Israel and the Gibeonites', *BA* 27 (1964), pp. 96-100.
44. 'Did a Treaty Exist between the Israelites and Kenites?', *BASOR* 175 (1964), pp. 51-54.
45. 'Die Hetitiese Beskawing en die Ou Testament', *NGTT* 6 (1965), pp. 26-34.
46. 'Die Evangelie van Thomas en sy Betekenis', *TL* 3 (1965), pp. 31-39.
47. 'Die Offer en Maaltyd by die Vorming van die Verbond in Ou en Nuwe Testament', *TG* 5 (1965), pp. 77-85.
48. 'Judas' Hand in the Bowl and Qumran', *RdQ* 18 (1965), pp. 259-61.
49. 'Wie en Wat is die Antichris volgens Thessalonisense?', *NGTT* 6 (1965), pp. 159-69.
50. 'Ps. 21—A Covenant Song?', *ZAW* 77 (1965), pp. 193-202.
51. 'Die Bybel en Egipte', *NGTT* 6 (1965), pp. 206-15.
52. 'Science of the Ancients', *Scientific South Africa* 3 (1965), pp. 635-36.
53. 'The Destruction of Mankind in the Near East', *AION* 15 (1965), pp. 31-38.

54. 'The Covenant-idea in the Book of Hosea', *OTWSA* 7-8 ([1964-65] 1966), pp. 35-49.
55. 'The Importance of the Covenant Idea for Ancient Israel', *Bargai*, Sept. 1966, pp. 129-30.
56. 'The Dog in Ex. XI 7', *VT* 16 (1966), pp. 504-507.
57. 'An Ancient Tradition of the Fertility of Palestine', *PEQ* (1966), pp. 166-67.
58. 'Winged Gods and Goddesses in the Ugaritic Tablets', *OrAn* 5 (1966), pp. 157-64.
59. 'The Burning of the Golden Calf and Ugarit', *IEJ* 16 (1966), pp. 191-93.
60. ''n Ontwerp vir 'n Historiese Grammatika in Bybelse Hebreeus', *NGTT* 8 (1967), pp. 20-22.
61. 'Enkele Gedagtes oor die Prosastyl van Exodus', *TL* 5 (1967), pp. 58-61.
62. 'Ugaritic and the Translation of the Old Testament', *The Bible Translator* 18 (1967), pp. 71-74.
63. 'A Possible Origin of the Concept of Day of the Lord', *Biblical Essays* (*OTWSA*), 1967, pp. 90-97.
64. 'The Curse of the Cross and the Renewal of the Covenant', *Biblical Essays* (*Neotestamentica* 1), 1967, pp. 219-26.
65. 'Geregtigheid in die Boek Miga en Parallelle uit die Ou Nabye Ooste', *TG* 7 (1967), pp. 416-25.
66. 'Covenant, Promise and Expectation in the Bible', *TZ* 23 (1967), pp. 305-22.
67. 'A Possible Explanation of the Name Baal-Zebub of Ekron', *ZAW* 79 (1967), pp. 361-64.
68. 'Shipwreck in Ugarit and Ancient Near Eastern Law Codes', *OrAn* 6 (1967), pp. 221-24.
69. 'The Subjective Conception of History and the Old Testament', *OTWSA* [1967], 1971, pp. 28-34.
70. 'Die Nuutste Debat oor die Hiksos en die Bybel', *NGTT* 9 (1968), pp. 1-8.
71. 'Sekere probleme in verband met die Klassifikasie van die Hamito-Semitiese Tale', *Taalfasette* 6 (1968), pp. 46-54.
72. 'Die Konvensie van Jerusalem—'n keerpunt in die geskiedenis van die Kerk', *NGTT* 10 (1969), pp. 32-38.
73. 'Ou-Testamentiese en Semitiese Studies in Suid-Afrika', *NGTT* 10 (1969), pp. 77-85.
74. 'The Obliteration of the Family as Motif in the Near Eastern Literature', *AION* 19 (1969), pp. 191-99.
75. 'The Son of a Handmaid in Northwest Semitic', *VT* 19 (1969), pp. 312-21.

76. 'Iron in the Ugaritic Texts', *OrAn* 8 (1969), pp. 209-13.
77. 'Aspects of Family Law in the Covenant Code in light of Near Eastern Parallels', *Dine Israel* 1 (1969), pp. 5-19.
78. 'Legal Activities of the Lord according to Nahum', *OTWSA* 1969, pp. 13-20.
79. 'The Battle between the Men of Joab and Abner as a Possible Ordeal by Battle', *VT* 20 (1970), pp. 356-57.
80. ''n Waardering van die Letterkunde van die Bybel', *Die Unie* 66 (1970), pp. 502-504.
81. 'The Change of the Situation of a Person in Ancient Near Eastern and Biblical Wisdom Literature', *AION* 31 (1971), pp. 155-64.
82. 'I am the Way, the Truth and the Life', *The Christ of John* (*Neotestamentica*) 1971, pp. 81-88.
83. 'Remarks on Certain Difficult Passages in Keret', *JNSL* 1 (1971), pp. 11-22.
84. 'The Covenant as Giving Expression to the Relationship between Old and New Testament', *Tyndale Bulletin* 22 (1971), pp. 82-94.
85. 'Some Remarks on the First Three Mythological Texts of Ugaritica V', *UF* 3 (1971), pp. 21-24.
86. 'Ter ere van W.F. Albright en Roland de Vaux', *NGTT* 13 (1972), pp. 32-33.
87. 'W.F. Albright (24/5/1891—19/9/1971)', *JNSL* 2 (1972), pp. 1-4.
88. 'Remarks on Keret 26-43', *JNSL* 2 (1972), pp. 37-52.
89. 'New Light from Ugaritica V on Ex. 32:17', *JNSL* 2 (1972), pp. 86-87.
90. 'Hesiodos, Spreuke en Hölderlin', *NGTT* 13 (1972), pp. 169-76.
91. 'The Good and Evil Eye in the Sermon on the Mount', *NTWSA*, 1972, pp. 51-58.
92. 'The First Ugaritic Texts in Ugaritica V and the Old Testament', *VT* 2 (1972), pp. 296-303.
93. 'Die Sumeriese Gilgamesj', *TL* 10 (1972), pp. 6-11.
94. 'Solomon Caesar Malan en die Assirioloog Austen Henry Layard', *TG* 13 (1973), pp. 58-62.
95. 'The Divine Subject of the Verb in the Book of Micah', *OTWSA* [1968] 1973, pp. 25-34.
96. 'Die verlede, hede en toekoms van Grammatikale Arbeid op Bybelse Hebreeus', *Taalfasette* 17 (1973), pp. 1-11.
97. 'Hebrews and Qumrân', *Neotestamentica* 5 (1971) 1974, pp. 9-21.
98. 'Love in the Writings of Qumrân and John', *Neotestamentica* 6 [1972] 1974, pp. 67-77.
99. 'Taalkundige en Letterkundige Probleme i.v.m. die Aanwending van Buitebybelse Materiaal vir die Nuwe Testament', *NGTT* 15 (1974), pp. 268-73.

100. 'Remarks on Keret 54-59', *JNSL* 3 (1974), pp. 26-33.
101. 'Die benaming Bybelse Argeologie, is dit houdbaar?', *TG* 15 (1975), pp. 12-17.
102. 'Medînâ in Ezra and Nehemiah', *VT* 25 (1975), pp. 795-97.
103. 'Remarks on Keret 59-72', *JNSL* 4 (1975), pp. 9-21.
104. 'Gen. XXXIV and Mari', *JNSL* 4 (1975), pp. 87-90.
105. 'Die Christen en die Letterkunde', *TL* 14 (1976), pp. 53-56.
106. 'Verhoudingsteologie in die Regsaspekte van die Ou Testament', *NGTT* 17 (1976), pp. 66-75.
107. 'The Poetic Form of the Hymn of the Day of the Lord in Zephaniah', *OTWSA* [1970-71], 1976, pp. 9-14.
108. 'The Rôle of the Lord in the Covenant Code', *VT* 26 (1976), pp. 262-74.
109. ''n Argeologiese opskudding: die ontdekking by Ebvla', *NGTT* 18 (1977), pp. 225-29.
110. 'Prof. P.J. van Zijl (9/2/1939—25/8/1976)', *JNSL* 5 (1977), pp. 1-2.
111. 'Transgression and Penalty in the Book of the Covenant', *JNSL* 5 (1977), pp. 23-41.
112. 'The Numeral Seventy in the Old Testament and the Family of Jerubbaal, Ahab, Panammuwa and Athirat', *PEQ* 109 (1977), pp. 113-15.
113. 'Probleme van die Nuwe Afrikaanse Bybelvertaling', *TL* 16 (1978), pp. 38-41.
114. 'The Use of the Suffix Conjugation and the Prefix Conjugation in a few Old Hebrew Poems', *JNSL* 6 (1978), pp. 9-18.
115. 'Remarks on Keret 73-79', *JNSL* 6 (1978), pp. 19-24.
116. 'Bibliography of Publications by South African Scholars on the Ancient Near East', *JNSL* 6 (1978), pp. 91-96.
117. 'Ruitery of Strydwabemanning in Exodus', *NGTT* 19 (1978), pp. 195-99.
118. 'Pehâ in the Old Testament and the Ancient Near East', *OTWSA* 19 (1979), pp. 44-52.
119. 'Hoe korreleer 'n mens die argeologiese resultate met die Bybel? 'n paar gesigspunte', *TG* 19 (1979), pp. 153-61.
120. 'Notes on Keret 79(b) - 89 (CTA 14:2:79(b) - 89)', *JNSL* 7 (1979), pp. 17-26.
121. 'The Semantic Field of *kly* in Ugaritic', *JNSL* 7 (1979), pp. 27-30.
122. 'Die tyd van Abraham is soos kwiksilwer', *NGTT* 21 (1980), pp. 140-57.
123. 'A Few Observations on the Polarisation between Yahweh and Baal in I Kings 17-19', *ZAW* 92 (1980), pp. 227-36.
124. 'Afrika suid van Egipte in die Ou Tyd (± 2500 v.C.—100 n.C.) soos uit historiese bronne bekend', *TG* 20 (1980), pp. 286-94.

125. 'Das Nicht-Haftbar-Sein im Bundesbuch im Lichte der altorientalischen Rechtstexte', *JNSL* 8 (1980), pp. 17-34.
126. 'Notes on Keret in CTA 14:90—103a', *JNSL* 8 (1980), pp. 35-47.
127. 'Neh. 9 and Pss. 105, 106, 135 and 136. Post-Exilic Historical Traditions in Poetic Form', *JNSL* 9 (1981), pp. 35-51.
128. 'Werktuie in Bybelse dae', *TG* 21 (1981), pp. 176-84.
129. 'Notes on Keret, CTA 14: 103b-114a', *JNSL* 9 (1981), pp. 53-66.
130. 'The Root b'r in Ugaritic and in Isaiah in the Meaning "to pillage"', *JNSL* 9 (1981), pp. 67-69.
131. 'Prof. T.C. Vriezen, a Tribute', *JNSL* 9 (1981), pp. 1-2.
132. 'Extrabiblical Material and the Hermeneutics of the Old Testament with Special Reference to the Legal Material of the Covenant Code', *OTWSA* 20/21 (1982), pp. 53-65.
133. 'Prof. Mitchell Dahood S.J. (2 Feb. 1922—8 March 1982)', *JNSL* 10 (1982), p. 1.
134. 'Prof. N.H. Ridderbos who passed away in 1982', *JNSL* 10 (1982), pp. 3-4.
135. 'Nebukadrezzar in the Book of Jeremiah', *JNSL* 10 (1982), pp. 53-65.
136. 'Die waarde van die Persiese leenwoorde vir 'n beter verstaan van die bronne van die boeke Esra-Nehemia', *NGTT* 24 (1983), pp. 5-14.
137. 'Die Siro-Efraimitiese Oorlog en Jesaja—'n historiese perspektief', *NGTT* 24 (1983), pp. 237-46.
138. 'Some Theological and Religious Aspects in Ezra and Nehemiah', *JNSL* 11 (1983), pp. 59-68.
139. 'Remarks on Keret 114b-136a (CTA 14:114b-136a)', *JNSL* 11 (1983), pp. 69-78.
140. 'Prof. Dennis J. McCarthy (14/10/24—29/8/83)', *JNSL* 11 (1983), pp. 1-2.
141. 'Die Hugenote van Stellenbosch', *Bulletin van die Hugenote-Vereniging* 21 (1983), pp. 28-29.
142. 'Dr. S.P. Heijns, die eerste Afrikaner om te promoveer in Teologie', *NGTT* 25 (1984), pp. 52-59.
143. 'Die Publikasie van 'n eerste Wetteversameling uit Ou Egipte', *TG* 24 (1984), pp. 31-40.
144. 'Waar kom die pleknaam Skeba vandaan in Afrikaans?', *TL* 22 (1984), p. 84.
145. 'Die Boekery van ds. Wilhelm van Gendt en Joachim von Dessin se Versameling', *Kwartaalblad van die Suid-Afrikaanse Biblioteek* 38 (1984), pp. 161-67.
146. 'Prof. Dr. Adrianus van Selms', *JNSL* 12 (1984), pp. 1-3.
147. 'Prof. J.H. Kroeze', *JNSL* 12 (1984), pp. 19-20.
148. 'Prof. Yigael Yadin', *JNSL* 12 (1984), pp. 21-23.

149. 'Prof. Dr. Walther Zimmerli', *JNSL* 12 (1984), pp. 25-26.
150. 'The Ugaritic Root tpt', *JNSL* 12 (1984), pp. 63-69.
151. 'The Marriage Metaphor in Hosea for the Covenant Relationship between the Lord and his People', *JNSL* 12 (1984), pp. 71-78.
152. Die Edik van Nantes en Madame de Maintenot', *Bulletin van die Hugenot-Vereniging* 22 (1984-85), pp. 36-38.
153. 'Die Verhoudingsteologie as 'n moontlike oplossing vir 'n Teologie van die Ou Testament', *NGTT* 26 (1985), pp. 246-59.

D. *Contributions to Multi-authored Volumes and Festschriften*

1. 'Legal Aspects of the Dream of Solomon', *Fourth World Congress of Jewish Studies, Papers* I, 1967, pp. 67-70.
2. 'Oerwortels. Wyn in die Nabye Ooste', D.J. Opperman (red.), *Die Gees van die Wingerd*, 1968, pp. 15-34. Festschrift of the K.W.V.
3. 'The Treaty between the Israelites and Tyrians', *Congress Volume Rome* (*Supplement Vetus Testamentum*) 17 (1969), pp. 71-87.
4. 'Ordeal by Battle in the Ancient Near East and the Old Testament', *Studi in onore di Edoardo Volterra*, VI, 1969, pp. 127-35.
5. 'The Treaty between Israel and the Gibeonites', *The Biblical Archaeologist Reader* 3 (1970), pp. 121-26.
6. 'Israel—'n Prinsipe in die Hermeneutiek', *Hermeneutica*, 1970, pp. 23-34. (Festschrift in honour of E.P. Groenewald.)
7. 'Oudste beskawings langs groot riviere aangelê', F.A. Venter (ed.), *Water*, 1970, pp. 473-81. (Publication for the Water Year, 1970.)
8. 'Water in die Bybel', F.A. Venter (ed.), *Water*, 1970, pp. 493-96. (Cf. 7 above.)
9. 'Father and Son as Terminology for Treaty and Covenant', H. Goedicke (ed.), *Near Eastern Studies in Honor of William Foxwell Albright*, 1971, pp. 121-35.
10. 'Problems in Connection with the Translation of Ancient Texts', *De fructi oris sui*, 1971, pp. 46-57. (Festschrift for A. van Selms.)
11. 'Afrikaans in die Kerk', B. Kok (ed.), *Afrikaans, ons pêrel van groot waarde*, 1974, pp. 56-65. (Commemorative volume, Afrikaans 100 Years.)
12. 'Die studie van die Ou Testament in die moderne wêreld', *Die Bybel en die Moderne Mens*, 1974, pp. 14-25.
13. 'Liability in Case of Negligence in the Old Testament Covenant Code and Ancient Legal Traditions', *Essays in Honour of Ben Beinart* (Festschrift for Ben Beinart), I, 1978, pp. 283-94.
14. 'Notes on Treaty Terminology in Ugaritic Epics', *UF* 11 (1979), pp. 265-74 (Festschrift for C.F.A. Schaeffer).
15. 'Oor tradisies in die Ou Testament', *Die Ou Testament Vandag*, 1979, pp. 26-38.

16. 'Letterkundige Kritiek en die Bybel', in *Van Leipoldt tot Letterkundige Kritiek*, 1982, pp. 12-25.
17. *Die Bybel leef*, 1982, pp. 55-66, 99-106.
18. 'Letterkundige Kritiek en die Bybel', in F.C. Fensham (ed.), *Van Leipoldt tot Letterkundige Kritiek*, 1982, pp. 12-25.
19. 'The Relationship between Phoenicia and Israel during the Reign of Ahab', *Atti del I Congresso Internazionale di studi Fenici e Punici*, II, 1983, pp. 589-94.
20. 'Die pad van die Akademie (1909-1984)', J.C. Moll (ed.), *Akademie 75*, 1984, pp. 3-18.

INDEX

INDEX OF BIBLICAL REFERENCES

INDEX OF AUTHORS

JOURNAL FOR THE STUDY OF THE OLD TESTAMENT
Supplement Series

1 I, HE, WE AND THEY: A LITERARY APPROACH TO ISAIAH 53
D.J.A. Clines

*2 JEWISH EXEGESIS OF THE BOOK OF RUTH
D.R.G. Beattie

*3 THE LITERARY STRUCTURE OF PSALM 2
P. Auffret

4 THANKSGIVING FOR A LIBERATED PROPHET: AN INTERPRETATION OF ISAIAH CHAPTER 53
R.N. Whybray

5 REDATING THE EXODUS AND CONQUEST
J.J. Bimson

6 THE STORY OF KING DAVID: GENRE AND INTERPRETATION
D.M. Gunn

7 THE SENSE OF BIBLICAL NARRATIVE I: STRUCTURAL ANALYSES IN THE HEBREW BIBLE (2nd edition)
D. Jobling

*8 GENESIS 1–11: STUDIES IN STRUCTURE AND THEME
P.D. Miller

*9 YAHWEH AS PROSECUTOR AND JUDGE: AN INVESTIGATION OF THE PROPHETIC LAWSUIT (RIB PATTERN)
K. Nielsen

10 THE THEME OF THE PENTATEUCH
D.J.A. Clines

*11 STUDIA BIBLICA 1978 I: PAPERS ON OLD TESTAMENT AND RELATED THEMES
Edited by E.A. Livingstone

12 THE JUST KING: MONARCHICAL JUDICIAL AUTHORITY IN ANCIENT ISRAEL
K.W. Whitelam

13 ISAIAH AND THE DELIVERANCE OF JERUSALEM: A STUDY OF THE INTERPRETATION OF PROPHECY IN THE OLD TESTAMENT
R.E. Clements

14 THE FATE OF KING SAUL: AN INTERPRETATION OF A BIBLICAL STORY
D.M. Gunn

15 THE DEUTERONOMISTIC HISTORY
M. Noth

16 PROPHECY AND ETHICS: ISAIAH AND THE ETHICAL TRADITIONS OF ISRAEL
E.W. Davies

17 THE ROLES OF ISRAEL'S PROPHETS
D.L. Petersen

18 THE DOUBLE REDACTION OF THE DEUTERONOMISTIC HISTORY
R.D.Nelson

19 ART AND MEANING: RHETORIC IN BIBLICAL LITERATURE
Edited by D.J.A. Clines, D.M. Gunn, & A.J. Hauser

20 THE PSALMS OF THE SONS OF KORAH
M.D. Goulder

21 COLOUR TERMS IN THE OLD TESTAMENT
A. Brenner

22 AT THE MOUNTAIN OF GOD:
STORY AND THEOLOGY IN EXODUS 32–34
R.W.L. Moberly

23 THE GLORY OF ISRAEL:
THE THEOLOGY AND PROVENIENCE OF THE ISAIAH TARGUM
B.D. Chilton

24 MIDIAN, MOAB AND EDOM:
THE HISTORY AND ARCHAEOLOGY OF LATE BRONZE AND IRON AGE JORDAN AND NORTH-WEST ARABIA
Edited by J.F.A. Sawyer & D.J.A Clines

25 THE DAMASCUS COVENANT:
AN INTERPRETATION OF THE 'DAMASCUS DOCUMENT'
P.R. Davies

26 CLASSICAL HEBREW POETRY:
A GUIDE TO ITS TECHNIQUES
W.G.E. Watson

27 PSALMODY AND PROPHECY
W.H. Bellinger

28 HOSEA: AN ISRAELITE PROPHET IN JUDEAN PERSPECTIVE
G.I. Emmerson

29 EXEGESIS AT QUMRAN:
4QFLORILEGIUM IN ITS JEWISH CONTEXT
G.J. Brooke

30 THE ESTHER SCROLL: THE STORY OF THE STORY
D.J.A. Clines

31 IN THE SHELTER OF ELYON:
ESSAYS IN HONOR OF G.W. AHLSTRÖM
Edited by W.B. Barrick & J.R. Spencer

32 THE PROPHETIC PERSONA:
JEREMIAH AND THE LANGUAGE OF THE SELF
T. Polk

33 LAW AND THEOLOGY IN DEUTERONOMY
J.G. McConville

34 THE TEMPLE SCROLL:
AN INTRODUCTION, TRANSLATION AND COMMENTARY
J. Maier

35 SAGA, LEGEND, TALE, NOVELLA, FABLE:
NARRATIVE FORMS IN OLD TESTAMENT LITERATURE
Edited by G.W. Coats

36 THE SONG OF FOURTEEN SONGS
M.D. Goulder

37 UNDERSTANDING THE WORD:
ESSAYS IN HONOR OF BERNHARD W. ANDERSON
Edited by J.T. Butler, E.W. Conrad & B.C. Ollenburger

38 SLEEP, DIVINE AND HUMAN, IN THE OLD TESTAMENT
T.H. McAlpine

39 THE SENSE OF BIBLICAL NARRATIVE II:
STRUCTURAL ANALYSES IN THE HEBREW BIBLE
D. Jobling

40 DIRECTIONS IN BIBLICAL HEBREW POETRY
Edited by E.R. Follis

41 ZION, THE CITY OF THE GREAT KING:
A THEOLOGICAL SYMBOL OF THE JERUSALEM CULT
B.C. Ollenburger

42 A WORD IN SEASON: ESSAYS IN HONOUR OF WILLIAM McKANE
Edited by J.D. Martin & P.R. Davies

43 THE CULT OF MOLEK:
A REASSESSMENT
G.C. Heider

44 THE IDENTITY OF THE INDIVIDUAL IN THE PSALMS
S.J.L. Croft

45 THE CONFESSIONS OF JEREMIAH IN CONTEXT:
SCENES OF PROPHETIC DRAMA
A.R. Diamond

46 THE BOOK OF THE JUDGES: AN INTEGRATED READING
B.G. Webb

47 THE GREEK TEXT OF JEREMIAH:
A REVISED HYPOTHESIS
S. Soderlund

48 TEXT AND CONTEXT:
OLD TESTAMENT AND SEMITIC STUDIES FOR F.C. FENSHAM
Edited by W. Claassen

49 THEOPHORIC PERSONAL NAMES IN ANCIENT HEBREW
J.D. Fowler

50 THE CHRONICLER'S HISTORY
M. Noth

51 DIVINE INITIATIVE AND HUMAN RESPONSE IN EZEKIEL
P. Joyce

52 THE CONFLICT OF FAITH AND EXPERIENCE IN THE PSALMS:
A FORM-CRITICAL AND THEOLOGICAL STUDY
C.C. Broyles

53 THE MAKING OF THE PENTATEUCH:
A METHODOLOGICAL STUDY
R.N. Whybray

54 FROM REPENTANCE TO REDEMPTION:
JEREMIAH'S THOUGHT IN TRANSITION
J. Unterman

55 THE ORIGIN TRADITION OF ANCIENT ISRAEL:
THE LITERARY FORMATION OF GENESIS AND EXODUS 1-23
T.L. Thompson

56 THE PURIFICATION OFFERING IN THE PRIESTLY LITERATURE:
ITS MEANING AND FUNCTION
N. Kiuchi

57 MOSES: HEROIC MAN, MAN OF GOD
G.W. Coats

58 THE LISTENING HEART: ESSAYS IN WISDOM AND THE PSALMS
IN HONOR OF ROLAND E. MURPHY, O. CARM.
Edited by K.G. Hoglund

59 CREATIVE BIBLICAL EXEGESIS:
CHRISTIAN AND JEWISH HERMENEUTICS THROUGH THE CENTURIES
B. Uffenheimer & H.G. Reventlow

60 HER PRICE IS BEYOND RUBIES:
THE JEWISH WOMAN IN GRAECO-ROMAN PALESTINE
L.J. Archer

61 FROM CHAOS TO RESTORATION:
AN INTEGRATIVE READING OF ISAIAH 24–27
D.G. Johnson

62 THE OLD TESTAMENT AND FOLKLORE STUDY
P.G. Kirkpatrick

63 SHILOH: A BIBLICAL CITY IN TRADITION AND HISTORY
D.G. Schley

64 TO SEE AND NOT PERCEIVE:
ISAIAH 6.9-10 IN EARLY JEWISH AND CHRISTIAN INTERPRETATION
C.A. Evans

65 THERE IS HOPE FOR A TREE:
THE TREE AS METAPHOR IN ISAIAH
K. Nielsen

66 THE SECRETS OF THE TIMES:
RECOVERING BIBLICAL CHRONOLOGIES
J. Hughes

* Out of print